A History of Ancient Egypt

Blackwell History of the Ancient World

This series provides a new narrative history of the ancient world, from the beginnings of civilization in the ancient Near East and Egypt to the fall of Constantinople. Written by experts in their fields, the books in the series offer authoritative, accessible surveys for students and general readers alike.

Published

A History of the Hellenistic World
R. Malcolm Errington

A History of the Ancient Near East, second edition
Marc Van De Mieroop

A History of the Archaic Greek World
Jonathan M. Hall

A History of the Classical Greek World, second edition
P. J. Rhodes

A History of the Later Roman Empire, AD 284–621
Stephen Mitchell

A History of Byzantium, second edition
Timothy E. Gregory

A History of Ancient Egypt
Marc Van De Mieroop

In Preparation

A History of the Roman Republic
John Rich

A History of the Roman Empire
Michael Peachin

A History of Babylon, 2200 BC–AD 75
Paul-Alain Beaulieu

A History of Greece, ca. 1300 to 30 BC
Victor Parker

A History of Ancient Egypt

Marc Van De Mieroop

WILEY-BLACKWELL

A John Wiley & Sons, Ltd., Publication

This edition first published 2011

© 2011 Marc Van De Mieroop

Blackwell Publishing was acquired by John Wiley & Sons in February 2007. Blackwell's publishing program has been merged with Wiley's global Scientific, Technical, and Medical business to form Wiley-Blackwell.

Registered Office
John Wiley & Sons Ltd., The Atrium, Southern Gate, Chichester, West Sussex, PO19 8SQ, United Kingdom

Editorial Offices
350 Main Street, Malden, MA 02148-5020, USA
9600 Garsington Road, Oxford, OX4 2DQ, UK
The Atrium, Southern Gate, Chichester, West Sussex, PO19 8SQ, UK

For details of our global editorial offices, for customer services, and for information about how to apply for permission to reuse the copyright material in this book please see our website at www.wiley.com/wiley-blackwell.

The right of Marc Van De Mieroop to be identified as the author of this work has been asserted in accordance with the UK Copyright, Designs and Patents Act 1988.

Wiley also publishes its books in a variety of electronic formats. Some content that appears in print may not be available in electronic books.

Designations used by companies to distinguish their products are often claimed as trademarks. All brand names and product names used in this book are trade names, service marks, trademarks or registered trademarks of their respective owners. The publisher is not associated with any product or vendor mentioned in this book. This publication is designed to provide accurate and authoritative information in regard to the subject matter covered. It is sold on the understanding that the publisher is not engaged in rendering professional services. If professional advice or other expert assistance is required, the services of a competent professional should be sought.

Library of Congress Cataloging-in-Publication Data

Van De Mieroop, Marc.
  A history of ancient Egypt / Marc Van De Mieroop.
      p. cm. – (Blackwell history of the ancient world)
  Includes bibliographical references and index.
    ISBN 978-1-4051-6070-4 (alk. paper) – ISBN 978-1-4051-6071-1 (pbk. : alk. paper)
1. Egypt–History–To 640 A.D.   2. Egypt–Civilization–To 332 B.C.   3. Egypt–Civilization–332 B.C.-638 A.D   I. Title.
  DS83.V36 2011
  932–dc22
                                      2010004730

A catalogue record for this book is available from the British Library.

Set in 10.5/12.5 pt Plantin by Toppan Best-set Premedia Limited
Printed and bound in Singapore by Ho Printing Singapore Pte Ltd

1   2011

Contents

Illustrations

Color Plates

Color plates appear between pages 200 and 201

Maps

Boxed Texts

Special Topics

Sources in Translation

Key Debates

Summaries of Dynastic History

Preface

Visitors to bookstores and school and public libraries easily find titles on ancient Egypt. Works on Egyptian gods, the Book of the Dead, tombs, and pharaohs are abundant and new ones continue to appear. Is another publication that does not introduce material newly excavated or rediscovered in a museum then really needed? As a historian I thought so – otherwise this would have been a futile project. Basic surveys of the history of ancient Egypt are remarkably rare and those that exist tend to be either brief and geared toward a very general audience or detailed and intended for people who have made Egyptology a lifetime pursuit. My aim here is to present something in between: an introductory overview of Egypt's ancient past in a single voice that, I hope, will encourage readers to delve further into one of the most fascinating civilizations in world history. This volume aims to serve as an introductory textbook for courses on ancient Egypt, but also to give the many people intrigued by its culture a general summary of the historical situation in the more than 3,000 years of its existence. As the author I had to make many choices about what to include and to omit and where to focus attention, and it may be useful to provide some clarifications on what inspired my decisions.

Even if scholars of ancient Egypt often complain that something is unknowable because of a lack of evidence – a great problem in the study of its history indeed – there still is a vast number of topics we can discuss. What I present here is a personal selection from a host of possibilities. I know that many readers will feel that I unjustly ignored or gave short shrift to subjects they find interesting: art, material culture, religion, war, women, and so on. I focus here on political history, but I also stress social interactions and give special attention to how later people – including we today – looked back on periods or individuals of ancient Egypt. I am well aware that others would have written a different book and would have focused attention on questions that concern them more, but I hope my choices are not too idiosyncratic and will appeal to many readers.

Although I organized the book according to the standard sequence of periods we recognize in Egyptian history, in the chapter narratives I have tried to avoid a format that many surveys use. The ancient sources encourage a presentation of Egypt's history as a progression of individual reigns nicely grouped into 31 dynasties. This framework is quite secure and provides a straightforward structure that is easy to follow, but it prevents the recognition of patterns and can be monotonous. Because the dynastic organization is so central to the way in which scholars study any aspect of ancient Egypt, however, in each chapter I have provided very brief summaries that highlight reigns and dynasties, so that readers can more easily connect information they read or see in other books, articles, museums, and TV programs to my discussions. But in the main narratives I have avoided a purely chronological account.

Introductory histories often present information without contextualizing the evidence. Even if they make meticulous reference to specific inscriptions or papyri, it is not always clear whether these sources are unique or selected from many similar ones. So I start each chapter with a brief survey of the ancient written evidence available on the period it covers. Because the analysis of primary sources is such an important part of a historian's task, I also discuss one or more documents in detail in each chapter. Reading ancient historical sources is not straightforward and they require much interpretation before they become the building blocks of the histories we produce. It is important thus to realize what the nature of the evidence is that historians use to investigate a particular period or question.

Finally, perhaps the most difficult challenge in writing introductory surveys is that they do not argue – they assert. Even if sentences are qualified by words like "seemingly" (often omitted to avoid clutter in the text), they give the impression that there is certainty. That is far from true. Every page, if not paragraph, of this book probably contains a statement that will offend someone who has argued differently in writing or lectures. It is impossible to acknowledge every scholarly opinion in an introductory book that covers the entirety of ancient Egyptian history. I chose to follow interpretations that I found the most convincing or appealing, and in the Guide to Further Reading I give preference to works that were the most useful in guiding my decisions. Like most of my colleagues, as a teacher I demand from my students that they acknowledge the sources they use when writing a research paper. It may thus seem that I set the wrong example here by not specifically referencing where I found an idea or what scholar's view I follow. If I had chosen to give full bibliographic references, I would have produced a very different book, longer and probably more daunting to a general reader. But, in order to counteract the impression that what I have written is generally accepted fact, I have included sections called Key Debates in each chapter to survey different views on a specific topic and give more detailed notes with scholarly references. In these sections I often stress how interpretations have evolved because of changing modern preoccupations rather than a clearer understanding. Historians do not live in a vacuum and their interests and explanations reflect their own conditions. I admit that even in these sections I could not acknowledge all that has been written on a topic; the bibliography is simply too vast.

I include a number of websites in my citations, which may seem to some colleagues as pandering to a technology that has not yet proven its scholarly validity. Indeed, one of the most annoying aspects about the treatment of ancient Egypt on the worldwide Web is the amount of hogwash that presents itself with the same authority as the results of high-level scientific investigation. The impact of the Web on our access to knowledge cannot be ignored, however, and (although I am not very savvy in its use) I refer to sites that seem useful and often have many images. As is the case for my references to print publications, they are partial. I should reiterate that this book is an introduction. I hope it will lead the reader into further exploration of the ancient Egyptian civilization, one of the greatest in human history.

Writing this book has been a long-term undertaking and I have to thank several people for their help and encouragement. Al Bertrand first interested me in the project and arranged for a team of scholars to read all or substantial parts of the work. I am much in debt to Ronald Leprohon, Gay Robins, Thomas Schneider, and Willeke Wendrich, who saved me from embarrassing mistakes and urged me to formulate ideas more clearly. John Baines read the entire manuscript with his usual insightfulness and attention to detail, and suggested improvements on every aspect of it. Katya Barbash (Brooklyn Museum, New York) and Robert Simpson (Oriental Institute, University of Oxford) updated and standardized the translations of Egyptian sources quoted. Richard Parkinson (British Museum, London) allowed me to quote several of his translations verbatim, as did Robert Simpson for the Rosetta Stone. As usual all remaining errors are my own responsibility.

The Wiley-Blackwell staff, as always, was very helpful and efficient. I thank Haze Humbert, who took over from Al Bertrand as acquisitions editor, Deirdre Ilkson, and Galen Smith. Finally, I am grateful for my students at Columbia University who over many years listened to my lectures on ancient Egyptian history and forced me to sharpen my thoughts and improve my methods of presentation. I am especially indebted to the group that took the course in the spring of 2009 (too many to name individually) and used the manuscript in progress as a textbook. I informed them that they were guinea pigs and they seem to have survived the trial quite well.

New York
November 30, 2009

1
Introductory Concerns

Rather make my country's high pyramides my gibbet and hang me up in chains. (Shakespeare, *Antony and Cleopatra* Act 5, scene 2)

The tourist to Egypt who sails up the Nile from Cairo to Aswan gazes upon an abundance of grandiose monuments, often remarkably well preserved despite their enormous antiquity. Many of them are icons of ancient Egypt and have been so for centuries. Shakespeare's audience recognized the image Cleopatra conjured up when she called the pyramids her gallows. Modern guided tours always include these same pyramids, as well as the great Amun temple at Luxor with the royal tombs across the river, and the much smaller temple of Isis at Philae between the old and the High Aswan dams. These monuments, spread over hundreds of miles, are all different from what surrounds the traveler at home, alien in their function, their form, and their use of images and writing. They share so many characteristics that it is easy to forget that their builders lived countless years apart. More time passed between the construction of the pyramids at Giza and the building of the Philae temple we now see, than between the latter temple's inauguration and us.

1.1 What Is Ancient Egypt?

Chronological boundaries

It may seem easy to look at something – a monument, coffin, statue, or inscription – and call it ancient Egyptian, but it is not so simple to draw the boundaries of ancient Egypt both in time and space. In the late fourth century AD, the Roman emperor Theodosius issued an edict closing all Egyptian temples and

dispersing the priesthood. His act ended the knowledge of Egyptian hieroglyphs, which could no longer be taught. Can we take the withdrawal of official
support for ancient Egyptian cults and writing systems as the end of ancient
Egypt? Theodosius's edict only affected a small minority of people that had
long been under threat. Ancient Egyptian cultural characteristics had been
immersed in a world inspired by Hellenistic, Roman, and Christian ideas for
centuries. Certainly in political terms Egypt had lost its separate identity hundreds of years earlier. From the Persian conquest in 525 BC on, but for brief
spells of independence, the land had been subjected to outside control. In native
traditions the Persian rulers were still considered part of the long line of
Egyptian pharaohs, but their successors were different. Modern historians do
not call the Greek and Roman rulers of Egypt pharaohs, although their Egyptian
subjects continued to represent them with full pharaonic regalia. Is "Egypt after
the pharaohs" no longer part of ancient Egyptian history then? Individual scholars and institutions use different approaches. Some histories of ancient Egypt
end with Alexander of Macedon's conquest in 332 BC, others at the death of
Cleopatra in 30 BC, yet others run into the Roman Period up to AD 395 and
Theodosius's reign.

It is always difficult to draw a line after an era in history, as all aspects of life
rarely changed simultaneously. More often the change in the sources that
modern scholars use determines where they end historical periods. In Egypt's
case the gradual replacement of the traditional Egyptian language and writing
systems by the Greek language and script necessitates a different type of scholarship. Most specialists of Egyptian hieroglyphic writing do not easily read
Greek sources and vice versa. Although the ancient Egyptian scripts survived
after the Greek conquest of the country, there was a constant increase in the
use of Greek writing, which turns the modern study of Egypt into a different
discipline. Yet, Ptolemaic and Roman Egypt in many respects preserved ancient
Egyptian traditions and customs, so I will include a discussion of that period
in this survey.

If the disappearance of ancient Egyptian writing in the late 4th century AD
heralds the end of the civilization, does its invention around 3000 BC indicate
the beginning? No single event announced a new era, but from around 3400
to 3000 BC fundamental changes that were clearly interrelated took place in
Egypt and forged a new society. Those innovations included the invention of
writing, a process that lasted many centuries from the earliest experiments
around 3250 to the first entire sentence written out around 2750. In the last
centuries of the fourth millennium the unified Egyptian state arose and that
period can serve as the beginning of Egyptian history despite its vague boundaries. Naturally, what preceded unification – Egyptian prehistory – was not
unimportant and contained the germs of many elements of the country's historical culture. Hence, I will sketch some of the prehistoric developments in
this chapter to make the influences clear, but the creation of the state with the
coincident invention of writing and other aspects of culture will indicate the
start of Egypt's history here.

Geographical boundaries

Where are the borders of ancient Egypt? Arabic speakers today use the same name for the modern country of Egypt as did the people of the Near East in the millennia BC, Misr. Other people employ a form of the Greek term Aegyptos, which may derive from Hikuptah, the name of a temple and neighborhood in the city Memphis. It is easy to equate the ancient and modern countries, but today's remarkably straight borders, which imperial powers drew in modern times, do not mark the limits of ancient Egypt. We can better envision those by using as a starting point what is and always was the lifeline of the country, the Nile. Running through a narrow valley south of modern Cairo and fanning out into a wide alluvial plain north of the city, the river enables people to farm, live in villages and cities, and build and create the monuments and other remains we use to reconstruct the country's history. From the first cataract at Aswan to the Mediterranean Sea it forms the core of Egypt, today as in the past. The people who lived in this core reached beyond it into the western and eastern deserts and upriver south of the first cataract. At times their reach was extensive, affecting distant places in the west, areas along the Mediterranean coast in the east and north, and parts of the Nile Valley deep into modern Sudan.

It is not always obvious how far ancient Egypt extended, and our ability to determine that often depends on research priorities and modern events. As tourists still do today, the earliest explorers of ancient Egypt focused their attention almost exclusively on the Nile Valley, where monuments and ancient sites are visible and in easy reach. It requires a different effort to venture into the deserts beyond the valley, very inhospitable and so vast that ancient remains are not always easy to find. Yet the ancient Egyptians traveled through this hinterland and settled in oases. In recent years archaeologists have spent much more time investigating these zones than they did before, a deliberate shift of research strategies. Sometimes the move is less voluntary. When the modern Egyptian state decided to construct the Aswan High dam in the 1960s, it was clear that the artificial lake behind it would submerge a vast zone with ancient Egyptian remains. Thus archaeologists rushed to the region, producing in a short time-span many more data than had been collected in a hundred years of earlier research.

Despite the greater attention that archaeologists now devote to the areas of Egypt outside the Nile Valley, they still spend most of their time in the core area, and conditions in the valley dictate to a great extent how we view the ancient country. It is easy to think that Egypt was a place of tombs and temples only, as those so dominate the ancient remains. Built of stone or carved in the rocks, they are well preserved, a preservation aided by the fact that they are often located at the desert's edge, out of the reach of Nile floods and of farmers who need the land they occupy for fields. Compared to tombs and temples, the remains of ancient settlements, built in mud brick in a valley that was annually flooded before the Aswan dam's construction, are paltry. Buried underneath thick layers of silt deposit they are mostly inaccessible and unidentified. The lack of knowledge about the settlements where the ancient Egyptians lived was so great that scholars long called ancient Egypt a civilization without cities. Even now that archaeologists make concerted efforts to explore more than temples and tombs, information about the living conditions of the ancient Egyptian remains limited and dispersed.

What is ancient Egyptian history?

The question "what is history" is much too wide-ranging and thorny to address here, but before embarking on reading a book-long history of ancient Egypt it may be useful to see how it applies to that ancient culture. Less than 200 years ago many would have said that ancient Egypt does not have history. In the early 19th century the influential philosopher of history, Georg Wilhelm Friedrich Hegel (1770–1831), proclaimed that cultures without accounts of the past resembling historical writings in the western tradition had no history. But the discipline has moved on enormously and today most literate cultures – including ancient Egypt – are considered worthy of histori- cal study. The field of "world history" goes further and includes the world's non-literate societies in its purview. This attitude erases the distinction between history and prehistory, a step whose consequences are not yet fully appreciated. It has the benefit for students of ancient Egypt that it removes the awkward problem of what sources they use in their research. Historians mostly consider textual sources to be the basis of their work, but in the case of Egypt we have to wait until the second millennium BC for a written record that is rich and informative about multiple aspects of life. Archaeological and visual remains are often the sole sources for earlier periods, and they stay very important throughout the study of ancient Egyptian history. Writing Egypt's history requires thus a somewhat different approach than for other periods and places where narrative and documentary sources provide a firm outline.

This book is called "A History of Ancient Egypt," because it is clear that many other "histories" can be written, each with their own focus and intent. Historians can concentrate on political issues, social, economic, or cultural ones, each of which will provide a different picture of the society they discuss. Most basic surveys build their structure around political history. This will also be the case here, although it does not monopolize the account, and I will also address other concerns. The choices I made are personal but inspired by other treatments of the subject. Ideally more attention would have been given to topics such as the visual arts, but this book is intended as an introduction only and hopes to inspire further reading and study.

Who are the ancient Egyptians?

When we think about peoples of the past, we intuitively try to imagine what they would have looked like in real life, to visualize their physical features, dress, and general appearance. Popular culture regularly portrays ancient Egyptians and the various ways in which this has happened shows how impressions change over time. Take Queen Cleopatra, for example, the last ruler of the country at least partly of Egyptian descent. The repeated filming of the story of Shakespeare's *Antony and Cleopatra*, quoted before here, shows how the image of this woman has changed. The 1963 Hollywood blockbuster featured the British-born Caucasian Elizabeth Taylor as the queen; in a 1999 movie made for TV a Latin-American actress of mixed Chilean-French parentage, Leonor Varela, played the part. A calendar issued somewhat earlier by an American beverage company entitled "Great Kings and Queens of Africa" included a depiction of Cleopatra as a black African woman. These changes in the queen's representation did not result from scholarly reconsiderations of ancient data, but from changing perceptions in the popular mind about the context of ancient Egypt.

It was only recently that scholars started to acknowledge the African background of Egyptian culture as a consequence of contemporary cultural identity politics that tried to replace the dominant western-centered views on world history with a greater focus on Africa's contributions. One manifestation of these ideas, Afrocentricity, highlights the ancient Egyptians as black Africans who brought about many of the cultural innovations credited to the ancient Greeks. Initially Egyptologists bluntly dismissed these proposals, but in recent years a greater willingness to engage with them has developed. This new attitude has not made it easier to visualize the ancient Egyptians, however, as their relationship with other African peoples is not obvious, as is true for Egypt's overall contacts with the rest of Africa. While ancient Egypt was clearly "in Africa" it was not so clearly "of Africa." Archaeological and textual evidence for Egyptian contacts in the continent beyond its immediate neighbors is so far minimal and limited to the import of luxury items. The contributions of Egypt to other African cultures were at best ambiguous, and in general Egypt's interactions with Asiatic regions were closer and more evident. Was the same true for the population of the country and did the ancient Egyptians leave any reliable data that could guide our imagination?

There exist countless pictures of humans from ancient Egypt, but it is clear that these were not intended as accurate portraits, except for some late examples from Ptolemaic and Roman times. Men and women appear in standardized depictions where physical features, hairdos, clothing, and even posture characterize them as Egyptians. The representations of foreigners are equally uniform: Nubians have dark skins and braided hair (Plate 1), while Syrians have lighter skins and pointed beards (Plate 2). Clothing often also sets apart various peoples. The artists were intent upon showing the opposition between Egyptians

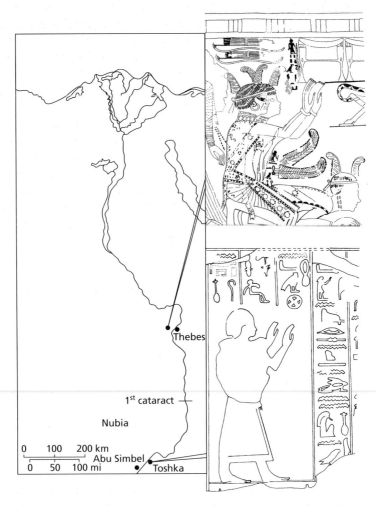

Figure 1.1   The Lower Nubian prince Hekanefer appears as an Egyptian in the representation in his own tomb at Toshka, while in a Theban tomb he is depicted as a typical Nubian

and foreigners, not to make clear their individual appearances. The perception of who was Egyptian could change according to the intended audience. For example, a prince from Upper Nubia in the 14th century, Hekanefer, appears in two different guises. In the tomb of the Egyptian viceroy at Thebes Hekanefer has typical Nubian features and dress, while in his own burial in Nubia he looks fully Egyptian (Figure 1.1). He wanted his own people to see him as a member of the Egyptian ruling class, whereas to the Egyptian viceroy of his country he was a Nubian subject, clearly distinct from Egyptians.

The homogeneity of Egyptians in ancient depictions is deceptive. Over the millennia Egyptian society constantly integrated newcomers with various origins, physical features, and customs. But unless there was a reason to make the difference explicit, they all appeared alike in stereotypical depictions. They were all Egyptians, not people with Nubian, Syrian, Greek, or other backgrounds. Some scholars have tried to determine what Egyptians could have looked like by comparing their skeletal remains with those of recent populations, but the samples are so limited and the interpretations so fraught with uncertainties that this is an unreliable approach.

Can we articulate any idea of what type of people we would have encountered when visiting ancient Egypt? I think we should stress the diversity of the people. The country's location at the edge of northeast Africa and its geography as a corridor between that continent and Asia opened it up to influences from all directions, in terms both of culture and of demography. The processes of acculturation, intermarriage, and so on probably differed according to community and over time. People must have preserved some of their ancestors' physique and lifestyles, and the degree to which they merged with neighbors with different backgrounds must have been variable. We cannot imagine an Egyptian population that was of uniform appearance. But somehow all these people at times saw themselves as Egyptians, different from people from the neighboring countries, and it is their common history we will explore.

1.2 Egypt's Geography

The Nile River

The Nile dictates how we can study the ancient Egyptians, and in many other respects the river shapes Egypt. Running through the eastern end of the Sahara desert, it essentially forms a long oasis. Wherever its water reaches the soil can be farmed; where it does not reach the earth is parched and it is impossible to grow anything on it. The contrast is so stark that one can stand with one foot in lush greenery and with the other in lifeless desert. The ancient Egyptians called the fertile area "the black land," the desert "the red land."

The Nile is the longest river on earth: some of its sources are located south of the equator and it runs for more than 4,000 miles (6,500 kilometers) northwards to empty into the Mediterranean Sea. In Egypt it has two distinct parts. The upstream part in the south, Upper Egypt, flows through a valley between 5 and 10 miles wide that is lined by cliffs restricting its course. Upper Egypt stretches for some 600 miles from modern Aswan to Cairo, located at a natural obstruction in the river that we call the first cataract. There are six numbered cataracts on the Nile, one in modern Egypt and five in modern Sudan. Cataracts are where the river is very shallow and rocky islands and boulders obstruct the water flow. These zones of narrow channels and rapids make navigation difficult and dangerous and consequently they constitute clear natural boundaries. Throughout ancient history the northernmost first cataract made up the southern border of Egypt's heartland and anything south of it was usually considered a different country. South of Aswan the Nile Valley is very narrow and it is only upstream of the third cataract that it is broad enough to include fields that allow sufficient farming to support substantial settled communities.

North of Cairo, the river's course is radically different. No longer enclosed by cliffs it spreads out into a huge triangle, which we call the Delta, with multiple branches. Because of its location downstream, the region is called Lower Egypt, bordering the Mediterranean Sea. The eastern- and westernmost points of the Delta are 150 miles (250 kilometers) apart, and the shortest distance between Cairo and the sea is 100 miles (160 kilometers).

All agricultural land in Egypt is made up of silt that the river annually deposited during its flood, prior to the construction of the Aswan dam. The river's water derives from three main sources. The White Nile, which originates in Central Africa, is most constant in its flow and does not carry much silt. But two tributary rivers, the Blue Nile and the Atbara that stem from the Ethiopian highlands, bring a sudden influx of water from heavy summer rains and both carry lots of silt. In Egypt the Nile is at its lowest level in the months of May and June and starts to rise in July because of rain in Ethiopia. It reaches its highest point in mid-September and recedes by mid-October (Figure 1.2). Its timing is in perfect harmony with the agricultural cycle, which makes farming in Egypt much less complex than in nearby regions and almost always guarantees that the population's needs are satisfied.

At one point in Upper Egypt the river water escapes the valley to flow into a large natural depression to its west, the Fayyum. From early prehistory on the accumulated water allowed for farming along the edges and, starting in the early second millennium, state initiatives tried to extend the agricultural zone by diverting the water into canals and controlling its flow. In the Ptolemaic and Roman periods these projects were very successful and the Fayyum became the breadbasket for Egypt and beyond.

The desert

The areas outside the reach of the Nile flood are arid desert. West of the Nile stretches out the Sahara, mostly uninhabitable but for its northern fringe along the Mediterranean Sea. In the vast desert plateau are some depressions where underground water surfaces to form oases (through Greek and Latin the English term derives from the Egyptian word *ouhat*). Up to 250 miles (400 kilometers) west of the valley they constitute places that the Egyptians controlled and settled, sometimes with penal colonies. Routes between the oases made it possible to travel from north to south avoiding the Nile Valley. The eastern desert

Figure 1.2 The Nile in flood near the Giza pyramids on October 31, 1927, before the building of the Aswan dams. Photograph by Mohammedani Ibrahim, Harvard University – Boston Museum of Fine Arts Expedition. Photograph © 2010 Museum of Fine Arts, Boston

is much less extensive as it borders the Red Sea some 60 to 200 miles (95 to 320 kilometers) east of the Nile. In Egypt its northern part is a hilly plateau, while the southern part contains high mountains that are difficult to cross. Dry riverbeds, wadis in Arabic, cut through these mountains, however, and make travel from the Nile to the Red Sea possible, although water is in short supply from wells only.

Under current climatic conditions the eastern and western deserts cannot support any farming and even the nomadic herding of animals is difficult. The eastern desert was a source of metals, including gold and hard stones, however, and thus of great interest to the Egyptians. East of the Delta the eastern desert leads into Asia, across the modern Suez Canal. The Sinai Desert to its east is mostly very inhospitable and some parts of it contain high desolate mountains. Travel through Sinai is limited to routes along the Mediterranean coast. The region contains some very desirable resources, such as copper and the semi-precious turquoise stone. Although Sinai formed a buffer between Egypt and Asiatic states, it was always in Egypt's orbit.

Climate

With its location just north of the Tropic of Cancer, Egypt is hot, especially in the summer, when average temperatures in Aswan easily reach 40 degrees Celsius. The country also receives very little rain and none of it in the summer. The current conditions did not always exist, however. Before the late third millennium BC, the climate was wetter and enabled people to live outside the valley collecting wild resources and doing some farming. The environment of Egypt in prehistory and early history was thus different from that in the later historical period and for the earliest developments scholars have to look beyond the valley to understand what went on.

Frontiers and links

Hemmed in by deserts and the sea, Egypt has a degree of isolation many other countries lack. In the west access is mainly restricted to a narrow strip along the coast, in the east the high desert separates it from the Red Sea coast. The Mediterranean coast was also a frontier and no harbor is known on it before the first millennium BC. Previously, boats had to sail inland before they could anchor. The first cataract delineated Egypt's southern border on the Nile. Traffic in and out of the country was thus easy to control and from early on kings established border posts at the first cataract and on the eastern and western points of the Delta to monitor it.

On the other hand, by its very location Egypt was at a crossroads. Any over-land movement between Africa and Asia had to pass through it. Thus early hominids from Africa crossed Egypt during their migration across the globe, while in the Middle Ages and later Egypt was the bridge between the heartland of the Islamic empires and their North African possessions. Through the Mediterranean, Egypt was connected by sea to southern Europe. In the late second millennium BC, ships sailing along the eastern Mediterranean coast went from Egypt to Greece and the Aegean islands passing by the Syrian coast. In later times overseas traffic between Egypt and Europe was intense, with huge cargo ships securing Rome's grain supply. The ancient Egyptians liked to portray themselves as separate from the rest of the world, with a long local pedigree and immune from outside interference, but that was a false image. Throughout its history Egypt was exposed to external influences as foreigners were drawn to the country. The longevity of ancient Egyptian culture was partly due to the readiness of others to absorb it.

1.3   The Makeup of Egyptian Historical Sources

Anyone with an interest in ancient Egypt is aware of the mass of material that is available to a student of the culture. Many museums have an abundance of objects on display, numerous TV documentaries show a seemingly unlimited array of buildings, wall paintings, statues, and the like, and whoever travels to Egypt itself sees ancient remains almost everywhere. Writing is very prominent in all this material: the ancient Egyptians liked to carve and paint texts onto their monuments. A major temple was incomplete if it did not have texts and images on every surface. A project ongoing since the 1920s continues to track where inscriptions are located and what scholars have published them. The catalogue is not yet finished.[1] This embarrassment of riches does not mean that every aspect of life is well documented, however, or that the sources are easy to use in historical research. Nor are they evenly spread over the millennia of Egyptian history. As I take writing as the historian's primary source, I will focus my remarks here on the written record.

Papyri and ostraca

The papyrus is almost as iconic of ancient Egypt as is the pyramid. The paper-like – the words are obviously related – sheets of plant-fibers hammered together are fragile and would not have survived were it not for Egypt's dry climate. The survival of papyri depends on where they ended up after use. Undoubtedly the ancient Egyptians kept business records and accounts in their houses and offices in towns and villages. Those were situated in the floodplain and consequently are now submerged underneath Nile deposit. Even if one could excavate the buildings where the papyri were stored, the humidity would have destroyed them. Likewise, there are few papyri from the Delta. The large majority of finds derives from the desert areas, where people included papyri in tombs or, more rarely, from administrative offices near burial complexes. In the Ptolemaic Period large amounts papyri were also used to enclose mummies in what we call cartonnage. The artisans bought them up in bulk to make a kind of papier-mâché coffin surrounding human and animal corpses, and mixed all sorts of writings together. These have survived because they were buried in the desert.

Papyrus was expensive. People regularly reused rolls, writing on the reverse and in spaces left blank in the midst of a text. They combined thus writings with very different content. We find, for example, magical spells written on the back of a papyrus with administrative records. This repeated use can lead to confusion; when various documents appear side-by-side but written over several decades do they relate to each other or are they fully independent? For daily purposes the Egyptians also used other materials that were cheap and abundant. Those included primarily the shards of broken pots and flat chippings of lime-stone on whose surfaces one could write in ink. Scholars refer to them as ostraca, from the Greek word for potshard, ostracon (Figure 1.3). Most often they contain brief business documents, but can have much more elaborate writing on them. For example, someone copied most of the literary *Tale of Sinuhe* on a limestone flake, 35 inches (88.5 cm) high with 130 lines of text on

Figure 1.3 Example of an ostracon from the late 19th dynasty. akg-images/Erich Lessing

it. Many ostraca contain sketches that often reveal an artistic spontaneity that is absent in official monuments.

Because of the problems of conservation over time, the record of papyri and ostraca available today is not an accurate reflection of what was written in antiquity. Only the materials that were kept in the desert survive, and those deal primarily with issues concerning the dead. If they are administrative, they often record the mortuary cult. Some archives recording the private affairs of people survived by accident by being discarded in desert tombs.

Literary works likewise survived when they were deposited in burials. Funerary compilations such as the Book of the Dead are thus more likely still to exist than other literature. An exceptional community of artists and workmen who built the tombs in the Valley of the Kings lived in the desert at modern Deir el-Medina. For those people we have the remains of their everyday writings and they are extensive and wide-ranging. Beside papyri more than 10,000 ostraca were excavated in the village. The writings include letters, business contracts, and accounts, but also a good number of excerpts of literary texts. Although this was an unusual community, with especially literate members, the documents probably reveal what would have been available elsewhere in Egypt. Some towns and villages from the Greek and Roman periods are the source of papyri, but these were almost all excavated unscientifically in the early days of Egyptian archaeology. Together with the official state records that make up the mass of papyri used in mummy cartonnage, they give a more complete picture of ancient writings than for earlier periods.

Monumental inscriptions

The most visible remains of Egyptian writing are on monuments, the buildings, statues, steles, and coffins that are so numerous and evident in museums and in the Egyptian countryside. These are most often official statements, honoring the donor of the monument or celebrating a military adventure, the construction of a building, or similar public accomplishments. The integration of text and image, jointly proclaiming a message, is greater in Egypt than in most other cultures. A statue, for example, is almost incomplete without the written name of whom it represents. Conversely, the statue itself can serve as a hieroglyph of writing. The inscribed name is carved in such a way that the figure of the statue appears at the end. In the Egyptian writing system a person's name needs to be followed by the determinative signifying a man or a woman. With male statues the sculpture itself often performs that function.

Historical criticism

Official statements require a skeptical reading. One of the hardest tasks for the scholar of ancient Egypt is to subject the textual record to historical criticism. Often a single source, or a set that presents the same point of view, provides the only information on an event or a practice. It is thus difficult to ascertain whether the outcome of a military campaign was as glorious as the author proclaims or even whether the campaign took place. In other fields of historical research the rule that a single testimony is no testimony is often invoked, but this attitude would leave ancient Egyptian history in tatters, as often we have to rely on one source only. Historians need to use great caution. They cannot just accumulate individual statements about a king's reign and present them as a reconstruction of the period.

A particular challenge arises with the use in historical reconstructions of what are clearly literary compositions. The Egyptians did not produce accounts that professed to be accurate investigations of the past. They did write stories, however, portraying historical figures. For example, in a Middle Kingdom piece of wisdom literature, *The Instruction Addressed to King Merykara* (see Chapter 4), Merykara, a known ruler of the preceding First Intermediate Period, hears a description of troubles and military action against internal Egyptian and foreign enemies. It is tempting to accept this narrative as fact and use it as an explanation of an otherwise documented decline of royal power in the First Intermediate Period. But the literary source was not written in order to explain history to a later audience. Its purpose was to inspire royal and elite conduct that could deal with adversity, and the challenges described may have been purely fictional. In earlier years of Egyptian scholarship the narrative was taken at face value, but today scholars use the *Instruction* as a source of information on the period of its composition, rather than on the period it depicts. The study of the First Intermediate Period needs to be based on other evidence.

1.4   The Egyptians and Their Past

Stories like *The Instruction Addressed to King Merykara* show that the Egyptians had a knowledge about their past and that they knew who had ruled the country in earlier times. This is not surprising, of course, as they could see ancient monuments and writings as we do today. But especially in the Late Period, in the first millennium BC, the past also had a special status, giving authority and prestige. King Shabaqo of the eighth century, for example, had a narrative about creation carved on a stone slab claiming that it was a copy made from a worm-eaten papyrus. The author of the text, *The Memphite Theology*, used a language modeled on that of the Old Kingdom, but it is most likely that the text was of much later date and was presented as ancient to give it greater clout. In the first millennium BC as well, people had their tombs decorated with imitations of scenes from third millennium tombs, carefully copying the ancient styles.

King lists

The prestige of antiquity especially applied to the office of kingship. All kings of Egypt were part of a lengthy sequence of universal rulers that went back to the start of history and even before. The Egyptians expressed this concept clearly in what we call king lists, a set of documents from the entirety of Egyptian history, which did not all have the same function in antiquity. The group of documents that survived is small and includes mostly fragmentary records. More material is bound to appear; very recently a scholar recognized a piece of a list written in Demotic during the late Ptolemaic Period in a collection of papyrus scraps.

Around 1290, King Sety I of the 19th dynasty had himself depicted with crown prince Rameses, to become Rameses II, on the walls of the temple at Abydos. The scene shows them giving offerings to a long line of 75 predecessors, each one represented by a cartouche, arranged in correct chronological

Figure 1.4 Fragmentary king list from the temple of Rameses II at Abydos. Werner Forman Archive/British Museum, London

order. The list is not complete, but edits history to remove discredited rulers, such as the foreign Hyksos and five kings of the 18th dynasty, which had ended in Sety's youth. The 18th-dynasty rulers omitted were Queen Hatshepsut, whose joint reign with Thutmose III was anathema to the idea of exclusive rule, and the four kings associated with the so-called Amarna revolution. A list comparable to Sety's, now damaged, stood in Rameses II's temple at Abydos (Figure 1.4), and a somewhat earlier representation at Karnak shows King Thutmose III making offerings to the statues of 61 predecessors, not in chronological order.

Non-royal people could also honor past kings. In his tomb decoration at Saqqara an official of Rameses II depicted the cartouches of 57 kings from the first to the 19th dynasty in correct order, but for the inversion of the 11th and 12th dynasties. A tomb in Thebes shows the priest Amenmose making offerings to the statues of 12 kings, including all those then considered legitimate kings of the 18th dynasty (as well as the queen of the dynasty's founder) and one of the Middle Kingdom. These lists are all evidence of a cult for royal ancestors, and they show knowledge of the names of past rulers and their correct sequence, although there was no attempt to depict them all.

Sety's list at Abydos starts with Menes, then considered the original unifier of Egypt, but kingship did not begin with Menes in Egyptian opinion. The Palermo Stone, a monument whose fragments are spread over several museums, lists predecessors of the kings of unified Egypt: first men wearing a crown later associated with Lower Egypt, then men wearing a crown later associated with Upper Egypt. For what we call the historical period the stone provides year-by-year annals, giving rulers' names and short entries on a special event for each year, as well as a measurement of the Nile's inundation height that year. The list ends in the 5th dynasty, which may have been when the stone was carved, although some scholars suggest that it dates much later.

The two longest and most complete king lists from Egypt take the concept of kingship even further back in time. The Turin King List and Manetho's *History of Egypt* start their lists with gods, who ruled for thousands of years. The sequence they provide reflects ideas of creation and the struggles between Horus and Seth that appear in other sources. After the great gods came lesser gods and assorted creatures, such as spirits, until Menes emerged as the first historic ruler. These lists assert thus that kingship arose at the time of creation.

Both the Turin King List and Manetho's *History of Egypt* attempt to give a full chronicle of Egyptian kingship including the names of all rulers and the length of their reigns. The list now in the museum of Turin, Italy, is a lengthy papyrus from the 13th century BC, which scholars often call the Turin Royal Canon. It allegedly was complete when discovered in the early 19th century, but is now in many pieces. It lists some 300 names of kings, from Menes to the end of the 17th dynasty, sometimes giving the time they ruled to the day. The list does not sanitize history and includes the despised Hyksos kings. At times it sums up, for example, 955 years and 10 days from Menes to the end of the 8th dynasty, which shows a concern to subdivide the long sequence of rulers.

The idea of subdivision is fully developed in the final, and today most influential, king list of Egypt. In the third century BC an Egyptian priest, Manetho, wrote a history of his country in the Greek language, the *Aegyptiaca* or *History of Egypt* (see Chapter 13). Preserved only in quotations and paraphrases of later authors, it attempted to account for Egypt's history with a king list into which Manetho inserted narratives. The latter often recall earlier stories about Egyptian rulers and show that Manetho had access to writings now lost. The long king list was a massive reconstruction of the names of rulers and the length of their reigns. For periods when power in Egypt was centralized Manetho lists individual royal names; when it was diffuse he often mentions only the number of kings, their capital, and the total number of years they ruled. His list includes all rulers from Menes to the last king whom Alexander defeated in 332 BC, the Persian Darius III.

The most influential feature of Manetho's organization was his division of the list of kings into "dynasties." He was the first to use this Greek term for a

Special Topic 1.1 *The five names of the kings of Egypt*

Although Manetho gives a full list of the kings of Egypt, we cannot always equate the names he provides with those we find in other king lists and in monuments. That is due to the fact that Egyptian royal names, at least from the Middle Kingdom on, contained five elements (there are some variations over time). For example, for a ruler of the 18th dynasty we call Thutmose IV the names were:

1. as the god Horus: Mighty Bull, perfect of glorious appearance (= Horus name);
2. as the Two Ladies, that is, the vulture and the cobra representing Upper and Lower Egypt: Enduring of kingship like the god Atum (= *nebty*-name);
3. as the Golden Horus: Strong of arm, oppressor of the nine bows.
In those three epithets he was shown as a god or as a pair of goddesses;
4. the first name in a cartouche, preceded with two signs that indicate Upper and Lower Egypt, the sedge plant and the bee: Menkheprura, which means "The enduring one of the manifestations of Ra" (= Prenomen, given when he ascended the throne);
5. the second name in a cartouche, the king's birth name with the indication "son of Ra": Thutmose, greatly appearing one; beloved of Amun-Ra (= Nomen).

Manetho could use any of the five names, often in abbreviated form, as the basis of his designations of kings; other king lists mostly used the prenomen while early monuments mostly gave the Horus name. Especially for the Early Dynastic Period it is often unknown what the correspondence is between Manetho's names and those on monuments.

Because Manetho wrote in Greek he reproduced Egyptian names in a manner not fully true to the original. Some of his names are better known in wide circles than the more accurate renderings. For example, he calls the builder of the great pyramid at Giza Cheops, while Egyptologists prefer to render the ancient Egyptian name as Khufu.

The modern rendering of Egyptian names – royal and non-royal – is a problem. Ancient Egyptian writing does not indicate vowels (see Chapter 2), so we do not know with certainty where to insert vowels between consonants and what vowels to use. Moreover, we do not know what some consonants would have sounded like. Scholarly opinion has changed over time and there has never been full agreement. Many different spellings of names appear: for example, Thutmose, Thutmosis, Tuthmosis, and Thotmose; Ramses, Ramesses, and Rameses. These inconsistencies may confuse especially newcomers to Egyptology, but quite soon they cease to annoy.[2]

Modern practice also often uses a distinctive term to refer to the kings of Egypt up to the Greek period: Pharaoh, often without the definite article. This habit derives from Greek translations of the Hebrew Bible, where the king of Egypt is called Pharaoh. The Greek term rendered the ancient Egyptian *per'aa*, which meant "great house" or "palace." In the 18th dynasty "palace" became a common way to designate the king, who was at the center of the institution, and in the 22nd dynasty it became an epithet of respect. Before the Greco-Roman Period ancient Egyptians hardly ever gave their kings the title pharaoh, but in modern studies pharaoh and king are synonyms. It is only because the special term is so broadly known that scholars continue to use it.

group of rulers in order to designate a succession of kings who shared common attributes, mostly that they represented several generations of a family. He broke the long sequence of rulers up into 31 dynasties.[3] His sections for each dynasty start with the number of kings and the capital city. Then he lists the names of individual rulers and numbers of years, and at the end he sums up the total number of years. For example:

> Dynasty 23, 3 kings from Tanis
> Petoubates: 25 years
> Osorkho: 9 years
> Psammous: 10 years
> Total: 44 years[4]

The subdivisions are mostly obvious as they acknowledge when a new family seized power or when the capital moved. But the reasons for Manetho's changes of dynasties can be unclear to us. He sometimes starts a new dynasty although the first king was the son of the preceding king in the list. Manetho or his sources must have noted breaks that are not evident to us.

Today's scholarship adheres closely to Manetho's organization of Egyptian history into dynasties. All people, events, monuments, and so on are provided a chronological context by stating to what dynasty they belonged. Subjects such as imperial policy or administrative structure are regularly studied as they are attested in a specific dynasty. The notion of dynasty is so strong that scholars now speak of a dynasty 0 to group together rulers who preceded Manetho's Menes. While dynasties provide a handy means to subdivide Egypt's long history, the rigorous adherence to Manetho's list can impose a restricted and misleading framework on historical analysis. Many surveys move from one dynasty to the next (sometimes giving each dynasty a separate chapter) and enumerate events reign-by-reign as if Egypt's history could only be an annotated king list, as it was in Manetho's work.

Egyptian concepts of kingship

All Egyptian king lists, including Manetho's, reflect an ideology of kingship that is not historically accurate to our way of thinking: there can only be one king at a time because his rule is universal. That was indeed true in times of centralized power, but in other periods multiple political centers and regional dynasties coexisted. For example, in the mid-second millennium the 13th through 17th dynasties overlapped. The 13th and 17th dynasties ruled the south, while the 14th shared power in the Delta with the 15th and 16th dynasties, which were both made up of foreigners. Manetho provides only six names of kings, those of the 15th dynasty, for the entire period, but he lists the five dynasties in succession with numbers of kings and regnal years. His totals come to 260 kings who would have ruled 1590 years. Manetho presented these kings as if they lived one after the other, because Egyptian tradition did not acknowledge the existence of parallel kings.

The Egyptians saw each reign as a complete era. When a king came to the throne, it was as if the world was created anew and would go through a full cycle of existence. All the king's deeds in the new era were in essence perform- ances of royal duties, which were like ritual acts that all his predecessors had already performed. This attitude led to assertions that can mislead the modern historian. Kings could claim accomplishments of a past reign as their own. King Pepy II of the 23rd century, for example, portrayed himself as defeating Libyan enemies, presenting a scene also attested from the reign of King Sahura who lived two centuries earlier. The 7th-century King Taharqo likewise duplicated Sahura's representation. While we see this as a falsification of history, the Egyptians considered each representation a ritual re-enactment of feats that were part of normal royal behavior. Kings like Rameses II started their reigns with massive building projects because they wanted to show that creation was repeated when they took power.

The modern concept of history is very different from the ancient Egyptian; we do not see the accession of each king as a new era that repeats earlier reigns. Moreover, although dynastic divisions provide a handy means to organize a millennia-long history, they do not always reflect the historical changes that interest us most. We try to see continuities and patterns over longer periods of time, and hope to determine how people built upon the work of their predeces- sors. One of the hardest challenges to a modern writer of Egypt's history is how to take documentary evidence that is as a rule organized on the basis of who reigned and to mold it into a narrative that seeks to identify long-term trends in diverse aspects of life. A listing of events reign-by-reign may have a clear structure, but it provides a skewed image of history.

1.5 The Chronology of Egyptian History

The dynastic lists do provide a great help in the reconstruction of the relative chronology of Egypt's history. We can almost always establish the sequence of rulers within a dynasty and of successive dynasties, if they did not overlap. Thus we know in what order the pyramids near Cairo were constructed, for example, something that would be much harder to find out from other evidence. The parallel dynasties are obviously a problem, but our understanding of Egyptian history is now secure enough to determine when these occurred, although we do not always know how long they coexisted.

Modern subdivisions of Egyptian history

The distinction between periods of successive and of parallel dynasties has led to a crucial modern subdivision of Egyptian history into Kingdoms and

Intermediate Periods. Today all Egyptologists use the terms Old, Middle, and New Kingdom to indicate when the state was unified, that is, when there was a single ruler for Upper and Lower Egypt, and they see a similar situation later on in the Late Period, when foreigners regularly ruled Egypt as a unified kingdom. In between those periods of centralized power scholars recognize Intermediate Periods, when various kings ruled simultaneously in multiple centers. An Early Dynastic Period precedes the entire sequence. Although the principle underlying these modern subdivisions is clear –centralized or decentralized power – there is no agreement on their chronological boundaries. Certain elements are standard: the 4th to 6th dynasties are part of the Old Kingdom, the post-reunification 11th and 12th of the Middle Kingdom, and the 18th through 20th of the New Kingdom. But some scholars, for example, include the 7th and 8th dynasties in the Old Kingdom, while others see that phase as part of the First Intermediate Period.

These designations impose a mental framework on Egypt's history that is largely erroneous. The alternation between Kingdoms and Intermediate Periods suggests that there were only two modes of political structure, and that all Kingdoms and all Intermediate Periods were alike. Perhaps this was to an extent true for the Kingdoms, which the Egyptians themselves saw as repetitions of the same conditions, but there were great differences between the various Intermediate Periods. Hence, in recent years scholars have suggested renaming the First Intermediate Period as the Period of the Regions, for example. The designation Late Period also suggests that it was an epilogue and that Egypt's true history ended with the New Kingdom. This universally accepted periodization should thus be used as a handy tool, but not uncritically.

Absolute chronology

Although the relative chronology of Egypt's history is secure, the absolute dates are not. Manetho's disregard of overlapping dynasties, as well as the numerous variants in the lengths of reigns in the different excerpts of his work, make it impossible to build a timeline counting back from Alexander's conquest. From the mid-second millennium on it is sometimes possible to relate events in Egypt to other cultures in the Near East (whose absolute chronology is firmer), especially in the first millennium when various Near Eastern powers invaded the country. In the second half of the second millennium dated evidence of diplomatic contacts with the Near East helps, but the occasions are few.

Another source for dating Egypt's history in absolute term derives from ancient astronomical observations of when the Sothis (Sirius or Dog Star) re-emerged on the eastern horizon just before sunrise after 70 days of invisibility, around July 19 in the modern calendar. Egypt's administrative calendar counted only 365 days in a year – rather than the 365¼ days of a full astronomical year

– and the moment Sothis appeared changed thus over time. Scholars used to take the very few recorded observations as firm anchors for dating periods, but now they are more skeptical of their value. Also the technique of measuring the decay of C14 in wooden and other objects can be of some help, but the results tend to be too inaccurate to settle issues of detail. The scholarly debate about Egypt's absolute chronology continues unabated.

1.6 Prehistoric Developments

Because of Egypt's location at the junction of Africa and Eurasia, many hominid migrations out of Africa passed through the country. It is no surprise then that early human stone tools were found there. The evidence of human activity in the Nile Valley from 700,000 BC to the beginning of Egyptian history around 3000 BC is scarce, however, and at many times nonexistent, and we cannot see a continuous development from these early times. The growth of an Egyptian culture becomes only clear in the last millennia of prehistory, from the mid-sixth millennium on. From 5400 to 3000 is a very long time, but developments in Egypt were rapid when compared to other prehistoric societies. They include a shift in subsistence from hunting and gathering to farming, and the evolution of a social and political structure with a clear hierarchy of power and wealth that culminated in the Egyptian state. Throughout these two-and-a-half millennia we do not see abrupt cultural changes or the sudden appearance of populations that brought new practices with them, so the evolution must have been indigenous, albeit with influences from the outside. The processes of formation of the Egyptian state accelerated around 3400, and we will look at them in the next chapter. Here we will focus on earlier events.

The beginning of agriculture

By 6000 BC the Egyptian climate and the Nile River had settled in patterns similar to the modern, although until 2200 it was more humid than today. It is only in the mid-6th millennium that agriculture emerged in the country, substantially later than in the neighboring Levant where people started to live in permanent farming communities by 7000 BC. The relative richness of wild natural resources may explain why the Egyptians adopted the new technology later than people in other areas surrounding the Levant. The Nile provided fish and waterfowl and in the desert lived game, while wild sorghum and other plants could be harvested. The technology of farming was clearly an import into Egypt as it involved plants and animals not available in the wild there: the primary domesticated animals were sheep and goats and the first cereals cultivated were emmer wheat and barley, foreign to Egypt and imported from the Near East. The domestication of cattle may have been inspired by practices farther west in Africa. The adoption of agriculture had different consequences in Upper and Lower Egypt.

In the Delta and the Fayyum people started to live a sedentary lifestyle like their neighbors in the Levant in the 6th millennium. They built villages and obtained most of their food from the cereals they grew. Few settlements are known, but they show that from around 5400 the northern Egyptians practiced farming. In Upper Egypt and Nubia people primarily engaged in pastoralism, the herding of sheep and goats. This made them more mobile and we do not find village settlements near the Nile Valley. The people spent much time in the desert – more fertile than it is now – and the only permanent remains we have of them are tombs. When we find traces of settlements, they contain ash and debris, but no architecture. The graves show that people produced nicely polished pottery and the first representations of humans in figurines, and that they chose to place valuable mineral and metal objects with the dead. Similar burial practices appear from Middle Egypt to Khartoum in Sudan, which suggests that the people over this large area shared common beliefs. We call their material culture in Upper Egypt Badarian after the archaeological site of el-Badari.

In the Nile Valley the extensive use of agriculture with permanent settlements nearby only arose after 4000 BC. This development only occurred north of the first cataract, distinguishing Egypt from Nubia. Large centers appeared and people went to live near the zones that the Nile flooded annually to work in the fields. Until the building of the Aswan dam, agricultural practices in Egypt were very different from those in the neighboring Near East and Europe. The country received too little rain to rely on its water to feed the crops, and the Nile was the farmer's lifeline. That river's cycle provided everything needed, however, and the Egyptians relied on natural irrigation. The water rose in the summer, washing away salts that impede plant growth and leaving a very fertile layer of silt on the fields bordering it. The water receded in time for the crops – all grown in winter – to be sown, and it left the fields so moist that they did not require additional water while the plants grew. Farmers harvested crops in the late spring and the fields were ready for a new inundation by July. The cycles of the river and the crops were in perfect harmony. The only concern was the height of the flood, which dictated how much land received water. The ideal flood was somewhat more than eight meters above the lowest river level. If the river rose too much villages and farms would be submerged; if it rose too little not enough land would be irrigated.

People could help the river by leading water in canals and building dykes around fields in order to regulate when the water reached the crops. Some of the earliest representations of kings from around 3000 may show such work (Figure 1.5), but they do not constitute major projects to extend agricultural zones substantially. Artificial irrigation that used canals and basins to store and guide the water into areas that the river could not reach only appeared later in Egyptian history, and scholars debate when it started. Probably the increased aridity in the later third millennium pushed people into controlling the water more. Most important was the management of water in the Fayyum depression;

Figure 1.5 The macehead of King Scorpion from ca. 3000 BC may show the king digging an irrigation canal. Werner Forman Archive/Ashmolean Museum, Oxford

during the Middle Kingdom and especially in Greek and Roman times, the state dug extensive canals to drain excess water and lead it to otherwise infertile sectors. Irrigation practices throughout Egypt basically remained the same for most of ancient history until the Romans introduced the waterwheel.

Naqada I and II periods

The most extensive remains of the fourth millennium are cemeteries, including a massive one with some 3,000 tombs at the site of Naqada in Upper Egypt.

This site gave its name to the archaeological culture that characterizes the last centuries of Egyptian prehistory. Scholars subdivide the Naqada Period into I (3800–3550), II (3550–3200), and III (3200–2900), with further subdivisions (IIIA, IIIB, etc.) to acknowledge changes in the material culture. The changes were gradual and the period divisions do not necessarily reflect major cultural differences. The archaeological periodization is thus a chronological framework within which historical processes need to be sited, not a principle to understand the processes.

The earliest Naqada burials show the beginnings of later Egyptian practices. The dead are facing west and gifts are set beside them. The manner of burial and the quality and quantity of grave goods demonstrate the changes in Egyptian society best. At first corpses were just placed in shallow pits, but over time the treatment of some bodies became much more elaborate. In Naqada II the first evidence of wrapping them with linen appears, which would ultimately lead to full mummification by the 4th dynasty. Tomb structures came to signal social distinction. While the majority of people remained buried in simple pits, some tombs became large and complex and after 3200 would develop into major constructions with multiple chambers and for some a superstructure that marked them clearly in the landscape. The grave goods accompanying the dead most clearly show how people's wealth started to differ substantially. While the majority received a set of pots, next to the bodies of some individuals were placed objects such as stone mace heads and palettes carved in the shapes of birds and animals. The distinctions between burials increased over time, which must reflect differences in wealth and status of the living. These processes of social differentiation would culminate in late prehistory and lead to the development of the Egyptian state.

While Naqada I was a regional culture, Naqada II remains appeared throughout Upper Egypt. It is clear that larger settlements existed near the cemeteries and those at Naqada, Hierakonpolis, and Abydos were the most prominent. One tomb in Hierakonpolis, tomb 100, was especially impressive because of its painted wall decoration, which displayed boats, animals, and fighting men. A man appears holding two lions with his bare hands, an artistic motif that scholars interpret as a sign that the buried person was a leader of the community. Archaeological assemblages show that the inhabitants of the Delta still adhered to a different culture, which we call Ma'adi, although they imported goods from Upper Egypt. They had close contacts with Palestine and imported copper from there as well as highly prized goods from farther afield, such as lapis lazuli ultimately from Afghanistan. They traded some of these commodities on to Upper Egypt.

By 3400 then, all of the elements of later Egyptian culture were in place. People knew how to farm relying on the Nile, they lived in settlements in the valley, and they buried the dead nearby. Their material remains show that Upper and Lower Egypt were distinct and that in each region the societies showed social differentiation, especially in the ways in which people were buried. Many other characteristics of later Egyptian ideology and world views

Special Topic 1.2 *Egyptian city names*

Thebes, Hierakonpolis, Memphis, ... We do not refer to cities with their ancient Egyptian names, but mostly with Greek designations. The Greeks used several ways to formulate the names of places in Egypt. When a city was most famous as the center of worship of an Egyptian god, they regularly named it after a manifestation of that god, often the animal form. Hierakonpolis meant "the city of the falcon" because it was a cult center of the god Horus, who was represented as a falcon. The Egyptian name was Nekhen. Heliopolis was "the city of the sun," after the sun god; its Egyptian name was Iunu.

The Greeks could base their names on ancient Egyptian designations of an entire city or an important structure within it, and they tried to imitate the original sound. Such names sometimes replicated those of cities in Greece itself. Egyptian Abedju became Abydos, a city name also found in northern Greece. Memphis, the city near the pyramids in the north, derived its name from Mennufer, King Pepy I's pyramid at Saqqara (a modern Arabic name that derives from Sokar, the god of the necropolis). In Late Egyptian language Mennufer became Memfe, which the Greeks rendered as Memphis. The Egyptians also referred to the city as Ankh-tawy "The Life of the Two Lands," because of its location at the junction of Upper and Lower Egypt.

At times, we do not know why the Greeks choose a name. The Egyptians called the religious center of the Middle and New Kingdoms Waset. The Greeks referred to the place as Thebes, which is also the name of one of the most important cities in central Greece. Although some scholars suggest that the Egyptian name of a district of Waset inspired the Greeks, it is possible that the city's leading status was at the basis of the selection.

Sometimes we use the modern Arabic designation of a site as the primary name to refer to a place. Thus scholars most speak of el-Kab and el-Amarna, which are the names of archaeological sites that contain the remains of the ancient cities of Nekheb and Akhetaten respectively. The modern Arabic name can contain traces of the ancient Egyptian one. For example, modern Qift derives its name from ancient Egyptian Gebtu, which became Kebto or Keft in Coptic. Other names show what impressed the later inhabitants in the ancient remains. The city Luxor derives its name from Arabic al-Uqsur, which means "the palaces."

Our modern designations are thus a mixed bag that we tend to use indiscriminately and we mostly ignore their source. The ancient Egyptians often tried to indicate what they thought to be a city's most important characteristic. For example, Naqada was near the city Nubt, which means gold, and it was called so because of its location across the Nile from the entrance of a wadi leading to gold mines. That may explain the area's wealth in late prehistory, but our modern term conceals that fact.

probably also developed in these prehistoric times. In order to understand these ideas better we have to study the more elaborate information of historic times, however.

NOTES

1. Porter et al. 1929– .
2. In this book I use the spellings of royal names found in Shaw, ed. 2000: 479–83. I also follow the dates for reigns provided in that list with some minor changes.
3. Many scholars believe that Manetho only listed 30 dynasties (a round number) and that the 31st dynasty was a later addition.
4. Verbrugghe & Wickersham 1996: 201.

2

The Formation of the Egyptian State (ca. 3400–2686)

He will take the White Crown; he will uplift the Red Crown.
He will unite the Two Powers; he will appease the Two Lords with what
   they wish.

(Prophecy of Neferty)[1]

Throughout ancient Egyptian history the idea that the state was a union between two lands, Upper and Lower Egypt, was sacrosanct. When the lands were not united – in the eras we now call Intermediate Periods – chaos ruled; it was a royal obligation to keep Upper and Lower Egypt together so that order and proper conditions prevailed. Many aspects of royal imagery and titulary expressed that ideal. Among the various crowns a king could wear were an elongated, white crown of Upper Egypt and a box-shaped, red crown of Lower Egypt. But more important was the double crown that combined the two. In statuary, the sides of royal thrones regularly contained a representation of sedge and papyrus plants knotted around a windpipe arising from lungs (Figure 2.1). The scene symbolized that the king seated on the throne provided unity, tying together Upper Egypt, symbolized by the sedge, and Lower Egypt, symbolized by the papyrus. In Egyptian the words *to unite* and *lung and windpipe* contained the same sequence of consonants, thus the drawing of the lungs and windpipe spelled out the king's action. Other imagery and many texts likewise showed the ruler as king of Upper and Lower Egypt, an idea explicitly announced in two of his five titles (see Chapter 1). The passage quoted above was just one of many expressions of this concept. It celebrated Amenemhat I, the founder of the 12th dynasty, as the king who brought together the two parts of Egypt and their tutelary gods, Horus and Seth.

Egyptian history starts with the unification of the state, a process that happened around 3000 BC and that established the ideal of political rule for millennia. The nature of the early Egyptian state is unusual, albeit not unique, in

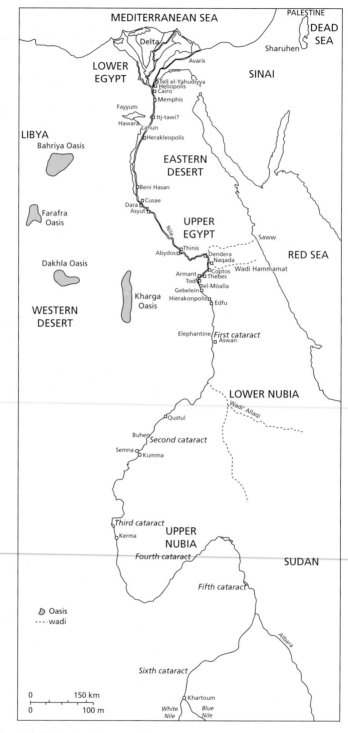

Map 1 Egypt and Nubia from prehistory to the Middle Kingdom

Figure 2.1   Unification symbol of Upper and Lower Egypt on the side of Rameses II's throne on the facade of Abu Simbel

world history. Whereas in other early cultures we see a gradual growth of political units mostly centered on city-states that merged into territorial states, Egypt developed rapidly from a village society into a large unified state. The unusual character of Egypt's state formation makes it more difficult to understand than other cases in history. The processes that led to a unified territorial state are mostly obscure, although the evidence is not scarce. Scholars continue to formulate theories to explain why the state developed, but none has convinced the entire academic community. Everyone agrees, however, that it was a momentous episode in Egyptian history in every respect. Not only was the political model of a united Upper and Lower Egypt established, but also the ideals of kingship as well as the means of glorifying and supporting the king. Writing originated and the canons of art and architecture were founded. The social, economic, and intellectual foundations of ancient Egypt emerged at this moment, and their influence pervaded the rest of the country's ancient history. It is thus important for us to grasp what happened. Scholars call whatever preceded the unification Predynastic, while the Early Dynastic Period covered the first centuries of Egyptian history until ca. 2686.

2.1 Sources

The formation of the Egyptian state happened when Egypt emerged from prehistory – the invention of writing is one of the characteristics of the early state – and the written evidence perforce is very limited. Most of our data are archaeological and within that record cemeteries dominate by far. Moreover, Upper Egypt is much better known archaeologically than the Delta.

Writing itself only slowly expanded into a rendering of the Egyptian language and its usages grew gradually to include more areas of activity. The first complete sentence written in Egyptian may only date to the late 2nd dynasty. Earlier inscriptions, often found on seals that were impressed on clay, were terse and provided little beyond people's names and titles. Royal names appear on a large number of objects, however. Wooden and ivory labels containing an image of the king, his name, and some other information are plentiful.

As is true for all of ancient Egyptian history we reconstruct dynasties on the basis of later king lists. The names that appear there do not fully correspond to those on Early Dynastic objects, which use different names and include many

---

Summary of dynastic history
Late Predynastic–Early Dynastic Period (ca. 3400–2686)

ca. 3400–3000	**Late Naqada Period** Growth of regional centers at Naqada, Hierakonpolis, and Abydos Monumental tombs at Abydos
ca. 3200–3000	**Dynasty 0** Kings Scorpion, Narmer, etc. First attempts at full unification of Egypt End of A-group culture in Nubia
ca. 3000–2890	**1st dynasty** Definitive unification of Egypt Capital at Thinis (near Abydos cemetery) Establishment of Memphis near junction of Upper and Lower Egypt
ca. 2890–2686	**2nd dynasty** First royal tombs at Saqqara (alongside Memphis) First known writing of entire Egyptian sentences

additional kings. Hence modern scholars developed the concept of a dynasty 0 to fit names attested epigraphically only. The annals on the Palermo Stone (see Chapter 1, p. 16) cover some kings of this period, and provide a year-by-year account of mostly ritual actions. The identification of the kings involved is not always certain, and the information provided is extremely terse.

There exists a very rich visual record for this period. Numerous stone palettes (flat slabs seemingly used to mix cosmetic paints) and other objects were decorated. The representations were often only animals, but some depict the king in action as a warrior, for example. The "reading" of such scenes is not easy, but they did present an important message the kings wanted to communicate. While in the past scholars saw scenes like the one on Narmer's palette (see below) as a commemoration of a specific event, today they tend to see it as a generic portrayal of a royal act. Such a reading changes the historical use of the object radically.

2.2 Royal Cemeteries and Cities

The Late Naqada culture

By 3400 people throughout Egypt surrounded themselves with similar tools and objects in life and in death, which shows us that they shared a common culture, coined Naqada IIC and III by modern archaeologists. But they did not live under a single political structure. Various centers of power coexisted within a network of villages that spread across the country. The three centers that seem to have been the most prominent were all located in a 125-mile (200-kilometer) stretch in the southern half of Egypt: Hierakonpolis, Naqada, and Abydos. Especially the cemeteries of these sites show that the processes of social stratification that had started centuries earlier had fully developed. Set apart from the great cemetery of Naqada a small number of brick-lined tombs became large in size and contained numerous grave goods, while at Hierakonpolis a richer set of large rock-cut tombs appeared.

The tendency to devote more resources to the burials of elite individuals culminated at Abydos, located to the north of Naqada. Here was the cemetery of the first kings of Egypt, but already before the unification of Egypt some people buried there received large tombs. One tomb, whose occupant is unidentified (the excavators call the tomb U-j), had 12 rooms and although it had been robbed before excavation, it still contained many bone and ivory objects, much Egyptian pottery, and remains of 400 jars imported from Palestine, which probably were filled with wine or oil originally. Among the ivory objects were some 200 square labels incised with images that scholars interpret to signify various regions of Egypt (Figure 2.2). They suggest that people from various parts of the country and beyond shipped goods to Abydos to honor the person buried around 3250 BC.

Figure 2.2   Inscribed labels from tomb U-j at Abydos

Dynasty 0

Tomb U-j was dwarfed in size by nearby tombs whose occupants are known to us from inscriptions. They include three kings from dynasty 0, six kings and one queen of the 1st dynasty, and two kings of the late 2nd dynasty. All are large subterranean complexes, with multiple rooms that were built of mud brick and became increasingly deeper. Above ground was probably only a low earthen mound. The names of the occupants appear sometimes on steles set up above the tombs, or we know them because of the writing found within the tombs on jars and on seal impressions and labels originally attached to goods. Although all tombs had been looted and burned in the third millennium, they still contained evidence of their original wealth when excavated in modern times. Beads of semi-precious stones, gold, and silver were strewn around while numerous vessels were stacked in the rooms. Among them were many jars from Palestine that held perfumed oil, which was highly valued. In the entrance of one tomb people poured oil three feet (90 centimeters) deep in order to make the air smell pleasant.

The king's body was placed in a wood-lined shrine while the secondary rooms often contained the corpses of people and animals. Analysis of the bodies shows that the servants were strangulated to accompany the king in death, while his pet dogs and lions, as well as some dwarfs, were killed to entertain him. Human sacrifice was a short-lived practice in Egypt, abandoned after the 1st dynasty. Its appearance at this time shows how powerful the kings were in society.

The cemeteries at Naqada, Hierakonpolis, and Abydos were attached to walled settlements whose remains are less well known as they were located in the flood plain. But it is clear that the people with special burials were prominent in life as well. They gained their wealth in part from importing goods from outside the Nile Valley. Naqada and Hierakonpolis were located near routes that led to mines of semi-precious stones and metals in the eastern desert. Hierakonpolis also controlled access to Nubia in the south. Abydos's elite seems to have had close contacts with Palestine in Asia, the source of semi-precious stones, metals, and agricultural products such as wine and oil. The people and towns with these distant contacts seem to have gained special prominence at home that gave them power over others. Egyptian society had become fully hierarchical with a select group on top, supported through the labor of the local agricultural populations. The elites surrounded themselves with specialists, such as craftsmen who created the art and architecture that confirmed their special status.

2.3 The First Kings

Images of war

Later king lists call the first ruler of the whole of Egypt Menes, but this name does not appear on any of the early monuments. There is thus uncertainty about who can claim the honor of having unified the land, the fundamental characteristic of kingship in Egyptian eyes. It must have been one of the men buried at Abydos, but scholars fail to agree on the identity of Egypt's first king. Today many suggest he was Aha, but Narmer and other candidates are equally likely. Moreover, the ideal of the unification of Upper and Lower Egypt seems to have been present for some time before the feat was irreversibly accomplished. That Egypt was created through military means is a basic concept expressed in the art of the period. A sizeable set of stone objects, including ceremonial maceheads and palettes, contain scenes of war and fighting between men, between animals, and between men and animals. The wall painting in tomb 100 at Hierakonpolis (see Chapter 1) seems to be an early example of that imagery, which dominated the art around the time the Egyptian state arose. Whereas in the past Egyptologists read the scenes of war literally as records of actual events, today they prefer to see them as stereotypical statements of kingship and the king's legitimacy. This new approach makes it impossible to date the unification of Egypt or attribute it to a specific individual on the basis of these

Figure 2.3 The palette of King Narmer, front and back. Werner Forman Archive/Egyptian Museum, Cairo

representations. But the art of the period shows that the Egyptians linked unification with conflict.

Many of the objects containing these scenes were excavated as a group at Hierakonpolis. Among them several inscribed with the name of Narmer stand out because of the detail of their scenes. We can read Narmer's palette, a 25-inch- (63- centimeter-) high thin flat slab, as one of the first royal inscriptions from Egypt (Figure 2.3). The front shows a king wearing the high white crown of Upper Egypt beating another man with a mace. Near the second man are two hieroglyphs that seem to denote the name of a region in the north or the victim's name. Above them is a falcon perched on a papyrus plant holding a rope around a man's neck, which we can read as the god Horus, represented as a falcon, handing over the conquered Delta to the king. On the back the same king, wearing the square red crown of Lower Egypt, reviews standard-bearing troops. To their right are two rows of decapitated bodies with heads at their feet. Two hieroglyphs in the top registers of both sides identify the king as Narmer. This monument declares that King Narmer of Upper Egypt defeated the Delta, and thus became king of Lower Egypt as well. Scholars now question the literal reading of Narmer's palette as an account of the first conquest of the Delta, but regard the representation as one of several statements that the Egyptian king was obliged to keep the country united, through military means, if needed.

Other men, perhaps earlier than Narmer, appear in similar martial settings. The Hierakonpolis deposit contains a 10-inch- (25-centimeter-) high limestone mace representing a king with the crown of Upper Egypt, possibly engaged in work on canals lined with papyrus plants, a symbol of the Delta. The top register shows lapwing-birds tied to standards that probably signify various districts of Egypt and we read the macehead as a celebration of their subjugation by the king (see Figure 1.5). Two signs in front of his mouth seem to render his name: a rosette and a scorpion. As we cannot read these phonetically, scholars refer to the man either as King Scorpion or as King Rosette-Scorpion.

The unification of Egypt

Historians now regard Scorpion, Narmer, and others to be part of dynasty 0, a group that preceded the traditionally acknowledged rulers of the 1st dynasty. The number of rulers and the length of the period involved are debated. Some read royal names on the tags excavated in the U-j tomb at Abydos from around 3250, others confine the use of the title "king" to later centuries. It is clear that the concept of kingship predated the unification of the state in Egypt, and that some who ruled only parts of the country had attributes, such as crowns, that were later reserved for kings of all of Egypt. Only with the establishment of the 1st dynasty was all of Egypt brought together in a firm union. Archaeological evidence does not support the idea that this was the result of the conquest of a northern state by a king from the south, as the art suggests. Especially in the Delta there is no indication of a centralization of power before the 1st dynasty's unification.

Most likely the area that incorporated Abydos, Naqada, and Hierakonpolis first grew into a territorial unit and then rapidly expanded into other areas to its north and south. The close connection between these three previously independent centers is clear from the fact that the names of early rulers often appear in more than one site. For example, Narmer was buried in Abydos, but his most significant monuments were in Hierakonpolis, while his wife's tomb may have been at Naqada. The annexation of Delta regions was the final act in this expansion.

Whatever the processes involved, we cannot really explain why a territorial union was pursued. Egypt is very resource rich, especially agriculturally, and there was no need for communities to seek fields faraway in order to feed themselves. The desire for luxury goods from Asia – minerals, semi-precious stones, oils, and wine – may have pushed people from the Abydos region to ensure guaranteed access, but the conquest of all intermediate zones seems a very laborious way to achieve that. Over the years Egyptologists have suggested numerous explanations for the creation of the Egyptian state (see Key Debate 2.1, p. 50). Originally a sudden military conquest was the preferred scenario; today scholars favor the idea of a gradual growth of a unified territory. When compared to other ancient cultures the creation of Egypt as a territorial state was a rapid process, requiring a few centuries only. Why it happened cannot be answered with confidence.

2.4   Ideological Foundations of the New State

The visual commemorations of the unification of the Egyptian state focus on the person of the king, represented as much larger than others and as the sole agent. The emphasis on the royal person pervades all aspects of early Egyptian society, and is one of the ideological pillars of Egyptian culture that endured throughout the country's ancient history. At the creation of the state the Egyptians formulated a vision of the world and its organization that was fundamental for all that followed in later millennia. They codified ideologies and established procedures and tools as the basis of official life, which would change and evolve in later history, but remained foundational.

Kings

The exaltation of the king is evident throughout the visual and written record of the earliest Egyptian dynasties, and had its roots in the Predynastic Period. He was at the center of all aspects of life, both religious and secular. The king was not a mere human; he was closely connected to the divine, albeit not a god himself. It was his duty to provide for the gods and the dead, and to maintain balance (*maat*) in the universe for the rest of humanity. The falcon god Horus was the king's patron and the king was Horus's earthly incarnation. At his accession the king received a name as Horus, which appeared on all his monuments. In the 1st dynasty the Horus names were often martial in character, such as "the fighting Horus" (Aha) or "Horus who strikes" (Den). From the Predynastic Period on, one symbol of the king was called *serekh* in ancient Egyptian, a word that literally means "to proclaim." It was the image of an upright rectangle with vertical stripes in the bottom half. On top of the rectangle perched a falcon, the god Horus. At first the *serekh* was empty, but soon the names of kings of dynasty 0 appeared in it. The *serekh* remained a powerful symbol: some large stone steles of the 1st dynasty merely showed the *serekh*. They were eloquent metaphors of royalty.

Cemeteries

The striped part of the *serekh* depicts the facade of the royal palace or palace enclosure, a mud-brick wall with recesses. Palaces must have dominated early political centers, although the excavated evidence for them is very slim. The earliest *serekhs*, painted on vessels placed in tombs, show that palaces predated the unification of Egypt. While we cannot say much about the king's abode in life, we do know a lot about his burial, and the tombs and mortuary monuments continue to proclaim his pre-eminence throughout Egyptian history. From King Aha on, the royal tombs at Abydos were surrounded by subsidiary burials, which contained the remains of wives and attendants. In the tomb of Aha the latter seem all to have been younger than 25 years at death, and probably they were purposefully killed to serve the ruler in the hereafter. The king's tomb retained its central importance in later Egyptian history. Hundreds of officials built their tombs around the great pyramids at Giza, for example, but in those days they were no longer put to death for the king. Early royal tombs were monumental: their superstructures were massive mud-brick edifices with niched facades that imitated the palace facades. Because these superstructures resemble in shape the clay benches in front of modern Egyptian houses, we refer to them with the Arabic word *mastaba*, that is, bench. Already in the Early Dynastic Period officials started to use the form as well as kings and throughout the Old Kingdom the mastaba remained the typical burial for elite members of Egyptian society.

Festivals

Many other visual expressions of royal power existed. The king wore crowns and had scepters and other regalia that were reserved for his office, and he participated in public festivals that reaffirmed his special status (Plate 3). The latter were ephemeral events whose format we can only vaguely reconstruct from depictions and later sources. One ceremony that seems to have been important from the Predynastic Period on and that continued to be practiced into the Greek Period was called *sed* in ancient Egyptian. Held occasionally in a king's life – in later periods only after 30 years of rule – it renewed his powers. Wrapped in a special cloak he appeared on a podium with the two thrones of Upper and Lower Egypt, while statues of the gods were placed nearby (Figure 2.4). During this celebration of his dual kingship he made a ceremonial run around boundary stones to reconfirm his territorial claims. Some of the earliest depictions of kings show them participating in the *sed*-festival, which seems to have become more important over time. The 3rd-dynasty step pyramid of Djoser contained a special *sed*-court to renew the king's reign into eternity, and in the 14th century King Amenhotep III built a massive complex to celebrate *sed*-festivals (see Chapter 8).

Figure 2.4 Label showing King Den participating in the *sed*-festival. © The Trustees of the British Museum

Royal annals and year names

Festivals of this type were considered to be so important that they were recorded in what we call royal annals. From the 1st dynasty on, the Egyptians designated years by identifying a special accomplishment that had happened, using very terse language, such as "Halting at Herakleopolis and the lake of the temple of Herishef." This had a purely practical side: administrators attached labels inscribed with such designations to goods to make clear the date of their delivery. But the labels also intimate to us what the Egyptians considered to be important royal acts. The authors of the now fragmentary Palermo Stone collected these data to provide a record of the first three dynasties. The events commemorated included cultic acts, such as the erection of a temple or a divine statue and visits to shrines in various towns. Very common was a biennial "following of Horus," probably a royal tour through the country to interact with the population and judge disputes. Military campaigns, so common in the depictions of the Late Predynastic Period, are rarely mentioned.

Gods and cults

The king's position in society was grounded in Egyptian views about the world of the gods. It is difficult, if not impossible, for us to understand how ancient Egyptians perceived gods and related to them. It is clear, however, that their attitudes differed from those of believers in Abrahamic religions, not only because the Egyptian pantheon knew numerous deities rather than one god. Egyptian gods were natural forces and could be terrifying characters that needed to be appeased. Families and communities had their preferred deities, and often selected those for reasons that escape us. In our study of Egyptian religion we have to remember that the abundant remains involving gods and goddesses available to us are almost exclusively from the official sphere and set up on behalf of the court. Personal religious feelings are nearly never accessible to us.

The king's duties included the support of the cults and temples, and his powers derived partly from his identification with the god Horus. In order for these concepts to work on a countrywide level, there had to exist a view of the gods that was valid throughout Egypt. Most gods had a strong connection to one specific town that in historical periods often housed their main temple. It is certain that many associations went back to prehistoric times, and scholars assume that almost all cults were originally local. But in the Early Dynastic Period there existed a unified Egyptian pantheon. Some scholars argue that the unification of Egypt led to an ideological merging of local systems, while others think that already in Predynastic times the regional pantheons fitted within a system that transcended political boundaries.

The art and texts of the Early Dynastic Period refer to gods attested throughout Egyptian history, although it is unlikely that they had the same definition as in later times when the evidence is clearer. We encounter Horus and Seth, connected to kingship, the cow-goddess Hathor (whose name means "Estate of Horus"), the fertility god Min, and other gods much better known later on. The annals report that the king visited their shrines or dedicated statues to them, and some archaeological remains of early temples exist. There must have been official ideas about their relationships and areas of competence that differed from Predynastic times, and officially sponsored gods gradually displaced local ones.

The newly established court formulated countrywide ways to express concepts such as temple, divine statue, etcetera. Whereas previously local traditions and preferences existed, the imposition of a union on the country led to common norms, at least in the official sphere. The later official Egyptian temple contained a limited set of small roofed rooms to house the divine statue, which one reached by crossing one or more courtyards, some open, others with columns that supported a roof. In Egyptian prehistory there was no uniform style of temple, however, and cults could focus on an earthen mound or a stone boulder, for example. The new form thus had to supplant existing customs.

Similarly, official Egyptian statuary – not well documented in the Early Dynastic Period but abundant in the Old Kingdom – followed strict rules of representation of the body that regulated the relative size of body parts, the position of the arms, and so on. In Predynastic times different conventions existed, which needed to be eliminated to make place for a common style. An example of an earlier tradition is a set of colossal statues of the god Min, excavated at his cult center Coptos. They show a style of human representation that is very unlike the dynastic one. They are gigantic (13.5 feet or 4.1 meters high), have unusual proportions, show the god as bald and with an atypical beard, and contain inscribed signs that do not resemble those appearing elsewhere. By the 2nd dynasty the new state had refashioned the image of Min to fit the common standards of divine representation. In general it instituted an official culture that gradually replaced the local traditions. The latter may have survived much longer than scholars usually suggest, but the novelty of a countrywide system was the result of the unification.

Bureaucracy

A state with Egypt's expanse required a structure that enabled the collection of resources and the communication of central demands throughout the territory. The strong focus on the king made the state's administration very centralized. Officials owed allegiance to him, not to an abstract concept of the state. As was the case for kings, we know officials best through their burials. At Saqqara, the cemetery overlooking the city of Memphis, appear a number of substantially sized mastaba-tombs of high officials and members of the royal family dating to the 1st and 2nd dynasties. The officials sometimes listed their titles, and their names appear on the labels found in royal tombs, which indicate that they were responsible for a delivery. These short writings show that a bureaucracy existed from the foundation of the Egyptian state on. The number of officials' tombs is relatively small, however, and it seems that the administration was not yet extensive. But it was the precursor of later Egyptian bureaucracies.

The men's duties included the collection of resources from all over the land. From the Late Predynastic Period on, royal tombs at Abydos accumulated goods from distant places. The labels found in tomb U-j seem to contain the names of estates from Upper and Lower Egypt whose produce was sent to support the buried dead. Throughout Early Dynastic times and later on the concept survived that domains in various parts of Egypt were set aside to provide for the king, in life and in death. Production in them was organized in such a way that a surplus existed for that purpose. Ideologically their countrywide distribution reaffirmed the king's role as a unifier of the land. At the same time all other producers probably owed some type of dues – in kind; currency did not exist – to the court, which administrators collected and used in support of the state's infrastructure. In order to assess the amounts each region could provide, the court undertook censuses. The "Following of Horus" event commemorated regularly in the Palermo Stone annals seems to have been such an exercise while from the early 2nd dynasty on took place a biennial cattle count, probably for the same purpose.

From the Early Dynastic Period on Egypt was subdivided into units that we call nomes after the Greek term for regional administrative districts. Each nome had its territory, name, and symbol, a system that was fixed by the 5th dynasty and survived into the Greco-Roman Period albeit with changes over time. An official was responsible for them and represented the king locally. The nome system enabled the administration of the country in a methodical and uniform manner. It made it easier to assess dues and to deal with local issues. The drawback for the king was that officials – we call them nomarchs – could develop a local power base, which in times of weak central government enabled them to gain autonomy.

At the apex of the entire bureaucracy was the king. The center of the state was wherever he was. Manetho, who lists the capital of each dynasty, states that the first two dynasties were from This or Thinis. Since all kings of the 1st dynasty and two of the 2nd were buried at Abydos and kings were buried near their capital in later periods, we locate the ancient city in Abydos's vicinity, probably beneath the modern town of Girga, where it is impossible to excavate. The capital's position near Abydos suggests that the dynasty 0 lords buried there were the main forces behind the unification of Egypt, but the location was not strategically ideal. It is thus no surprise that the administrative capital of Early Dynastic Egypt was farther north, at Memphis alongside the officials' burial site at Saqqara. In the Old Kingdom Memphis did become Egypt's political capital. The city's location was ideal for that purpose as it lies just south of where the Nile Valley and Delta meet, and the early high administrators of the state were in closer contact with the two parts of the land there than at Abydos. One of the ancient names of the Memphis region was Ankh-tawy, "The Life of the Two Lands," which reasserted the ideological union of Upper and Lower Egypt.

The ideology of the Early Dynastic state thus incorporated all the elements that defined ancient Egypt for 3,000 years or more afterwards. It was a union of Upper and Lower Egypt held together by the king, whose powers as an incarnation of the god Horus ensured order in the universe. Official norms and beliefs had a countrywide impact: The gods were organized in a single pantheon, official art and architecture adhered to court standards, and all people in Egypt handed over part of their labor to the state. An administration carved the country up into units and collected dues, while embodying the king's power locally.

Special Topic 2.1 *Canons of Egyptian art*

State formation and the imposition of a common rule over the entire country came with a reform of artistic practices that applied to all official art and remained the canon throughout Egyptian history into Roman times. The imposition of these rules was absolute. Even carvings on rock surfaces in the desert confirmed to the new iconography of the state, which focused on the king. From the Early Dynastic Period on all formal monuments – reliefs, paintings, and statues – adhered to the same principles.

Figures were firmly placed on a level horizontal base line and the representation of the rest of the body started from that line. In the Middle Kingdom a grid with 18 equidistant horizontal lines contained the body up to the hairline: six lines for the distance from the soles of the feet to the knees, nine to the buttocks, 10 from the knees to the neck, and two from the base of the neck to the hairline. A vertical line from the ear down bisected the torso. Various periods used somewhat different proportions and figures could be squatter or more slender, but the basic ideas remained the same.

Egyptian artists wanted to show as much of the body as possible. In relief sculptures they depicted a person in profile, but represented certain elements in full view forward so they could be seen clearly. They showed the chest frontally and placed an enlarged eye near the side of the head. They attached a woman's breast in profile to the frontal chest. A man's legs were set apart so that the one farthest from view was visible; a woman's legs were together.

Artists represented elite members of society in select poses only and in perfect physical condition and of an ideal age. For men the age was full-grown, either youthful or more mature; for women it was youthful only. In some periods men appeared with signs of fatigue or old age on their faces, but that is rare. The flesh was painted in conventional colors: men, who spent time outdoors, were red-brown; women, who stayed indoors, yellow. Non-elites appeared in more varied poses – doing manual labor, for example – but with the same skin colors and proportions. Foreigners were shown as caricatures almost: Syrians had pointed beards, Nubians curly hair, and so on.

The aim of the artists was not to present a portrait of the person but an idealized form without a specific visual identity. The inscription on the representation stated who it was. It was thus easy to usurp an image: one could just remove the existing name and replace it with one's own.

2.5 The Invention of Writing

All these ideological structures of the Egyptian state were facilitated, if not made possible, by the existence of writing. The origins and development of early Egyptian script formed a seminal part of the creation and maintenance of the state, paralleling the processes of state formation in many respects. The earliest evidence of a coherent system of notation comes from tomb U-j at Abydos around 3250 BC, while all the elements of the standard Egyptian hieroglyphic script are clear in the mid-1st dynasty around 2900, and the fully developed usage is attested from the late 2nd dynasty on, around 2750. As is the case for the origins of the state, the earliest stages of writing are not entirely clear to us, and scholars debate what elements of the later Egyptian script they already include. Moreover, the reasons why writing originated are also disputed. The discussion here is thus one of several potential reconstructions.

Precursors at Abydos

Among the grave goods in tomb U-j at Abydos were a number of inscribed objects. Some 200 square bone and ivory labels, which were originally tied to bales of cloth or other goods, contained incised signs, while about 100 jars had one or two signs painted on them. Often there are multiple examples of the same inscription. The total number of distinct signs is only some 50, most of them found on more than one object. Those on the labels include numerals and word signs, but almost never on the same object. The jars contain word signs only. The numerals include single digits and a sign for 100. All other signs are pictorial and they mostly depict birds. The excavator of the tombs believes that some signs render entire words, and others the sound of parts of words, as was the case in later Egyptian script, but the evidence is inconclusive. Most of the signs on labels and jars probably indicate the provenience of the products, the name of a region or an estate, while others may render the names of kings. Any actual reading is tentative, however. Yet, the material shows that people at the places of origin and destination of the products all understood the same system.

Hieroglyphic script

The invention of hieroglyphic writing as it would be used for millennia in Egypt took place in Late Predynastic and Early Dynastic times. It made the rendering of the sounds and meanings of the spoken language possible, although writers did not aim at a complete recording of all elements of speech. Especially the earliest inscriptions were terse and only indicated the essential concepts of a message. They did not provide grammatical forms or all the components of a sentence in the spoken language. We do not know whether or not people spoke a common language throughout Egypt at the time writing was invented, although it is clear that they wrote only one language.

The hieroglyphic script contained two basic types of signs: those that indicate a word through meaning (we call them logograms or ideograms) and those that indicate a word or part of it through sound (we call them phonograms). The same sign can have both functions, and oftentimes the ancient scribe drew a short vertical stroke underneath a sign to show that it should be read as a logogram. Hieroglyphic signs are pictorial and their origins lie in drawings from which one can often extrapolate meaning. The picture of the sun ☉ can mean "sun" and semantically related words such as "day." The pronunciation of the word was not indicated at all, and one could only read the logogram aloud if one knew the language recorded. Some such signs were never pronounced. A group of them were what we call determinatives. They appeared after almost every word to clarify its nature. For example, when the determinative of a man followed the logogram that indicated the basic idea "to write," it indicated, "scribe"; when the determinative representing a roll of papyrus followed the sign, it meant, "writing." Determinatives were very common in ancient Egyptian writing, guiding the reader in choosing the right meaning of the logographic signs.

Logograms by themselves can convey much information, but they allow room for error. They also cannot render most names, which were central to the earliest inscriptions, and nonfigurative notions such as "good" or "to desire." Thus the Egyptians developed a set of signs that could be read phonetically, containing one to three consonants. They did not indicate the vowels that accompanied the consonants and each sign had multiple readings. The sign for the consonant m, for example, could represent the syllables ma, me, mi, etcetera. Among the phonograms are 24 signs that cover the consonants of the Egyptian language. Theoretically these could be used to write out any word, as in an alphabet. Those are the signs that shops in Egypt today use to write out tourists' names in hieroglyphs. But the ancient Egyptians never limited themselves to those. They saw them on the same level as signs that record two or three consonants, such as *nr* or *nfr* with any combination of vowels. Phonograms appear in the earliest inscriptions to write out dynasty 0 or dynasty 1 royal names. We speak of the palette of Narmer because of the appearance of the *n`r* and *m`r* signs in the *serekh*. Our understanding of these early writings is restricted, however. Narmer's name appeared in inscriptions from all over Egypt and Palestine and multiple ways to write it out existed. We may be mistaken in our reading of it.

The earliest inscriptions show little else than the royal name, but in the mid-1st dynasty they become more elaborate. From the reign of King Den, around 2900, derive many labels that contain multifaceted statements (Figure 2.4). One of them shows the king's name in the *serekh* written with the phonograms d and n. The right side of the label is lined with the sign for year and next to it is a depiction of the *sed*-festival, which we read as a year name. The label also gives the name of an official, Hemaka, and his title "seal bearer of the king of Lower Egypt," and it indicates that oil was involved in the transaction recorded. The reading of such a label is still highly impressionistic as it merely shows names, titles, and words without indicating their grammatical relationship. In the 1st dynasty the order of signs was also very loose and modern decipherers have to read them by analogy with what would make sense in later Egyptian texts. But the uses of writing certainly increased and the first known roll of papyrus, with no signs on it, comes from the tomb of Hemaka.

Perhaps the first preserved continuous sentence in Egyptian script that indicates all elements of the spoken language appears on a sealing of the reign of Peribsen of the late 2nd dynasty, "Sealing of everything of Ombos (Naqada): He of Ombos [i.e., the god Seth] has joined the Two Lands for his son, the Dual King Peribsen."[2] It shows a fully developed script, but not the final stage of hieroglyphs' evolution. The number of hieroglyphic signs varied over time. While initially one or two thousand appeared, they were reduced to some 750 in the Middle Kingdom when spellings became institutionalized in schools. In the Greek and Roman periods, however, scribes created many new signs for religious and monumental texts (see Special Topic 2.2).

Why did the Egyptians invent writing? The earliest preserved records were administrative in character, keeping track of the movement of goods, and it is logical that a state of Egypt's size and complexity required a flexible system of accounting that could keep information on the nature of goods, their quantities, provenance and destination, the people in charge of them, and the date of the transaction. In Babylonia, where writing originated around the same time, bureaucratic concerns are obvious in the earliest texts, and many scholars suggest the same impetus in Egypt. But others stress how important display was in the earliest Egyptian inscriptions. The visual commemorations of the unification of Egypt, the tomb steles inscribed with nothing but the *serekh*, and many other inscriptions of the third millennium have no bureaucratic goal, but honor the gods and the king. Throughout Egyptian history the hieroglyphic script was prominently displayed to celebrate someone or something. The glorification of the king may have been one of the driving forces in the script's invention. If not, it was certainly soon adopted for that purpose.

Special Topic 2.2   *Languages and scripts of ancient Egypt*

No one today speaks the ancient Egyptian language and we can only reconstruct it through the documentation of the past. The written record of ancient Egyptian is spread over an enormous time-span. It is clear that the language the writings rendered changed constantly due both to internal and external influences. Moreover, despite the great conservatism in writing, practical considerations pushed the Egyptians to adapt the script for its diverse usages and they used several forms simultaneously. We cannot speak then of a single Egyptian language and script, but of multiple stages and various scripts.

Egyptian is an Afroasiatic language combining elements found in such North African language groups as Berber with Semitic characteristics. It stands alone within the languages of Africa because of its closeness to Semitic, which reflects the geographical location of Egypt. The history of the language needs to be pieced together from written evidence that did not mirror the changes immediately. We identify several stages. The Old Egyptian form, known primarily from official inscriptions, was relatively close to Middle Egyptian, which was written from around 2100 to 1750. Middle Egyptian became the classical language of Egypt, because authors used it to compose the literary works that Egyptians continued to copy out for centuries later on. It is the form of the language that modern students of Egyptian initially learn. In the New Kingdom starting around 1500 the Egyptians spoke the Late Egyptian form that gradually appeared in their business documents and letters. By the seventh century Demotic took over, also mainly found in writings of daily use. In the fourth century AD the Christians of Egypt began to write the Coptic form of the language, which survived as a vernacular into the 12th century and is still used today in the liturgy.

The changes in the script do not necessarily reflect changes in the spoken language, although we use the same terms to refer to the different stages of both. Four basic scripts appear: hieroglyphic and its derivatives hieratic and Demotic, which all use a mixture of logograms and phonograms, and Coptic, an alphabet. Hieroglyphic – a Greek term that means "sacred carved writing" – is pictorial and requires great care in writing. It was reserved for monumental and ornamental inscriptions until AD 395. Some less elaborate forms, which we call cursive hieroglyphs, appear in religious texts. Probably from the very beginning scribes used a rapid way of writing hieroglyphs for everyday purposes. We call that script hieratic – a Greek term meaning "priestly." From the early first millennium on some monumental inscriptions in hieratic script appear.

In the mid-first millennium people also started to write demotic – the Greek for "of the people" – a script that today requires specialist training to read as it has little obvious relationship to hieroglyphic or even hieratic, from which it descended. The Egyptians used it to write business documents and literature, and gradually also religious and some monumental texts. After Alexander's conquest of Egypt in the late fourth century Greek became a parallel language of administration and literature. The famous Rosetta Stone, key to the modern decipherment of the hieroglyphic script, contains the same royal edict in hieroglyphs, Demotic script, and Greek (see Chapter 13).

Greek script also influenced the writing of Egyptian. The Coptic script, first attested in the second century AD, was an alphabet that included vowels and was derived from the Greek with seven signs borrowed from Demotic to indicate sounds not present in Greek. The earliest Coptic writings were magical spells whose correct pronunciation was important and which required an explicit indication of the vowels. Soon Coptic became the script of the Egyptian Christian church.

All the forms of the script had their variants, which we call cursive, abnormal, and so on. Variations were temporal, regional, and also depended on who wrote. Reading Egyptian always involves a degree of decipherment and requires a good knowledge of the language, which itself constantly changed. Because all scripts except for Coptic rendered vowels only in special circumstances and no one speaks ancient Egyptian any longer, we are uncertain about how to vocalize words. Thus some speak of the god Re, others of Ra. Many Egyptological publications quote terms and titles by their consonants alone, which is disorienting to the beginner but reflects Egyptian practice.

In ancient Egypt writing always remained a restricted skill and the preserve of the privileged, most often men and some women attached to the court. We cannot estimate the literacy rate at any time, but it was certainly very low in the beginning and only gradually grew with the expansion of bureaucracies in the Old Kingdom. The esoteric character of writing gave those who knew it a special power. While many Egyptians may have seen inscriptions, only a few could understand them.

2.6   Foreign Relations

Egypt's location on the junction of Africa and Asia made it natural that it was in contact with cultures on both continents, and the development of the Egyptian state had a great effect on neighboring regions. There are also indications that outside cultures may have triggered events in Egypt, but historians differ much in opinion on this question.

The Uruk culture of Babylonia

The fourth millennium was also a period of crucial change in Babylonia – the region of southern Iraq and western Iran – that culminated in the appearance of the state. In contrast to Egypt the focus of the state in Babylonia was the city and several city-states existed side-by-side. But many characteristics of the ancient Egyptian state appeared in Babylonia as well, such as social stratification, monumental architecture, bureaucracies, and writing. The development in Babylonia seems to have been more gradual than in Egypt, and may have concluded slightly earlier, around 3200 rather than 3000. But the absolute dating of the archaeological data that underlie our reconstructions has such a margin of error that it is not a reliable means to determine precedence. Moreover, unified Egypt can no longer be considered the earliest state there, and it is unclear when its predecessors can be called true states.

Fourth-millennium Babylonia was dominated by the Uruk culture, which had a widespread regional impact although its core was in the south of Iraq. By 3200, Uruk itself was a large city with many monumental buildings and a distinct culture that is visible in its material remains. One of the culture's most remarkable features was its influence throughout western Asia, a phenomenon of the mid-fourth millennium we call the Uruk expansion. People living in the peripheries of southern Iraq – in Iran, northern Iraq and Syria, and southern Turkey – adopted elements of the Uruk culture to different degrees. Some people in northern Syria surrounded themselves fully with Uruk-style goods, and many scholars think that they were colonists coming from southern Iraq. In other places, Uruk and local cultural features occur in varying proportions. Some elements of the Uruk culture, especially a type of container we call the

Beveled Rim Bowl, appear over an enormous area from Pakistan to the Syrian coast, and historians assume that trade relations caused this widespread cultural influence. It is thus logical that the Uruk expansion may have reached Egypt as well.

In the art and architecture of Late Predynastic Egypt appear several elements that have a strong Babylonian flavor. Their foreign origin is suggested by the fact that that they existed only briefly in Egypt whereas in Babylonia they became part of the defining features of the culture. A common scene in the rich visual record of the period is the domination of animals by one or two men. The "master of animals" already appears in the wall painting of tomb 100 at Hierakonpolis of the Naqada II Period, and in some examples of the image the men seem to wear distinctly Babylonian clothing. The motif soon disappeared from Egyptian art but flourished in later Babylonia. Similarly short-lived in Egypt was the use of the cylinder seal, a small stone carved with a picture that becomes visible only when rolled on clay. The Egyptians used cylinder seals in the third millennium only, whereas the Babylonians continued to produce large numbers of them for 3,000 years. Also the use of mud-brick niched facades in Predynastic and Early Dynastic tombs, and most likely palaces, resembles Babylonian architecture where mud-brick construction dominated throughout its history. These elements have inspired many scholars to suggest a strong Babylonian influence on early Egypt. Some have credited Babylonians with inspiring Egyptian ideas of the state and writing even though these differed in nature from their Babylonian counterparts. But others point out how limited the Babylonian material is and that Babylonian practices do not necessarily predate Egyptian ones. They also stress that no evidence of the Uruk expansion appears in the region between northern Syria and Egypt, which would have been the natural passage from Babylonia to Egypt. It is interesting that no Egyptian or Egyptian-style material occurs in Babylonia. Today scholars prefer to stress indigenous forces in the evolution of early Egypt and they see the Babylonian features as the result of intermittent trade contacts, which may have been across the Persian Gulf and Red Sea rather than overland via Syria.

Late-fourth-millennium Nubia

Late-fourth-millennium evidence from Nubia north of the second cataract shows the development of a social hierarchy there. Some of the tombs excavated at the site of Qustul were much larger and richer than the surrounding ones and indicate the presence of specially honored people. In one tomb archaeologists found a fragmentary incense burner decorated with Egyptianized royal imagery: A man wearing the crown of Upper Egypt sits in a boat surmounted with a *serekh*. The scholar who published the tomb claimed that these distinctly royal elements predated evidence from Egypt and suggested that the idea of kingship originated in Nubia and then inspired Egypt. Later research showed, however, that the Qustul tomb was of the same date as the Late Predynastic royal-style tombs of Egypt. Because there is evidence of the processes that led to state formation in Egypt and not in Nubia, it is much more probable that Egyptian events influenced Nubia rather than the other way around.

Indeed the rise of the Egyptian state had an impact on its immediate peripheries. Whereas Egypt and Nubia had shared a material culture before the fourth millennium, the Naqada culture was purely Egyptian. Contemporaneous Nubians continued to emphasize materials like ceramics and ostrich shells that had lost their importance in Egypt. We label the Nubian archaeological remains with the term A-Group. The emerging elites in Late Predynastic Egypt desired luxury products, such as gold, ivory, and ebony, which they obtained from or through Lower Nubia in exchange for foods including cheese, oil, and honey. The vessels used in the transport as well as some luxury objects, such as stone palettes and copper tools, ended up in the tombs of the Nubian elites. The tomb at Qustul with the royal incense burner seems to have been an extreme example of that trend. These trade relations gave way to hostilities, however, and the Egyptians began to portray the Nubians as enemies, stereotypically depicted as bound naked men overcome by Egyptian royal might. The disappearance of A-Group material around the beginning of the 1st dynasty in Egypt is probably a result of this change in attitude.

Late-fourth-millennium Palestine

To the north of Egypt in Palestine people had developed an urban culture in the late fourth millennium. It is clear from objects in Late Predynastic tombs – especially pottery – that the Egyptians imported wine, oil, and copper from that area. The trade does not seem to have required a permanent Egyptian presence, as we find no Egyptian archaeological remains in Palestine of the Late Predynastic. The situation changed in dynasties 0 and 1, when many archaeological sites in Palestine contained Egyptian materials, such as imported pottery. Some sites had typical Egyptian architecture as well as pots in Egyptian styles but made of local clay, which suggests that Egyptians had moved into the region and set up colonies. Yet the earliest Egyptian kings were militarily active in Palestine as well. Possibly even the Narmer palette shows an attack on Palestinian settlements, and in the 1st dynasty originated images of kings defeating men whose depiction became the stereotype for the hostile "Asiatic" in later Egyptian iconography. Thus both in Palestine and Nubia the original trade relations with Egypt that had benefited local elites seem to have been replaced by Egyptian military aggression under dynasties 0 and 1. The growth of the Egyptian state with its economic and military powers had thus a great effect on its periphery.

In the earlier 2nd dynasty the Egyptian presence in Palestine and the import of goods from that area declined strikingly. Instead long-distance overseas

Key Debate 2.1 *The impetus to state formation in Egypt*

Egypt stands out among early states in world history. In most other cases – but not all (Trigger 2003: 104–13) – political entities incorporating limited territories, usually a city and its surroundings, for long periods of time preceded the existence of the territorial state. In Egypt the unification of Upper and Lower Egypt, a vast territory, initiated the state. Why did the evolution there lead almost immediately to a territorial state?

Over the years scholars have formulated many explanations under the influence of various ideological and intellectual trends (cf. Wenke 2009: 326–60). Early investigators, inspired by European ideals of historic progress through imperialism, thought that an outside force was responsible. A "dynastic race" arrived from the north and unified Egypt by conquest – archaeologists thought they could even identify their skeletons in early dynastic cemeteries (as discussed by Bard 1994: 1–5). The Egyptian visual evidence suggested otherwise, however. The Narmer palette and similar objects showed that Egyptians defeated other Egyptians. For a long time historians thought that at first two kingdoms (Upper and Lower Egypt) existed, becoming one at the start of Egypt's historical period. They debated what kingdom was victorious and what king accomplished the unification. Inspired by later mythology some thought that the Delta subdued the Nile Valley (Sethe 1930: 70–8); more believed that the south conquered the north. Much discussion revolved around who was the first to unite the two countries. Narmer seemed a likely candidate, but the somewhat earlier King Scorpion appeared with both Upper and Lower Egyptian symbols as well (I. Edwards 1971: 1–15). The idea that there existed two equivalent states was deemed unlikely, however, especially since the Delta showed no central political organization before the overall unification of Egypt (Frankfort 1948: 15–23). Thus the theory that a regional elite expanded its power gradually over the entirety of the country by eliminating other elites gained hold. The process started long before the ultimate unification of the country (Kaiser 1990).

This still did not explain why territorial unification occurred. Theories that the concept was inspired from abroad – Babylonia and Nubia have both been suggested – are mostly rejected now (cf. Midant-Reynes 2003: 275–307), and scholars prefer to focus on indigenous forces. Many think that centers of production and exchange developed along the Nile Valley and that elites in them sought increased territorial powers to gain access to trade items and agricultural areas. When the zones of influence of neighboring centers started to intersect, conflict arose, which was settled through either war or alliances (Bard 1994: 116–18). But Egypt was rich in resources and had a small population in late prehistoric times, so why would people have competed over them? Non-materialist motives may have driven expansion. People who settled down became territorial and like players in a Monopoly game tried to expand their holdings. Thousands of such games took place along the Nile and increasingly fewer players became more powerful until one triumphed (Kemp 2006: 73–8). Conquest was not necessarily the main force of unification; peaceful arrangements (marriages, etc.) may have been more important (Midant-Reynes 2003: 377–80).

In recent years the view that the valley was the primary locus of change has been under attack. Remains in the desert, which was more fertile in the fourth millennium BC than it is now, show that pastoralists flourished more than the early farmers of the valley. Part of the evidence on them derives from rock art in the eastern desert (T. Wilkinson 2003: 162–95), other evidence comes from the western desert oases (Riemer 2008). For centuries the people who moved around outside the valley were more active and wealthier than those who farmed. They developed a greater social hierarchy and an elite that controlled resources and they ultimately unified the whole of Egypt – valley, Delta, and desert regions – into a vast territory with a bureaucracy to administer it (Wengrow 2006). The question still remains, however: why?

contacts with ports farther north commenced, especially with Byblos in Lebanon. There the Egyptians could obtain long beams of cedar wood as well as agricultural products, which could be shipped by boat. These long-distance trade contacts would flourish in the Old Kingdom. Ports like Byblos also gave access to luxury items, such as lapis lazuli from Afghanistan, which previously reached Egypt through overland trade.

Tomb U-j, constructed at Abydos around 3250 BC, was the first of a long series of tombs in ancient Egypt whose inhabitants had a very special status. Although the tomb was a relatively small construction, it was filled with grave goods that came from all over Egypt and Palestine. The ability of one man to command these resources from far afield was the result of a centralization of power in Upper Egypt where early centers had joined together. The people of this region seem to have gradually extended their control over the rest of the country so that by 3000 a single king ruled Upper and Lower Egypt, thereby initiating Egypt's dynastic history. The new state required new ideologies and methods of government and administration, which developed in parallel with kingship and included ideas about the gods and how to honor them, bureaucratic techniques, and writing. Their invention was a process that needed several centuries to be completed. Yet compared to many ancient cultures, it was rapid. By the end of the 2nd dynasty, around 2686 BC, Egypt had developed into a stable territorial state under a strong king and an effective administration. The basis for further developments was fully in place.

NOTES

1. Parkinson 1998: 138, quoted by permission.
2. Baines 2007: 137.

3

The Great Pyramid Builders (ca. 2686–2345)

Soldiers, forty centuries look down upon you from these pyramids. (Napoleon Bonaparte in Egypt, July 21, 1798)

The 3rd through 5th dynasties, which ruled Egypt from around 2686 to 2345, are possibly unparalleled in world history for the amount of construction they undertook. Most of the 20-some kings compelled thousands of laborers to quarry, transport, put in place, and decorate vast quantities of stone, in order to construct royal mortuary monuments. They diverted enormous resources from the entire country for this purpose, filling a 70-kilometer-long stretch of the desert edge along the west bank of the Nile near modern Cairo with huge monuments still awe-inspiring today despite the ravages of time (see Map 2).

It may be a mistake to focus on stone monuments for the dead when studying this period as they represent just one aspect of the Egyptians' activities. Historical surveys regularly warn against this. But evidence on other aspects of life is relatively rare, and especially the textual sources on Egypt in this period are restricted in nature and quantity. We do not know the exact number of rulers in some dynasties. Nevertheless, the various stages leading to the pyramid form and the experiments with other forms of mortuary monuments exemplify how several ideas competed for recognition in the state and how much change was a characteristic of the period. Moreover, the complexes eloquently show what the Egyptians could accomplish in technical and organizational terms in this period. The pyramids are an index of royal power and allow us to speculate on Egypt's wealth, on the state's structure and its governmental practices. They show how that power was supreme and was put to use for the glorification of the king. It is thus fully proper that we see this as the first kingdom period in Egyptian history: the Old Kingdom.

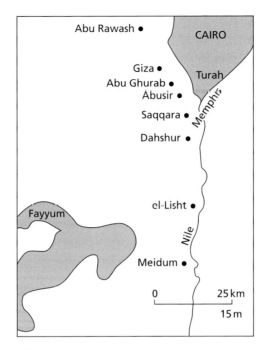

Map 2 Pyramid locations

3.1 Sources

Pyramid complexes are gigantic constructions but they are not the most eloquent of historical sources. They do not contain lengthy inscriptions detailing the king's actions in life. It is even not always easy to determine who built a pyramid and scholars rely on a variety of references from contemporary and later sources. Sometimes the king's name appears on buildings attached to the pyramid or the surrounding tombs of officials indicate the dead king's name. In some cases we depend on identifications made long ago by Greek historians like Herodotus.

The textual sources from the Old Kingdom are very restricted in number and contents, and this greatly limits our ability to study the period's history. It is clear that writing was widely used in Egypt – we find graffiti in the desert and on blocks used to build the pyramids – but much material has disappeared. Especially papyri have disintegrated and all finds recording the business of institutions and private people are fortuitous. Inscriptions carved on stone often survived only because the stones were reused later on, which makes it very difficult to reconstruct their original context. Not surprisingly the large majority of written evidence comes from a mortuary context: inscriptions in tombs, and papyri of the administrations of mortuary temples in the desert.

The basic structure for the history of the 3rd to 5th dynasties derives from king lists, at a minimum composed a millennium later. There are inconsistencies in the names of kings and the number of years they ruled. The Palermo Stone gives year-by-year information on these dynasties' kings, usually of a ritual nature, but it is very damaged (see Chapter 1). The kings left very few inscriptions, and written declarations of their actions did not yet exist at this time. King Sahura commemorated military activity in pictorial scenes of his mortuary temple, but this is an unusual record. The large majority by far of inscriptions are from officials' tombs, where they chronicled their careers, mentioning the kings they served. Scholars call these inscriptions somewhat misleadingly "biographies" because they recount aspects of a person's life. They are mostly stereotypical statements that grew out of earlier lists of titles and formulas appealing to visitors to pronounce prayers to the dead. Biographies first appeared in the 4th dynasty and continued in use throughout the 5th dynasty and beyond; the genre was popular in Egypt until the Roman Period. Those of the 4th and 5th dynasties all originate from cemeteries near the capital Memphis and give access to a wealth of officials' names and titles. Some inscriptions cite royal decrees that protected a temple's assets. We hear the king's voice in them and get some sense of how he governed.

Other written evidence of the period itself is restricted to rock inscriptions outside the Nile Valley reporting mining expeditions and a few papyrus archives. The Abusir papryi are best known (see below). A private archive, probably from the 4th dynasty, found in a box at Gebelein in 1935, has not yet been published in translation.

In the Old Kingdom Egyptians started to put in writing religious and wisdom texts, which date mostly to after the 5th dynasty. Later Egyptians looked back on the Old Kingdom as a grand period of their history and falsified texts to make them sound as if composed then, for example, King Shabaqo's stone of the eighth century (see Chapter 12). Also Middle Kingdom authors, who composed major works of Egyptian literature, liked to set their stories and instruction texts in Old Kingdom times. Such sources used to be considered valuable for the reconstruction of Old Kingdom history, but historians today are much more skeptical.

The history of the 3rd through 5th dynasties is thus mainly architectural. By far most of the archaeological remains of the period come from the area of Memphis; some derive from Abydos in the center and Elephantine in the south, while the western desert has begun to yield some material. Historians surveying the Old Kingdom tend to place the great monuments of the period in a sequence provided by the king lists, and to collect other data regarding their builders from sundry sources. It is an unsatisfactory situation, but one that cannot be changed. Even were new sources to appear, those might provide more detail, but they are unlikely to alter fundamentally our ability to investigate the era.

Summary of dynastic history
Old Kingdom (ca. 2686–2345)

ca. 2686–2613	**3rd dynasty**
	Memphis becomes the royal burial site
ca. 2686–2648	King Djoser
	Builds first stone mortuary complex at Saqqara
ca. 2613–2494	**4th dynasty**
ca. 2613–2589	King Sneferu
	Builds three pyramids at Meidum and Dahshur
ca. 2589–2566	King Khufu
	Builds Great Pyramid at Giza
ca. 2566–2558	King Djedefra
	Begins pyramid at Abu Rawash
ca. 2558–2532	King Khafra
	Builds second pyramid at Giza and Great Sphinx
ca. 2532–2503	King Menkaura
	Builds third pyramid at Giza
ca. 2503–2498	King Shepseskaf
	Builds colossal mastaba at Saqqara
ca. 2494–2345	**5th dynasty**
ca. 2494–2487	King Userkaf
	Builds pyramid at Saqqara and solar temple at Abusir
	Widow Khentkaus I may have held kingship briefly
ca. 2445–2421	King Nyuserra
	Builds pyramid at Abusir and solar temple at Abu Ghurab
ca. 2375–2345	King Unas
	Earliest preserved Pyramid Texts appear in his tomb

3.2 The Evolution of the Mortuary Complex

The last two kings of the 2nd dynasty were buried in Middle Egypt at Abydos next to their 1st-dynasty predecessors, but earlier 2nd-dynasty rulers had chosen a northern site on the desert edge alongside the city Memphis for their tombs. All the major burials of the kings of the 3rd through 5th dynasties were near Memphis as well. According to Manetho that city became Egypt's capital with the start of the 3rd dynasty, a shift that made sense because of Memphis's strategic location near where Upper and Lower Egypt meet.

Djoser's step pyramid at Saqqara

Under the first king of dynasty 3, Djoser – this name from later king lists is much more widely known than the Egyptian Horus name Netjerikhet that appears on all his monuments – the construction of mortuary complexes underwent a fundamental change: they started to be built of stone. Earlier complexes at Abydos and at Saqqara near Memphis had been massive but they were of mud brick. A few elements only were of stone. Djoser's Step Pyramid complex at Saqqara was the earliest construction of its size in world history fully made of stone. Credit for this innovation must go to Imhotep. Much later Egyptian tradition calls Imhotep King Djoser's chief architect, and an inscription found at the site of the Step Pyramid confirms his existence and role. On the base of a statue of Djoser appears Imhotep's name, with some titles including "the chief of sculptors." It was highly unusual for the name of a non-royal to appear on a king's statue, so Imhotep must have been considered very important. In his entry on Djoser, Manetho states that he invented building in cut stone, which was either a transfer of the architect's accomplishment to the king or an accidental omission of Imhotep's name.

Imhotep reproduced in stone what had been previously built of other materials. The facade of the enclosure wall had the same niches as the tombs of mud brick, the columns resembled bundles of reed and papyrus, and stone cylinders at the lintels of doorways represented rolled-up reed screens. Much experimentation was involved, which is especially clear in the construction of the pyramid in the center of the complex. It had several plans with mastaba forms before it became the first Step Pyramid in history, piling six mastaba-like levels on top of one another. The final structure measured 121 by 109 meters in area and was 60 meters high. The weight of the enormous mass was a challenge to the builders, who placed the stones at an inward incline in order to prevent the monument breaking up.

The king was laid to rest in a granite chamber underneath the Step Pyramid reached through a maze of tunnels. Those were filled with tens of thousands of stone vessels, many of which bore inscriptions of earlier kings, whose grave goods may have been recycled. These vessels' contents and that of the massive grain storage areas in the southwest area of the complex were supposed to provide for the king in the hereafter. The complex was more than a burial, however. Imhotep made provisions for the mortuary cult and for a *sed*-festival in which Djoser would participate in eternity. In the southeast part were stone replicas of structures used in the *sed*-celebration and in the great courtyard boundary markers indicated where the king had to make his ceremonial run to mark his territorial claims. On the north side of the pyramid was a mortuary temple to maintain the dead king's cult. A small closed room – we call such a room *serdab* after the Arabic word for cellar – contained a life-sized seated statue of the king, the first large royal sculpture surviving from Egypt. All these elements were enclosed with a massive stone wall forming a 500 by 250 meter rectangle, with only one narrow door. The entire complex was revolutionary because of its daring use of stone and its grandeur. It remained partly unfinished.

Sneferu's three pyramids

The next crucial moment in the development of the pyramid was the reign of Sneferu, the first king of dynasty 4. He constructed three large pyramids, the combined mass of which by far surpassed that of other rulers' monuments. The earliest was a Step Pyramid with seven stages at Meidum, standing by itself some 28 miles (45 kilometers) south of the dense concentration of tombs near Memphis (Figure 3.1). At some point an eighth step was added and later the steps were filled in to form a smooth outer casing, thus creating a true pyramid. The outer layer did not adhere well to the finished surface of the Step Pyramid, however, and at some unknown moment collapsed so that the monument now looks like a tower on a heap of debris.

Figure 3.1 Sneferu's pyramid at Meidum

Sneferu's architects were the first to plan a real pyramid from the onset, yet they failed at their first try. At Dahshur, just south of Saqqara, they started one with a 55-degree angle, and midway they realized this was too steep, when they continued at 43 degrees using smaller blocks of stone. The result was the Bent pyramid. Two kilometers north of it they successfully constructed the first true pyramid with straight sides on a 43-degree angle. They used reddish limestone, and the resulting Red pyramid, which measured 220 by 220 meters at the base, was surpassed in area only by Khufu's pyramid.

The Great Pyramids at Giza

Around 2550 BC, Sneferu's successor Khufu, whose name the Greeks later rendered as Cheops, was the recipient of the largest pyramid ever built, the Great Pyramid at Giza. It was one of the seven wonders of the ancient world and throughout history has not failed to fascinate visitors, including Napoleon, quoted at the start of this chapter. The size boggles the mind: it was 146 meters high and measured 230 by 230 meters at the base. We estimate that it contained 2,300,000 blocks of stone with an average weight of 2¾ tons, some weighing up to 16 tons. Khufu ruled 23 years according to the Turin Royal Canon, which would mean that throughout his reign annually 100,000 blocks – daily about 285 blocks or one every two minutes of daylight – had to be quarried, transported, dressed, and put in place. The blocks fit tightly together with only a thin layer of mortar, which was possible because their surfaces were planed precisely level.

The construction was almost faultless in design. The sides were oriented exactly toward the cardinal points, and were at precise 90-degree angles. We can only speculate on how the builders determined the location of the north so accurately. The pyramid's interior contained several chambers and tunnels constructed in such a way that the enormous weight on top did not crush them. A smooth casing of limestone originally covered the outside, but in the Middle Ages local residents used the pyramid as an endless supply of stone for their building projects.

Khufu's son and second successor, Khafra, built a slightly smaller pyramid (143.5 meters high and 215 by 215 meters at the base) just south of his, and his grandson Menkaura raised the smallest of the three, still 65 meters high and 105 by 102 meters at the base. These already massive constructions need to be seen within their context, which makes the mortuary complexes even more astounding. Starting with Sneferu's Bent pyramid at Dahshur, a complete complex not only contained the king's burial in the large pyramid, but also subsidiary pyramids, a pyramid temple, a causeway, and a valley temple. These were laid out on an east–west axis so that the progress of the dead king's body from the valley temple to the tomb paralleled the movement of the sun through the sky.

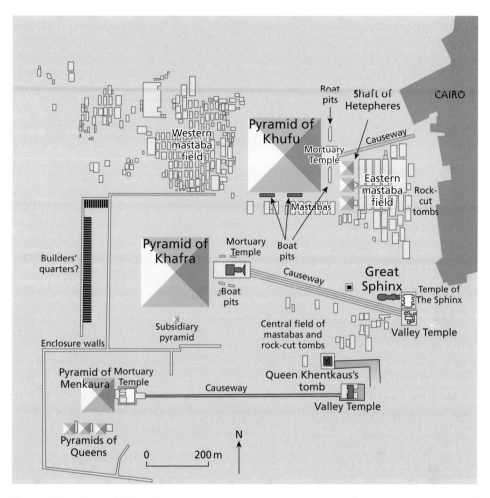

Figure 3.2 Plan of Giza plateau

The valley temple held multiple statues representing the king. Many of those are preserved for Menkaura and show him together with the goddess Hathor and personifications of Egypt's nomes. The temple gave access to the causeway leading up the plateau. Khafra's causeway stands out because of the sphinx guarding it, which artists carved in the natural rock. It was the first truly colossal statue in Egyptian history, not equaled in size until a thousand years later. At the end of the causeway was the pyramid temple on the east facade of the pyramid, in which the cult of the dead king was celebrated for decades after his death. The pyramid itself contained the tomb. With its mass, its secret tunnels and chambers, and its stone doors, the builders hoped to protect the king's body in eternity, but they failed. All three pyramids were robbed a long time ago (Figure 3.2).

The kings were not buried in isolation. Besides their tombs were located subsidiary pyramids intended for queens, and officials of the state had mastaba tombs on the Giza plateau. They were laid out in neat rows to allow as many as possible of them to rest near their masters in eternity. The plateau contained a mass of underground chambers, rock-cut tombs as well as later burials. Near Khufu's causeway were two boat-shaped pits, possibly intended to aid the king on his voyage to the sky, while two rectangular pits on the south side of the pyramid contained dismantled wooden boats, which may have been the original ones used to take the king's body across the Nile. Archaeological research continues to reveal unexpected finds beneath the plateau.

We can marvel about the Giza pyramids for many different reasons. Their sizes, orientation, and intricate plans have inspired numerous theories, some so outlandish that they involve extraterrestrials. On a more mundane level we should consider the logistical problems that faced the builders. Those varied according to local circumstances but were always daunting. Most obviously, the heavy stone blocks had to be pulled and lifted by sheer manpower alone, and no one has yet explained satisfactorily how this was done (see Key Debate 3.1). The projects required careful planning of the use of space on the Giza plateau, a problem that became more acute as the area filled up. In order to situate the three pyramids on the same level the southern ones had to be farther into the desert than Khufu's to adjust for a dip at the southeast edge. The base of each pyramid had to be exactly horizontal so as not to create a slant. This required the construction of a level platform to adjust for the unevenness of the plateau. In the center of Khufu's pyramid is still a natural mound around which the architects worked. In Khafra's case part of the plateau was leveled, while on the other side a platform was built.

Most likely workmen pulled the stones on ramps of mud and chippings of stone and other debris that needed constant rebuilding. The area available to position the ramps became smaller when the plateau filled up with tombs and other constructions, and they most likely circled around the parts of the pyramid already completed. They needed to be discarded afterwards, and with a volume of about two-thirds of that of the pyramid they served this demanded a lot of space.

The thousands of workers participating in the projects required housing, kitchens to prepare their food, and workshops for their tools. South of Menkaura's pyramid archaeologists have uncovered remains of a village that could have housed 4,000 people in dormitories, and they found a set of alabaster workshops and kilns southeast of the pyramid. But much more logistical support was needed. The question of manpower is especially intriguing. People from all over Egypt must have been conscripted in the effort, which meant that some of them had to travel for hundreds of kilometers. Scholars now estimate that about 25,000 of them were active at the same time, working three-month stints. If the general population of Egypt at the time was 1.5 million, as some scholars reckon, this would have represented some 5 percent of the adult male population. They had to abandon their usual tasks at home, which may have been possible in periods when agricultural duties were limited. If work on the pyramids was only seasonal rather than year-round, however, the number of people involved and amount of labor to be done in a day would have been larger. Later Greeks stated that Khufu was a tyrant who forced his subjects to do this (see below), but it is more likely that the Egyptians saw the work as a normal duty in honor of their ruler.

While the builders used local stone quarries for the mass of the pyramids they also brought special limestone from Turah across the river, as well as granite from distant Aswan for the outer casing of some pyramids. Together with other materials and labor, this meant that the whole country contributed to the effort. These were monuments that required the entire state's support, and the complexity of the bureaucratic organization behind them can only be imagined.

Solar temples of the 5th dynasty

Although the three mortuary complexes at Giza may seem to represent the culmination of a long evolution, later kings continued to experiment. The last king of dynasty 4, Shepseskaf, built a huge sarcophagus-shaped mastaba at Saqqara, which seems to indicate a desire to express another ideology. The kings of dynasty 5 returned to pyramids for their tombs at Abusir and Saqqara, although they were much smaller and with cores made of small stones. But in addition they constructed temples with a focus on the sun god, whose cult further increased in importance (see below). The remains of two solar temples are known, both of which had several phases in which various plans were tried out. In the end the complexes contained a valley temple, a causeway, and a walled courtyard with a huge masonry obelisk on a platform as its focal point. Next to the court stood a large stone boat. The courtyard held several slaughterhouses and magazines, and it seems that the function of these complexes was to provision for the mortuary cult at the pyramid. Their imagery was strongly connected to the sun; the obelisk was a monumental sunray and the boat represented the boat in which the sun traversed the sky.

The final pyramid of the 5th dynasty belonged to King Unas, who was the first to carve spells of a mortuary book, the Pyramid Texts, onto the walls of the interior chambers. The burial room was also decorated with white alabaster panels incised to look like reed and wood structures, as in Djoser's complex a permanent stone rendering of ephemeral structures. The pyramid tomb survived under the 6th dynasty and was the standard royal tomb in the Middle Kingdom as well. In the New Kingdom it ceased to be used for the kings' burial.

In the 325 years of the 3rd through 5th dynasties, and continuing into the early 6th dynasty, the people of Egypt were constantly engaged in the construction of these enormous complexes. The building demanded the contributions of labor and materials from the entire country and the immense effort of numerous people from all levels of society. Regularly there was not enough time in a king's life to complete the original grandiose plans and a complex was finished in mud brick so that the builders could turn to the next project. But still, the

Special Topic 3.1 *The afterlife of the mortuary complexes*

Today the pyramids stand isolated in the desert, abandoned when the last tourist leaves, but in ancient times that was not the case. The mortuary complexes were meant to provide the dead with offerings in perpetuity, and although that ideal was never realized and cults ceased typically after a couple of generations, they needed personnel to do the job. Priests were assigned those duties in shifts and had to move into the complex. They set up house near or inside mortuary and valley temples and built themselves shelters. Their presence and natural decay caused damage to the temple architecture, which they tried to patch up with wooden beams and bricks. Over time these buildings became ramshackle, and the stately monuments we may imagine turned into small villages where people cooked, washed, discarded rubbish, and so on.

It was impossible for Egyptians in later periods to maintain all of the Old Kingdom monuments, and most of them were deserted. Some had a special appeal, however, and remained important. Djoser's complex at Saqqara was a pilgrimage site from the New Kingdom on, with many visitors leaving offerings especially to his architect, Imhotep. On the plateau around it people from the Middle Kingdom into the Roman Period built tombs, and from the New Kingdom on the mummified Apis bull was buried there (see Chapter 12). Rameses II started underground galleries for the animal's burial, which continued to expand into the Roman Period.

Also the sphinx at Giza had a special fascination. The New Kingdom king Amenhotep II commemorated how he visited the monument when he was still a prince, and how he "observed the excellence of the resting-place of Kings Khufu and Khafra, the justified." Thutmose IV left a stele recording a dream he had while resting beside it, in which the statue promised him kingship if he removed the sand covering its body. Later kings repeatedly claimed to have cleared the sculpture as well as repairing damage, and restorations into the Roman Period are still visible today. According to legend the nose broke when Napoleon's soldiers fired a cannonball at it, but most likely the damage occurred centuries earlier.

remains towered over the capital city of Memphis and no one traveling along the Nile could avoid seeing them. They stood there across the ages as silent reminders of the kings' grandeur.

3.3 Administrating the Old Kingdom State

Neferirkara's archive at Abusir

We can scarcely imagine the administrative supervision that was needed for the building projects of the Old Kingdom; we do not have official records of the work. We do know, however, that the Egyptian state at the time wanted to manage closely the economic activity under its purview and that it had the ability to do so. It employed a bureaucracy that could utilize systems of collection and distribution of resources and the means of accounting to keep track of them. The activity is best documented in papyrus archives from mortuary temples at Abusir of the 5th dynasty. Those of King Neferirkara, his queens, and his successor are best known, recording temple affairs in the late 5th and early 6th dynasties (see Sources in Translation 3.1). Some of the papyri list methodically the amounts of food contributions, their place of origin, and who delivered them. The accountants regularly used a tabular format with separate columns for different kinds of contributions and rows to keep track of their sources. They kept records of the yields of the estates provisioning the temple,

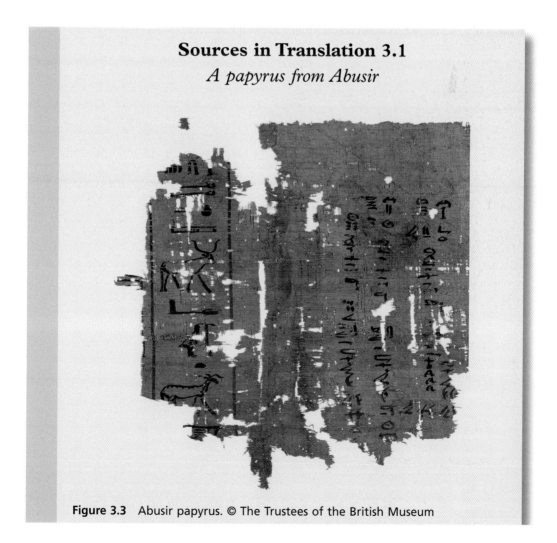

Sources in Translation 3.1

A papyrus from Abusir

Figure 3.3 Abusir papyrus. © The Trustees of the British Museum

This fragment is the beginning of a papyrus roll found in the mortuary temple of the 5th-dynasty king Neferirkara at Abusir. The left column is written in hieroglyphs and reads: "The year a[fter] the fourteenth occasion of the counting of all the great and small herds [ ]," which we know indicates the 27th or 28th year of King Djedkara Izezi, the penultimate ruler of the 5th dynasty.

To the right another scribe wrote an account in hieratic script:

First month of Shemu, last day: Giving the [ ] gallons of grain issued to Tjesemy and Nefernemtet: THIS IS WHAT IS MEASURED EVERY DAY.

2nd month of Shemu, day 2: Giving the [ ] gallons of grain issued to Tjesemy; day 6: Giving the 5½ gallons of grain issued to Tjesemy: THIS IS (WHAT IS MEASURED EVERY DAY).

(Translation from Parkinson 1999: 89, quoted by permission)

including grain, fruit, vegetables, milk, wine, fats, poultry, and meat. Other papyri listed the timetables of priestly duties and kept inventories of the temple's tools and cult objects.

The expenditures of the institutions were accounted for in the same way. These involved primarily the support of personnel on all levels. The Egyptian economy did not use money. Payments for services were in kind, especially bread and beer, meat and fowl, and emmer wheat and barley. Each level of worker received a set amount of these products, and in order to keep track of the distributions quantities had to be clearly defined. Loaves of bread and jars of beer had standard sizes. Since institutions employed large numbers of people, their kitchens had to prepare huge amounts of food, whose ingredients had to be accounted for as well. The mortuary temple of Neferirkara was a relatively small enterprise. The bookkeeping tools used there had all the characteristics needed for the massive projects of pyramid building, however. These just required many more accountants.

Officialdom

The Old Kingdom state had a large number of officials whose titles appear primarily in short inscriptions in tombs. They combined numerous titles, which tend to be so nondescript that we cannot infer responsibilities from them. Hesira, a prominent man in Djoser's reign, for example, was, among other things, "greatest of the tens of Upper Egypt" (Plate 4). This does not reveal what he did. Because of the bureaucratic nature of the Egyptian state, scribes were important, and their number must have increased substantially to deal with the massive projects, although still only a small percentage of the population was literate. People in various levels of the administration were able to read and write, and "scribe" became the most basic attribute in their titularies. The structure of the administration remains unknown but was certainly very hierarchical. By the early 3rd dynasty on the king's right-hand man was the vizier, who throughout Egyptian history oversaw all aspects of the state administration. In the 4th dynasty, the king seems to have granted most high officials titles that claimed a blood relationship to him, but this was probably a fiction to stress one's closeness to the center of power. From the 5th dynasty on this practice disappeared.

The state not only rewarded administrators when they were active, but also gave support for their burials. In the shadow of the Great Pyramid at Giza, for example, stand rows of mastaba tombs for officials built by royal craftsmen as a gift to them, and, like the king, these officials received offerings to provide for them in the afterlife. The diversion of the country's resources to the administrative center was thus exacerbated with the growth of the bureaucracy. The concept that the entire country supported the king and his entourage in life and in death was indeed a central aspect of the political ideology of Egypt, and in practice it required a rigorous organization. The idea dated back to the Early Dynastic Period and even before (see Chapter 2), and the subdivision of Egypt into nomes facilitated the practice. Depictions of the king in the pyramid complexes stressed his connections to the nomes, which probably numbered around 40 at the time. The most stunning set of sculptures of Menkaura, for example, excavated in his valley temple, show the king with the goddess Hathor beside a series of personifications of nomes, that is, women bearing the nome symbol on their heads (Figure 3.4). In Nyuserra's solar temple at Abu Ghurab a long relief showed the procession of nome representations.

Agricultural estates in the nomes provided the food for the mortuary cults of kings and officials. In Sneferu's complex at Dahshur a relief shows the personifications of such estates – women carrying a tray of food offerings with the name of the estate carved above their heads – in a procession organized by their nomes. The preserved part includes 34 estates from 10 nomes in Upper Egypt and four from one nome in Lower Egypt. They were spread over the entire country from the first cataract to the Delta, and were often named after the king, for example, "Joy of Sneferu." Likewise, officials' support derived from various regions. The estates involved could be very small, such as half a hectare, and their dispersal was partly for ideological reasons: the entire country supported the court. In order to facilitate the collection and shipping of these resources, local administrations had to be in place. The main population center in each nome became a regional capital and the local nomarch resided there to represent the state.

Special Topic 3.2   *Egypt's Administration*

From its very creation the Egyptian state required a bureaucracy that at a minimum kept track of the resources owed to the center of power. Many preserved documents from the entire ancient history of the country deal with this issue. Some of the first records we have are bureaucratic: objects from the tombs at Abydos contained sealings with indications where they came from. We have to assume that in all periods, and especially when the country was unified, a large administration existed. At the same time, it is clear over the long period that ancient Egypt existed many changes took place.

We can see certain basic patterns, however. The king was at the center of the administration and his person gave it authority. State resources were for the king to collect and distribute. In order to facilitate work, different departments existed: treasury, agriculture, and labor. The titles of the officials who headed these changed little over the centuries. They dealt with all assets of the state: goods, produce, and manpower. They supervised the collection of dues and corvée labor and their allotment for varied purposes.

The large country was divided into provinces, which we designate with the term nome. By the 5th dynasty Upper Egypt was divided into 22 nomes, while the systematization of Lower Egyptian nomes is clear to us only late in Egyptian history. Nomarchs ideally represented the king's interests, but in intermediate periods gained much independence.

The huge central bureaucracy had many levels. Throughout Egyptian history a vizier acted as second-in-command to the king; in some periods two viziers shared the numerous tasks. It is always difficult for us to determine what administrators did. The titles themselves do not indicate it, and many officials combined various titles and accumulated several responsibilities. Alongside the civil administration existed temple and military administrations, each with their ranks and tasks. The latter is totally unknown from Old Kingdom records. Egypt's bureaucracy was so large that it represented a burden when the state was weak. Its participants not only received rewards in life, but the king also gave many the resources to build a lavish tomb and support a mortuary cult that ideally would last forever.

3.4 Ideological Debates?

The continual experimentation with the layout and elements of the mortuary complex is but one indication that the principles of kingship were in flux during the Old Kingdom. The sequence of massive buildings may give the impression that royal power was stable, but there were many occasions when succession was contested and groups with different ideologies acquired power in turn. The study of these issues is difficult because the textual sources of the period are extremely restricted. It seems clear, however, that differing views find their expression in the remains of the Old Kingdom.

Figure 3.4 King Menkaura with the goddess Hathor and the personification of the Hu nome of Upper Egypt. Werner Forman Archive/Egyptian Museum, Cairo

Problems of royal succession

Historians suspect that princes regularly fought over the succession to the throne. Each ruler had several wives, and the sons of different mothers could allege to be the legitimate heirs, each probably with the support of diverse lobbies in court. Our understanding of these events is greatly hampered by the fact that we often do not know the exact kinship between the members of the court whose names appear in the sources. But the current tentative reconstruction of the royal families suggests that disputes were frequent in the Old Kingdom.

Sneferu's accession to the throne and the start of the 4th dynasty, for example, seems to have been awkward. His relationship to the last king of the

3rd dynasty is unclear, and some scholars believe that he married his half-sister, Hetepheres I, to gain legitimacy, although we do not know the role of women in royal succession at the time. The fate of Hetepheres's body is a mystery. Next to the pyramid of her son Khufu archaeologists found a sealed deep shaft, filled with exquisite mortuary equipment including a sarcophagus. But the sarcophagus was empty. Was she buried elsewhere on the Giza plateau or near Sneferu's complex at Dahshur?

At the death of Khufu, the Great Pyramid builder and clearly a very powerful man, two of his sons vied for the throne. The original crown prince had been Kawab, but he died before his father. The first successor was Djedefra, who may have married Kawab's widow, Hetepheres II, in order to strengthen his claim to kingship. Djedefra decided not to build his pyramid at Giza but at Abu Rawash, some eight kilometers to the north, which many scholars interpret as a sign of his devotion to the sun god whose main cult center was across the river at Heliopolis. Khafra, a son of Khufu by another wife, soon replaced his half-brother and sited his mortuary complex next to his father's. Some scholars state that he had Djedefra's tomb methodically destroyed, but archaeological evidence suggests that this happened many centuries later.

At the end of the 4th dynasty, King Shepseskaf, may have promoted a new ideology by moving his tomb to Saqqara and building it in the shape of a mastaba. His successor was Userkaf, the first king of the 5th dynasty, known to have favored the cult of the sun god Ra. His wife was Khentkaus I, who was also buried in a mastaba tomb, but at Giza near the Great Pyramids. As "Mother of two Kings of Upper and Lower Egypt" she probably gave birth to the next two rulers of dynasty 5. Most startling is that she appears with regalia and a title that suggests that she held kingship for a while. Some scholars believe that she represented the lobby in the court that promoted the solar cult, an ideology she may have displayed in the shape of her tomb.

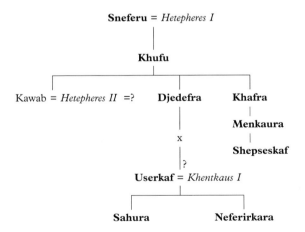

Tentative family tree of the 4th and early 5th dynasties (selected family members only)
Bold: kings; italics: queens; =: marriage

The gods Horus and Ra

The moves from one burial site to another, the experimentations with the shapes of tombs, and the use of new titles all suggest that the kings of the Old Kingdom sought different ways to assert their relationship to the divine world and their destiny within it. From the inception of kingship the god Horus had been the main patron of the king, who was the god's earthly embodiment. That ideology survived into the Old Kingdom Period. The statue where the falcon god cradles King Khafra in his wings is a vivid expression of this ideology: the falcon not only protects the king with his wings but he also merges with the king so that there is no distinction between the bird's breast and the back of the king's head (Figure 3.5). Mythology makes clear that the Egyptians saw Horus as the successor of Osiris and that they equated the living king to the former and the dead king to the latter god. Horus's lengthy struggle to wrestle kingship from the god Seth was one of the most elaborate tales of Egyptian mythology. The Old Kingdom Pyramid Texts already allude to it and over the centuries, into the Roman Period, various versions of it appear. The two gods were perpetual antagonists and seem to have represented two competing ideologies in the Early Dynastic Period. One king of the 2nd dynasty, Peribsen, used a Seth name instead of a Horus name, while his successor (Khasekhemwy) placed images of both gods above his *serekh* and used "The Two Lords are at Peace in Him" as an epithet that followed his name.

In subsequent history the Horus name was one of the king's most important titles and rulers such as Djoser used that name alone in their inscriptions. The sun god Ra as the source of all life was also crucial for kingship, however, and his role seems to have grown during the Old Kingdom. The increase may have been due to the capital's proximity to the main cult center of the sun god, Heliopolis (Greek for "city of the sun"), across the Nile from Memphis. Many innovations in the representation of the king relate to his relationship to the sun. In Sneferu's reign the symbol of royalty that we call cartouche (the French term for artillery shell) became standard. It is an oblong circle with a base line into which the king's name was written, and signifies the king's power over everything the sun encircled on its daily course (see Figure 2.1). The king was "son of Ra" as well as the embodiment of Horus, in mythology Osiris's son. Solar imagery was very strong in the mortuary complexes. The pyramid itself was a sunray and a means for the king to ascend to heaven to join the sun. Its cap was modeled on the *benben* stone, an incarnation of the mound on which the sun god had created the universe. The original *benben* stone was located in Heliopolis, where kings from no later than Djoser built temples to the sun god. Moreover, the entire pyramid complex was laid out on an east–west axis to parallel the sun's path through heaven.

The king's connection with Ra found its strongest expression in the monuments of the 5th dynasty. The sun temples that provided the mortuary cults with offerings contained open courtyards where the sun could readily

Figure 3.5 King Khafra and the god Horus. Egyptian Museum, Cairo, © 2010. Photo Scala, Florence/BPK, Bildagentur für Kunst, Kultur und Geschichte, Berlin

participate in the cult rituals performed in front of an obelisk, that is, a stone sun ray. Later tradition (see below) presented the first three kings of the dynasty as the physical sons of Ra, which may have been an attempt to explain the special status of the sun god in the 5th dynasty.

Yet the Horus ideology did not disappear. The relationship with his father Osiris remained the model for that between the living and dead kings, and in essence Osiris was the force through which one generation produced the next. His mummy resided in the netherworld where he ruled as king. At the very end of the 5th dynasty, the Pyramid Texts – spells to guide the king to his place in the hereafter (see Chapter 4) – started to be carved in the royal tombs. These combined the ideologies of Osiris and Ra, which were both seen as forces of rebirth. During the day the sun, identified with Horus, traveled through the sky as the source of all life. At night it merged with Osiris in the netherworld to be reborn at daybreak. The Pyramid Texts guided the king to his place alongside the sun. It is possible that the merging of the Osiris and Ra ideologies inspired some of the conflicts we see in Old Kingdom times.

3.5 Foreign Relations

The existence of a rich and powerful state naturally had consequences for the neighboring regions, although Egypt perhaps was more isolationist in the Old Kingdom than in previous and later times. The ideology of the king as warrior and conqueror, which had been so strong at the start of the dynastic period, was not very prominent in the period's visual arts, but it did survive. At this time it had to involve foreigners as Egypt was at peace inside its borders. The mortuary temple of Sahura contained a record of that king's campaigns in Libya. It shows images of Libyan chiefs and their families, with captions giving their names, and of captured animals, whose numbers are recorded (Figure 3.6). These scenes became an archetype for the representation of Libyan wars later on, and many scholars believe that Sahura himself may have copied earlier examples. In any case, Egypt must have been engaged militarily abroad, but the extant record is slim.

Contacts with Nubia

One documented campaign involved Sneferu who marched into Lower Nubia and perhaps assured Egyptian presence in the region for the next 250 years. Buhen at the northern edge of the second cataract was the site of a fortress, and graffiti and inscribed seals attest that Egyptians lived there to regulate traffic along the Nile and to interact with people farther south. Only limited evidence appears of an indigenous Nubian population between the first and second cataracts, and it seems that the Egyptians exploited the region fully for their own benefit, investing nothing in its infrastructure or the local people. By the end of the 5th dynasty, however, Nubians gradually reasserted themselves and replaced Egyptian dominance in Lower Nubia with a confederation of chiefdoms. This forced Egypt to seek other ways to stay in contact with the people farther upriver (see Chapter 4).

Contacts with Asia

During the Old Kingdom, the political situation in the Syro-Palestinian area was very unlike that in Nubia, so Egypt's relations with that region were

Figure 3.6 Bears captured as booty by King Sahura on his Libyan campaigns. Werner Forman Archive/Egyptian Museum, Berlin

different. The Levant had an urban culture of city-states that were economically well off and technologically advanced. The Egyptians had to interact with people there as equals: they traded rather than exploited the region. The mountains of Lebanon produced strong timber that was unavailable elsewhere, and Egyptian ships – some of them represented in Sahura's temple reliefs – sailed to Byblos to procure it. Interestingly, the crews on them were represented as non-Egyptians. It is no surprise that excavations in Byblos revealed objects with the names of many 4th- and 5th-dynasty kings. Assorted Egyptian objects appear farther away, such as in the northern Syrian city of Ebla, but there is not much. Conversely few names of Levantine cities appear in Egyptian texts. It was only in Sinai – an intermediate zone between Egypt and Asia with nonsedentary populations – that Egyptian presence was constant from the 3rd through 6th dynasties, as inscriptions of royal names found there document. The aim was to mine turquoise and copper, and there was no reason to annex the region.

No contacts are documented between Egypt and Babylonia, the urban culture that flourished in southern Iraq and had a strong cultural reach into western Syria. The Egyptians had done away with all the cultural elements that had a Babylonian flavor, such as cylinder seals and some artistic motifs. As pointed out in Chapter 2, these may have been of marginal importance in any case. It is remarkable, however, that no evidence shows that the peoples of Egypt and Babylonia were aware of each other in the mid-third millennium.

3.6   Later Traditions about the Old Kingdom

The pyramids and their builders still make a great impression on us today. It is no surprise then that later Egyptians wondered about these men and their achievements and that they spun tales around them. Especially three kings appeared in stories written from the Middle Kingdom to the Roman Period: Djoser, Sneferu, and Khufu. The tales are not always flattering and can depict the kings in negative terms. A rich corpus exists, only a few elements of which can be addressed here.

Djoser and Imhotep

The first great builder Djoser was respected for his monument at Saqqara, which became a pilgrimage site from the New Kingdom on. Many visitors left graffiti behind that show us that they knew Djoser's name. In the New Kingdom Turin Royal Canon (see Chapter 1) the king appears as the only one whose title "King of Upper and Lower Egypt" is written in red ink, a sign that the author saw him as the start of a new era. The earliest preserved story involving the king is from the Greek Period in an inscription carved on the rocks of an island in the first cataract. It tells the story of a famine in Djoser's reign, which ended when Imhotep made offerings to the god Khnum. The inscription professes to record the king's decree to make these offerings permanent. Even later is a Demotic tale of the 1st or 2nd century AD that relates how Djoser and Imhotep campaigned in Assyria and faced witchcraft, which was a popular subject in the Roman Period.

The figure of Imhotep was crucial to Djoser's legacy, and it was the architect whose memory flourished most in later Egyptian tradition. Nothing special about him appeared before the New Kingdom, but then several sources presented him as a great wise man of the past. In the 1st millennium BC, he became regarded as the son of the creator god Ptah, and many statues portrayed him as a sage reading a papyrus. A cult developed around him in Memphis, which spread all across Egypt and gained popularity in all levels of society. Many pilgrims came to his tomb at Saqqara and deposited votive offerings, which mostly consisted of a mummified ibis – the bird associated with the god of wisdom Thoth – in a jar. Thousands of these were excavated northeast of Djoser's complex.

Just before the Greek conquest Imhotep became honored as a great healer and when the Greeks governed the country they equated him to their healing god Asklepios. The Romans honored Imhotep as a god, who knew architecture, interpreted divinatory signs, and helped the ill, infertile, and pregnant. His fame was so great that Arab scholars of the Middle Ages still referred to him as a sage.

Sneferu

The first king of the 4th dynasty, Sneferu, was popular in Middle Kingdom tales as the patron of advisors who could predict the future. In one tale, priest Neferty entertained Sneferu by telling him how – ostensibly centuries later – King Amenemhat would reunite the country. The tale calls Sneferu an excellent king. More elaborate was the story in the Westcar papyrus. Its setting was the court of King Khufu whose sons told him stories as distraction. Bauefra recounted how Sneferu sought relaxation in a boat rowed by 20 young women. When one of them lost a pendant, he ordered a magician to fold the lake in such a way that the charm could be recovered. This was mere entertainment, but may have been intended to show how benevolent Sneferu was. That aspect certainly appealed to Middle Kingdom Egyptians, who honored him as a god and often invoked his name in that of their children.

The Great Pyramid builders

Sneferu's son Khufu may not have been remembered so kindly from the start. The Westcar tale set in his court also contained a story about this king. The narrator was his son Hardjedef, whom Middle Kingdom Egyptians saw as a sage like Imhotep. Hardjedef told of a man who could reattach heads to bodies, and Khufu demanded a demonstration on a prisoner. The magician refused, however, and showed his skills with a goose and an ox. He then went on to tell Khufu a story about future kings of the 5th dynasty, born as sons of the sun god Ra (see Sources in Translation 3.2). The tale seems to be an explanation why that dynasty was especially devoted to the solar cult.

Greek historians had no doubts about Khufu's cruelty. Herodotus (5th century BC) and Diodorus (1st century BC) described how he compelled tens

Sources in Translation 3.2

A Middle Kingdom tale about the 5th dynasty

The Westcar papyrus, written in the Second Intermediate Period but probably the copy of a Middle Kingdom tale, relates the birth of the first three kings of the 5th dynasty, the sons of the sun god with a mortal woman, Ruddjedet. When it was time for her to deliver, Ra sent four birth goddesses and the divine creator of humans to assist the woman. The goddess Isis encouraged each of the children not to harm the mother with statements that were puns on the kings' names.

> They then entered before Ruddjedet.
> Then They sealed the room with her and Them in it.
> Then Isis placed Herself before her, Nephthys behind her,
> and Heqet was hastening the birth.
> Then Isis said, "May you not be powerful in her womb,
> in this your name of Userref!"
> And this child slipped out onto Her arms,
> as a child one cubit, with strong bones,
> the appearance of whose limbs was gold,
> whose head-cloth was true lapis-lazuli.
> And They washed him, when his navel cord had been cut,
> and he was placed on a sheet as a pillow.
> Then Meshkenet presented Herself to him.
> Then She said, "A king who will perform the kingship
> in this entire land!"
> <And> Khnum made his limbs healthy.
> (Translation from Parkinson 1998: 117,
> quoted by permission)

The name the gods gave the king in this tale was Userref, which contains the verb *user* "to be powerful," after the admonition of Isis to the child not to stay in the womb. It served as an etymology of the actual name of the first king of the 5th dynasty, Userkaf. The story goes on to explain the names of Sahura and Neferirkara Kakai in the same way, associating these kings with the god Ra.

of thousands of men to work on his tomb, brought misery to the country, and shut down temples. Herodotus claimed that Khufu, whom he called Cheops, even forced his daughter to prostitute herself to help finance the building. Both historians portrayed Khafra in similar terms, but they showed Menkaura as a caring ruler who reopened the temples. Diodorus related how the people of Egypt hated the two tyrants so much that they threatened to tear their corpses apart. These authors were certainly inspired by the scale of the pyramids, which

Key Debate 3.1 *How was the Great Pyramid built?*

Khufu's pyramid at Giza is the one wonder of the ancient world still standing and its massive size does not cease to amaze. Many of the blocks used in it are so gigantic – weighing up to 16 tons – that every visitor wonders how the ancient Egyptians were able to transport and lift them into place, reaching a height of 146 meters at the top. The ancients already speculated about it. In the 5th century BC the Greek Herodotus stated the builders used wooden lifting devices, without giving details; the first-century-BC historian Diodorus said ramps had been used because the Egyptians did not know cranes when the pyramids were built (cf. Verner 2001: 82). Modern scholars and amateurs continue to publish explanations, regularly drawing popular attention because the question is so mystifying. Leaving aside suggestions of extraterrestrial forces, these range from crediting Egyptians with skills now lost or at best rare – such as the power of sonic levitation (Lawton & Ogilvie-Herald 1999: 220) – to theories based on careful investigations of the Giza plateau and its non-monumental archaeological remains. In the last few decades this research has produced impressive results that support the idea that ramps were used. Archaeologists found vast amounts of stone chips and mortar, which likely are the debris of such ramps (C. Smith 2004: 150–77). There are still scholars who argue for lifting devices with such technologies as pulleys (cf. Verner 2001: 82–93), either alone or in combination with ramps (Lauer 1989), but the enormous weight of the interior blocks makes this unlikely. Perhaps they were only used for the exterior layer of Turah limestone (Vercoutter 1992: 276).

It is most probable that men, perhaps assisted by oxen, dragged the stones on sledges up ramp that were covered with a mixture of chips, gypsum, and Nile mud to decrease friction (Bard 2008: 140). Some say oil was added to the mixture (cf. www.pyramidofman.com/blog/photo-how-were-the-pyramids-built), although one wonders how the men pulling did not lose their footing. Different types of ramps could have been constructed and also more than one type in the same project. They could have been long and straight, spiraled around the pyramid, or zigzagged upward. They could have been fully on the exterior or partly inside the mass of the pyramid (Arnold 1991: 98–101; Lehner 1997: 215–17). Since the interior of each pyramid contained steps, it is possible that each level was used as an interval in the ramps. Most scholars seem to agree that ramps would not have been straight because they would have covered an enormous surface not readily available at Giza, but others object that a spiraling ramp needed to narrow as the size of the pyramid layers decreased and would have become useless at the top (Lauer 1989). A suggestion that the pyramids were not constructed of cut stone but of concrete poured into molds (Davidovits & Morris 1988), has very little support among Egyptologists.

Many other logistical questions remain. One is the number and the source of the workers. They were not slaves, as Cecil B. DeMille portrayed them in *The Ten Commandments*. An unwilling workforce equipped with copper and stone tools could not be controlled by soldiers whose weapons were basically of the same types. It is not that there were not enough prisoners of war, as some suggest (Hornung 1999a: 22–4); using them was impossible. The laborers were Egyptians who worked voluntarily, probably when they were not needed in agriculture. The main force came from two teams of 2,000 men each, assisted by others for building ramps, cooking, tool manufacture, and so on, and supervised by architects. The total workforce at one time was probably between 20,000 and 25,000 (Lehner 1997: 224–5).

they could only imagine to have been built through forced labor of the masses. Menkaura's smaller tomb would have been a sign of his kindness. Several scholars claim that Sneferu's reputation needs another explanation, as he moved more stone than any other Old Kingdom ruler. His name, which is formed from the word "good," may have inspired the idea of his benevolence.

Later Egyptian tales about Old Kingdom kings contained much fantasy and magic. The visible monuments of these kings probably inspired the stories. The sun temples of the 5th dynasty may have led to the belief that its first rulers were the sons of Ra, rather as the sizes of the pyramids of Khufu and Khafra gave these men a reputation for cruelty. Egyptians after the Old Kingdom were very much in the same situation that we are in today when looking at the period. Little evidence is available to enable the reconstruction of people's deeds. The mortuary monuments are the most awe-inspiring remains, but despite their mass they leave many questions unanswered.

4

The End of the Old Kingdom and the First Intermediate Period (ca. 2345–2055)

I let the plow lands be inundated while every neighborhood thirsted. Everyone had Nile water to his heart's content, and I gave water to his neighbors so that he should be at peace with them. (Khety, nomarch of Asyut under the 10th dynasty)[1]

The 3rd to 5th dynasties, discussed in the previous chapter, stand out in Egypt's ancient history because of the grandeur of their mortuary complexes. The immense building activity to honor just one man continued into the 6th dynasty, but ended around 2200. Between kings Pepy II of the 6th dynasty and Mentuhotep II of the 11th, two centuries later, no major royal monument arose. If we take tomb construction as an index of power, this clearly indicates a weakening of the king's ability to command the country's revenue. Instead resources became more widely distributed over the upper classes of society. State officials in the provinces built themselves grand mortuary complexes in which they often expressed local traditions rather than the court's uniform style. In inscriptions carved in their tombs, men like Khety, quoted above, professed achievements previously only possible as royal acts. The regions of Egypt gained an importance unthinkable at the height of the Old Kingdom. The waning of central power led to a political fragmentation, however, and from the end of the 6th dynasty to the middle of the 11th several "kings" coexisted, an abomination in later Egyptian eyes. In our modern framework of the country's history such an era constitutes an Intermediate Period. Many scholars argue that later Egyptian literature portraying famines and social disturbances reflects on this period. The interpretation of these depictions is not straightforward, however, and instead of an overall decline of the country we should see the First Intermediate Period as a time when the regions shared the wealth that the center had previously monopolized.

4.1 Sources

For some 200 years after Pepy II, kings no longer left many monuments or written remains. We know of the names of numerous rulers from some later king lists, while other lists ignore the period from Pepy II to the 12th dynasty altogether. No complete record of the royal names of the period is available. Royal annals of the early 6th dynasty existed, but the stone onto which they were carved was reused as sarcophagus lid and the text is almost fully illegible. The main inscriptional evidence is found in tombs where officials describe their careers. The accounts are more detailed than those from before the 6th dynasty, and they appear all over Upper Egypt, thus giving us different regional perspectives. They are not numerous but they are a crucial source for the period. Mortuary texts from the 6th dynasty and later – Pyramid and Coffin Texts – are important for the study of religious beliefs.

The First Intermediate Period appears in several literary works of the Middle Kingdom, always in negative terms as a time of disturbance. While historians in the past took these descriptions as accurate reflections, today we see these

Summary of dynastic history
Late Old Kingdom and First Intermediate Period (ca. 2345–2055)

ca. 2345–2181	**6th dynasty**
ca. 2321–2287	King Pepy I
	Period of prosperity
ca. 2278–2184	King Pepy II
	Longest rule of ancient Egyptian history in Manetho's list
	Regionalization of power becomes visible
ca. 2181–2160	**7th and 8th dynasties**
	Numerous kings from Memphis often called Neferkara in imitation of Pepy II
ca. 2160–2025	**9th and 10th dynasties**
	Rulers from Herakleopolis with power limited to northern Middle Egypt and the Delta
ca. 2125–2055	**11th dynasty, first half**
	Rules southern Egypt only from Thebes
ca. 2112–2063	King Wahankh Intef II
	Starts to use title King of Upper and Lower Egypt

works, written at least 50 years after the reunification of Egypt, as expressing anxieties of Middle Kingdom people. They are not a source for the First Intermediate Period, which remains difficult to study.

4.2 The Rise of the Regions and Political Fragmentation

Nomes and nomarchs

The amazing monuments of Old Kingdom Egypt could only be built and maintained with the participation of the entire country: people from all the nomes contributed labor and supplies to enable the court to construct the kings' burials and care for their mortuary cults with offerings. Throughout the Old Kingdom, rulers liked to show their personal associations with the nomes, visually depicted as gods carrying standards. Estates set aside to grow supplies for the mortuary cults were spread over Egypt to symbolize that the entire population honored the kings. In order to make this complex operation possible, the court required regional representatives, and each nome was under the charge of a royal official, the nomarch, and his staff. While royal appointees, they were local men, who were much closer to the population than was the king and who probably had much autonomy, as long as they fulfilled their nome's obligations. Only a strong central power could keep them in line.

During the 6th dynasty the power of the center declined. Nomarchs and other provincial officials no longer obtained their appointments from the king but instead passed their offices on to their sons, as if they made up dynasties. In the past royal officials had been buried near their masters, a trend that culminated in the reigns of Unas, the last king of the 5th dynasty, and Teti, the first of the 6th, around whose pyramids was the densest concentration of private tombs in the Memphis area. But after Teti, nomarchs and other officials saw fit to be buried at home rather than in the capital's cemeteries. They constructed tombs that equaled those near Memphis in grandness, and instead of adhering to the court styles, over time they increasingly followed local traditions and tastes. In the Theban area, for example, they dug huge courtyards in the side of the cliff, in the back of which they cut rows of pillars in front of facades with burial chambers behind them. We call these tombs *saff* today after the Arabic word for row (Figure 4.1). In Dendera, just north of Thebes, they constructed mastaba tombs with a different layout from those at Memphis. Even the modestly well-off had sufficient assets to pay for grave goods especially made for the purpose. They often placed wooden models of people, animals, and workshops in their tombs, for the production of which a class of provincial craftsmen was needed. In earlier times access to such materials and their producers had been a privilege of the elite in the capital

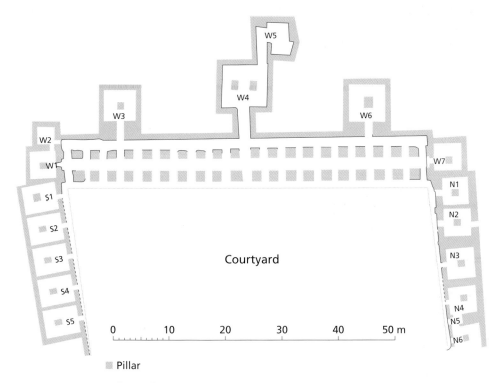

Figure 4.1 Plan of a *saff* tomb

Mortuary texts

Another sign of the disintegration of royal power and privilege showed in the mortuary texts accompanying the dead. Only late in the 5th dynasty the Pyramid Texts, intended to guide the king to his rightful place in the hereafter, started to be carved on royal tomb walls. Several 6th-dynasty kings and queens received such guidance in their burials, but the spells appeared solely with royals. Yet, already in the 6th dynasty mortuary texts were given to non-royals as well. Wealthy individuals commissioned coffins with spells that presented them as ascending the sky and merging with the sun. The Coffin Texts became much more prominent in the later First Intermediate Period and in the Middle Kingdom, but they are first attested in the 6th dynasty in places distant from the capital. The Pyramid Texts inspired many of the Coffin spells, which is a telling indication of how the king's prerogatives had dissipated. Some scholars called the Coffin Texts evidence of a "democratization of the hereafter," an expression that fits the general social trends in the First Intermediate Period, although we have to remember that the people affected were still all part of the elite.

Special Topic 4.1   *Pyramid Texts and Coffin Texts*

Mortuary books present one of the most intriguing genres of Egyptian literature, but also one of the most difficult ones. They constantly evolved over their long history from being the earliest religious writings in Egypt, and in world literature, to some of the latest. They all aimed at protecting the dead and guide him or her to a continued joyful existence in the hereafter, but they took many different forms.

The oldest preserved texts were carved on the walls of the underground chambers and corridors of ten Saqqara pyramids from the late Old Kingdom. Eight were for kings and queens of the 6th dynasty, one for the last 5th-dynasty king, and one for a king of the 8th dynasty. We call them Pyramid Texts, and their earliest attestations appear in royal contexts only (Figure 4.2). In the Middle Kingdom and later on officials

Figure 4.2   Pyramid texts from the pyramid of King Unas. Werner Forman Archive

cited the Pyramid Texts in non-royal burials, however, sometimes copying almost the entire sequence found in earlier royal tombs.

The Pyramid Texts were spells of very varied lengths carved in vertical columns of hieroglyphs. More than 800 spells in total are known, and while many occurred in more than one tomb, each collection was unique. They do not form a unified composition and have miscellaneous origins and dates, but their order was not random. They were situated in such a way in the tomb that they served the dead in various ways. One major concern was the protection of the body against danger and defilement, and the outer walls of the sarcophagus chamber contained spells with that aim. The body needed to be prepared to receive the mortuary offerings, something that was also accomplished through the recitation of the proper words. Another goal was to guide the spirit of the deceased to its rightful place in the hereafter, that is, with the gods. Daily the spirit would resurrect to find a place in heaven and spells on the walls of the corridor leading away from the underground chambers aided that.

The language of the Pyramid Texts is often obscure and the texts contain allusions to a variety of myths that are not always fully known to us. The role of the sun god was central, although Osiris, god of the netherworld, was fully integrated in the sun's realm.

Starting in the 6th dynasty rich Egyptians outside the capital started to have spells painted on the insides of their wooden coffins. The Coffin Texts had affinities with the Pyramid Texts in that they shared the same aims, but they were available to non-royals and they were written in the Middle Egyptian dialect. Most of the Coffin Texts date to the 12th dynasty. We know close to 1,200 spells, many appearing in one coffin only. They are painted in vertical columns and some have illustrations beside them, most impressively the Book of the Two Ways, a group of spells written on the floors of some coffins (Figure 4.3).

The aim of the Coffin Texts was to make it possible for the dead to enjoy eternity. The spells enabled the reception of offerings, and protected and guided the dead body so that it could join the sun on its daily journey. The god Osiris was more prominent here than in the Pyramid Texts. His corpse resided in a place called Rosetau situated "at the boundary of the sky," and the Book of the Two Ways provided a map of the roads to him. The dead were so closely associated with Osiris that the god's name was inserted before their own. The idea that only kings would join the gods after death had thus totally disappeared from these texts.

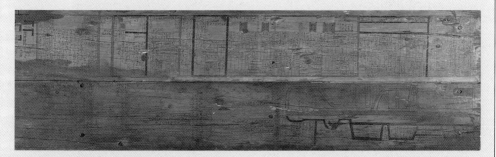

Figure 4.3 Book of the Two Ways. akg-images/Erich Lessing

Officials' biographies

Both in the provinces and in the capital officials seem to have stressed their individual personalities more than in the previous age. They had biographies carved in their tombs in which they stressed their own achievements, rather than the king's favors to them. Three men buried at Elephantine on Egypt's southern border, for example, described how they led trading expeditions deep into Nubia during the early 6th dynasty. And although they acknowledged their masters in Memphis, they downplayed their importance. At Abydos another official called Weni the Elder proclaimed his personal importance. Under King Pepy I he judged a royal wife accused of treason and led five military campaigns into Asia. Then he became governor of Upper Egypt under Pepy's successor Merenra. Earlier officials did not announce such activities publicly. They either did not direct such important initiatives or – more likely – did not receive the same credit for them as in the 6th dynasty because royal power had been so absolute.

Pepy II

Now that the central and local officials asserted their powers and claimed more of the country's resources for themselves, the king's unique position became diluted and his importance decreased. The last great ruler of the Old Kingdom was Pepy II, a man with an unusually long reign. Manetho claims that he came to the throne at the age of six and lived to be 100. This could easily be an exaggeration but records of his reign point to a rule of at least 65 years, which is similar in length to Rameses II's well-documented 67 years in the 13th century. Pepy's successors in the 6th dynasty were weak; we do not even know how many there were. The conditions for the king deteriorated in the 7th and 8th dynasties, both of which still resided at Memphis. According to one version of Manetho's list, 70 kings who reigned for 70 days made up the 7th dynasty and 27 kings who reigned for 146 years (that is, an average of 5.5 years) made up the 8th. He provides no further details. Some royal names of these dynasties appear in the Abydos king list, but only a few of them left any remains, a sign of weakness and instability. Several kings of these dynasties called themselves Neferkara after Pepy II's throne name, a probable indication that they sought to regain his stature. This does not mean that an economic collapse paralleled that of political power, however. Egypt's wealth was more equally shared among the upper classes of society and it was consumed locally rather than diverted to the center. It is even possible that the economy flourished at this time because of better use of the agricultural potential.

Sources in Translation 4.1

The tale of Pepy II and his general

Not all the stories about kings discussed in this chapter were of doom and gloom. A tale known from three manuscripts of the New Kingdom and later deals with King Neferkara, probably Pepy II, the last great king of the Old Kingdom. The composition is probably from the Middle Kingdom. It relates how the king had a homosexual relationship with one of his military commanders – something the Egyptians disapproved of. A man called Tjeti, son of Henet found out, and decided to spy on the king.

> Then he noticed the Majesty of the King of Upper and Lower Egypt:
>   Neferkara going out at night,
> all alone, with nobody with him.
> Then he removed himself from him, without letting him see.
> Henet's son Tjeti stood,
> thinking: "So this it!
> What was said is true –
> he goes out at night."
> Henet's son Tjeti went,
> just behind his god –
> without letting his heart misgive him – to see all he did.
> He (Neferkara) arrived
> at the house of General Sasenet.
> Then he threw a brick, and kicked (the wall),
> so that [a ladder(?)] was let down for him.
> Then he ascended,
> while Henet's son Tjeti
> waited until his Person returned.
> Now after his Majesty had done what he desired with him,
> he returned to his palace,
> Tjeti went back to his house.
> Now his Majesty went to the house
> of General Sasenet
> when four hours had passed of the night,
> he had spent another four hours in the house
> of General Sasenet,
> and he entered the palace when there were four hours to dawn.
>   (Translation Parkinson 1991: 56, quoted by permission)

The end of the story remains unknown and we can only guess what happened. It is clear, however that this tale, like those of the Westcar papyrus, belongs to a popular form of literature that was willing to show kings outside their normal surroundings. Almost certainly, it also contains criticism of the king. The man who followed him, Tjeti, hoped to use Pepy's nocturnal adventures to discredit him.

Why did the Old Kingdom dissolve?

How could this have happened? Contemporary sources do not discuss such questions, and we have to explain the situation through inference from our understanding of the Old Kingdom state. One man alone never held the all-encompassing powers of the center, even if the rhetoric of the Old Kingdom made the king the source of all authority. Kings needed officials to run the complex operations of the court and had always rewarded these people, including with gifts of burials and of mortuary cults that received provisions from estates set aside for the purpose. These donations diverted royal wealth into the hands of officials' families. Moreover, many administrators probably acted quite independently, especially those active in the nomes. They may have obeyed royal orders at first because of respect and fear, but the king's personality needed to be strong to sustain this. Perhaps Pepy II's long reign was a disaster for the king's image. A young boy at his accession, he needed advisors to run the state (Figure 4.4). And, even if he did not reign a full 94 years as Manetho claims, his advanced age at the end of his reign may have prevented him from exercising full control.

The regionalization of power may also have been forced upon the state due to climate change, although the two events may be purely coincidental (see Key Debate 4.1). Before 2200, Egypt's climate had been wetter than it is today and this made it possible for people to grow some crops with the help of rain besides relying on the Nile's natural irrigation. Around 2200 the humidity decreased, however, which forced people to live in the Nile Valley, depending on the river only to water their crops. It is probably at this time that they started to develop artificial irrigation systems to expand the agricultural zones. Scholars have suggested opposing scenarios as a result of the desiccation. Many envisage famines and an inability of the state to feed its population. They relate the appearance of burials throughout Egypt to an increased death rate caused by natural disasters. Others, however, suggest that local officials organized agriculture, as the complex state bureaucracy was incapable of micromanaging the new processes of irrigation. This gave local officials great influence regionally and increased their status, enabling them to build themselves lavish tombs. These elaborate constructions made them much more visible in the archaeological record than their Old Kingdom predecessors.

The result is clear. Royal power dissipated and provincial lords became the men in charge. This situation is well reflected in the account that the official Ankhtify had carved in his tomb at el-Mo'alla, some 30 kilometers south of Thebes. The tomb itself was cut in a pyramid-shaped mountain with a courtyard before it, a causeway, and a mortuary temple. It stood in the center of a cemetery of subsidiary burials, perhaps for his officials. The inscription states that Ankhtify was the governor of the two southern nomes of Edfu and Hierakonpolis. There is only one marginal reference to a King Neferkara in the

Figure 4.4 Young King Pepy II on his mother's lap. © Brooklyn Museum/Corbis

tomb. Most scholars place Ankhtify in the 9th dynasty, but it is possible that he lived earlier, in the 8th dynasty or even before.

Ankhtify relates how the god Horus made him governor of the Edfu nome and how he needed to bring order to the region. He then made an alliance with the general of Armant, a city to his north that was under attack by forces of Thebes and Coptos. When his troops approached the opponents they hid away in their cities, afraid to commit to battle. Ankhtify's humanitarian deeds equaled his military successes. He claimed that the whole of Upper Egypt was starving and arranged for food supplies to be imported. He had thus no qualms stating:

> I was the vanguard and the rearguard of mankind, since nobody like me has existed nor will he exist; nobody like me has been born nor will he be born. I have

surpassed the feats of my ancestors, and those who come after me will not be able to equal me in any of my feats in this million years. (Translation after Seidlmayer 2000: 128–9)[2]

Such arrogance would be unheard of in Old Kingdom times, when only kings could allege to be so important that the wellbeing of the land depended on them. Ankhtify was not alone. At Dara near Asyut in Middle Egypt, a local lord named Khui built a pyramid in the midst of a cemetery for his officials in the period when the 10th dynasty of Herakleopolis officially ruled his territory. Such men, and probably several others, usurped royal prerogatives. They acted independently as military men and provided for their people. They had become small kings. The ideological impact of this shift must have been enormous. In the heyday of the Old Kingdom Egypt's population contributed to the construction of massive mortuary monuments of one man, often located at a great distance from the places where they lived. When the resources were regionally utilized, they labored for someone in their own vicinity, who did not have royal status. The kings of the past claimed close association with the gods; the new rulers did not. How the people of Egypt were persuaded to accept this change we cannot say.

4.3 Foreign Relations

Nubian independence

The weakness of the Late Old Kingdom state must have had an effect on Egypt's interactions with its neighbors, but we have to be careful not to see it as the sole cause of what happened abroad. Already in the late 5th dynasty Lower Nubia, just south of Egypt's border and previously under its control, had become independent and 6th-dynasty sources attest to a confederation of

Table 4.1 Dynasties of the First Intermediate Period

Memphis	Herakleopolis	Thebes
<-Dyn. 6 ca. 2345–2181 -->		
Dyn. 7		
ca. 2181–2160		
Dyn. 8		
	Dyn. 9	
	ca. 2160–2025	Early dyn. 11 ca. 2125–2055
	Dyn. 10	
<-- Later dyn. 11 ca. 2055–1985 -->		

Nubian chiefs in the region. The people left behind archaeological remains that we now call C-Group. They seem to have been originally nomadic and during the Old Kingdom they entered Lower Nubia, which had been mostly abandoned since the disappearance of the A-Group around 2900. When Egypt's influence south of the first cataract waned around 2350, C-Group people settled in the valley and preserved a discrete culture until the start of the New Kingdom. The archaeological evidence for them is mostly limited to graves and associated pottery. At first the tombs were round or oval pits with a ring of stone filled with gravel as the surface marker. Nearby stood sandstone steles. After the Middle Kingdom in Egypt, some of the burials included large superstructures and chapels, probably in imitation of Egyptian practices. The C-Group people always remained hostile forces to the Egyptians, and the latter's ability to influence them varied with the extent of their power in Lower Nubia.

South of the second cataract grew up a more centralized state centered on the town of Kerma near the third cataract. Some scholars think that the Egyptians referred to that state as Yam, others think Yam was located much farther upriver near the fifth cataract. Yam provided exotic sub-Saharan African goods, such as incense, panther-skins, ivory, and ebony wood. The biography of Harkhuf, carved on the facade of his tomb on the island of Elephantine, devoted much attention to expeditions there. He made three journeys in the reign of Pepy II. For the final one he chose not to follow the valley route along the Nile but used a trail that ran through the oases of the western desert. When he reached the lord of Yam he received an escort to travel north into Lower Nubia, and met up with the confederate chiefs. All the relations on these trips seem to have been peaceful, and the Nubians guided him back home.

One of Harkhuf's greatest achievements was that he obtained a pygmy, which pleased the young Pepy II more than anything else. Harkhuf reproduced the king's letter on the wall of his tomb including these instructions:

> Come north to the residence at once! Hurry and bring with you this pygmy, whom you brought from the land of the Horizon-Dwellers. May he live, prosper and be healthy, in order to dance for the god, and gladden and delight the heart of the king of Upper and Lower Egypt, Neferkara (= Pepy II)! When he goes down with you into the ship, get worthy men to be around him on deck, so he does not fall into the water. When he sleeps at night, get worthy men to sleep around him in his tent. Inspect ten times at night! My Majesty wishes to see this pygmy more than the tribute of the Mine-Land (= Sinai) and Punt. (Translation after Strudwick 2005: 332–3).

Not all the expeditions into Nubia were peaceful, however. Slightly later Pepy II sent the commander Pepynakht on a military mission (see Sources in Translation 4.2), but this was not an attempt to reoccupy the region and perhaps only a raid to capture slaves.

Sources in Translation 4.2

The inscription of Pepynakht Heqaib

In an elaborate tomb on the island of Elephantine appears the biography of Pepynakht Heqaib, who was an official and military commander under King Pepy II. As was usual at the time, he accumulated many titles and described activities in the civilian and military spheres.

> Custodian of the domain and scribe of a phyle of the pyramid of Neferkara, bearer of the royal seal, sole companion, overseer of foreigners, Heqaib. Overseer of the pyramid town of Pepy I, sole companion, ritual priest, overseer of foreigners, who brings the products of the foreign countries to his lord, Pepynakht. The leader of the phyle of the pyramid of Merenra, he who instills the terror of Horus in the foreign countries, the revered Heqaib, count, sole companion, chamber attendant, herdsman of Nekhen, lord of Nekheb, overseer of all foreigners, revered before the great god, Pepynakht.
>
> I am a speaker of perfection and a repeater what is desired, I never said anything evil to a superior against any man, because I wish my name to be perfect in the sight of the Great God. I gave bread to the hungry and clothes to the naked. I never judged my fellows in such a way that a son was deprived of his father's property. I am the beloved one of his father, the favored one of his mother, and beloved by his siblings.
>
> The majesty of my lord sent me to devastate the land of Wawat and Irtjet. I did what pleases my lord and killed a great number there, including the chiefs' children and the commander of the excellent Nubian troops. I brought a great number of them to the court as prisoners, I being at the head of the expedition, a large and strong force, as one who is strong of heart, and my lord was delighted with me as he was with every mission on which he sent me.
>
> ......
>
> The majesty of my lord sent me to the land of the Aamu (Asiatics) to bring back (the body of) the sole companion, warden of Nekhen, Kaaper's son, the overseer of the foreigners Ankhti. He had been building a reed boat there to travel to Punt, when the Aamu and Sand-dwellers killed him and the armed division of the expedition, which was with him.
>
> ......
>
> I drove the murderers among them away.
>
> (Translation after Strudwick 2005: 333–5)

Pepynakht made several statements that were common boasts for officials in this period, for example, that he fed and dressed those in need. He emphasized his military achievements most, however. The raid into the Nubian areas of Wawat and Irtjet left the greatest impression in later times, it seems. His mortuary chapel became a cult site where Middle Kingdom Egyptians honored him as the patron of travelers to the south and as an intermediary for the living with the realm of the gods and the dead. They left offerings at the chapel, and in their inscriptions they exclusively used his second name, Heqaib.

Beyond the Nile Valley

Pepynakht's military skills were so great that Pepy II withdrew him from the south to lead troops into the eastern desert in order to recover the bodies of Egyptians who had been killed by nomads. The Egyptian state's ability to control zones east from the Nile seems to have waned and mining expeditions to Sinai ended after Pepy II's reign. Military activity in Asia is last reported in the biography of Weni the Elder from the early 6th dynasty, and the trade contacts with ports farther north seem to have ceased. While the names of many kings of the 4th dynasty to King Pepy II appear in Byblos, no later ones occur until the 12th dynasty.

Yet, Egypt's control over the western desert was strong in the late Old Kingdom and continued into the First Intermediate Period. The copy of a decree of King Pepy II found at the site of Balat in the Dakhla oasis reports that he established the mortuary cult for an official there. The settlement nearby contained a governor's palace, storerooms, and workshops, and in the cemetery associated with it stood six large mud-brick mastabas, the earliest of which dates to the reign of Pepy I. The tomb owners included a son of Pepy II. Very remarkable is the find at Balat of a set of clay tablets with hieratic text incised on them when the clay was still moist, which suggests that papyrus was scarce in the oases. The texts are accounts, list of names, and letters. The integration of the western oases into Egypt's domain explains how Harkhuf could use the desert road connecting them for his travels to Nubia. How firm the control was is unclear, but the settlement at Balat survived throughout the First Intermediate Period.

Mercenaries

Egypt's military adventures, internally and abroad, required troops. Originally the army had been made up of local men who fought as part of their duties to the state, and, later on, to their local lords. Starting in the 6th dynasty armies, such as Weni's expeditionary force, included mercenaries from Nubia and Libya, and these foreigners would become a permanent fixture, even when the Egyptian state reunified under the Middle Kingdom. The integration of these people in Egyptian society was remarkably fast. In Ankhtify's tomb at el-Mo'alla, mentioned above, appear representations of some Nubian soldiers. More remarkable, however, is that across the river at Gebelein several mortuary steles were found that Nubian mercenaries had set up (Figure 4.5). They used an Egyptian type of monument and adopted Egyptian styles in their representations as well as Egyptian names oftentimes, but they depicted themselves with a darker skin color and Nubian hairdo and sometimes explicitly stated that they were Nubian in the inscription. They seem thus to have fully accepted Egyptian mortuary customs but wanted to preserve their separate identity.

Figure 4.5 Mortuary stele of the Nubian soldier Nenu, Egyptian, Egypt. Said to be from el-Rizeiqat. Museum of Fine Arts, Boston Purchased by A. M. Lythgoe. 03.1848 © 2009 Museum of Fine Arts, Boston/The Bridgeman Art Library. All rights reserved

4.4   Competition between Herakleopolis and Thebes

Herakleopolis

Despite the confusion of local lords, the concept that there was one legitimate king for all of Egypt seems to have survived, albeit in name only. Around 2181 the seat of that kingship moved south from Memphis to Herakleopolis at the entrance of the Fayyum. The Herakleopolitan kings of the 9th and 10th dynasties saw themselves as heirs of the Old Kingdom and one was even buried at Saqqara, but their powers were limited and they did not have full dominance over Middle Egypt, it seems. It was perhaps also at this time that Ankhtify, the governor of the very south, was free to campaign inside Egypt. Yet, the 9th- and 10th-dynasty rulers had the status of king and it was against them that a newly emerging power directed its struggles for supremacy.

Thebes

To the south of the regions where political power had been concentrated since Early Dynastic times developed a new center that would dominate Egypt for many centuries: Thebes. The populations of two previously minor towns on the east bank of the Nile merged under the leadership of an "overseer of priests" called Intef. Around 2125 he started a rival dynasty to the one at Herakleopolis, which we now call the 11th. The basis for his power is unknown, but he had the ability to command the constructions of a huge *saff* tomb across the river. Intef initiated a sequence of stable and lengthy rules that led to a pacification of the south. From this base his successors started to push north, annexing territories the rulers of Herakleopolis claimed as their own. The Thebans restored the prestige of the king. Officials acknowledged their dependence on him and the king again was the recognized sponsor of temple building throughout the territory. Already the second king of the dynasty, Wahankh Intef II, had taken the title King of Upper and Lower Egypt, which did not mean that he controlled both the valley and the Delta, but revealed his aspirations clearly.

Thebes's ambitions ended the First Intermediate Period. Its armies caused the Herakleopolitan system to collapse, and some scholars think that they hacked its royal tombs to pieces. The king in charge of the final thrust was Mentuhotep II who changed his titles repeatedly to celebrate his successes. In his 20th year he adopted the Horus name "Divine of the White Crown" to indicate his dominance of Upper Egypt, and in his 39th he became the "Uniter of the Two Lands." With his reunification of Egypt he started a new era, the Middle Kingdom. Later Egyptians did not forget this. He received a posthumous cult, and in the 13th century Rameses II honored him as the creator of the Middle Kingdom. A relief from that king's mortuary temple shows Mentuhotep's statue next to those of Menes, the first unifier of Egypt, and Ahmose, the founder of the New Kingdom.

4.5 Appraising the First Intermediate Period

Middle Kingdom literary reflections

Mentuhotep II was a great man in Egyptian eyes: he had returned the country to its proper condition of a unified state. Intermediate periods did not appeal to Egyptian elites, who saw them as times of chaos. But how bad was the situation in the First Intermediate Period really? Until recently many modern historians imagined a time of great disruptions, political discord, social upheaval, famines, and external threats. It was not difficult to find sources to argue this view, especially in the writings of the Middle Kingdom. The Middle Kingdom was a period of much creativity, and for the rest of their history the Egyptians saw it as the classical era of literature. With few exceptions the narratives composed then were set in the past; we have already seen those that treated the Old Kingdom. One composition especially has contributed to the idea that the First Intermediate Period was one of disaster, *The Admonitions of Ipuwer*, known from one 19th-dynasty manuscript only, but its language dates it to the Middle Kingdom. Its first modern editor saw it as a reflection on the First Intermediate Period, an idea that long had almost general acceptance among Egyptologists.

In this lengthy text Ipuwer, a man not known from other sources, depicts a terrible situation. The land is without a king and rebels rule lawlessly. Crime is rampant and foreign soldiers roam freely. Towns are destroyed and the countryside has become a wasteland. Ipuwer focuses especially on the social conditions, which show a topsy-turvy world, for example:

> "Poor men have become men of wealth, he who could not afford sandals owns riches;"
> "The robber owns riches, the noble is a thief;" and
> "Gold, lapis lazuli, silver, and turquoise, carnelian, amethyst, and ... are strung on the necks of female slaves. Noblewomen roam the land."

The text provides no historical reference at all and it is pure conjecture that it talks about First Intermediate Period times. The reading of Ipuwer's *Admonitions* as a depiction of this period's disturbances influenced the interpretation of other texts greatly, however.

We do find historical figures in another text, possibly from the First Intermediate Period itself, but much more likely composed in the Middle Kingdom: *The Instruction Addressed to King Merykara*. Merykara was a king of the Herakleopolitan 10th dynasty; the speaker was his father Khety, but we cannot determine which one of the several kings with that name was meant. The address, damaged at the start, urges the young man to treat his officials and soldiers well, to be just, and to strengthen the land against foreign enemies. The speaker mentions how he fought not only against outsiders, but also inside Egypt, and he deplores how this led to the destruction of monuments at Abydos. Many scholars saw the text as proof that during the 10th dynasty Egypt had been riven by internal strife and was under threat from foreign invaders. Yet, this is not clear at all, and the work fits well as a piece of wisdom literature where a father advises his son on how to behave, portraying the negative repercussions of unwise rule.

The atmosphere of doom is not limited to texts that postdate the First Intermediate Period. Also the tomb biographies of worthies of the 6th to 10th dynasties regularly portray difficulties, which are presented in such a way that the tomb owners emerge as saviors. They gave food to the hungry, clothed the naked, and protected the people from foreign attackers. These men were always successful and just.

Historical critique

Recently historians of Egypt have interpreted this material much more critically than in the past, although they are at a loss to determine how much of it they can believe. The negative images were certainly an exaggeration. The tomb owners wanted to magnify their accomplishments by making the situation more dismal than it was in reality, a procedure later Egyptian kings would also use. The Middle Kingdom literary works were not historical accounts but belonged to various genres with different purposes. The counsels to Merykara are part of a genre of advisory texts that appear throughout Egyptian literature and intend to guide young men to proper behavior. Ipuwer's account is a lament that reflects on chaos in general. It provides a standard depiction of social upheaval that regularly features in world literature in general. The Middle Kingdom may have been a period when such reflections were appropriate. Elite Egyptians feared chaos and made it the king's responsibility to avoid it. By exaggerating the dangers of instability they championed strong rule, something that re-emerged in the Middle Kingdom.

Key Debate 4.1   *Climate change and the First Intermediate Period*

What explains the end of the Old Kingdom? The powerful and highly centralized state that built massive pyramids dissolved around 2200 into small regions whose monuments seem pitiful in comparison. Egyptian literature that seems to reflect on the First Intermediate Period contains many references that suggest a collapse of agriculture. The *Admonitions of Ipuwer*, for example, read, "O, but the Nile flood is rising and they have not prepared for it," and "O, but the desert is throughout the land; the nomes are ravaged" (Parkinson 1998: 171–3). Nomarchs like Ankhtify of el-Mo'alla and Khety of Asyut boast of their ability to feed their people while the rest of the country suffers from famine (Vandier 1936: 1–19).

Since agriculture in Egypt depended on Nile floods, which did vary yearly, low levels caused hardship. The Palermo Stone (see Chapter 2) records that levels fell one meter between the 1st and the mid-2nd dynasties and then remained more or less the same into the 5th dynasty, when the record ends. A one-meter decline represented a 30 percent reduction of agricultural land in the 19th century AD (Butzer 1984: 106). Archaeologists have looked for physical evidence of drier conditions in Egypt. At the end of the Old Kingdom people in Elephantine built on lower levels than before and sand dunes seem to cover several Middle Egyptian sites (cf. Moeller 2006). Adding these data together the idea that climate change caused the decline of the Old Kingdom emerged. The dry conditions affected not only Egypt, but also a wide zone from the Mediterranean to the Indus Valley where several cultures collapsed around that time (B. Bell 1971; Hassan 1997, 2007). The idea, briefly popular in the 1970s, has become widespread in recent years, and textbooks on climate change assert it as fact (e.g., Burroughs 2007: 289).

The evidence is not that secure, however. A major problem in using geophysical evidence is that it is impossible to correlate its dates to the chronology of Egyptian history, which has a wide margin of error in the 3rd millennium. And not all scholars think that the Nile levels were low in the First Intermediate Period. Evidence from east Africa and the Delta suggests that they were exceptionally high between 2150 and 1900 (Butzer 1997: 257). The textual evidence is also suspect. The information of the Palermo Stone – which in any case shows lower Nile levels at the height of the Old Kingdom – could be factual (Seidlmayer 2001: 87) or fictional (O'Mara 1996). The literary depictions of the First Intermediate Period are not historical sources. Although some scholars insist that *Ipuwer's Admonitions* contain a description of the collapse of the Old Kingdom (Hassan 2007), the composition has no clear referent to the period. The nomarchs' boast of feeding the people while the rest of Egypt dies of hunger is a literary topos; they are great leaders in a world of chaos (Moreno García 1997: 1–87). The case for climate change is thus unproven (Moeller 2006). Its popularity is more a sign of modern preoccupations than of historical reality.

NOTES

1. Translation after Lichtheim 1988: 28.
2. The texts are fully translated into German in Schenkel 1965: 45–57. An English paraphrase with translations of many of the texts appears in Assmann 2002: 93–105.

5
The Middle Kingdom
(ca. 2055–1650)

A man has perished: his corpse is dust,
and his people have passed from the land;
it is a book which makes him remembered
in the mouth of a speaker.
More excellent is a (papyrus) roll than a built house,
than a chapel in the west.
It is better than an established villa,
than a stele in a temple.
(From a 19th-dynasty praise of scribes)[1]

Mentuhotep II's defeat of the rival 10th dynasty of Herakleopolis started a new period of unification in Egyptian history, which was to last for nearly 400 years. While both the modern term Middle Kingdom and the ancient presentation of Mentuhotep on a par with Menes and Ahmose (see Chapter 4) may suggest that this period parallels the Old and New Kingdoms in many respects, it is more difficult to define the Middle Kingdom than those other periods. In simplistic terms we can point to the pyramids as the Old Kingdom's defining characteristic and at the empire for the New Kingdom; no comparable single feature describes the Middle Kingdom. It was a period of transformation. Much aware of Old Kingdom and First Intermediate Period traditions, the Egyptians of the Middle Kingdom established a number of practices that were fundamental for subsequent periods. This was perhaps true the most in the cultural domain. Throughout later history, ancient Egyptians regarded literary compositions of the Middle Kingdom as the classics. The quote above is from a New Kingdom eulogy of that literature: its impact lasts longer than that of men and their buildings. Also in administrative practices and foreign policy the Egyptians of the Middle Kingdom laid the basis for later times. The period represents the completion of processes that had started many centuries before, while the era's accomplishments inspired Egyptians for more than 1,500 years.

5.1 Sources and Chronology

From several kings of the period survive a large number of statues representing them as humans or human-headed sphinxes and inscribed with their names. We know of some 70 for Amenemhat III alone, for example (Plate 5). The kings of the Middle Kingdom were eager to represent themselves in stone and invested much effort in the enterprise. Not only kings but also other members of the elite set up inscriptions, including thousands of steles at Abydos. These officials continued the late Old Kingdom and First Intermediate Period tradition of narrating parts of their careers until the late-12th dynasty when the mortuary texts on steles became hymns to gods, especially Osiris.

The most numerous surviving official writings were brief reports on military or mining expeditions, graffiti or inscriptions on rock surfaces in the eastern desert, Sinai, and Nubia, and probably better preserved due to the arid conditions. In this period the first lengthy written announcements of royal feats carved in stone appear. Senusret I and Amenemhat II left annalistic, that is year-by-year, accounts of their deeds, giving more detail than the earlier annals that treated the Early Dynastic and Old Kingdom periods. Unfortunately these inscriptions are preserved in fragments only. While the known inscription of Senusret focused fully on donations to the temple of Ra at Heliopolis, Amenemhat mentioned other accomplishments, including military and trading expeditions, and a royal hunt. Kings of the Middle Kingdom also lined the mud-brick walls of temples with stone in order to enable decorations with relief sculpture. Although most of these were later dismantled and incorporated into New Kingdom temples, they reflect a changing attitude in royal display.

The administration of state institutions and private enterprises was recorded on papyri, which survive only in unusual circumstances. One important group derives from the town of Lahun built near the pyramid of Senusret II in the desert. It contains three separate archives, including a temple library and administrative records. The slightly earlier papyri of a private landowner, Heqanakht, still exist because they were discarded in a tomb, and they reveal aspects of life on an agricultural estate.

The Middle Kingdom was an era of great literary creativity when many classics of Egyptian literature were composed. These include a number of texts set in the reigns of actual Middle Kingdom kings, especially tales that involve rulers of the early 12th dynasty. We have to see these as works of fiction, however, rather than as historical narratives of these kings' actions and their times.

Archaeological material from the Middle Kingdom derives from the entirety of Egypt, continuing the geographical spread from the First Intermediate Period. The remains from the new capital of Thebes in the southern part of the country become much more prominent, and also various excavations in the Delta yield Middle Kingdom materials.

The chronology of the period is relatively firm. All king lists provide solid information on the 12th dynasty, although several of them ignore most of the 11th and 13th dynasties. Other data allow for a reliable reconstruction of the

11th dynasty, but there are uncertainties about the identity of rulers and the total length of the 13th dynasty. The absolute chronology may seem secure but it is not. A priest wrote in a letter from the 7th year of an unnamed king, most likely Senusret III, found at Lahun: "It is on the fourth month of *peret*

Summary of dynastic history
Middle Kingdom (ca. 2055–1650)

ca. 2125–2055	**11th dynasty, first half** Rules southern Egypt only from Thebes
ca. 2055–1985 ca. 2055–2004	**11th dynasty, second half** King Mentuhotep II Terminates the competing dynasty of Herakleopolis Constructs mortuary temple at Deir el-Bahri
ca. 1992–1985	King Mentuhotep IV Confusion at court
ca. 1985–1773 ca. 1985–1956	**12th dynasty** King Amenemhat I Re-establishes order Founds new capital at Itj-tawi
ca. 1956–1911	King Senusret I Builds extensively all over Egypt, including at Amun temple in Karnak Builds pyramid at Lisht Campaigns in Lower Nubia
ca. 1911–1877	King Amenemhat II Leaves annalistic account of his reign (now fragmentary)
ca. 1877–1870	King Senusret II Starts the development of the Fayyum region
ca. 1870–1831	King Senusret III Campaigns in the Levant and especially in Nubia Office of nomarch disappears from the official record
ca. 1831–1786	King Amenemhat III Further develops the Fayyum
ca. 1777–1773	Queen Sobekneferu Last ruler of the 12th dynasty
ca. 1773–after 1650	**13th dynasty** Numerous kings, mostly ephemeral, but some with long reigns Royal court moves from Itj-tawi to Thebes, ca. 1700

(= growing season), day 16 that the heliacal rising of Sothis (= Sirius) will occur,"[2] predicting an astronomical event that can be dated in absolute terms (see Chapter 1). For long scholars accepted that this year was close to 1870 and built the chronology of the Middle Kingdom around that date. But we are much less confident now. The place where the Sothis star was observed affects the dating. If it was in the north of Egypt, 1870 seems correct, but if it happened in the very south, the year would be later. Today most scholars consider the information on Sothis to be of secondary importance, and rely more on other data for the absolute chronology.

5.2   Kings and Regional Elites

In the early 20th century BC, King Amenemhat I (ruled 1985–1956) built the first substantial pyramid since Pepy II finished his in the late Old Kingdom, some 200 years earlier. He did so at the modern site of Lisht, midway between Meidum and Dahshur where Old Kingdom pyramids stood. As filling he used sculpted stone blocks taken from Old Kingdom royal buildings from Giza and Saqqara, and their decorations inspired his own sculptors in their carving of reliefs. The artists imitated Old Kingdom styles rather than those that had developed more recently. The complex was a symbol of the return of royal power as a central force in Egyptian society and a revival of Old Kingdom ideals. Middle Kingdom pharaohs worked hard to centralize authority once more and to establish dynastic stability. Especially those of the 12th dynasty were successful in this effort, but they never fully thwarted the power of provincial elites. The struggle between centralizing and regional forces in Middle Kingdom Egypt may have been the dominant theme of its domestic history. For slightly more than two centuries under the 12th dynasty (1985–1773) the center seems to have had the upper hand, but it was not all-powerful. Regional families abandoned their local bases in return for appointments at court. This arrangement may have been detrimental for royal power, however, and in the 13th dynasty rotating kingship seems to have replaced strong dynastic rule.

Reunification and the 11th dynasty

The 11th dynasty, which ruled from Thebes, originated during the First Intermediate Period and for some 70 years shared power with a Middle Egyptian dynasty at Herakleopolis. King Mentuhotep II (ruled 2055–2004) changed this situation by eliminating the rival dynasty and thus reunifying Upper and Lower Egypt. This was not necessarily due to military victory, but may have been a negotiated settlement after he annexed parts of the other state. The process seems to have been slow, and Mentuhotep II updated his Horus name repeatedly to proclaim his accomplishments. Only in his 39th year did he become Sematawy, "Uniter of the Two Lands," which we take to declare his final success.

As sole ruler of Egypt Mentuhotep II had the capacity to build several impressive monuments, including a majestic mortuary temple at Deir el-Bahri on the west bank of the Nile at Thebes. But the court's influence was restricted. All over Egypt local worthies announced their special status by erecting steles inscribed with biographies where they focused on their own achievements, and in many respects this era shows the same cultural diversity as the preceding period. The limits on royal power may have led to chaos at the end of the 11th dynasty. Very little is known about Mentuhotep II's second successor (called Mentuhotep as well), who is not even named in later king lists.

The start of the 12th dynasty and the foundation of Itj-tawi

The founder of the 12th dynasty restored order. Amenemhat I, who most likely was Mentuhotep IV's vizier, seized the throne around 1985. He was the true architect of the Middle Kingdom, which came to fruition in the 12th dynasty. For the next 200 years one family ruled the country with unity at home and a strong impact on neighboring regions. Amenemhat I initiated radical changes in Egypt's government. His court left Thebes for a newly founded capital, called Itj-tawi in Egyptian. The name means "(Amenemhat is) he who takes possession of the Two Lands," stressing the concept of a unified Egypt. The exact location of Itj-tawi is unknown, but we are confident that it was close to Amenemhat's pyramid at Lisht, somewhat to the south of Memphis. The foundation of a new capital was a drastic step. It removed the court from the Theban families that had dominated government in the 11th dynasty and brought it closer to other political centers: Herakleopolis, the home of First Intermediate Period dynasties, and especially the Old Kingdom capital Memphis, the largest population center in the country. Thus, on the one hand the court separated itself from existing power structures, while on the other hand it could draw on a larger variety of people for its staff. Itj-tawi may have been primarily an administrative town with royal mortuary complexes nearby. In documents of the time it is often referred to as the "Residence."

The kings of the 12th dynasty were eager, however, to give Itj-tawi its own infrastructure and identity. They devoted much attention to the surrounding region, especially the Fayyum basin west of the Nile. Senusret II (ruled 1877–1870) initiated its development as a major agricultural resource. His engineers drained parts of the lake in its center with a system of canals. This enabled them to lay out new fields and increase agricultural production. The Middle Kingdom Fayyum was only temporarily successful, but did inspire later Ptolemaic and Roman developments that turned the area into the breadbasket of the Mediterranean world.

In cultural terms Itj-tawi had a distinct character from the rest of the country, at least in the first century of its existence. All but the last two rulers of the 12th dynasty built pyramids and mortuary complexes in the surroundings, and filled them with royal statuary, relief sculptures, and the like. Thus they patronized numerous architects, who experimented with different layouts and building techniques. The pyramids of the first two kings, both at modern Lisht, to a great extent imitated the classical examples of the Old Kingdom from Giza, but they were placed on platforms following a Theban practice. The architects of later kings used other sources of inspiration, such as Djoser's complex at Saqqara, from which they took the form of a rectangular enclosure. Some of their works became very famous in antiquity. The mortuary temple of the final major pyramid of Egypt, Amenemhat III's at Hawara, was known as "The Labyrinth" in classical times and foreign visitors came to see it as a tourist attraction.

Many artists worked at Itj-tawi producing statues and relief sculptures for the kings. They developed a royal style that at first was unique to the capital's surroundings. Elsewhere artists often continued to use the regional styles that had developed in the First Intermediate Period, and it was only slowly, especially in the reign of Amenemhat III, that the court style dominated throughout Egypt. This uniformity was ephemeral, however. With the loss of royal prestige in the 13th dynasty, much artistic production reverted to the provinces and local styles re-emerged. At that time the number of royal monuments decreased dramatically, while that of private sculptures in the round and in relief increased. A general decline in quality is visible, however, as many of the provincial artists had received less training in design and in the carving of hieroglyphs.

The royal house at Itj-tawi sought to keep kingship in the same family and avoid usurpations of the throne. They initiated the practice of co-regency: the ruling king trained his successor by giving a chosen son the status of junior king. Although it conflicted with the principle that one person only could be king at one time, we find inscriptions that date an event in the reign of two kings. They indicate, for example, that the 30th year of Amenemhat I was also the 10th year of his son, Senusret I. It is unclear how senior and junior kings shared responsibilities, and scholars debate the lengths and very existence of many co-regencies (see Key Debate 5.1). For the rest of ancient Egyptian history kings used co-regencies as a means to select an heir, although the practice was rare between the Middle Kingdom and the Ptolemaic Period. The method made the transition of power much more secure, as the younger man had the time to establish his own support base before his father's death. The system seems to have worked well for the 12th dynasty: For some 200 years members of one family only ruled Egypt.

The end of the 12th dynasty may have been due to the absence of a male heir with whom such an arrangement was possible. The last ruler was Sobekneferu, the first woman of Egypt firmly attested in contemporary monuments as holding full royal powers. And she did not hide that she was a woman, unlike the later Hatshepsut who gradually took on male attributes (see Chapter 7). Sobekneferu's statues show her as a woman with female clothing (although in one she wears a man's head cloth and kilt). The queen's reign was brief, close to four years only, and she probably inherited the throne from her husband, Amenemhat IV, when he had no male heir. With her the family of Amenemhat I lost the kingship of Egypt.

Provincial powers in the early Middle Kingdom

The 12th dynasty kings at Itj-tawi were powerful, but they were not alone in possessing wealth and social standing. For a long time during the Middle Kingdom the provincial elites that had been more-or-less independent in the First Intermediate Period kept their local authority, albeit within a setting where a king ruled the entire country. Their resilience is most visible in their archaeological remains, as two examples will illustrate.

Near the modern village of Beni Hassan in Middle Egypt are located the cemeteries of officials who governed the 16th Upper Egyptian nome in the late 11th and 12th dynasties. Thirty-nine rock-cut tombs belonged to the nomarchs and high administrators and their important family members. They are large in size and 10 of them are decorated with elaborate wall paintings, depicting domestic scenes, entertainment, and hunts. Twelve tombs contain inscriptions that describe the owners' careers. On the low desert beneath the rock-cut tombs are 900 shaft-graves belonging to mid-level administrators who joined their masters in death, just as royal courtiers did in the cemeteries of the capital. These remains show that members of the same family governed the region for almost one century during the early 12th dynasty. While they acknowledged that the king had appointed them, the passing on of the office from one generation to the next shows that the latter had little choice. The grandeur of the tombs and their decorations suggest that these local administrators acted as kings on a small scale. They dated events according to the years they had been in office and maintained courts with officials who bore titles that paralleled those in the capital. They engaged in diplomatic marriages with neighboring governors and they interacted with foreign delegations. The last of the Beni Hassan governors, Khnumhotep II, depicted in his tomb how people from the eastern desert visited him bearing gifts, for example (Figure 5.1).

Likewise, the nomarchs of Elephantine, the strategic point at the first cataract where Egypt and Nubia meet, had the ability to build large tombs, inscribed with biographical accounts. Those indicate that the men accepted the power of the kings of Egypt, but that they too were all members of the same family for most of the 12th dynasty. We know of these men not only through their tombs; they also had the wealth to build chapels in the sanctuary dedicated to Heqaib, the late Old Kingdom commander who campaigned in Nubia. He had become the patron of travelers and his tomb was a cult site (see Chapter 4). The governors' attention to his sanctuary shows how they promoted local traditions.

Figure 5.1 Tomb painting from Beni Hassan showing desert people bringing gifts to governor Khnumhotep II. akg-images/Erich Lessing

Royal interference in the provinces

Two competing, yet interacting, power structures thus seem to have existed in Middle Kingdom Egypt into the 12th dynasty: local lords with independent sources of wealth and influence, and the royal court, which sought to re-create the centralized state of Old Kingdom times. The court's reach into the provinces increased gradually, and to promote it the kings may have used a policy of internal colonization. That is, they may have established a network of points that they controlled independent of local institutions. Throughout Egypt and in Lower Nubia archaeologists have uncovered several settlements that were newly created during the Middle Kingdom. The state seems to have built them for the special purpose of housing personnel for the maintenance of mortuary cults or – when placed in strategic positions on Egypt's borders – as military colonies. The layout of these settlements reveals ideas on how to organize communities, although interpretation is difficult and controversial.

The prime example of a planned settlement is the town constructed to provide for the mortuary cult of Senusret II beside his pyramid's valley temple near the modern village called Lahun (Egyptologists also refer to it as Kahun) at the entrance to the Fayyum. The walled town was almost square, and its interior was organized on a gridiron pattern with straight streets along which rectangular homes of standardized sizes were built. Most houses were small (some 33 by 33 feet or 10 by 10 meters with 4 to 12 rooms). At the northern end of the town was a row of large units (some 190 by 130 feet or 60 by 40 meters and with up to 80 rooms), including one on a raised platform, to house the community leaders and perhaps even, at times, the king. The total population was probably around 3,000. As people abandoned Lahun in the 13th dynasty its remains are not concealed beneath later occupation layers, and the excavators discovered many tools and domestic items. They also found hundreds of fragmentary papyri that account for the laborers and their supervisors. The men worked in gangs that provided service for set amounts of time. Other documents include census records of households, which could own domestic servants, often men and women of Asiatic descent.

Other Middle Kingdom settlements had the same planned layout as Lahun. Some were located in the center of Egypt, for example, at South Abydos, others on the borders: at Avaris in the eastern Delta, Abu Ghalib in the western Delta, and Elephantine at the first cataract. The Egyptians also built a set of forts to guard the second cataract (see below). Inside the massive walls the houses and official buildings show the same standardization.

How do we interpret these settlements? Some scholars see the gridiron city plans and standardized layout and sizes of houses as the reflection of an ideology of strict state supervision and control. They consider the appearance of two house-sizes only as an indication that society was rigorously divided into two classes: a large class of commoners and a small elite. But others have pointed out that the special purpose settlements are not a true reflection of Middle Kingdom Egyptian society. Other archaeological sources, such as tombs and the shrines and votive objects people left near religious sites, suggest that a variety of classes existed, including a vibrant middle class, and that social mobility was possible. The wall paintings in the tombs at Beni Hassan also show multiple social levels. People from all over Egypt could make careers, for example in the army, which became professionalized in the Middle Kingdom. Some declared in biographical inscriptions that they acquired wealth and social status outside the state administration, and the idea that Middle Kingdom Egypt was a prescriptive society is at least an exaggeration. The kings may have wished to impose order, but it is unlikely that they oversaw all that happened in their country, as some scholars suggest.

Another way in which Middle Kingdom pharaohs reached out into the provinces was through a policy of building and restoring temples to local deities. Several 12th-dynasty kings were very active in this respect. Senusret I, for example, renovated many, if not all, important temples throughout the country and started several new ones. He developed the Amun temple at Karnak, which

Figure 5.2 List of nomes on Senusret I's temple at Thebes. akg-images/Erich Lessing

became the greatest building project of New Kingdom and subsequent kings. His work there was incorporated into later construction or it was dismantled to reuse the stones. The latter practice preserved in pieces the chapel built to celebrate Senusret I's *sed*-festival. On its walls were listed the nomes of Egypt and their lengths along the river. The king ruled over *all* of Egypt (Figure 5.2).

Administrative centralization

Finally, in the mid-12th dynasty, the regional and central power structures seem to have negotiated an arrangement that benefited both. Under Senusret III (ruled 1870–1831) the title nomarch disappeared from the record and three large administrative districts replaced the nomes: those of the north, the south, and the so-called "head of the south." The first encompassed Lower Egypt north of the capital, the second Middle Egypt, and the third the area from just north of Abydos to Elephantine. Two main centers coordinated the administration: Itj-tawi in the north, and Thebes in the south. At the same time the monumental provincial tombs disappeared. Members of powerful regional families did not lose their influence, however. On the contrary they joined the royal bureaucracy and thus gained new ways to acquire wealth and power within the context of a centralized state. Khnumhotep III, the son of Khnumhotep II of Beni Hassan, for example, was not buried at home but in Dahshur nearer to his lord, Senusret III. He had made a career at court and had probably risen to the post of vizier, the highest administrator in the country. Other sons of local elites likewise moved to the "Residence" in the capital, and we see a massive expansion of the cemeteries near Itj-tawi with large mastaba tombs.

Royal power in the 13th dynasty

The 12th dynasty survived for some 50 years after Senusret III's death and kingship seems to have been stable as long as a male heir existed. The 200-year-long rule by one family ended with Queen Sobekneferu. When a new dynasty started, still residing in Itj-tawi, the situation changed dramatically. The only king list that reports royal names of the 13th dynasty, the Turin Canon, includes 57 kings and, as the papyrus is fragmentary, more kings may have existed. Manetho just states that 60 kings ruled for a total of 453 years, a high number that scholars usually regard as a mistake for 153. They estimate the dynasty's duration to have been about 150 years, and that many of the kings ruled a few years at best. Kingship changed hands rapidly and without apparent rules of succession. Contemporary records reveal only one clear father–son sequence. Our understanding of the period is further complicated by the fact that most of the 13th-dynasty rulers left very few remains that enable us to study their accomplishments.

The image of chaos is contradicted, however, by the contemporary documentation on court officials, which shows that the governmental practices of the 12th dynasty continued for a long time afterwards. The bureaucracy flourished and its members were able to erect statues and steles all over Egypt. It seems that a well-organized bureaucracy ran the country through established procedures. Some families were able to hold on to offices for a long time. A man called Ankhu, for example, was the son of a vizier, while two of his own sons held that position as well. The highest civilian office of the land was thus inherited while kingship was not.

The weakness of the king should not be exaggerated. The officials acted in a palace structure that depended on him. Kingship no longer was the preserve of one family, however, but may have rotated between various ones. As each king had to assert his authority by a means other than lineage, it took more time for him to leave an impression on the historical record, that is, as a builder or warrior. But he was not a mere figurehead in a structure dominated by others. Kingship did not always change hands rapidly: in the middle of the dynasty a set of longer-ruling kings appeared, who were able to build and restore monuments.

The royal court resided at Itj-tawi for perhaps more than a century in the 13th dynasty and the country remained unified. That situation ended around

Special Topic 5.1   *The Heqanakht papyri*

The existence of a private economic sector beside the state-run is revealed to us by chance through a group of four letters and four accounts found in the debris dumped in a tomb at Deir el-Bahri. They report on the affairs of Heqanakht, a priest for the mortuary cult of an official Ipi, whose estate was located near Thebes. Heqanakht probably lived in the time of Senusret I. While he was away on a business trip in the north he wrote to his eldest son, Merisu, whom he had left in charge at home.

Heqanakht's primary concern was the preparations for the coming agricultural year. He seems to have rented most of his land from colleagues and neighbors, and had negotiated the fees, which he insisted his son pay exactly. Another worry was the support of his extended family, that is, his mother, wife, and children, and their servants. These received barley rations, carefully accounted for, and clearly some had complained that they were insufficient. Heqanakht retorted that he was living in worse conditions, using hyperbolic language that we do not need to take literally:

> Look, one should say hunger only about real hunger. Look, they have started to eat people here. Look, there are none to whom this salary is given anywhere. You should conduct yourselves with diligent hearts until I have reached you.

And:

> But as for anyone who will reject this salary, woman or man, he should come to me, here with me, and live as I live.[3]

The likes and dislikes of the family members come through clearly in these letters. Heqanakht favored his youngest son, Sneferu, he scolded Merisu for denying his sister or aunt Hetepet access to a hairdresser, and he complained that his family abused his new wife Iutenhab, whom he wanted sent to him.

Letters like these are much more candid than the other written sources we have from ancient Egypt and give a glimpse of the lives of people we may otherwise not encounter. Unfortunately they are rare and not easy to interpret, as often we do not know the context of the issues writers address.

1700, when competing dynasties set up in the Delta. This resulted from Egypt's position in the wider world, a topic that is also important for our understanding of Middle Kingdom history.

5.3   Kings as Warriors

From the beginning of Egyptian history conquest and warfare had been royal obligations, and military campaigns across the country's borders featured in the pictorial imagery of kings. In the Middle Kingdom that aspect of royal behavior acquired much greater importance, and the role of the king as vanquishing outsiders became emphasized in official writings. Whoever lived outside Egypt's control was automatically hostile and uncivilized and needed to be defeated. Middle Kingdom rulers could only think of annihilating Nubians, while they talked of "wild men of Asia" who had to be kept in line. Literary texts from the Middle Kingdom mention "Walls of the ruler" at the northeast edge of the Delta, which were intended to control the Asiatics just as the second cataract forts did the Nubians. The most elaborate Middle Kingdom presentation of foreigners as enemies to be crushed comes perhaps from what we call Execration Texts, written out on ceramic objects to be ritually smashed (see Sources in Translation 5.1). They list names of peoples and places from Syria, Libya, and Nubia in great detail, and demonstrate accurate geographical knowledge of these areas. The lists must have been based on reports of people who traveled abroad, albeit not necessarily as warriors. Their basic credo was that all the inhabitants of these regions were enemies.

Sources in Translation 5.1
The Execration Texts

The Egyptians saw magic as a means to restore order and guarantee harmony. They could employ substitutes when seeking to destroy sources of chaos, and an action against such items would affect the intended target. In order to subdue foreign and domestic enemies they wrote out their names on statuettes of bound prisoners or on vessels and smashed those so that the hostile powers would be obliterated (Figure 5.3). Such objects first appeared in the 6th dynasty and they are most numerous in the Middle Kingdom, when several collections were found in Egypt and one in Nubia. A few examples are known from the Second Intermediate Period and the New Kingdom, while the practice probably continued with uninscribed figurines of bound people in foreign dress.

The lists include detailed names of individuals and places (regions and cities), but in order to be encompassing they often ended with broad summaries, like this one:

> Every rebel who plans to rebel
> in this entire land:
> all the Medjay of Webat-sepet;
> all the Nubians of Wawat, Kush,
> Shaat and Beqes,
> [their] heroes, [their] runners,
> all the Egyptians who are with them,

Figure 5.3   Execration figurine. Musée du Louvre, Paris. Photo © RMN/Les frères
Chuzeville

all the Nubians who are with them,
all the Asiatics who are with them,
...
all the Tjemhu of the western hill-countries of the
land of Tjemhu,
of He[ ]kes and Hebeqes,
their heroes and their runners;
the dead man Intefiqer
born of Satsasobek,
and born of Intefiqer;
Senusret, born of Imas.[4]

The list includes domestic enemies, and the people to the east (*Medjay*), south (Nubia), north (Asia), and west (*Tjemhu* in Libya). It ends with two specific Egyptian enemies, Intefiqer and Senusret, identified by their own name and that of their parents. One of them was already dead but his spirit could bring harm. Sometimes there is a catch-all phrase to include any man, woman, or transsexual who may plot rebellion.

The rhetoric of royal military prowess was especially strong in the 12th dynasty, perhaps most so under King Senusret III. For example, he set up steles at the second cataract, Egypt's southern border at the time, taunting the Nubians:

> Aggression is bravery;
> retreat is vile.
> He who is driven from his boundary is a true back-turner,
> since the Nubian only has to hear to fall at a word:
> answering him makes him retreat.
> One is aggressive to him and he shows his back;
> retreat and he becomes aggressive.
> Not people to be respected –
> they are wretches, broken-hearted!
> My person has seen it – it is not an untruth;
> for I have plundered their women, and carried off their underlings,
> gone to their wells, driven off their bulls,
> torn up their corn, and put fire to it.[5]

A long hymn in honor of that king written on a papyrus found at Lahun also devotes much attention to his role as warrior:

> The one who protected the land and extended its borders,
> Overwhelming the foreign lands with his crown,
> Enclosing the Two Lands with the deeds of his hands,
> Encompassing the foreign lands with the strength of his arms,
> Slaying the bowmen (= people of the north), without striking a blow,
> Shooting an arrow, without drawing a bow.
> Terror of whom strikes the cave-dwellers (= probably Nubians) in their land,
> Fear of whom slays the nine bows (= enemies of Egypt),
> Whose slaughtering causes thousands to die among the barbarians,
> And the enemies who approach his borders.[6]

The rhetoric regarding Senusret III certainly had an impact on later generations. Starting in the New Kingdom he was honored as a god in Nubia, and his fame as a warrior thrived in the first millennium. Classical sources depicted him as a great hero and adventurer. The Greek historian Herodotus stated that Sesostris (his rendering of the name Senusret) subdued tribes in Europe, sailed the Indian Ocean, and ruled Ethiopia. A tale possibly composed in the third century AD makes Sesonchosis (another Greek rendering of Senusret) second only to Alexander of Macedon in military accomplishments. Other kings likely contributed to this grossly exaggerated image, but the fact that the Greeks called Senusret Egypt's greatest warrior attests to the Middle Kingdom ruler's reputation.

The military ideal was not pure rhetoric. Middle Kingdom evidence shows that Senusret III campaigned in Nubia in his 8th, 10th, 16th, and 18th years. Graffiti by soldiers and official inscriptions carved on rocks in Nubia, the eastern desert, and Sinai attest to military acts under other rulers. The official record can refer to distant places, it seems, but the interpretation is difficult. Some scholars have read the annals of Amenemhat II, for example, as evidence that Egyptian troops reached southern Anatolia and that the navy attacked the island of Cyprus. The identification of the place names in that text is too uncertain, however, for such conclusions. These annals clearly expose the aim of military actions: they list the amounts of booty the army brought back, including captives, metal and wooden objects, and other valuables. The same interest dominates in the New Kingdom accounts of foreign wars.

Although our knowledge of the military in the Middle Kingdom is very limited, it seems that its role in society was much greater than in the Old Kingdom. The army was well organized and in the 12th dynasty it had a core of professional soldiers. They served for prolonged periods of time and were regularly stationed abroad. The army provided an outlet for ambitious men to make careers. The bulk of the troops continued to be recruited from the populations of the provinces and participated in individual campaigns only. How many troops were involved and how long they served remains unknown.

The annexation of Nubia

The primary target of Egypt's military aggression in the Middle Kingdom was Nubia to its south. During the First Intermediate Period Lower Nubia was in the hands of a confederation of chiefs whose people were buried with remains to which we give the archaeological designation C-Group (see Chapter 4), while south of the second cataract existed a more centralized state whose capital was the town of Kerma. Shortly after Middle Kingdom reunification, Egyptian kings started to campaign in the area between the first and second cataracts, but this does not seem to have resulted in a permanent occupation.

It is even possible that an ephemeral competing Nubian dynasty existed briefly in Lower Nubia, recorded in a set of hieroglyphic rock inscriptions with the Horus names of three kings that are otherwise unknown from Egyptian sources. The inscriptions' style leads some scholars to date them to the late

11th or early 12th dynasties, although they could be later. We know nothing more about these "Nubian kings." Were they Egyptians ruling Nubia or Nubians with Egyptian names and titles? Possibly the 11th-dynasty Egyptian campaigns had encouraged Lower Nubians to set up a state in resistance, but this is mere guesswork.

The 12th-dynasty kings Senusret I and III took an unambiguous stance toward Lower Nubia: they campaigned there in order to annex the region and firmly established a border at the second cataract. They implemented this policy by building fortresses throughout Lower Nubia, especially at the second cataract where under Senusret III the number was increased to 11. That cataract is not a single narrow point in the river, but a sequence of rapids and islands over some 30 miles (50 kilometers). At the southernmost point the Egyptians built the fortresses of Semna and Semna South on the west bank, Kumma on the east bank, and Uronarti, some 3 miles (5 kilometers) downriver on an island. Buhen, which already existed in the Old Kingdom (Chapter 3), may have been the central fortress at the northern side of the cataract. This was unmistakably the southern border of Egypt. Farther north, along the 250 miles (400 kilometers) between the first and second cataracts, the Egyptians constructed a line of forts in strategic places, notably at the entrances of wadis that gave access to mines and stone quarries. They gave these forts such names as "Warding off the Bows" and "Curbing the Foreign Lands," clearly announcing their martial character.

The fortresses were remarkable examples of military architecture with huge walls, ramparts and ditches, bastions, and fortified gates with drawbridges. Inside them were barracks, magazines, workshops and offices, as well as small temples for Egyptian gods. The interior planning used the same gridiron pattern as the Middle Kingdom settlements in Egypt itself (Figure 5.4). Large granaries contained the rations to feed the troops and personnel stationed there.

The function of these forts is obvious from their architecture. They were well-protected points from which the Egyptians could monitor activity in the region. They must have considered the local inhabitants to be dangerous, otherwise there would have been no need for such elaborate defenses. A group of documents attests to the Egyptian concerns. A papyrus found in Thebes contains copies of administrative reports from the reign of Amenemhat III, the "Semna dispatches." They describe how patrols tracked the movements of locals and how Nubian traders were received in the forts. No one could go north without permission. The Egyptians also used the fortresses to collect the resources they mined in the region, especially gold, and to prepare them for shipment home.

Most of the local people were not involved in these activities. The forts' inhabitants were Egyptians who were sent from the homeland and regularly rotated. The remains in the locals' graves and settlements show a continued use of objects manufactured in the regional style, the so-called C-Group culture. Originally there was no acculturation and relations could hardly have been cordial. The Egyptians were an occupying force sheltered behind secure walls.

Figure 5.4 Aerial view showing a re-creation of the Fortress of Buhen (12th dynasty, ca. 1878–1843, on the ancient Egyptian–Nubian border) generated from a 3D computer model originally created in 1993 by Bill Riseman and updated by the Institute. © 2010 Institute for the Visualization of History, Inc.

They sometimes used mercenaries to venture outside, whom they recruited from the nomads of the eastern desert. Some scholars see the monumentality of the defenses as overreacting to a low-level threat and more intended to impress on people how powerful Egypt was than for actual use, but the amount of energy and resources the Egyptians expended on these forts suggests that pragmatic concerns were important as well.

5.4   Egypt in the Wider World

The early Kingdom of Kush

The C-Group Lower Nubians may have been a source of fear, but they did not form a well-organized opposition. Such an enemy confronted Egypt farther south, upriver from the second cataract. From the late Old Kingdom on a state had developed between the second and third cataracts around the town of Kerma. At that time the Egyptians may have called the region Yam; in the Middle Kingdom they started to refer to it as Kush. The Kingdom of Kush flourished during the late Second Intermediate Period, when it presented a strong rival to the Egyptian state. The leaders of this society benefited from the kingdom's location. They acted as intermediaries between sub-Saharan Africa and Egypt for the acquisition of such luxury products as elephant ivory, ebony, and animal skins. That the Egyptians traded with them is clear from the many Egyptian objects found at Kerma. They may have seen the people of Upper Nubia as enemies, but they could not ignore them if they wanted access to African goods.

The occupation of Lower Nubia was successful for more than 200 years under the 12th dynasty and into the 13th, when the waning of royal authority affected the state's power abroad. The regular rotation of troops seems to have stopped. Many of the Egyptians in the Nubian fortresses did not leave, however, but stayed as civilians rather than soldiers. They turned their barracks into homes where they lived with wives and children for several generations. Archaeological evidence of Nubians in the forts increases although it remains limited. The expatriate Egyptians had to work together with the ascendant Kerma state, which would become a rival to Egypt in the Second Intermediate Period.

The eastern desert and Sinai

The Egyptians' interactions with their neighbors to the east were very different from those with Nubia. In the east they first encountered the eastern desert and Sinai, sources for stones and minerals. Beyond Sinai lay the regions of Syria and Palestine, home to urban cultures under the leadership of local kings.

East of the Nile, in the inhospitable mountainous desert that stretches into the neighboring Sinai region, the Egyptians found materials lacking in the Nile Valley: hard stone for statues and sculptures, copper for tools and decorative objects, and semi-precious stones such as turquoise, for jewelry and the like. From the very beginning of the Middle Kingdom into the 13th dynasty Egyptian kings sponsored expeditions to obtain such goods. Senusret I, for example, claimed to have sent 17,000 people into the Wadi Hammamat to bring back stone for 150 statues and 60 sphinxes. In Sinai the Egyptians set up bases near mines, especially turquoise mines, and they involved locals in the exploitation. The main base was at Serabit el-Khadim, where a small temple for the goddess Hathor "Lady of turquoise" was built.

The inhabitants of these areas had a life that was fundamentally different from the Egyptian: they were nomads rather than town or village people. The lack of water made agriculture largely impossible, so people raised herds of sheep and goats and guided them to pasture following the seasons. In the eastern desert their archaeological remains are limited to shallow graves, which we call pan-graves after their round shape. The dead were not mummified and received only a few pots as grave goods. Pan-graves appear in a large stretch of the eastern desert from northern Upper Egypt to Central Sudan. The Egyptians referred to the inhabitants of that region as *Medjay*, and they had both hostile and peaceful interactions with them. On the one hand the lower Nubian forts seem to have been intended partly to control the nomads (one of them was called "Repelling the *Medjay*"); on the other hand the Egyptians recruited men from their ranks to monitor the region. In the Middle Kingdom and especially in later periods, the *Medjay* acted as police forces, at first in the desert only, later in the Nile Valley as well.

Also people in Sinai and much of Palestine lived as nomads. The essential difference between that lifestyle and the Egyptian was much developed in a literary text from the Middle Kingdom: the *Tale of Sinuhe*. The tale mentions the transfer of power from Amenemhat I to his son Senusret I, and may date to soon after the latter's reign. It relates how Sinuhe, a royal courtier, panicked at the death of the old king, and fled into Sinai where he almost died of thirst. Nomads saved him, and Sinuhe ended up living as the guest of a man called Amunenshi – a Syro-Palestinian name – who was the ruler of Upper Retenu, that is, northern Palestine. Sinuhe became very successful as a member of Amunenshi's tribe and lived an idyllic life with abundant food. His people brought him fruits, wine, honey, cereals, fowl, and game. His success was crowned when he defeated the champion of another tribe in hand-to-hand combat.

Sinuhe never fully adjusted to the nomadic life, however, and when King Senusret summoned him he immediately returned to Egypt. There the king reinstated him with great pomp and Sinuhe became a true Egyptian once more, putting on fine linen garments and sleeping in a bed. Perhaps most importantly an Egyptian tomb was prepared for him, provided with mortuary equipment, and assigned an estate to supply it. Although the tale dwells on Sinuhe's time with the nomads, the author's lack of knowledge about such life is striking. Sinuhe is said to be the member of a nomadic tribe, but the luxuries surrounding him were those of a wealthy landowner in Egypt. The Egyptian writer did not understand the world of the nomad: it was essentially non-Egyptian, but what that exactly entailed was unclear. Nomads were exotic, and meeting them could be portrayed as a special event. In his tomb at Beni Hassan, Khnumhotep II prominently depicted a delegation of desert nomads who brought him gifts. A note on a tablet handed to Khnumhotep in the painting stated:

> In year 6 under the Majesty of the Horus, one who guides the Two Lands, the King of Upper and Lower Egypt, Khakheperaa [Senusret II]: the number of Asiatics that the governor's son Khnumhotep brought on account of eye-cosmetic was 37.[7]

Syria and Palestine

The Sinuhe tale focuses on the hero's life among the nomads and only in passing mentions cities. The archaeological reality of the region paints a very different picture: in the early 2nd millennium the whole of Syria and Palestine north of Sinai was made up of city-states with fortified urban centers. The rulers of these states were in contact with one another and with kingdoms in Mesopotamia and western Iran, but in their correspondence they do not refer to Egypt. Contacts with Egypt existed, however. A very recently reconstructed inscription on the mastaba of Khnumhotep III at Dahshur, mentioned above, relates how sailors from Egypt reached Byblos and witnessed a conflict between that city and a northern neighbor. The Egyptians obtained cedar from the Lebanon Mountains near Byblos, crucial for building projects and for coffins, and the resin that came from such trees, needed in mummification. Some Egyptians may have resided permanently there and may have established a temple devoted to Hathor as "Lady of Byblos." The interaction with Egyptians had a great impact on the elites from Byblos. From this period date nine tombs built to imitate Egyptian ones in shape and decoration. Frequently the local leaders had their names written out in hieroglyphs and they used the Egyptian title of "mayor."

Elsewhere in the Levant the Egyptians obtained foods, such as olive oil and wine, which were transported in Syro-Palestinian jars found in excavations all over Egypt. People imported Egyptian objects or imitated them. Sphinxes and statues of Egyptian kings appear at various sites, which do not imply Egyptian control but suggest that local people saw such objects as collectors' items to show off that they were in touch with Egypt. Altogether the number of Egyptian objects in Syria and Palestine is limited, however.

The world beyond

Some Egyptian objects made their way farther north, possibly via Syria, including to Crete, where Minoan culture flourished at the time. Egyptian stone vessels were so popular there that people made local imitations. Conversely some Minoan pottery appeared in Egypt, and at Lahun people replicated the style. The appeal of precious foreign objects is most clearly demonstrated in a deposit found beneath the temple of the god Montu at Tod, just south of Thebes. In four copper boxes inscribed with the name of Amenemhat II archaeologists found a mass of silver objects and some gold ones, chunks of lapis lazuli, and some cylinder seals that are typically Mesopotamian. Chemical analysis of the silver shows that some of the objects came from the Aegean and others from Anatolia. The lapis lazuli originally derived from Afghanistan. All these objects could have passed through many hands before they reached Egypt, and we do not know how they ended up at their final destination, as gifts, trade items, tribute, or loot.

The Egyptians also tried to obtain goods from sub-Saharan Africa without Nubian intermediaries, and developed sea-faring trade on the Red Sea for that purpose. Recent excavations on the coast of the Red Sea, reached via wadis to the east of Thebes, revealed the remains of Middle Kingdom harbor installations at Saww (modern Mersa/Wadi Gawasis). They include man-made caves in which equipment such as ship rope was stored, while in front of them lay timber beams of cedar imported from Lebanon. Inscriptions on the site indicate that several 12th-dynasty kings sponsored expeditions to lands called Punt and Bia-Punt. The name Bia-Punt is unknown elsewhere, while scholars have long debated the location of Punt. It is clear that it was somewhere on the southern Red Sea coast and that it was a source for much-desired exotic materials, such as incense, wild animal skins, gold, ivory, and ebony. The port at Saww was not fortified and does not include large constructions, but it survived at least into the early 18th dynasty; Hatshepsut may have used it to launch her famous expedition to Punt (see Chapter 7).

Rhetoric and practice in foreign relations

In the Middle Kingdom the official rhetoric regarding non-Egyptians became more hostile and the need to subdue them was more loudly proclaimed than had been the case before. But in reality the Egyptians had to interact with foreign people. As we have seen, they had trade relations with surrounding regions. They also allowed foreigners to immigrate into Egypt or invited them to settle there to provide labor. Nubians were present from the Old Kingdom, and people from Syria and Palestine became numerous during the Middle Kingdom. People with Syro-Palestinian names or explicitly identified as Asiatic were common (see Sources in Translation 5.2). They were often servants, especially women, who appear in the accounts of various households. Some of those seem to have had more foreigners than Egyptians in their staff.

The influx of Asiatics seems to have increased in the 13th dynasty, and many of them settled in the eastern Delta. The settlements and burials show that these people held on to their traditions, and archaeologists find much Syro-Palestinian pottery and weaponry. The newcomers seem to have started to organize politically, and around 1700 some initiated dynasties in competition with the 13th at Itj-tawi. When their power in the north grew, that dynasty relocated to Thebes, starting the Second Intermediate Period.

Sources in Translation 5.2
A lawsuit of the 13th dynasty

Our knowledge of the role and rights of women in Middle Kingdom society is woefully deficient as royal records are mostly silent on this topic and documents of daily use, such as those from Lahun, also focus on men in society. Some exceptional sources exist, however, and they suggest that women were not without legal rights. An important document in this respect is a papyrus now in the Brooklyn Museum in New York (Papyrus Brooklyn 35.1446) and probably originally from Thebes. When found it was in more than 500 pieces; scholars have painstakingly pieced together a still-fragmentary scroll that is some 2 meters long and 30 centimeters wide. The papyrus is covered on both sides with hieratic script, written over more than a century under 12th- and 13th-dynasty kings. Scholars disagree on the relationship between the seven documents the papyrus contains. Some see it as a century-long record of the same family property, others as several disparate accounts.

The latest entries, written on the back of the papyrus in the 13th dynasty, seem to belong together. They include a long list of names of servants that were part of a donation made in the second year of King Sobekhotep III. Originally the list included 95 names (78 are preserved), at least 45 of whom are of people explicitly identified as Asiatic, mostly women. This shows how numerous the foreigners were in Thebes, at least in the servile class.

The list seems to have been part of a legal dispute. In the final section of the document an unnamed defendant accuses his daughter, Tihenut, of making false claims on the servants, whom he intends to give to his new wife, Senebtisy, and her children. He states:

> My daughter, Tihenut, is bringing suit and saying: "My father has committed a wrong. Belongings of mine, which were given to me by my husband, are in his possession. But, he (=my father) gave this property to his wife Senebtisy. Let it be returned to me," so she says.[8]

The record becomes very fragmentary afterwards. Although the exact details remain unclear, the papyrus confirms information from other sources that a woman in the Middle Kingdom had the right to her own property and that she could start a court action. The fact that the document is written from her father's point of view suggests, however, that she lost the case.

5.5   The Cult of Osiris

Changes in mortuary religions that had begun in the late Old Kingdom came to full fruition in the Middle Kingdom and especially involved the god Osiris. The Coffin Texts, which gave great prominence to that god, became widespread in the elite burials of the period and it is clear that at least in the upper levels of society people sought a connection with him in death. Because Osiris was the judge of the netherworld people wanted to be in his favor.

The site of Abydos became very important in this respect. Some time in the Old Kingdom Osiris was assimilated with the jackal-headed god, Khentyamentiu of Abydos, whose name means "foremost of the westerners," that is, of the gods of the netherworld. Pepy I of the 6th dynasty built a temple for Osiris in this syncretized form, which later kings restored and expanded. In the Middle Kingdom, the tomb of the 1st-dynasty king Djer at Abydos was reputed to be the tomb of Osiris, and an annual festival started that commemorated the god's death and his rebirth as ruler of the netherworld. During the festival people took the cult statue out of his temple, carried it to his tomb in the desert, and returned it in a pageant that involved staged events, such as attacks on the procession. A 12th-dynasty stele of the overseer of the treasury Ikhernofret describes how King Senusret III had sent him to Abydos to adorn the statue and provide it with a palanquin made of gold, silver, lapis lazuli, amethyst, and special woods. The text continues with a narrative of the procession and states that Ikhernofret "felled the foes of Osiris."[9]

Osiris's popularity was so great in the Middle Kingdom that people from all over Egypt made pilgrimages to Abydos or sent others to present offerings on their behalf. They also desired to be buried near him, but few managed to do so. Senusret III may have chosen Abydos for his burial rather than Dahshur where he had a pyramid. Many other people, both kings and elite, established monuments resembling mortuary constructions at Abydos while their tombs were elsewhere. Egyptologists call these monuments cenotaphs or memorial chapels (Figure 5.5). People from a surprising social range built chapels in order to receive mortuary offerings, in which they set up steles engraved with representations of themselves and sometimes accounts of their lives. Later in the Middle Kingdom the inscriptions became hymns to Osiris with a mention of the deceased's name. The size of the chapels and the steles inside them varied enormously; poorer people had tiny buildings with a small inscribed stone in them. The practice of setting up cenotaphs got so out of hand, that King Wegaf of the 13th dynasty tried to regulate it, unsuccessfully however.

The aim of all this was to have a close association with the cult of Osiris, an ideal that continued in later times. A few New Kingdom kings had cenotaphs at Abydos, while commoners brought offerings to King Djer's tomb, which they believed had housed Osiris's body. They deposited so many bowls and vessels that the modern Arabic name of this part of the Early Dynastic cemetery is Umm el-Qaab, "mother of pots."

Figure 5.5 Cenotaphs in Abydos. From O'Connor, D. (2009) *Abydos: Egypt's First Pharaohs and the Cult of Osiris*, London: Thames and Hudson

Other gods received greater official recognition in the Middle Kingdom than they had before. The Theban origin of the 11th dynasty made the city's main god Amun an important rival to the sun god Ra from the north. The two gods merged together as Amun-Ra, a new supreme divinity for Egypt, and Thebes became the city of the sun (Heliopolis) of the south. The prominence of the Theban pantheon is also clear from the royal names of the 12th dynasty: Amenemhat invokes Amun, while Senusret means "Man of Wosret," perhaps referring to a Theban goddess who may have been Amun's original companion.

5.6 Middle Kingdom Literature and Its Impact on Egyptian Culture

The promotion of the cult of Osiris was not the only cultural element that the Middle Kingdom conferred on later Egyptians. The period was especially important for its impact on literature. Many of the works known today were composed in the Middle Kingdom, and later Egyptians saw several of them as classics. The burst of creativity in this respect is remarkable. Some private mortuary inscriptions and the Pyramid Texts of the late Old Kingdom had shown skilled literary use of language, but the range of written expression had been limited. That changed in the Middle Kingdom, when a large variety of genres appeared. There is much uncertainty about the context of this creativity, as we do not know the date of composition of most texts. Until recently scholars used to suggest that it started in the First Intermediate Period when the greater personal freedom of people may have encouraged literary expressions, but today most see the 12th dynasty as the crucial period. It is clear that some of the major works cannot have been composed earlier because they contain references to that dynasty: the *Tale of Sinuhe* (see above), the *Prophecy of Neferty* (see Chapter 3), and the *Teaching of King Amenemhat I*. It is possible that the court sponsored literature in general, some have suggested, because many compositions praise the benefits of order over chaos.

The works were often set within a historical context. The *Prophecy of Neferty* used the court of 4th-dynasty king Sneferu to predict that chaos would engulf the country but that King Ameny – a short version of the name Amenemhat I – would restore order by reunifying Egypt and keeping outsiders away. Other compositions refer to kings Khufu (4th dynasty), Merykara (10th dynasty), and others. They can also involve esoteric creatures, however, such as the giant serpent that tells how its family was killed by a falling star in the *Tale of the Shipwrecked Sailor*.

Later Egyptians used Middle Kingdom works to educate scribes. For some compositions we have dozens of copies students made in the New Kingdom, and it seems that there was a set curriculum they had to learn. As the Middle Kingdom literary dialect was, for a long time, the only proper language for certain official and religious texts, that choice is no surprise.

By far the majority of the texts' authors remain anonymous, and even when a name appears it is probably fictitious. Many works belong to a genre of literature we call instructions or teaching because they contain wise sayings. The Egyptians honored the sages who pronounced those words; their memory lasted longer than that of great builders or others. The praise of scribes from the 19th dynasty, quoted at the top of this chapter, continues with these words:

> Is there any here like Hardjedef?
> Is there another like Imhotep?
> There is none among our people like Neferty,
> or Khety their chief.
> I shall make you know the name of Ptahemdjehuty and Khakheperresonbe.
> Is there another like Ptahhotep,
> or likewise, Kaires?[10]

Those were great men in Egyptian eyes, and their words were recorded in the Middle Kingdom so that later generations could hear them. This was one of the various ways in which the period fundamentally shaped the history of the country.

Special Topic 5.2 *Reading Egyptian literature*

Egyptian literature of the Middle Kingdom is poetry. According to the Egyptians its aim was to render "perfect speech," that is, to be aesthetically pleasing and persuasive. The formal aspect of the language was thus very important, as is the case in all poetry. One of the Middle Kingdom compositions is called *The Tale of the Eloquent Peasant* where a poor man, robbed of his donkey by a corrupt official, wins his case before a higher authority because of his eloquence.

How can we today appreciate the poetic strength of this material? We are separated from the original language by several degrees. Most of us do not know ancient Egyptian, and even those who do cannot determine how a verse would have been pronounced. The absence of vowels in most Egyptian writing is a major problem and we are not certain how exactly the consonants sounded. A careful reading of the lines certainly helps and gives some idea of the effects the author sought in the choice of words. Read this passage, for example:

dd.jn-shtj-pnhsfw	And this peasant said, "The thirsty man's
n-jb m-mww	approaching water,
dʒt–rʒ n-hrd n-sbnt	the nurseling's reaching of a mouth
m-jrtt ntf-mt	for milk – he dies,
nhjj–mʒ:f n-jj:f	while for him who prays to see it come,
jj wdf-mt:f-r:f	death comes slowly."[11]

The repeated use of the consonants *n* and *m* throughout and of *jj* and *f* in the final two lines must have been intended for effect. Part of the vocabulary was chosen to pun with words in adjacent passages. Scholars have also pointed at meter and stress as poetic elements.

Because the sound is so difficult to access, scholars often focus on content to see poetic merit. The passage here uses irony. The thirsty man and baby are denied life-saving water and milk although they are close by, but at the same time someone who wishes to die has to wait a long time. The entire *Tale of the Eloquent Peasant* has a clever structure where nine speeches that use different techniques in trying to convince his audience are inserted in a simple narrative of events. It is very skillfully crafted and organized. Our reading of it will always remain imperfect, however.

Key Debate 5.1 *Co-regencies*

In political systems – such as Egypt's – where power is concentrated in the hands of one person, transfer of rule is always a problematic moment. The new king needs to establish authority immediately and convince others to obey him as they did his predecessor at the same time that he needs to learn the ropes of the job. In order to smoothen transition the Egyptians at some point in their history conceived the idea of co-regency: the king selected an heir and made him his equal before the actual transfer of power. The system had great benefits, as the desired successor was clearly identified and had the opportunity to create the authority needed to rule alone. It poses problems to the historian, however. As Egyptians ideologically could only conceive of a single king at a time, they portrayed the two reigns as successive rather than overlapping in later king lists, which are the basis of our chronologies. Dynasties seem thus longer than they were in reality (von Beckerath 1997: 74–5). Moreover, when we try to identify who was responsible for certain actions or ideas, it makes a difference whether only one ruler was involved or two who collaborated.

All aspects of the practice have stimulated much scholarly debate. We do not know when it first occurred: some find traces in the Old Kingdom (Kaplony 1977: 286–93), others in the First Intermediate Period (Schaefer 1986). But most historians see the Middle Kingdom as the time when the practice became regularized. The specific co-regencies are contested, however.

The example that seemed most secure for the greatest length of time was the co-regency between Amenemhat I and his son Senusret I at the start of the 12th dynasty. The stele of a man called Antef contains two dates: the 30th year of Amenemhat (his last year) and the 10th of Senusret. Hence Egyptologists long accepted a 10-year-long co-regency (Murnane 1977: 2–5). They found confirmation of the idea in another private stele with both kings' names and in a literary text, *The Teaching of Amenemhat*. In the latter the old king addresses his son as "Lord of All," which is a royal designation (Parkinson 1998: 207), and describes a failed assassination attempt, which many see as the reason why he elected Senusret as co-regent. But the so-called double date on Antef's stele was reinterpreted as an indication of a period of 30 years in Amenemhat's reign and of 10 years in that of Senusret (Delia 1979, contested in Murnane 1981, with a rejoinder in Delia 1982). Some scholars call into question all double dates of the Middle Kingdom (Obsomer 1995) and date the *Teaching of Amenemhat* to a later period, so that it would be irrelevant to Middle Kingdom times (Grimal 1995). More recently new data appeared that seem to support the idea that the rules of Amenemhat and Senusret partly overlapped (Schneider 2006: 170–2).

Every other possible co-regency until the Ptolemaic Period when the practice is confirmed has been contested (cf. Murnane 2001). In particular the possible overlap between Amenhotep III's reign and that of his son Akhenaten is controversial, and whether or not it took place affects the way in which scholars interpret the origins of the latter's reforms (see Chapter 8).

NOTES

1. Parkinson 1991: 150, quoted by permission.
2. Translation after Wente 1990: 73.
3. Translation after Allen 2002: 17.
4. Translation Parkinson 1991: 125–6, quoted by permission.

5. Parkinson 1991: 45, quoted by permission.
6. Translation after Simpson (ed.) 2003: 302.
7. Translation after Shedid 1994: 61.
8. Translation after Hayes 1955: 115.
9. Lichtheim 1988: 99.
10. Parkinson 1991: 130, quoted by permission.
11. Parkinson 2002: 127, quoted by permission.

6

The Second Intermediate Period and the Hyksos (ca. 1700–1550)

The Canaanites who fled from *Joshua*, retired in great numbers into *Egypt*, and there conquered *Timaus*, *Thamus*, or *Thammuz* King of the Lower *Egypt*, and reigned there under their Kings *Salitis*, *Boeon*, *Apachnas*, *Apophis*, *Janias*, *Assis*, &c. untill the days of *Eli* and *Samuel*. They fed of flesh, and sacrificed men after the manner of the *Phoenicians*, and were called Shepherds by the *Egyptians*, who lived only the fruits of the earth, and abominated flesh-eaters. (Sir Isaac Newton, *The Chronology of Ancient Kingdoms Amended*, 1728: 9)

The 13th dynasty had its original seat at Itj-tawi and at least 24 of its mostly short-term rulers were accepted as kings all over Egypt. But some time in the middle of the dynasty, around 1700, the royal court moved to Thebes and lost control over the region north of Abydos. That moment started the Second Intermediate Period, a time when Egypt was once more politically divided and when several dynasties coexisted. Unlike in the First Intermediate Period, when various Egyptian lords continued to share power, in the Second Intermediate Period foreigners were in control of much of the country. These outsiders acknowledged their non-Egyptian roots: they called themselves Heqau-khasut, "rulers of foreign lands," a term that later Greek accounts rendered as Hyksos, the name we now use. Later Egyptians stressed the otherness of the Hyksos and depicted them in very negative terms, but in reality the Hyksos were eager to absorb Egyptian culture and preserve it, and they lived alongside Egyptian people and kings for more than a century with little evidence of hostile interactions. The Hyksos have become the symbol of the Second Intermediate Period, because we have long accepted Egyptian portrayals – especially the one Manetho wrote in Greek – of a period of confusion and calamity. Sir Isaac Newton's 18th-century depiction of the Hyksos as cannibals is typical for the view that dominated until very recently. Opinions on the Second Intermediate Period

Summary of dynastic history:
Second Intermediate Period (ca. 1700–1550)

ca. 1700–1650	**Later 13th dynasty** Court leaves Itj-tawi for Thebes Egypt loses control over Lower Nubia
ca. 1700–1650	**14th dynasty** Minor rulers in northern Egypt
ca. 1650–1550	**15th dynasty** Six Hyksos kings rule northern Egypt from Avaris King Apepi confronts the Theban ruler Kamose
ca. 1650–1580	**16th dynasty** Minor rulers in northern Egypt, subject to the Hyksos
ca. 1650–1550	**17th dynasty** Theban successors to 13th dynasty King Seqenenra Taa dies violently, possibly in battle King Kamose initiates campaign against Hyksos and the Kingdom of Kush, ca. 1555
ca. 1750–1500	Classical Kerma phase in Nubia

have changed in the last few decades, and today more scholars believe that the Hyksos made up part of a political and cultural complexity in which both Egyptians and foreigners played important parts.

6.1 Sources and Chronology

King lists and inscriptions provide a large number of royal names for the Second Intermediate Period, but the contemporary sources are scant and quite uninformative. While the Hyksos rulers in the north had the ability to undertake building projects, they and their officials left few inscribed remains, mostly scarab seals, which sometimes include royal names unattested in king lists. The historical value of such seals is limited. A handful of written sources derive from the south of Egypt and Lower Nubia. We have thus little to work with to describe events. Later Egyptians wrote about the Hyksos with much acerbity, and we have to use these biased accounts carefully. Archaeological data and objects help us to elaborate the picture of the period.

Also chronologically the Second Intermediate Period is a nightmare. The only king list that provides names of rulers, the Turin Canon, devotes five or

Table 6.1 Dynasties of the Second Intermediate Period

Avaris	North of Egypt	Thebes
	Dyn. 14	Late dyn. 13
	ca. 1700–1650	ca. 1700–1650
Dyn. 15	Dyn. 16	Dyn. 17
ca. 1650–1550	ca. 1650–1580	ca. 1650–1550

six columns, which could have contained some 27 names each, to the 13th through 17th dynasties. The papyrus is very damaged, however, and little chronological information can be gleaned from it. Manetho gives high numbers of kings for all but the 15th dynasty, whose six kings he explicitly names. As a result the number of kings and lengths of reigns are very elusive. The Second Intermediate Period ended around 1550. Its exact duration is debated; I follow those who assign it about 150 years, a solution that is tentative.

6.2 Avaris: The Multiple Transformations of a Delta City

A history of Avaris

During the Middle Kingdom, King Amenemhat I founded a town on an eastern branch of the Nile in the Delta, inland yet close enough to the sea to serve as a harbor and connected to Sinai by overland routes. The history of this settlement, which was called "The (royal) estate of the district" Hutwaret in Egyptian and rendered as Avaris in Greek, characterizes the political and cultural developments of the Delta and the rest of Egypt in the next 450 years. Twelfth-dynasty Avaris included workers' quarters laid out as a planned settlement with the same gridiron arrangement as Lahun, next to a hitherto unexcavated town. Its location near the border with Asia made it a popular destination for immigrants from that area, and by the end of the dynasty the house architecture started to show Near Eastern rather than Egyptian styles. The newcomers used Egyptian-style pottery, however, and imported liquid products from southern Palestine (oil and wine) shipped in jars produced there. A high number of the men were buried with weapons of a Syro-Palestinian origin and it is likely that mercenaries recruited there formed part of the population.

The Asiatic character of Avaris became stronger under the 13th dynasty when a large palace was built on top of the earlier settlement, Egyptian in layout but with non-Egyptian elements. Most unfamiliar were the burials. While in Egypt these were always away from residential areas, in the Near East people buried their dead in or near their houses. The 13th-dynasty palace at Avaris contained a series of tombs within its walls, something Egyptians would never have done. Moreover next to these tombs – albeit Egyptian in construction – were pits in which one or two donkeys were interred, a practice that was entirely foreign to Egypt after the 1st dynasty. The excavator of Avaris believes that these animal burials reveal the tomb owners' status and profession: they were caravanners who traveled back-and-forth between Egypt and Palestine for trade and carried their goods on donkey-back. The paintings in Khnumhotep II's tomb at Beni Hassan (see Figure 5.1) depict such a caravan. The mixture of Egyptian and Near Eastern cultures is visible in other remains of the period as well. The inhabitants used both Egyptian scarab seals and Near Eastern cylinder seals, the latter seemingly also carved in Egypt.

Later in the 13th dynasty this palace was abandoned and people built a new settlement with houses in Near Eastern style that had tombs in their courtyards. An epidemic seems to have hit the town late in the dynasty and shallow burials with several occupants indicate a sudden drop in the population. Avaris recovered, however, but it was no longer under Egyptian political control. A king of the 14th dynasty named Nehesy chose it for his capital. Temples built at the time show both Egyptian and Near Eastern ground plans. Much of the material culture of the city was Asiatic, although Nehesy and his officials used hieroglyphic writing.

The city grew into one of the largest settlements of the Near East in the 17th century. Its success was crowned when the Hyksos dynasty set up court there. Avaris was the center of a kingdom that reached into Middle Egypt and had contacts with the rest of Egypt, Nubia, and the eastern Mediterranean. Much pottery came from Cyprus. The city was very wealthy if we can believe the accounts of its captor Kamose, who claimed he seized hundreds of ships filled with gold, lapis lazuli, silver, turquoise, bronze weapons, oils, fats, honey, and woods when he looted it.[1] At first it was not a military stronghold, but late in the Hyksos Period the rulers chose a strategic site on the riverbank at the western edge of the site to build a massive citadel, 12.35 acres (50,000 square meters) large. The citadel had thick walls and bastions, and its construction is a sign of the increased military tensions in the mid-16th century when Thebes and Avaris started to compete for supremacy. The Egyptians won the conflict and tore down the citadel, while the rest of the city was mostly abandoned. In the early 19th dynasty kings Sety I and Rameses II founded Piramesse two kilometers to the north, superseding Avaris.

Cultural hybridity

The city reflects the cultural and political history of the Second Intermediate Period well. It shows a hybrid culture in which Near Eastern elements merged with Egyptian customs. From the late 12th dynasty on many of its inhabitants seem to have been Asian-born or descendants of such immigrants, honoring their own traditions but also absorbing Egyptian ones. They maintained their burial practices, which were very alien to those of the Egyptians, yet saw fit to write out their names in hieroglyphs or took Egyptian names (Figure 6.1), and

Figure 6.1 Stele of the official Mentuhotep. Alongside the small mummified figure between the man's legs is the text "The Syrian woman Sat-Hathor," identifying his deceased wife as a Syrian woman who had an Egyptian name. Aegyptisches Museum, Berlin. Photo: Juergen Liepe. © 2010 Photo Scala, Florence/BPK, Bildagentur für Kunst, Kultur und Geschichte, Berlin

entombed Egyptian-style objects with them. They maintained strong commercial links with the Levant, and their city was probably a favorite destination for people from that area, but they also traded with Upper Egypt and Nubia. Avaris was a port-of-trade between Asia and Africa, open to cultures from both continents.

The arrival of the Asiatics brought several benefits to Egypt, especially in the technological sphere, where the country had lagged behind its eastern neighbors. The Asiatics used a fast wheel for pottery production and seem to have practiced more advanced bronze-working and weaving techniques, although the evidence is inconclusive. Their armory was more efficient: they shot with composite bows rather than the earlier Egyptian straight bow, had special battle axes, scimitars and daggers, and may have had full body-armor. The fact that men were buried with these weapons shows the importance they gave to military activity. An unsolved question is whether or not they introduced the horse and war chariot into the military. After the Second Intermediate Period the Egyptian army started to include a chariotry, as did all other armies of the Near East, where the innovation came slightly earlier. We do not know when exactly the technology entered Egypt and under what impulse. Perhaps the Hyksos started the chariot's use, but it is also possible that only later kings adopted this important military advance. In a more peaceful sphere, the Asiatics introduced new musical instruments. They were not barbarians tearing down a high civilization, as later Egyptians wanted us to believe, but they injected new energy into an ancient system.

Other immigrants

Asiatics were not the only foreigners who gained a foothold in Egypt at this time. In addition the nomads from the eastern desert, the *Medjay* (see Chapter 5), had easier access to the valley. Their simple tombs, called pan-graves because of their shape, show their presence from the region of Memphis to Kerma, south of the third cataract. In the subsequent centuries the *Medjay* would become the police force of Egypt. The newcomers and the political disunity of Egypt led to a cultural fragmentation, where each region had its unique mixture of elements, some more attached to earlier traditions than others.

6.3 The Hyksos

The name Hyksos

Avaris attained its most successful period, and its greatest size, when it became the political capital of a dynasty, the 15th in Manetho's count. He and other Egyptian sources looking back at the period stressed the foreign origin of its kings. The first-century-AD historian Flavius Josephus quoting Manetho called them "Hyksos," which he mistakenly explained as "shepherd kings." The term was a Greek rendering of the Egyptian Heqau-khasut, "rulers of foreign lands," the singular of which was Heqa-khasut. That was not a new label for the Second Intermediate Period, however, nor was it reserved for these kings. From the late Old Kingdom on foreign people like Asiatics and Nubians could be identified as such. In the tomb of Khnumhotep II, next to the leader of the Asiatic visitors was written his name Abisha and that he was a Heqa-khasut. Into the Ptolemaic Period Egyptians would continue to use the term to refer to foreigners.

When the Turin Royal Canon or other New Kingdom sources call the rulers from Avaris Hyksos we should not be surprised then. More remarkable is the fact that the first four rulers of the 15th dynasty used the term in their own inscriptions: They owned seals that gave their names followed by the word Heqa-khasut. The term also appears in an inscription on a monumental door-jamb. The Hyksos did not hide their foreignness nor were they ashamed of it.

Hyksos origins

Where did they come from? No explicit information exists and scholars usually rely on the names of Hyksos kings and commoners to determine their origin (see Key Debate 6.1). As the names were written in hieroglyphs it is not easy to establish their exact reading, but whenever we can recognize the language it is west Semitic, that is, from the Syro-Palestinian area. This observation fits well, of course, with the strong Syro-Palestinian influence in the material culture of Avaris, which appeared before the Hyksos kings set up court there. It is thus likely that from the ranks of Asiatic immigrants in the eastern Delta region grew a royal dynasty that became the recognized authority and had its capital in Avaris. Whether or not this involved military action is unclear. The Hyksos are often portrayed as warriors because the men buried at Avaris had weapons in their tombs. But that was a characteristic of Syro-Palestinian burials in general, and the interpretation is much influenced by later descriptions of the Hyksos, and the negative bias in them makes them highly problematic historical sources (see below).

Egyptian cultural influences

Despite their clearly acknowledged foreignness, the Hyksos wanted to be known as Egyptian kings as well. Three of the six members of the 15th dynasty appear in their inscriptions with several of the five royal names that were standard by that time (see Chapter 1). Apepi, for example, also used the throne names Aauserra "The one who is great of strength of Ra," and Seqenenra, "The one who is great of valor of Ra." They had no qualms about being called "sons of Ra" and – as was typical for Egyptian kings – restored temples to Egyptian gods and dedicated cult objects to them. They wrote their names on statues and sphinxes – admittedly reusing those of Middle Kingdom rulers, but that was normal practice. The Hyksos were not opposed to Egyptian culture; they pre-served and promoted it. The so-called Rhind mathematical papyrus (see Sources in Translation 6.1) was copied from a 12th-dynasty original in the reign of

Sources in Translation 6.1

The Rhind mathematical papyrus

Probably the most elaborate document from the Second Intermediate Period is a 202-inches- (513 cm-) long papyrus written in the reign of the Hyksos ruler Apepi. It contains 87 mathematical problems covering various aspects from simple multiplications to calculations of volume. The text uses a format where a problem is stated and then the ways to solve it are expounded. Some of the problems have accompanying drawings (Figure 6.2).

The Rhind papyrus is one of a few surviving mathematical texts from Egypt. Architectural remains show, however, that the Egyptians must have been very skilled at the science and their success in engineering suggests that many more such writings may have existed. It is difficult to connect the topics of the Rhind papyrus to actual concerns in architecture. Some of the problems deal with the pyramid shape, and the one quoted here asks the reader to calculate the unit of slope, the *seked*, "which measured the lateral displacement in palms for a drop of a royal cubit of 7 palms."[2]

Figure 6.2 Detail of the Rhind mathematical papyrus. © The Trustees of the British Museum

Example of calculating a pyramid. If the side of its base is 360 cubits (618 feet) long, and the height is 250 cubits (429 feet). What is its *seked* (= slope of the sides)? Take ½ of 360; it makes 180. Multiply 250 so as to get 180; it makes ½ ⅕ ¹⁄₅₀ of a cubit. A cubit is 7 palms. Multiply 7 by ½ ⅕ ¹⁄₅₀

1	7
½	3½
⅕	⅓
¹⁄₅₀	¹⁄₁₀ ¹⁄₂₅

Total: ½ ⅕ ¹⁄₅₀.

5⅕ palms is its *seked*.[3]

This problem has no practical value in pyramid building, however, and must have been intended to teach mathematical methods for their own sake. Other problems solved on the papyrus may have had real-life applications, but these are hard to ascertain.

The papyrus provides some information on the end of Hyksos rule as well. Its writer noted that he copied it from a Middle Kingdom original in the 33rd year of King Apepi's reign. On its reverse is a statement that some towns were captured in the 11th year of an unidentified king. Most likely this refers to the battle between Hyksos and Thebes, but which king was involved, remains unknown.

Apepi. That king depicted himself as close to traditional scribal culture. He rewarded a scribe called Atju with the gift of a wooden scribal palette. On it was written:

Palette, made by the king, scribe of Ra, whom the god Thoth himself taught and in whose mouth the goddess Seshat spat.[4]

The king adopted expressions Egyptian officials of the Middle Kingdom had used before in order to advertise scribal skills. The male and female Egyptian deities of writing, Thoth and Seshat, had taught him personally. He placed himself within an Egyptian cultural context.

Political history

Because of the scarcity of sources it is hard to piece together the political history of the 15th dynasty. Manetho lists six names, while the damaged Turin Royal Canon speaks of "6 rulers of foreign lands (Heqau-khasut) ruling for 108 years." Some of Manetho's names can be connected tentatively to inscribed material of the period. The large majority of these are short scarab inscriptions.

King Khyan is noteworthy because his name appears on objects found far from Egypt at Knossos in Crete and Hattusa in Anatolia. King Apepi was the opponent of Theban kings of the 17th dynasty, and he appears thus in the sources that document that conflict.

Scholars usually assume that during its about 100-year-long existence the 15th dynasty gradually expanded control over northern Egypt from a core in the eastern Delta. That core is characterized in archaeological terms by the presence of Syro-Palestinian remains such as tombs, pottery, and architecture. The most informative site is Avaris. Farther south, near Heliopolis, was a site with similar remains, Tell el-Yahudiyya, where excavators discovered massive ramparts and many examples of a jug we associate with the Hyksos, "Tell el-Yahudiyya Ware." This type of pottery appeared throughout Egypt, Nubia, Palestine, and on Cyprus, which indicates trade contact with distant areas. The Hyksos seem to have extended their dominance from the eastern Delta heartland farther west and south until they reached the Middle Egyptian town of Cusae, just south of Beni Hassan. Some inscriptional evidence with Hyksos royal names appears south of Thebes, but it is likely that was taken there in a later period and does not show Hykos control throughout Upper Egypt.

The 14th and 16th dynasties

The Turin Canon lists other kings beside those from Avaris and Thebes, and contemporary inscriptions on seals report even more names. Some of those are west Semitic in type, others Egyptian. We group them into the 14th and 16th dynasties, collections of short-lived kings who ruled small territories only, especially in northern Egypt. We do not know who should be counted as members of these dynasties, whose very existence is disputed. A large number of people claimed kingship, but when and where they lived is often unclear. Some appeared when the 13th dynasty had withdrawn to Thebes and predated the Hyksos rule from Avaris. One such man left inscriptions throughout the Delta including several at Avaris. His name was Nehesy, which may mean "the Nubian." It is also possible, however, that this is an abbreviated name from the Syro-Palestinian area, and that Nehesy had no Nubian connections at all. With the growth of the 15th dynasty's influence in northern Egypt, many of these local "kings" became subjects of Avaris. The written evidence reveals nothing about political contacts, however.

Hyksos rule in Palestine?

Another mystery is how far Hyksos power extended into Asia. That was the homeland of the dynasts, and the archaeological remains show continued contact with the region. When the Theban ruler of the 18th dynasty, Ahmose, ended Hyksos rule in Egypt, his military officer, also named Ahmose, portrayed the sack of the city Sharuhen in southern Palestine as the final blow. But was the whole of Palestine politically united with the eastern Delta? No evidence for political control of the Hyksos of Avaris beyond the very south of Palestine exists. Syria and Palestine were home to many city-states with fortified centers and seemingly often in conflict with one another. Such military adventures seem unlikely to have been tolerated by a central power that dominated the region.

6.4 Nubia and the Kingdom of Kush

The independence of Lower Nubia

The dissolution of Egypt under the 13th dynasty had a negative effect on the country's control over Lower Nubia, annexed and guarded by forts in the Middle Kingdom. Late 13th-dynasty kings were no longer able to supply the forts with new troops, and the archaeological remains of some show evidence of violent destruction, the causes of which are uncertain. The result is clear: Egypt's occupation of Lower Nubia ended. The Egyptian soldiers who had been stationed there remained in the forts, however, as we can see from the steles with hieroglyphic inscriptions that some of them left behind, just like their Middle Kingdom predecessors. They maintained trade contacts with Egypt. In certain forts were found thousands of sealings – lumps of clay impressed by a scarab – recording the names of 13th-dynasty kings, and even later ones, including some Hyksos. Those sealings were originally attached to sacks and jars with goods imported from Egypt, and trade seems to have been intense at least in the early Second Intermediate Period.

The Kingdom of Kush

The absence of strong Egyptian military backing exposed the region to pressure from the south, where the "Kingdom of Kush" had developed as a centralized state with its core just south of the third cataract. That region was rich in agricultural fields and pastures where cattle could graze, and it had thus a denser population than other parts of Nubia. The kingdom's capital was located at Kerma, a site that in the previous 700 years had shown the growth of political and military power. There is no indigenous written evidence to put names on the people of this kingdom, and Egyptian sources are scarce. Some Middle Kingdom Execration Texts name leaders from Kush and their parents, while for the period of the Second Intermediate Period the only royal name known comes from a hieroglyphic inscription found at Buhen: Nedjeh (see below).

Kerma

The archaeological study of Kerma is complicated because the 18th-dynasty Egyptians who conquered the site thoroughly destroyed most of the buildings. The cemetery to the east of the settlement provides the best-preserved information, with at least 20,000 burials covering a period of almost a thousand years. They display practices different from those in Egypt. The Nubians did not mummify the dead, and buried them in underground chambers below an earthen mound – we call this a tumulus – surrounded with stones at the perimeter. The pottery in them is typical for the region and very different from what contemporary Egyptians used (Figure 6.3). The tombs started out being quite simple in the 3rd millennium, but over time some became grander and more

Figure 6.3 Vessel in the Classical Kerma style. © The Trustees of the British Museum

elaborate than others, showing that the society began to include people with different levels of wealth. As in Egypt, the Nubians provided for the dead with mortuary offerings and they built chapels near the tombs for that purpose. It seems that cattle were sacrificed in mortuary rituals and their skulls and horns were placed around the tumulus. One tomb of the early 2nd millennium accumulated some 4,500 skulls of oxen over time.

The increase in tumulus size and number of offerings culminated in the so-called "Classical Kerma" phase, which lasted from ca. 1750 to 1500. Some of the latest tombs of the eastern cemetery were nearly 320 feet (100 meters) in diameter. Besides the primary occupants, who must have been kings and queens, were buried several hundreds of people, who seem to have been sacrificed to serve them in death (Figure 6.4). Near these tombs are the remains of two mortuary temples, perhaps in partial imitation of Egyptian practices. One of them was decorated with colorful wall paintings, which depict scenes of nature and an idealized daily life. They show two different surroundings: a land that looks Egyptian, where people fish and sail boats as in Egyptian tomb paintings, and a Nubian land inhabited by African animals: hippopotami, oxen, and especially giraffes. At the very end of the city's existence a huge royal burial was constructed nearby, which victorious Egyptians later hacked into pieces.

The changes in the burials were paralleled in the architecture of the Kerma settlement. It started in the late 3rd millennium as a small town around a religious complex, and grew into a larger and more complex settlement with artisans' quarters in the early 2nd millennium. At that time a limited core area was surrounded with a defensive wall with bastions and with a dry moat. The layout inside was almost rectilinear, like contemporary planned settlements in Middle Kingdom Egypt. During the Classical Kerma phase, the town flourished to such an extent that people started to live outside this walled area and created a satellite harbor district near the river, which contained a vast administrative building with walls of stone. Inside the building were discovered numerous sealings, which show the existence of a supervisory authority that guaranteed the contents of containers. Many of the seals were imported from Egypt and some included the names of Hyksos rulers, demonstrating contacts between Kerma and the Delta.

In the center of the main town was a religious district that somewhat resembled Egyptian temple complexes in its general layout but not in its component parts. The core was a massive brick construction, 80 by 160 feet (25 by 50 meters) and still preserved to a height of almost 65 feet (20 meters). The structure is called the western Deffufa today, after the Nubian word for brick ruins. Its ground plan was of a local style and it became increasingly large and built of sturdier materials including baked brick and stone. As in Egyptian temples, around it were subsidiary buildings, such as smaller temples, workshops, and depots. Nearby was a great round hut, 50 feet (15 meters) in diameter, which was built with wooden posts and had a thatched roof, and probably served as an audience hall for the kingdom's leaders. In the Classical Kerma phase a

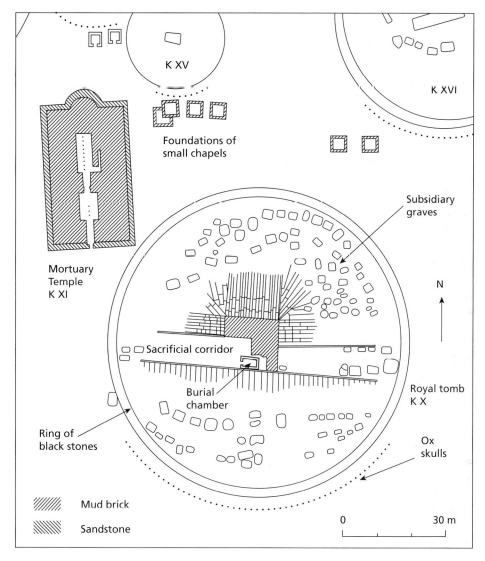

Figure 6.4 Plan of a royal tomb at Kerma (K X), with subsidiary graves, a corridor with human sacrificial victims, and a mortuary temple

palace in which Nubian and Egyptian architectural features were combined replaced that typically Nubian building.

The leaders of this community sought to portray themselves as true kings, queens, and noblemen, and looked to Egypt for inspiration. They acquired statues of former Egyptian kings and officials to exhibit in their palaces and town houses. The only ideal of kingship they could emulate came from the north. Thus, like the Hyksos in the Delta, the Kushites created a hybrid culture, continuing their own practices and merging them with Egyptian ones.

The extent of the Kingdom of Kush

The kings of Kush expanded their influence north into Lower Nubia, where the fortress residents started to work for them and acted as intermediaries with Egypt. A stele found at Buhen acknowledges the dependence on Nubian kings without hesitation (Figure 6.5). Its inscription reads:

> A gift that the king gives (to) Osiris, Lord of Busiris, the Great God, Lord of Abydos, and (to) Horus, Lord of Foreign Lands, that they may give an invocation offering consisting of bread and beer, oxen and fowl, and all things good and pure, on which a god lives, which heaven creates and earth makes, which Hapy (the Nile Inundation) brings as his perfect offering, for the spirit of the official Ka. It is the son of his daughter, who makes his name to live, namely the official Iah-user. He (Ka) says: "I was a valiant servant of the ruler of Kush. I washed my feet in the waters of Kush in the following of the ruler Nedjeh. I returned safe and sound (and) my family (too)."[5]

In Lower Nubia, Kush gained access to the gold resources from the desert east of the Nile, rich mines that had inspired Egyptian annexation in the Middle Kingdom. The virtual monopoly over the metal enabled Kush to import

Figure 6.5 Buhen stele that acknowledges the Nubian ruler Nedjeh

Egyptian goods and probably also craftsmen who could produce luxury items in Egyptian style. Conversely, finds of pottery produced in Kerma at various Egyptian sites show that products other than gold made their way north from Nubia as well. Kerma's relations with Egypt seem at first to have been strongest with the Theban area. In that region appear tombs that contain Egyptian objects (Plate 6), as well as Kerma-made pottery.

Egypt's weakness may have encouraged people from Kush to raid that country, in addition to pursuing trade relations. An inscription from a governor's tomb of the region south of Thebes mentions that the occupant fought an army of Kushites supported by Medjay and people from Punt. The attack could have been one of many incursions in order to gain access to Egyptian objects, such as statues and steles, which the people at Kerma admired. At the same time the Kingdom of Kush probably extended its power farther upriver to the south, reaching the fourth cataract if not beyond, which gave access to the African luxury goods that the Egyptians still desired. It was also in contact with the Red Sea via overland routes. Kerma pottery appears in the Kassala region of eastern Sudan, near modern Eritrea. Kush's trading and political powers were thus great; by the year 1600 the Kingdom of Kush had full control over the Nubian Nile Valley south of Egypt.

6.5 Thebes in the Middle

In between the Hyksos kingdom, in the Delta and Middle Egypt, and the Kingdom of Kush south of the first cataract, was squeezed the only "true" Egyptian dynasty, the 17th in Thebes. The kings there behaved as successors of the 13th dynasty, and indeed in many respects they carried on ancient Egyptian traditions. The chronology of the 17th dynasty is very uncertain and the king lists provide little help. Manetho includes 43 shepherd kings, that is, Hyksos, and 43 Theban rulers, without giving any names, and the Turin Canon is damaged in this section. Some other contemporary and later sources give us a sense of who ruled at this time, but the sequence of kings and the length of their reigns as well as of the entire dynasty are not certain. Probably numerous kings of various families were part of the dynasty. We assume it lasted about 100 years and coincided with the Hyksos dynasty in the north.

Royal tombs

The 17th dynasty's presence in Thebes is archaeologically well attested through burials on the west bank of the Nile. Its kings chose a site within a cemetery of the 13th dynasty for their tombs, at a place now called Dra Abu el-Naga. It was located near the entrance of the Valley of the Kings, which later housed most of the tombs of New Kingdom rulers. The 17th-dynasty kings experimented with new forms for their tombs. They constructed walled complexes with courtyards and a deep vertical shaft at the bottom of which were chambers to hold the mummy. Recently archaeologists discovered the remains of a mud-brick pyramid for King Nubkheperra, which was capped with a pyramid-shaped stone inscribed with the king's name and titles. Other such structures probably existed nearby.

These tombs were disturbed in ancient and modern times, and the inscribed remains recovered from debris in the area provide the only written sources for most kings of the 17th dynasty. A papyrus written 500 years after the Second Intermediate Period describes an investigation into whether or not burials in the area had been robbed; it lists six or seven tombs from this dynasty, some intact, others attacked by robbers. The threat of desecration of the royal bodies led priests of the late New Kingdom to remove some and rebury them in a secret place (see Chapter 11).

Seqenenra Taa

One such mummy belonged to the earliest 17th-dynasty king of whom we know more than his name, Seqenenra Taa, who died violently at an age between 30 and 40 years. He received blows on his head from several axes and his face was cut and smashed. Who killed him? Many Egyptologists assume that he died in battle with the Hyksos, and sometimes even reconstruct the sequence of blows and the shape of the axes that killed him. Opinions diverge on what exactly took place. Some conclude that he was prostrate when killed and may have been asleep, others that he stood on a low platform, perhaps a chariot. The poor quality of the mummification suggests that it was done hastily. Whatever happened, the events that led up to his death impressed his contemporaries. The inscription on his coffin calls him "the brave."

It is no surprise that scholars blame the Hyksos for Seqenenra's death, as the struggle between Thebes and Avaris defined the late 17th dynasty. The Thebans saw it as a war of liberation, and it was a drawn-out conflict that Seqenenra may have initiated. Why he chose to confront the Hyksos is not clear: evidence from the late 17th dynasty suggests that Thebans and Hyksos had friendly relations. The find in a Theban tomb of a vase with the name of a Hyskos princess has led to the suggestion that the two royal houses had concluded a diplomatic marriage.

On the other hand, a papyrus of the 19th dynasty, 500 years later, contains a fragmentary tale of antagonism between Seqenenra and Apepi, the penultimate Hyksos king. The latter sent a messenger to Thebes with a strange challenge: "Do away(?) with the hippopotamus-pool, which is on the east of the city, for they prevent me sleeping day and night."[6] Whatever the "real" message behind these words may have been, the story suggests that later Egyptians thought that Apepi challenged Seqenenra. The latter may have replied by initiating the fight against the Hyksos, but neither the story nor other evidence substantiates this idea. It is possible that Seqenenra moved the capital some 20 miles (30 kilometers) north of Thebes to a location called Deir el-Ballas today. Archaeologists found there the remains of two large palaces and a planned town, and an inscription on a lintel mentions Seqenenra. The (unpublished) ostraca from the town show a centralized system of rations with supplies and manpower coming from Thebes. The Thebans may have used it as a base in their war against the Hyksos, and soon after they were successful they abandoned the town.

Kamose's war

Contemporary evidence of the war against the Hyksos dates to the reign of Seqenenra's successor. King Kamose, the last king of the 17th dynasty, reported on his actions in an account that reads like a story. It starts with Kamose sitting in council with his advisors and complaining about the division of Egypt.

> To what end do I know my (own) strength? One chief is in Avaris, another in Kush, and I sit (here) associated with an Asiatic and a Nubian! Each man has his slice in this Egypt and so the land is partitioned with me! None can pass through it as far as Memphis (although it is) Egyptian water! See he (even) has Hermopolis! No one can be at ease when they are milked by the taxes of the Asiatics. I shall grapple with him that I might crush his belly, (for) my desire is to rescue Egypt, which the Asiatics have destroyed.[7]

Kamose's advisers pointed out, however, that relations with the Hyksos were fine and that the border with Nubia was safe. Using a literary device that would become common in New Kingdom royal inscriptions, the text goes on to tell how the king ignored them and attacked. The army sailed north and soon reached Avaris, where the inhabitants were so frightened that the women became infertile. Kamose claims to have plundered the city. He also captured a messenger from the king of Avaris to his colleague at Kush, and his account quotes the message in full.

> Aauserra, son of Ra, Apepi greets my son the ruler of Kush. Why have you arisen as ruler without letting me know? Do you see what Egypt has done to me? The Ruler which is in her midst – Kamose-the-Mighty, given life! – is pushing me off my (own) land! I have not attacked him in any way like all that he has done to you; he has chopped up the Two Lands to their grief, my land and yours, and he has hacked them up. Come north! Do not hold back! See, he is here with me: there is none who is expecting you here in Egypt. See, I will not set him free until you arrive! Then we shall divide the towns of Egypt, and Khenthennofer (Nubia south of the second cataract) shall be in joy.[8]

This message is the only evidence we have of diplomatic contacts between Hyksos and Nubians. It does suggest that Kamose also attacked the south, a statement confirmed by the find of a damaged stele he left at Buhen in his third year. The two adversaries of Thebes may have tried to join forces; whether they failed or not remains unknown.

Kamose's story of his campaign against the Hyksos ended with a description of the general joy of Egypt's population and the instruction to a courtier to carve all the events in stone. This is a typical victor's account, biased and hard to evaluate for its veracity. The only other explicit account of the war, the biography of soldier Ahmose son of Ibana (see Chapter 7), credits the defeat of the Hyksos, in which he participated, to Ahmose, Kamose's successor and the first king of the 18th dynasty. Later Egyptians saw that man as the founder of the New Kingdom. Rameses II placed his statue beside those of Menes and of Mentuhotep, the earlier unifiers of Egypt. Kamose probably laid the groundwork for the reunification, but how much he accomplished is hard to say.

Ahmose's reign takes us into the New Kingdom and will be discussed in the next chapter, as the expulsion of the Hyksos initiated a long process of Egyptian military expansion. The Second Intermediate Period ended thus at some time in the reign of Ahmose, and only then was Egypt truly reunified. From Kamose's account on, the depiction of that reunification was one of military defeat of foreigners. That image became the main focus of later portrayals of the Hyksos, which had a long history.

6.6 The Hyksos in Later Perspective

We cannot say much about Hyksos religion. As these people came from the Near East and maintained several of the customs that were rooted in religious beliefs, such as burial practices, scholars assume that they would have continued to honor Syrian deities. But the evidence for such cults is very limited. On the contrary, the few official sources we find from Hyksos kings show an adherence to Egyptian cults. The last kings of the 15th dynasty adopted traditional titles that made them the "sons of the sun god Ra." This image is in sharp contrast with the later Egyptians' portrayals of the Hyksos: those focused on their aberrant religious beliefs.

Queen Hatshepsut

The Hyksos cast a long spell over later Egyptian history. The writings about them are not numerous, but they continued to be created into the Roman era. The descriptions contemporaneous with the Hyksos expulsion – by King Kamose and soldier Ahmose – portray that event as a war between two kingdoms. We know that King Ahmose terminated all Hyksos political influence around 1550. It is thus somewhat of a surprise that almost 80 years later Queen Hatshepsut brought the Hyksos up again as enemies. She did so in an inscription in a small rock-cut temple she built near Beni Hassan, which aimed to underscore the legitimacy of her rule. Her reference to the expulsion of the Hyksos shows how the memory of these people still lingered, but Hatshepsut added a new element to the disruption they caused.

> I have restored what was destroyed, I have raised up what had been shattered, since the Asiatics were in the Delta at Avaris, when the nomads among them were overturning what had been made. They ruled without the god Ra, and did not act by divine decree right down to my Majesty's time.[9]

Hatshepsut claims that the Hyksos ruled without Ra, the god whom she invokes in the rest of the inscription as the one who ordained her to rule the land. Their neglect of that god was an abomination that no earlier source mentioned. Hatshepsut does not deign to indicate what god the Hyksos honored instead of Ra.

The gods Ra and Seth

Hyksos religion becomes an issue in the story of Apepi and Seqenenra Taa, mentioned above. The exact date of its composition is unknown; the only manuscript available is from the 19th dynasty. The tale states that Apepi honored no god besides Seth and worshipped him as if he were Ra. The conflict between Thebes and Avaris was thus framed in terms of the cities' cults, and the event became a religious clash between the Egyptian and the foreign. In the Middle Kingdom the sun god Ra, of the northern city of Heliopolis near Memphis, had been merged with the god Amun, chief deity of Thebes. Amun-Ra had become the king of all Egyptian gods (see Special Topic 6.1). In the story of Apepi and Seqenenra Taa, Seth was portrayed as Ra's equivalent in Avaris. Seth was one of the oldest gods of the Egyptian pantheon, and he embodied confusion and disorder. In the New Kingdom he became increasingly connected with foreign lands and their deities: Seth was the Syrian Baal, the Libyan Ash, or the Hittite Teshub. It was thus logical that the Thebans associated him with the Hyksos, and indirect evidence suggests that Seth had a temple in Avaris. The New Kingdom portrayal of the conflict between Thebes and Avaris does not mean in reality the Hyksos honored Seth at the expense of other gods. They were equally familiar with Ra and others.

With the rise of the 19th dynasty the god Seth gained greater official recognition. Sety I, whose name means "He of the god Seth," and Rameses II moved the country's capital to the Delta and showed great respect for Seth's cult. Rameses set up a stele in honor of that god, portraying him as

Special Topic 6.1 *Egyptian gods*

Many gods are among the best-known names from ancient Egyptian culture today. Who has not heard of Ra or Isis? The study of gods and an understanding of their importance and functions is one of the most difficult areas of Egyptology, however. Egyptian religious beliefs and their relationship to gods differed fundamentally from those of most modern people, and the Egyptians were able to assign a god multiple characteristics that may seem contradictory to us. Moreover, the cults of most gods had a history of more than 3,000 years with many changes and developments over time. It is dangerous to combine evidence on a god from the 3rd millennium BC with that from the 1st centuries AD. In many respects, the Egyptians seem to have been very conservative, and the representation of deities often remained the same for millennia. But their perception of individual gods was never static and acquired new characteristics over time.

One of the elements that can be confusing to us is that Egyptians could merge two gods into one, combining their attributes. Such developments could be the result of political changes. When the capital of Egypt moved from the north to Thebes in Upper Egypt, the Theban god Amun received an enormous boost in his official recognition. He acquired the status of the earlier chief deity, the sun god Ra of Heliopolis near Memphis. The combination of Amun and Ra made the god all encompassing. Amun was a hidden god, Ra the sun god visible to all in the sky. Amun-Ra was both the hidden and the perceived. As well as acquiring solar aspects, Amun also took on characteristics of the fertility god Min.

Although the pantheon was large from the start of Egyptian history, it had room for expansion. Some mortals became gods long after their death, such as Imhotep, Djoser's architect (see Chapter 3). Immigrants brought their deities, who found a place in the Egyptian pantheon. The newcomers were often associated with existing gods who had similar characteristics. The Syrian storm god Baal became merged with the Egyptian god of confusion, Seth. The foreign gods could keep their names and could be integrated into Egyptian divine families. The Syrian goddess Astarte, for example, became the companion of the Egyptian Ptah.

The abundance of evidence does not mean that we have an insight into the religious beliefs of the Egyptians in general, however. The countless temples, chapels, altars, relief sculptures, and paintings are mostly signs of officially endorsed expressions of worship. How people felt about the gods and the role they had in their personal lives is something much harder for us to access.

Ra's champion. This stele was dated in the 400th year of Seth's reign, and scholars used to suggest that this fixed the moment when the Hyksos established their dynasty in Avaris (i.e., ca. 1650). These kings did not honor the Hyksos. The king lists carved in this period at Saqqara and Abydos (see Chapter 1) omitted them for the list of ancestors, as they did for all kings from the 13th to 17th dynasties.

Manetho and Josephus

The longest and most detailed account of Hyksos rule in Egypt dates altogether later. When Manetho wrote a history of Egypt in the third century BC he did not ignore them in his king list. He even made a brief digression about the 15th dynasty, at least in the version preserved to us in the work of the third-century-AD author Africanus. Manetho wrote:

> 6 kings of the Shepherds. They captured Memphis and founded a city in the Sethroite nome. From there they set out to conquer the Egyptians.[10]

The account then lists six names and the lengths of their reigns, amounting to 284 years.

The conquest of Memphis before the founding of Avaris in the eastern Delta (the nome of Seth) is not known from older sources. That idea was developed much further by another ancient historian, who quoted Manetho extensively, Flavius Josephus of the first century AD. In his work *Against Apio*, where he argued for the antiquity of the Jewish people and their religion, he relied on Manetho as a native Egyptian source. He claimed to quote that author literally when he told a story of invaders from the east who captured Egypt easily. They burned down cities and temples and enslaved the people. One of them, Salitis, was enthroned as king, first at Memphis, then in a newly founded city in the Sethroite nome at Avaris, which he fortified heavily. Salitis started a dynasty of six rulers "always making war and always more and more destructive in their desire to destroy the Egyptians root and branch."[11]

Josephus then went on to interpret the name of the invaders, Hyksos, as "shepherd kings," but he also noted that some claimed they were Arabs, while others translated the name as "captives," something he felt to be "more persuasive and closer to ancient history."[12]

The image of the Hyksos as violent conquerors and oppressors of Egypt, written 1,300 or more probably 1,700 years after the events, has left a great impression in modern times. It inspired Sir Isaac Newton's words, quoted at the beginning of this chapter. There is no evidence from the Second Intermediate Period that substantiates it, however. Josephus's story reads like an elaboration of Hatshepsut's claim that the Hyksos "were overturning what had been made."[13] Scholars have tried to demonstrate the Hyksos's warlike character by pointing out that they placed weapons in their burials and fortified their settlements. But these practices do not validate the historicity of the late accounts, which remains a matter of belief rather than evidence-based.

Josephus went on to describe what happened to the Hyksos according to Manetho. After they ruled for 511 years (much longer than the 284 years Manetho assigns Salitis's dynasty) the people of Thebes rebelled and a long war broke out. Josephus claimed that the New Kingdom ruler Thoummosis (Thutmose) won the war, that is, decades after Ahmose's success in contemporary record. The victory was not an annihilation of the Hyksos, however. They withdrew to Avaris, which the Thebans tried to capture with 480,000 men. Finally an agreement was reached in which the Hyksos left the city and migrated to Syria, where they built Jerusalem. Josephus thus connected the departure of the Hyksos to the biblical Exodus and used them to show how much older than the Greeks the Jewish people were.

His account of the Hyksos did not end there, but later in the book Josephus continued to quote Manetho on the Hyksos, now accusing the earlier author of lies and fantasy. Manetho told how some two or three hundred years later a rebel king with an army of lepers, who had been given refuge at Avaris, invited the Hyksos back to fight with them against the Egyptian king Amenophis, who escaped to Ethiopia. For 13 years the rebels ruled Egypt in a horrible way, destroying towns, temples, and divine statues, and eating sacred animals. Manetho ended with the statement that the rebel leader changed his name to Moses. According to Josephus the Egyptian Amenophis and his grandson Rameses liberated Egypt from this scourge, and then the author denounced Manetho's story. This second tale is rarely quoted in modern studies of the Hyksos, because of its fantastic nature, and it has a complex intellectual background that relates more to later events in Egyptian history, namely the reign of Akhenaten (see Chapter 8). It shows clearly, however, how careful we have to be when using later tales in the reconstruction of Egyptian history. If we dismiss the historicity of the second story, we cannot consistently accept the first account as truth.

Josephus's writings were known and studied in modern times before alternative written and archaeological evidence on the Hyksos appeared. They gave these people much prominence and they have greatly affected how we view them. Josephus's aims were very different from those of modern historians. His primary source, Manetho, may have lived much closer in time to the Hyksos than we do, but he was still separated from them by 1,300 years and he clearly mangled his facts, as the contradictions in his account show. We cannot rely on him to write our history of the Hyksos. Later Egyptian writings on the Hyksos, culminating perhaps with Manetho, show how these people came to be perceived as anathema to the Egyptian ideal of order. That concept appears to have started 80 years after the Hyksos expulsion, when Hatshepsut presented them as a force of chaos that she eliminated. Such an idea was a common theme in royal rhetoric, however: every king restored order and re-enacted the original creation of the universe, which had been the initial removal of chaos. The image of the Hyksos as evil foreigners grew ever after.

We are not yet in a position to counter this negative portrayal fully, but archaeological data from the Second Intermediate Period suggest a very different picture. They indicate that the Hyksos emerged out of earlier immigrants from the Near East as a strong political force that had its center in the eastern Delta and exerted influence over Lower Egypt and the northern Nile Valley. They introduced cultural and other innovations, but adhered to Egyptian traditions as well. Nubians in the south achieved comparable political success and developed a hybrid culture as well. Both foreign groups looked to Egypt as a source of great traditions and high culture.

Stuck in the middle, the people of Thebes and Upper Egypt experienced much less foreign influence and were politically "independent," but they maintained contacts with Nubians and Hyksos that seem to have been mostly peaceful. They took the initiative to restore the unity of Upper and Lower Egypt, which meant removing foreign rulers. They started a process that would extend Egypt far beyond its traditional boundaries.

Key Debate 6.1   *Who were the Hyksos?*

Josephus's tale of the Hyksos' arrival in Egypt is very explicit: they conquered the country and mistreated its inhabitants. Also the name Hyksos clearly indicates that they were foreigners, and the question arises logically: where did they originate? Earlier scholars read the account literally and saw the question in the context of large population movements that supposedly took place in the Near East in the 19th through 16th centuries. Historians of the early 20th century thought that people with an Aryan background invaded Anatolia and northern Syria at the time. Those in northern Syria were the so-called Hurrians – the people who created the Mittanni kingdom there (see Chapter 7). These people would have reached Egypt during their migration (cf. von Beckerath 1964: 113–21), and some scholars thought they created an empire that stretched from the Euphrates to the Nile (Albright 1960: 86). Others saw a more limited territorial control but a clear Hurrian origin for the Hyksos (Helck 1971: 100–6).

But both the Hurrian connections to the Aryans and to the Hyksos were doubtful, because of a lack of linguistic and archaeological evidence, and historians started to look for other origins for the Hyksos. One changed his opinion from Hurrians to sea raiders from Cyprus and southern Anatolia who wanted to control Egypt's trade with the Levant (Helck 1993). More common is the idea that west

Semitic people with a strong state in Palestine took advantage of Egypt's internal weakness to invade (Redford 1992: 100–6).

The 13th-dynasty Execration Texts (see Chapter 5) contradict the idea that Palestine was politically united (Ryholt 1997: 103). There is also no evidence beyond Manetho and Josephus that there was a conquest, while the archaeology of Avaris shows a gradual increase of western Asian influence in the Delta. Thus many scholars now argue that the descendants of immigrants from the Levant who started to arrive in Egypt during the Middle Kingdom acquired political influence. Several 13th- and 14th-dynasty royal names are west Semitic. Many consider the most important Hyksos dynasty, Manetho's 15th, to derive from the same background and to have seized power over a large territory around 1650 (Bietak 1994: 21–3; 1997: 113). Some doubt the Levantine roots, however, and point out that too few names are preserved to determine the kings' background (Ryholt 1997: 126–30). The archaeological evidence seems quite convincing, however.

How far did the Hyksos kingdom reach into Asia? Eighteenth-dynasty accounts mention Sharuhen in southern Palestine as the last Hyksos stronghold (see Chapter 7). Possibly the entire region along the coast from eastern Egypt to northern Israel was united, with dependent vassals farther inland (Bietak 1994:

25–6). We have very little evidence of 15th dynasty kings in that region, however (Ryholt 1997: 130–2).

Why do the Hyksos arouse so much passion? The earlier proposed Aryan connections fitted European dreams of Indo-European supremacy, now discredited. The continued interest seems due to presumed biblical associations, which already inspired Sir Isaac Newton in the 18th century. Many Bible scholars still see the story of Joseph and his brothers entering Egypt as a reflection of the Hyksos (Albright 1940: 184; Sarna 1986: 17). This leads, of course, to questions about the Exodus, which Josephus had already connected to their expulsion from Egypt.

NOTES

1. Redford 1997: 14.
2. Robins & Shute 1987: 15.
3. Translation after Chace 1927: 96–7.
4. Translation after Morenz 1996: 167.
5. Translation after W. Davies in Welsby & Anderson (eds.) 2004: 100.
6. Redford 1997: 18.
7. Translation after Redford 1997: 13.
8. Translation after Redford 1997: 14–15.
9. Translation after Redford 1997: 17.
10. Verbrugghe & Wickersham 1996: 139.
11. Verbrugghe & Wickersham 1996: 157.
12. Verbrugghe & Wickersham 1996: 158. That statement may refer to the claim that the Hyksos were Arabs.
13. Redford 1997: 17.

7

The Birth of Empire: The Early 18th Dynasty (ca. 1550–1390)

I made the boundaries of Egypt to the extent of what the sun encircles. I made strong those who were in fear, for I repelled evil from them. I made Egypt superior to every land. (King Thutmose I)[1]

Egyptian tradition saw Ahmose, a king from Thebes, as the one who initiated the third period of political unification. He extended Thebes' control all over Upper and Lower Egypt and expelled the Hyksos from the country, thereby starting what we call the New Kingdom. That somewhat pedestrian designation disguises the novelty of the era. Indeed Egypt was politically one, as it had been in the Old and Middle Kingdoms, but its interactions with neighboring regions were crucially different from before, both because of Egypt's own actions and because of the world it encountered across its borders. The militarism and ideals of foreign conquest that had developed in the Middle Kingdom burst into aggressive imperialism directed against all its neighbors. A king, like Thutmose I quoted above, could boast that Egypt ruled supreme over the entire world. Yet, unlike in the past when Egypt had only fought the militarily much weaker, in the New Kingdom its armies engaged equal and even superior opponents. In reality, instead of dictating the terms of international relations the pharaohs had to negotiate with the rulers of other great states and tried to avoid all-out war.

The New Kingdom dazzles modern audiences. More of its rulers are famous today than for any other era of Egyptian history: Hatshepsut the female king, Akhenaten the heretic, Tutankhamun the boy-king buried with gigantic treasure, Rameses II the great warrior. Few educated persons today have not heard of these individuals and many with an interest in the ancient world know of others: Thutmose III, Tiye, Nefertari, Merenptah, and so on. While to an extent this is accidental – Tutankhamun's tomb happens to be the wealthiest tomb of Egypt found so far – much of the fame is justified. Egypt's situation

Summary of Dynastic History
Early 18th dynasty (ca. 1550–1390)

ca. 1550–1525	King Ahmose Expels the Hyksos and conquers Sharuhen in southern Palestine Raids Nubia south of the second cataract Builds last royal pyramid at Abydos
ca. 1525–1504	King Amenhotep I Campaigns in Nubia at least as far as the third cataract Possibly establishes workers' village at Deir el-Medina
ca. 1504–1492	King Thutmose I Campaigns in Nubia between fourth and fifth cataracts Defeats the Kingdom of Kush and destroys Kerma Campaigns in Syria as far as the Euphrates River Fathers Thutmose II and Hatshepsut with wives Mutnofret and Ahmose respectively
ca. 1492–1479	King Thutmose II Confronts rebellion in northern Kush
ca. 1473–1458	Queen Hatshepsut Acts as regent for young Thutmose III, 1479–1473 Becomes king of Egypt in or before 1473 Sends expedition to land of Punt Builds mortuary temple at Deir el-Bahri Disappears from the record around 1458
ca. 1479–1425	King Thutmose III Rules Egypt in name only while Hatshepsut is in control, 1479–1458 Campaigns extensively in Syria and Palestine, 1458–1449 Fights battle of Megiddo, 1457 Possibly establishes full Egyptian control over Nubia Initiates much temple construction
ca. 1427–1400	King Amenhotep II Presents himself as great huntsman, charioteer, and archer Initiates diplomatic contacts in the Near East after period of military campaigns
ca. 1400–1390	King Thutmose IV Marries Mittanni princess

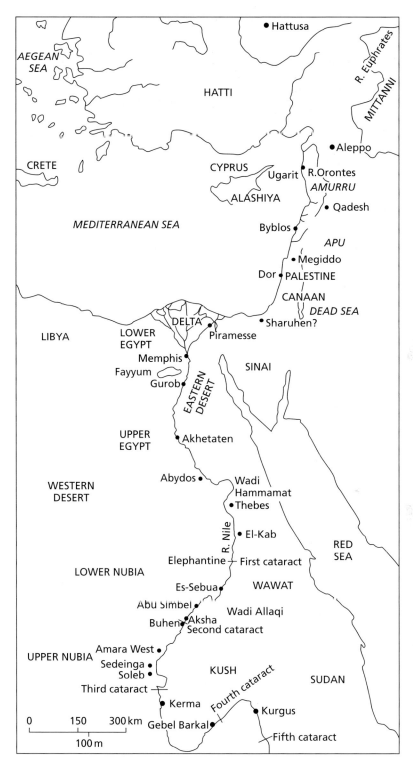

Map 3 Egypt and surrounding territories in the New Kingdom

in the New Kingdom enabled its pharaohs to build great monuments. Perhaps it also led them to reconsider their position in the universe and relationship to the gods (notably Amenhotep III and Rameses II). They even questioned the nature of the divine (in the case of Akhenaten). We may be in danger of being mesmerized by the opulence of the period and the profusion of its remains, but the New Kingdom was clearly something special. Due to the near-embarrassment of riches of its sources we can describe the period in greater detail than earlier periods, and therefore the next four chapters will deal with it.

7.1   Egypt in a New World Order

Before engaging on a survey of Egypt's New Kingdom it is important to sketch the international situation in this period. Egypt's history always involved foreign relations, and whenever the country was internally strong and unified it actively reached beyond its borders. In the Old and Middle Kingdoms the Egyptians had directed their military actions primarily southwards and into areas of Asia that were close by, while their trade contacts had stretched much farther into Nubia beyond the second cataract and along the Mediterranean coast to harbors of modern-day Lebanon and Syria. In these periods western Asia had known a series of strong and centralized states as well, in the regions of western Iran, northern Syria, and central Anatolia. Yet, although Egypt may have had contacts with these states, they were at best sparse, and the country kept a distance from its counterparts in western Asia.

The situation changed fundamentally in the mid-16th century. Coincident with the emergence of Egypt's New Kingdom an entirely new world arose in western Asia and beyond. Throughout the region there developed a set of large territorial states that survived for hundreds of years. These states made up an eastern Mediterranean system in which they all participated in political, military, economic, and cultural terms. Contacts among them were constant and intense. The main powers – beside Egypt – were southern Mesopotamian Babylonia, northern Mesopotamian Assyria, north Syrian Mittanni, and the Anatolian Hittite state called Hatti. At the periphery of these great states existed the Aegean Mycenaean world, Cyprus, and western Iranian Elam. In the center of the region western Syria and Palestine only remained politically fragmented; it was an area over which powerful neighbors fought. Each of the states had ups and downs and there was much change over 400 years. But the international character of the age persisted and had a fundamental effect on each state's individual history, including Egypt's.

In the New Kingdom Egypt's attitude toward western Asia differed from earlier periods – both as a participant in the creation and survival of the international system there and in reaction to its existence. Egyptian rulers campaigned actively in the region in an attempt to annex territory and to exert political influence. They thus came in direct contact with the rulers of other states who were politically powerful and militarily strong and had expansionist aims of their own. Many Egyptian pharaohs of the time boasted of their military valor and victories, as did their western Asiatic counterparts. But the interactions were not purely hostile; all kings realized the benefits of diplomacy. They formed a "Club of the Great Powers," whose members exchanged diplomatic messages, gifts, and brides. They engaged in wars but also concluded peace treaties and alliances. Egypt was a very active participant in the system, but not the dominant one – no single state was – and unlike in its earlier international affairs, it could not dictate the rules of engagement.

The history of the eastern Mediterranean system from 1550 to 1150 can be written through an abundance of sources not only from Egypt, but from the other states as well. The situation is almost unique for ancient history in that we can investigate a question such as the competition over western Syria from multiple points of view, including that of the victims of imperial expansion, taking us far beyond the history of Egypt. The New Kingdom has to be seen against this background, however, to understand both Egypt's international affairs and its domestic issues.

7.2   Sources and Chronology

With the New Kingdom the historian encounters a veritable explosion of sources, both written and archaeological. One author recently remarked that the mass of material made it impossible for him to continue his approach to earlier periods where he had taken into account every single scarab. New Kingdom kings, members of the royal family, officials, and others left abundant written remains, which can include so-called biographies of their lives (see Chapter 3). Official accounts of military actions are more detailed than before. The annals of Thutmose III are the most elaborate example of this genre and, for the first time in Egyptian history, allow for a systematic reconstruction of the king's military activity.

Besides written accounts kings also commissioned depictions of battles, and in the middle of the New Kingdom these regularly became gigantic relief sculptures carved on temple gateways and other large surfaces. These representations include Rameses II's battle at Qadesh, multiple copies of which provide a narrative of events in parallel with lengthy written descriptions. Royal accomplishments were not always military: Queen Hatshepsut commissioned ornate depictions of an expedition to the land of Punt and of the transport of gigantic obelisks.

In addition to official inscriptions in hieroglyphic script there exist a large number of documents written in hieratic script. Administrators wrote brief notices including a royal name and the year in the reign, which sometimes allow us to confirm the number of regnal years assigned to rulers in the king lists. The administrative archives of some secular and religious institutions are partly preserved and can include lengthy and detailed accounts. Also private individuals produced legal documents, letters and the like. The largest find by far of such material in the New Kingdom comes from the village of Deir el-Medina where the builders of the royal tombs resided in the desert. The dry environment preserved the material, which includes more than 10,000 ostraca and numerous papyri; the former mostly contain receipts, work rosters, and lists, the latter contracts, letters and some literary material. This was an unusual community in that more people in it seem to have been literate than on average in Egypt of the time, but their material still indicates how important the use of writing became in society at large.

An entirely new source for international history derives from the diplomatic correspondence of New Kingdom Egypt, not written on papyri in Egyptian scripts, but on clay in cuneiform rendering the diplomatic *lingua franca* of the time, Babylonian. In the late 19th century AD local peasants found some 400 such tablets in the ruins of Akhenaten's capital at modern Tell el-Amarna. About 350 of them are letters mostly written to the Egyptian king: a small number derive from the other great rulers of the time, the majority from Egypt's vassals in Syria and Palestine. The Amarna archive was not unique. Isolated finds from the later capital at Piramesse and Egyptian royal letters in archives in Asia show that diplomatic exchanges using cuneiform happened throughout the period.

The written material for the New Kingdom is thus substantially larger than for preceding periods, although many crucial gaps remain. The riches allow for a quite secure relative chronology of the period: we know all the rulers and mostly have a good idea about how long they ruled. There is still debate about the duration of certain reigns, however. Much argument exists over the length of certain co-regencies; king lists record all reigns as successive, but we know that fathers and sons sometimes ruled jointly. This question complicates the dating of the late 18th dynasty, for example.

A papyrus contains a Sothic date (see Chapter 1) for the 9th year of Amenhotep I, which scholars originally took as a firm anchor for the absolute chronology around 1546. But today they are less confident about the use of such dates and divergent proposals for dating the New Kingdom exist, generating intricate debates that often involve international contacts with more securely dated histories in Asia. The chronology I use here takes the middle road and starts the New Kingdom around 1550. The entire period lasted about 500 years until around 1069, which is similar in length to the Old Kingdom's 500 years and close to the Middle Kingdom's 400.

Manetho subdivided the New Kingdom into dynasties 18 through 20. Both the 18th and 19th dynasties started with a series of strong and long-lived rulers but descended into a confusion of royal succession. All members of the 20th dynasty belonged to the same family and the last one had to share power with a regional lord, which initiated the Third Intermediate Period. Because of the wealth of information and the range of subjects we can investigate, I will structure the four chapters on the New Kingdom slightly different from Manetho's dynasties, devoting two chapters to the 18th dynasty and spreading the discussion of the 19th and 20th dynasties over two chapters.

7.3 Egypt at War

War and society in the New Kingdom

New Kingdom Egypt was an imperialist state: the country annexed territories outside its traditional borders and controlled them for its own benefit. This policy had its roots in earlier periods, when military conquest was a regular part of royal duties, but peaked in the New Kingdom when Egypt was in an almost permanent state of war. The preoccupation had a fundamental impact on Egyptian society in general.

The war against the Hyksos initiated the New Kingdom, and from that moment on the country's army was on campaign on a regular basis for the next 150 years. In the later 18th dynasty military activity abated somewhat, but it picked up again in the 19th dynasty, when the conflict with the Hittites over Syria climaxed. The official record of texts and images may be somewhat misleading in that it portrays all campaigns as major events, while many of them were merely shows of force, but the attention devoted to war shows how the Egyptians saw it as central to the king's behavior. The king was a warrior and a war-leader, whose courage set him apart. Not only were the enemies cowards who retreated from the Egyptian army, but also the Egyptian troops and their commanders were not on a par with the king in bravery. Battle accounts regularly presented the army as a hindrance to the king's prowess. Advisors recommended caution but the king took the dangerous road and succeeded brilliantly. Troops started to loot the enemy camps before the battle was won and the king had to save the day through personal heroism. In the huge battle reliefs the king towered over friend and foe, single-handedly massacring opponents. The king had other roles as well – he was a priest, a diplomat, and an administrator – but his responsibilities as a warrior received much attention in the official record.

Naturally, the army was crucial for the king's success, and in the New Kingdom it underwent important changes. During the Second Intermediate Period a new technology in warfare appeared throughout the eastern Mediterranean: the chariot. Drawn by two horses, the light vehicle – merely a wooden platform with a low guard on two wheels with spokes – allowed an archer to approach enemy troops or hunting prey rapidly and shoot off his arrows. In battle the charioteer's only protection was a shield bearer who possibly used a spear to ward off attackers. The chariots look very fragile and the terrain must have been quite level and unencumbered by rocks to allow for their use (Figure 7.1). The impact of the chariot on warfare in the mid-2nd millennium was enormous, however, and every state of the eastern Mediterranean had a chariotry. Egypt was relatively slow in integrating that division into its army – perhaps only in the 19th dynasty – but from the start of the New Kingdom on kings rode to battle in chariots and the equipment was prominently mentioned in accounts and depictions. The first representations of

Figure 7.1 Image of the tomb owner Userhat, royal scribe of Amenhotep II, hunting from his chariot. Werner Forman Archive/E. Strouhal

horses and chariots in Egyptian art appear in the mortuary temple of King Ahmose at Abydos.

Charioteers were trained fighters and also men of wealth, who provided their own equipment. They received greater rewards than other soldiers and had a high social status. In all societies in the eastern Mediterranean charioteers formed an elite class with great economic and political influence. Egyptian war accounts report thus with special pride the numbers of foreign charioteers captured.

The bulk of the army was made up of the same troops as in the past, sailors and infantrymen. Ships had always been important as a means of transporting troops along the Nile. When the Egyptians entered western Asia they went mostly over land, thus reducing the navy's role. Some kings still sent naval expeditions along the Syrian coast in support of the army. Foot soldiers must have been the most numerous. How many of them fought in any battle remains a guess. The Egyptian account of Rameses II's battle at Qadesh against the Hittites in 1275 mentions about 37,000 infantry opponents (besides 3,500 chariots) and historians usually assume that the Egyptians fielded a similar number of men. These figures are exceedingly high, however, and make one wonder about the logistics of moving such a large army – with its attendants and baggage train – for hundreds of miles from the Egyptian heartland.

Professional soldiers made up the core of the army and they seem to have remained in service for long periods. A couple of biographies of the early 18th dynasty cover careers of more than 50 years. Men could climb the ranks and attain positions in the civil and religious administrations at the end of their service. Military men were prominent members of the court and of society in general. They could even become kings. The last ruler of the 18th dynasty, Horemheb, obtained the throne as general, not through inheritance. Alongside the professional army fought men recruited for individual campaigns and mercenaries. The latter derived from groups that often lived on the fringes of the Egyptian state, such as Libyans from the western desert.

The empire not only required soldiers but also bureaucrats to administer the new territories. Egyptians settled in Nubia and western Asia to represent the state, while a bureaucracy at home dealt with foreign affairs. Large regions of Nubia and some of Syria-Palestine near Egypt became integral parts of Egypt, and the civil bureaucracy must have grown to deal with them. Local people from the conquered territories were included in the administration. Some settled in Egypt, and although Egypt had always known immigration from abroad the number of foreigners in the New Kingdom increased. While they adopted Egyptian practices in many ways, they also introduced their own customs in cultural and religious life.

The fact that Egypt was an empire in the New Kingdom impacted many aspects of society. Military achievements gained more prominence, bureaucrats expanded their horizons, and Egyptians and foreigners influenced one another. The empire also brought in an enormous amount of wealth that benefited all parts of the state. Soldiers received rewards for their valor, temples obtained lavish endowments, and government administrators were involved in large projects at home and abroad. All these elements started with the beginning of the 18th dynasty and continued throughout the New Kingdom.

The "war of liberation"

The start of the New Kingdom was an eventful time during which Egypt reversed its situation as a rump state encircled by powerful neighbors to become a dominant force throughout the region including nearby parts of the Nile Valley and western Asia. Our knowledge of events is very limited, however, and primarily derives from the laconic account of one soldier who describes his long career in a tomb inscription at El-Kab. He was Ahmose son of Ibana, who joined the navy as a young man under King Ahmose and retired half a century later under Thutmose I. The first military successes he relates were at the expense of the Hyksos. King Ahmose's predecessor Kamose had boasted of his siege and capture of the Hyksos capital Avaris (Chapter 6). According to Ahmose son of Ibana, however, the Hyksos were still ensconced there two decades later. Scholars interpret some admittedly vague references to indicate that Hyksos also occupied Lower Egypt and Memphis in Ahmose's days. Because these foreigners held a part of Egypt, modern scholars often call the fight against them a war of liberation, an idea Egyptians themselves promoted. Ahmose son of Ibana recounts how the army laid siege to Avaris and raided nearby Hyksos settlements. The two parties seem to have reached an agreement and the Hyksos left the city. Despite Ahmose son of Ibana's claim that Avaris was sacked, archaeological work on the site shows no destruction except in the citadel. The town may have been abandoned.

With the expulsion of the Hyksos Egypt once more was politically unified – hence Egyptologists consider the New Kingdom to start at this time. Unlike in earlier periods, when Egyptians accepted that their border with Asia was at the eastern edge of the Delta, King Ahmose had grander ambitions. He tore down the citadel of Avaris and established a military base with hundreds of grain silos to feed soldiers. Nearby were camps with huts and campfires, which were in use for many years. A large group of men were buried in the area in simple pit graves. The pottery found alongside them was often of Nubian manufacture and it seems that Ahmose incorporated many soldiers from that region into his army. Avaris became the base from which to conduct wars in Asia.

Soon the Egyptian army marched into southern Palestine and besieged the Hyksos fortress of Sharuhen, probably located just south of modern Gaza at the site of Tell el-Ajjul. The siege lasted three years and it is likely that the army undertook numerous raids in the surrounding area. Archaeology uncovered numerous destruction layers in fortifications throughout Palestine that are dated around this time, albeit spread over a century. Scholars debate their cause. Some think they resulted from internecine wars between the city-states in the region; others blame Egyptian military activity starting with Ahmose. The effect on the region was drastic as the destructions were widespread and only half of the cities were rebuilt later on. Much of the population seems to have abandoned urban life. If the Egyptians were responsible, the desire to eradicate opposition, be it from Hyksos or from other people, probably inspired them. When Sharuhen finally fell the Hyksos disappeared as opponents.

The military activity in the north was paralleled in the south. Ahmose son of Ibana mentioned three campaigns there in areas we cannot identify with certainty. Matters were somewhat different in Nubia in that Kamose had already re-established Egyptian control over the second cataract forts that had been built in the Middle Kingdom. King Ahmose could use the Buhen fortress, which he restored, as the base for actions farther south. We know little of the details. South of the third cataract was still located the Kingdom of Kush with its capital at Kerma. Ahmose's predecessor Kamose and Ahmose himself may have penetrated deep into that kingdom's territory, if not beyond it in raids along the Nile, and they weakened that state. The annihilation of Kush was a later project, however.

The annexation of Nubia

Over the next two decades Ahmose's successors dealt definitively with the Kingdom of Kush. Our sources remain limited to soldiers' accounts listing the various campaigns in which they participated: Ahmose son of Ibana, already mentioned, and Ahmose Pennekhbet, who served kings from Ahmose to Thutmose III. It seems that Thutmose I (ruled 1504–1492) gave the final blow to the Kingdom of Kush. According to Ahmose son of Ibana he captured its king and hung him by his feet from the mast of a ship (see Sources in Translation 7.1). The Egyptians devastated the city of Kerma, hacking monuments to

Sources in Translation 7.1
The biography of Ahmose, son of Ibana

Ahmose, son of Ibana, was a sailor under the first three kings of the 18th dynasty and participated in 10 campaigns both to the north and the south of Egypt. In his tomb at El-Kab he recounts how the kings rewarded his valor with gifts of gold, fields, and slaves, and how he constantly rose in rank. In the following passage he describes how King Thutmose I dealt with Nubian rebels.

Then I conveyed the King Aakheperkara (= Thutmose I), the justified, when he sailed south to Khenthennefer (= Nubia, south of the second cataract), to crush rebellion throughout foreign lands and to repel the intruders from the desert region. I was brave in his presence in the bad water while towing the ship over the cataract. Thus, I was made crew commander.

Then his Majesty was informed that the Nubian … His Majesty became enraged like a leopard at this. His Majesty shot and his first arrow pierced the chest of that foe. Then, those enemies turned to flee, helpless at his Uraeus. A slaughter was made among them and their dependants were carried off as living captives. His Majesty journeyed north, all foreign lands under his control. That wretched Nubian bowman was head downward at the bow of his Majesty's ship "Falcon." They landed at Ipet-sut (= Karnak).[2]

pieces, and they established a much smaller settlement near the river. Thutmose I's troops also marched far upstream to a place between the fourth and fifth cataracts called Kurgus, where he left an inscription to commemorate the event. The location was of strategic and symbolic importance as it gave access to desert routes to its north.

The challenge of subduing Nubia lasted until late in the reign of Thutmose III (ruled 1479–1425), however. He also reached Kurgus and left an inscription next to his grandfather's. Although not well documented in the annalistic account of his reign, it seems that Thutmose III spent considerable efforts to destroy opposition in the northern part of Upper Nubia. But by the end of his reign that goal was accomplished and Egypt's hold was so secure that his successors could set in place a system of government to last for the rest of the New Kingdom.

As natural barriers the cataracts provided ideal boundaries to subdivide the Nile Valley. The Egyptians sometimes referred to the entire area of Nubia south of the first cataract as Kush, but mostly distinguished between Wawat and Kush, the former referring to the region between the first and second cataracts, the latter to the area farther south. The annexation of Wawat had been an easy affair, which Kamose had already accomplished before the start of the New Kingdom. Middle Kingdom policies seem to have made the region an almost integral part of Egypt with the second cataract as the southern border. Because the New Kingdom controlled the river upstream the forts there could be turned into civilian settlements rather than fortified guard posts.

Historians disagree on how New Kingdom Egyptians controlled the region to the south of the second cataract. The Egyptians had full dominion over the area up to the fourth cataract, but there is uncertainty over whether or not they administered it in the same manner throughout. Most likely there was regional variation. In the part between the second and third cataracts they built many fortified settlements in Egyptian style, including temples devoted to Egyptian gods and storage magazines. The inhabitants of these settlements were Egyptian immigrants and local people who had to assimilate Egyptian customs in order to fit in. The government was in the hands of an official called "King's son of Kush." The title is documented first in the reign of Thutmose IV although the office probably originated when the conquest of Nubia began. Despite the designation he was not an Egyptian prince, but a viceroy who sometimes was on close personal terms with the king. He administered the region as if it were an integral part of Egypt, with similar organizational structures. The integration with the heartland of Egypt was so strong that in the reign of Amenhotep III the authority of the King's son of Kush was extended northward up to the city of Hierakonpolis.

Beyond the third cataract the Egyptians' rule was less direct. They set up a few fortified settlements only in strategic locations, such as Gebel Barkal (named Napata), which controlled the river below the fourth cataract. The care of daily affairs was in the hands of Nubian princes as vassals to the Egyptian king. In their youth they spent time in Egypt to be educated in Egyptian manners and government practices. They lost their local roots, took on Egyptian names, and constructed Egyptian-style tombs for themselves. Yet, they knew Egypt's control over the region was not absolute, so they continued to attempt rebellions (at least in Egyptian eyes) for years after the introduction of this administration. They held the title "Overseers of southern foreign lands."

The region beyond the third cataract was thus a buffer zone between firmly held Egyptian territory and African lands upstream and inland from the river. Egypt invested little in its occupation. Local vassals were in charge, and only when they did not fulfill their obligations did the Egyptian army intervene. North of the third cataract the territory was fully integrated into Egypt and governed as an Egyptian province. The effect on Nubian culture seems to have been disastrous. Nubians who could afford it commissioned Egyptian tombs, and local cemeteries of the C-group culture (see Chapter 5) almost fully disappeared. The few remaining tombs in that style were of the poor. Some scholars have concluded from the mortuary information that local people disappeared, but it seems more likely that they Egyptianized and are therefore no longer identifiable as separate in the archaeological record.

Although Nubians adopted Egyptian customs, the Egyptians did not consider them to be like them. We have seen the case of Hekanefer before (Chapter 1). He was a prince of Miam, a region between the first and second cataracts, and had an Egyptian name. In his own tomb at home he appears with Egyptian dress and hairdo beside an inscription where he praises the god Osiris. The tomb could have easily been of an Egyptian-born administrator in the region. But Hekanefer is also represented in the tomb of the King's son of Kush under King Tutankhamun, located in western Thebes. There he is part of a group of Nubians, with stereotypical Nubian clothing, hairdo, and physical features. He prostrates himself before the tomb-owner and there is no doubt that he is a foreign subject. The Egyptians did not care for Nubian culture and adopted none of its ideas, customs, or artistic practices. Kings did marry Nubian women, and some Nubians entered Egypt and rose to prominent positions, but they had to shed most of their Nubian identities in order to succeed.

The Egyptian interests in Nubia seem to have been purely economic. From the reign of Thutmose III on Nubia's economy was integrated into the Egyptian and probably its greatest contribution was gold, the mined amounts of which ran into the hundreds of kilograms a year. The mines of Wawat in particular were in remote places and their exploitation was very difficult, even deadly for many of the workers. No description of the work exists for New Kingdom times, but since the mines were in use for millennia later accounts give us some idea. A Greek author of the Ptolemaic Period claims that families of chained slaves did all the work, laboring day and night under armed supervision. They cracked the rock by lighting fires in the shafts and dislodged the blocks with hammers and picks. In the New Kingdom the tools used must have been made primarily of hard stones, as bronze was rare in Egypt and copper too soft. Boys removed the stones from the shafts, adult men pounded them into smaller pieces, and women and old men ground them using stone mills. The pulverized stone was then washed to recover the gold dust. It has been estimated that at most 10 grams of gold could be extracted in this way from one metric ton of rock.

The work was worth the trouble, however. It provided the gold for gilding monuments like obelisks, and for sumptuous grave goods – Tutankhamun's inner gold coffin alone weighs 243 pounds (110.4 kilograms). Moreover, as Egypt had a virtual monopoly over the metal in the eastern Mediterranean, its kings used it in exchange for precious goods from other countries. These exchanges had a commercial value, but more importantly perhaps, they were diplomatic and tied the great kings of the time together, as we will discuss later on.

While the area between the first and third cataracts had little agricultural land and mining was the only economic enterprise, upriver from the third cataract the valley widened and allowed for farming and cattle raising. The Egyptians imported a surprising array of agricultural products from that zone and it seems that they coordinated production in order to maximize yields. They also seem to have organized manufacture to supply an Egyptian market. Nubian craftsmen made furniture and the like in Egyptian styles partly to satisfy the local demands and partly for transport to Egypt. These policies were only possible because of the military activity of early 18th-dynasty kings. By the end of the reign of Thutmose III in 1425, Nubia seems to have been mostly pacified and the system of control established there remained in use for some 300 years.

Wars in western Asia

The political conditions in western Asia were very different from those in Nubia at the start of the New Kingdom. In Nubia, the Kingdom of Kush presented a centralized opposition to Egypt's immediate south and its annihilation reduced local resistance to disparate forces only. Western Asia close to Egypt was politically fragmented into city-states while around the same time that Egypt reunified in the late 16th century an equivalent power emerged at some distance from Egypt in northern Syria. The Mittanni created there a centralized kingdom that stretched from the Mediterranean coast of southern Turkey to the northeast of modern Iraq. The heartland of the Mittanni state was east of the Euphrates but it controlled vassals in Syria west of the river. Egypt's military actions in the region were thus bound to reach the Mittanni sphere of influence at some point.

After the elimination of the last Hyksos opposition early 18th-dynasty pharaohs continued to raid along the Mediterranean coast according to the accounts of some soldiers who fought for them: Ahmose son of Ibana and Ahmose Pennekhbet. Thutmose I claims to have reached the Euphrates River, where he may have clashed with Mittanni forces. The main opponents of Egyptian armies were the small rulers who had sworn allegiance to the Mittanni king, however. For a century under the early 18th dynasty the campaigns were more raids than attempts at annexation. The Egyptians set up fortresses in some sites of southern Palestine; beyond that region they forced local rulers to be obedient to them through the threat of military action.

When Thutmose III became sole ruler of Egypt in 1458 he changed the policy toward western Asia. The annals he carved on the walls of the Karnak temple relate at least 15 campaigns in the period when he ruled alone, not all of them equally significant (see Sources in Translation 7.2). The first campaign

Sources in Translation 7.2
The Annals of Thutmose III

The longest Egyptian account of a succession of military actions comes from late in the reign of Thutmose III, who summarized some 15 campaigns in Syria over 20 years of his reign as the sole king of Egypt (much of the inscription is damaged). The record appears on the walls that surround the boat shrine of the Amun temple at Karnak and is based on earlier sources, including a type of record scholars call daybooks. Those accounted briefly for the king's where-abouts on a daily basis and listed acquisitions he made. The Annals of Thutmose III treat most campaigns very summarily. They devote much attention to the first campaign, however, which took place immediately after Thutmose III had become king by himself. The culmination of the story is the battle of Megiddo. The long composition shows how the king personally led the troops through a dangerous and narrow pass against the advice of others, who wanted to use a safer but longer road.

Year 23, first month of *shemu* (= summer), day 16, at the town of Yehem. His Majesty ordered a consultation with his mighty army, saying the fol-lowing: "That vile enemy of Qadesh has come and entered Megiddo and is there at the moment. He gathered round himself the princes of all the foreign lands that used to be loyal to Egypt, and those from as far as Nahrin, consisting of … the lands of Khor and Kedy, their horses, their armies, their people. And he says – it is reported: "I will wait and fight his Majesty here in Megiddo." Tell me how you feel about that?

They said to his Majesty: "How will it be to go on this road which becomes narrow, when it is reported that the enemies are waiting out there and they are numerous? Will not horse go behind horse and soldiers and people too? Will our vanguard be fighting while our rearguard is waiting here in Aruna, and unable fight? There are two other roads here. One of the roads is suitable for our lord – it comes out at Taanach. The other one is on the north side of Djefti, so that we can come out to the north of Megiddo. May our mighty lord proceed on whichever of these seems best to him. Do not make us go on that covert road!"

... The speech of the Majesty of the palace: "I swear as the god Ra loves me, as my father, the god Amun, favors me, as my nostrils are refreshed with life and dominion, my Majesty shall proceed on this Aruna road! Let him of you who wishes go on the roads you spoke of. Let him of you who wishes come in my Majesty's following. Otherwise they, the enemies whom the god Ra detests, will say: "Has his Majesty gone on another road because he is afraid of us?" So they will say.

They said to his Majesty: "May your father, the god Amun, Lord-of-the-Thrones-of-the-Two-Lands, who presides over Ipet-sut (= Karnak), do as you wish! We are followers of your Majesty wherever your Majesty goes! A servant follows his lord."[3]

At the end of the first campaign's description the text lists in detail the booty Thutmose III captured, including prisoners, horses, chariots, bronze armor, and livestock. These valuables seem to be what the account stresses the most, and the descriptions of other campaigns are mostly limited to them.

was crucial, however, and led to one of the most famous battles of ancient Egypt, the battle of Megiddo. Thutmose III claims that several vassals in southern Syria and Palestine had rebelled against the Egyptian garrison at Sharuhen. When the king retaliated the rebels sought refuge in the city of Megiddo, where he laid siege for seven months. With their defeat Thutmose III was free to raid farther north, which he continued to do in later years. This practice culminated in his eighth campaign when he reached the Euphrates and the land of Mittanni. Other states of western Asia, including Babylonia, Assyria, and the Hittites, were so impressed with Thutmose III's military achievements that they sent embassies. This shows not only that Egypt's international standing was guaranteed, but also that other great states had arisen with whom Egypt had to interact. Thutmose III's campaigns did not lead to a conquest of territory up to the Euphrates. The Egyptians held firmly onto southern Palestine only, while they continued to tolerate vassals ruling quite independently farther north.

Military competition with Mittanni ended during Amenhotep II's reign. His successor, Thutmose IV, seems to have concluded a peace treaty with the north Syrian country and married a Mittanni princess, whose name is unknown. The change benefited both states. Mittanni felt the threat from the rising powers of the Hittites and Assyrians to its north and east and needed to secure its southern border. Egypt was free to exploit the rich regions of southern Syria and Palestine, importing vast amounts of luxury products and some agricultural goods. It could also tap more easily into the trade networks of the eastern Mediterranean, which gave them access to products from Syria and the Aegean world.

7.4 Egypt and the Outside World

A side effect of Egypt's wars in Syria and Palestine was that the country's contacts with the cultures of the eastern Mediterranean intensified vastly. In earlier times Egypt had been in touch with the regions of western Asia, Anatolia, and the Aegean, and the presence of the Asiatic Hyksos in the Second Intermediate Period had its cultural impact on the country. But Egypt's involvement in Syria and Palestine during the New Kingdom gave it unprecedented direct access to the highly developed cultures of Asia. These gained an enormous influence on Egyptian elites, and one can even argue that those used their access to foreign goods and ideas as a means to set themselves apart from the rest of the population.

With the growth of the empire members of the military, bureaucracy, and priesthood became able to build grand and highly decorated tombs across the Nile from the country's religious center, in western Thebes. Among the scenes painted on the walls of these Theban tombs appear foreigners bearing gifts to the king or the official as the king's representative. These foreigners include primarily the subjected people of Syria, Palestine, and Nubia, who are depicted with stereotypical characteristics, such as pointed beards for Syrians. Included in fewer tombs are people of regions farther afield that were not under Egyptian political control, Hittites from Anatolia, Mittanni from northern Syria, and inhabitants from the distant lands of Keftiu and Punt (cf. below). While the Nubians mostly bear materials such as metal rings, elephant tusks, and animal skins, the Syrians and other eastern Mediterranean people often carry finished craft goods, such as decorated vessels and jewelry, depicted in great detail.

Royal inscriptions such as Thutmose III's Annals also account for gifts from distant Asiatic countries, including the great states of the Hittites, Assyria, and Babylonia. On a relief on the walls of the Karnak temple Thutmose III showed the gifts he made to the god Amun after his successful campaigns in Syria, and they included numerous craft objects such as vessels of precious metals and stones, statuettes, jewelry, and others.

There was thus an influx of luxury goods into Egypt, which affected Egyptian craft production. For example, among the imports were vessels and ingots of glass made in northern Syria and Assyria where the technology to make them first developed. The Egyptians continued to import glass but also recruited foreign glassmakers to set up their own production, which always remained limited, however. The chariot was another import from Syria, which had a radical effect on Egyptian warfare and society. Moreover, the presence of such foreign craft objects inspired the Egyptians to decorate their own products with Asiatic art designs.

The imports from Syria also included the cults of certain gods. Those could be attached to an imported technology such as the war goddess Astarte, who was associated with the chariot. Syria's leading deity, the storm god Baal, found adherents in Egypt as well. Literary tales about him started to appear in the Egyptian language in the reign of Amenhotep II.

Among the gift bearers represented in the Theban tombs appear eight groups of men identified as from Keftiu or from "the islands in the middle of the Great Green," in brief accompanying inscriptions. These terms referred to the island of Crete and to the rest of the Aegean islands, which at the time of the early 18th dynasty were home to the Minoan culture. Scholars debate whether the men were part of actual missions from the Aegean to Egypt, perhaps even to arrange diplomatic marriages, or merely stereotypical images of distant foreigners who paid homage to the Egyptian king or his representative. The gifts they carried were typical products from the Minoan world, especially elaborately decorated vessels.

Figure 7.2 Cretan tribute bearers depicted in the tomb of Menkheperrasonb. akg-images/Erich Lessing

At the same time painted Minoan pottery appeared in various Egyptian sites, and it is clear that the art of that region had a strong impact on Egypt. In the former Hyksos capital, Avaris, appeared three palaces the excavators think date to the reigns of Thutmose I to Thutmose III (ca. 1500–1425), which were decorated in Minoan – and very un-Egyptian – style. Paintings on lime plaster applied to the mud-brick walls contained scenes of people jumping over bulls, of ox heads and spirals, all common in the Minoan palace at Knossos on Crete. These motifs were popular in other palaces of the eastern Mediterranean at this time. Their appearance at Avaris at the same time that Minoans were depicted in Theban tombs suggests close contacts between Egypt and the Aegean, be they limited to trade or also involving diplomatic missions.

In the opposite direction from the Aegean early New Kingdom Egyptians were in contact with a land they called Punt. They reached Punt by seagoing boat and found it a country very unlike their own. The representations of houses, animals, and plants suggest a location in northeast Africa along the Red Sea coast, possibly the region of modern Eritrea, although a locale farther inland has also been suggested. Punt was a destination for Egyptian expeditions from the 5th dynasty on, but in the early New Kingdom it received unprecedented attention, at least in the record available to us. On the walls of the middle colonnade of her mortuary temple at Deir el-Bahri Queen Hatshepsut represented two events of special importance to her: her divine birth (cf. below) and an expedition to Punt. The latter scene, covering a wall some 90 feet (30 meters) long and 15 feet (5 meters) high, shows in detail Egyptians sailing to Punt, collecting gold ingots and other precious materials from the local queen and her husband (Figure 7.3), and returning with a huge cargo. Among the goods imported were complete incense trees as well as loose incense, an expensive fragrant tree extract that was used in the cult as an offering to the gods. The expedition gathered enormous heaps of it, and the accompanying inscription asserts that such amounts had never before been acquired. The relief's prominence indicates how proud Hatshepsut was of the expedition's achievements. It opened up trade contacts with sub-Saharan Africa and thus guaranteed access to exotic goods, such as elephant ivory, ebony, and wild animal skins. Importing foreign goods was a crucial aspect of successful rule. Egypt's contacts with the outside world in the New Kingdom were vital for establishing the country's importance internationally and for reaffirming the elite's position at home.

7.5 Domestic Issues

Royal succession

The unprecedented successes in military expansion of the early 18th dynasty may lead to the assumption that the royal house at home had a smooth and

Figure 7.3 The queen and king of Punt provide gifts to Hatshepsut's emissaries. Werner Forman Archive/Egyptian Museum, Cairo

straightforward sequence of strong rulers. That was not the case, however. The rules of royal succession in Egypt preferred the heir to be a son of the chief queen. If such a man were unavailable, the son of a secondary queen or the husband of the chief queen's daughter would do. When a king wanted to secure the succession he desired, he could appoint his chosen heir as co-regent, and the two would overlap for a number of years. In case the new king was a minor preferably a female relative acted as regent, most often his mother. Women were thus central in royal succession, and kings early in the dynasty regularly married sisters to strengthen their legitimacy.

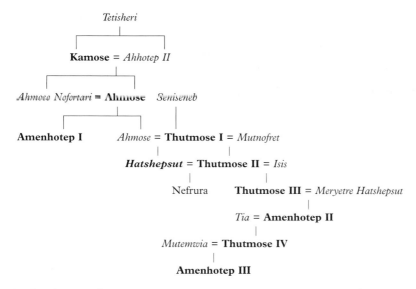

Tentative family tree of the late 17th and early 18th dynasties (selected family members only)
Bold: kings; italics: queens; =: marriage

It is not easy to study the succession of kings in the early 18th dynasty or to reconstruct relationships between the members of a court bloated in size. Family ties were often not expressed or they were indicated with such terms as "King's daughter" that may have been honorific rather than factual. King lists do not indicate periods of co-regencies and we do not know exactly when they occurred or how long they lasted. The scholarly literature provides thus many different scenarios of succession to the throne and of relationships between various people.

It is clear that several times in the six transitions of power during the early 18th dynasty the new king was not the son of the predecessor and his main wife, and that often he was a minor. Thus several "King's mothers" took care of business when the kings were young. Amenhotep I, for example, the second king of the 18th dynasty was a child when he came to the throne so his mother Ahmose-Nefertari seems to have acted as regent for him. Mother and son were venerated together in later time. Amenhotep I had no son when he died and Thutmose I, who seemingly was not related by blood, succeeded him. Possibly before he ascended the throne Thutmose I married Amenhotep I's sister, Ahmose, while his mother-in-law, Ahmose-Nefertari, whom he honored in his early monuments, seems to have supported his claim to power.

Hatshepsut

After his accession Thutmose I took a secondary wife, Mutnofret, who gave birth to the next king, Thutmose II. His first wife Ahmose already had given him a daughter, named Hatshepsut, who has become one of the most celebrated and controversial women of Egypt and the ancient world in general (Plate 7). Some years after her husband's death, in or shortly before 1473, she was crowned king of Egypt, a rise to power for which she seems to have prepared for two decades but whose repeated justification tells us how unorthodox it was. Hatshepsut was older than her half-brother Thutmose II whom she married. She was very prominent at court during his reign, which lasted perhaps 14 years: few representations of the king do not include her as well. Hatshepsut had the title of "God's wife" of Amun, which made her the highest priestess of the Amun temple at Karnak, an office that came with substantial endowments of land and other property.

Hatshepsut and Thutmose II had a daughter, Nefrura, who would succeed her mother as "God's wife." Thutmose II also had a son with a woman called Isis, Thutmose, who would become his successor (Thutmose III) in 1479. But, because Thutmose III was still a child Hatshepsut acted as regent, taking care of the country while she acknowledged her nephew's kingship. This state of affairs raised no eyebrows, as it replicated earlier cases where a woman of the previous generation was regent. Some officials referred explicitly to Hatshepsut's regency in their biographies. One Ineni, for example, stated in his tomb inscription:

> When he (Thutmose II) died, he joined the gods. His son (Thutmose III) stood in his place as king of the Two Lands, assuming rulership on the throne of the one who begot him, while his sister, the God's Wife, Hatshepsut, took charge of the affairs of the country, in that she took care of the Two Lands. Egypt served her with bowed head, the beneficent seed of the god, which came from him.[4]

Most likely in the 7th year of this arrangement, the relationship changed. Hatshepsut took royal names, including the prenomen Maatkara, and titles, which she rendered in the grammatically feminine form. Whereas she had been represented as a woman in earlier statues and relief sculptures, after her coronation as king she appeared with male dress and gradually became represented with male physique. Her breasts did not show and she stood in a traditional man's posture rather than a woman's. Some reliefs were even re-carved to adjust her representation to appear more like a man. For the next 15 years Hatshepsut ruled as king of Egypt, sponsoring construction work, such as her mortuary temple at Deir el-Bahri, trade expeditions, such as the one to Punt, and some military action, including in Nubia. She acknowledged the existence of Thutmose III as king, often representing him with her on monuments, albeit behind her to show an inferior status. All documents of the time are dated according to Thutmose III's regnal years, sometimes with her name as well. Her position as king was thus unusual as she was not alone.

The unorthodox nature of her kingship required justification, something Hatshepsut provided in several inscriptions and monuments. Some scholars have argued that her accession to the throne was not a coup d'état as she already held all strings of power starting under her husband's reign. Still, the event could not remain unexplained because her kingship was blatantly unconventional. The most extensive narrative appears on her mortuary temple at Deir el-Bahri, on the walls of the middle colonnade as a counterpart to the celebration of the Punt expedition (cf. above). There she claimed that the god Amun came to her mother in the form of Thutmose I.

> He (Amun) in the incarnation of the Majesty of her husband, the King of Upper and Lower Egypt, Aakheperkara (= Thutmose I) found her sleeping in the beauty of her palace. She awoke at the divine fragrance and turned towards his Majesty. He went to her immediately, he was aroused by her and he imposed his desire upon her. He allowed her to see him in his form of a god and she rejoiced at the sight of his beauty after he had come before her. His love passed into her body. The palace was flooded with divine fragrance, and all his odors were those of the land of Punt.[5]

Hatshepsut declared herself thus to be the daughter of Amun, who took on Thutmose I's form to beget her. Elsewhere she wrote that Amun issued an oracle proclaiming her to be king.

> An oracle before this good god magnificently predicted for me kingship of the Two Lands, with the north and the south fearing me; and it gave me all the foreign lands, illuminating the victories of my Majesty. Year 2, second month of the growing season (peret), day 29, the third day of the festival of the god Amun ... being the foretelling to me of the Two Lands in the broad hall of the Southern Opet (= Luxor temple), while his Majesty (Amun) delivered an oracle in the presence of this good god. My father, the god Amun, Chief-of-the-Gods, appeared in his beautiful festival.[6]

Perhaps in order to show how rightful her rule was, Hatshepsut also alleged that she restored Egypt from Hyksos rule, a feat that had been accomplished almost 80 years earlier (see Chapter 6).

Hatshepsut ruled as king for some 15 years. In Thutmose III's 22nd regnal year she disappeared from the scene, probably because she died. Thutmose III ruled another 33 years on his own, and perhaps two decades after Hatshepsut's disappearance he had her names and images removed from the numerous monuments she had erected (Figure 7.4). The statues she had set up in her temple of Deir el-Bahri were smashed and the pieces were thrown in a stone quarry nearby. The proscription was carefully done and often removed only the parts of her name and titles that showed she had been king. The reasons for the attacks are much debated (see Key Debate 7.1). They wiped Hatshepsut's reign from the memory of ancient Egyptians, however, and later king lists ignore her (see Chapter 1). The exception is Manetho, whose source in this matter remains a mystery. Josephus's rendering of Manetho states that she ruled 21 years and nine months and was the sister of Amenhotep I.

Modern scholars and others have found in Hatshepsut a perfect figure of antiquity to express their views on gender roles and family relationships. The

Figure 7.4 The erased image of Hatshepsut in the temple of Karnak

mere fact that she can be called Thutmose III's stepmother has led to an assort-
ment of suspicions of conflict between the two. Was she a "shrewd, ambitious
and unscrupulous woman," as some say?[7] Should we imagine that her kingship
was a culmination of the extraordinary influence of royal women in court politics, a process that started a century earlier? Employing elementary psychology,
many have suggested that Thutmose III's far-reaching military exploits when
he became sole king were the release of the pent-up frustration of a young man
browbeaten by his aunt. It seems that the relations between Hatshepsut and
Thutmose III were amiable during her rule, however, and the sources deny us
closer knowledge of what inspired both their actions.

Hatshepsut's reign did not represent a disruption in 18th-dynasty history,
domestically or in foreign affairs. It is impossible to determine to what extent
this was due to herself or to a central administration that functioned along
established lines irrespective of who was king. We know that some courtiers
became very important in Hatshepsut's reign and one man especially stands
out: Senenmut, whose relationship to Hatshepsut has been the subject of much
conjecture. He was a man of undistinguished birth who rose to prominence at

court. Several statues show him holding princess Nefrura, whose mentor and steward he became before Hatshepsut's accession. During her reign Senenmut acquired a long list of offices and titles. He was in charge of all of Hatshepsut's building projects, including her temple at Deir el-Bahri, although the suggestion that he was its architect is unproven. Senenmut had two tombs, one inside Hatshepsut's mortuary temple complex, which contained a quartzite stone sarcophagus, something otherwise reserved for royals at the time. At least 25 statues representing him are preserved. What explains his status? Speculation that he was Hatshepsut's lover is rife, but based on weak evidence. Crudely drawn graffiti in a cave above Hatshepsut's Deir el-Bahri temple show sexual intercourse between a man and a flat-chested woman with a large wig. Some people interpret the couple as Senenmut and Hatshepsut, the masculine-looking queen, who is wearing a royal wig. This interpretation is pure conjecture and more a reflection of modern-day preoccupations than of ancient reality. Senenmut's treatment after death is also somewhat of a mystery. Unknown parties erased his name from many of his statues and his tomb, something that occurred separately from Hatshepsut's proscription. Why this happened is unclear.

In the eyes of later Egyptians who compiled the king lists Hatshepsut's reign was a disruption in the usual sequence of kingship. She may not have been the last early 18th-dynasty ruler whose rise to the throne was irregular or whose kingship was challenged. Thutmose IV also took pains to legitimize his rule. He left behind a stele at the feet of the great sphinx at Giza in which he related the dream he had when as a prince he took a nap between the statue's legs. The sphinx prefigured his kingship, if Thutmose would clear away the sand. In other inscriptions as well, he stresses how gods anticipated his kingship when he was a youth. While the facts are often imprecise, it is apparent that the succession of kings was not secure in the early 18th dynasty.

Royal mortuary customs

Many New Kingdom rulers are best known today because of their tombs. Most tourists to Egypt visit the Valley of the Kings hidden in the mountains west of the Nile. Albeit emptied long ago, the deep tunnels cut in the rock and their painted walls do not fail to impress. The most famous king of ancient Egypt, Tutankhamun, owes his popularity to the rich finds in his tomb, the only one ancient robbers left largely intact. Its riches probably paled in comparison to what other tombs originally contained. The burial of kings and queens in valleys of the mountains of the western desert was an innovation of the 18th dynasty.

Middle Kingdom kings of the 11th dynasty were buried in various districts of western Thebes in tombs that were integrated in the complexes for their mortuary cults. King Mentuhotep II, for example, had a large temple set against the cliff at Deir el-Bahri with a tomb chamber dug into the rock behind it.

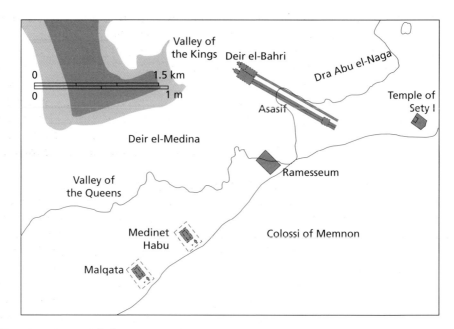

Map 4 Western Thebes

Seventeenth-dynasty kings chose the site of Dra Abu el-Naga for their burials, where they established complexes, some of which included mud-brick pyramids. The first king of the 18th dynasty, Ahmose, commissioned the last royal pyramid of Egypt, a relatively modest one with a core of loose sand and rubble, and a mortuary temple nearby in the ancient cemetery of Abydos. His tomb probably was in Thebes.

The next king, Amenhotep I, buried in Thebes, may have introduced a new practice that remained the rule for the rest of the New Kingdom. Instead of the tomb and mortuary complex being located in the same place, they were separated, with the tomb dug into a hidden location, probably to protect it against looting. The mortuary temples were prominent and close to the cultivated zone on the west bank. The best-known example is Hatshepsut's temple at Deir el-Bahri, located next to Mentuhotep's and inspired by it in its plan and appearance. A long causeway ran from the valley temple at the Nile (now lost) to the mortuary temple's lower court. Ramps led up to the second and third levels with courts, colonnades, and chapels. In the back of the complex was a small sanctuary for the boat of Amun. Many of the walls were decorated with painted relief scenes, including the story of Hatshepsut's birth and the expedition to Punt.

Two tombs were constructed for Hatshepsut. The earliest was a shaft in a cliff in the mountains behind western Thebes, about a mile to the west of Deir el-Bahri. As queen, she chose to be buried in the earliest royal tomb we can identify with certainty in the Valley of the Kings (KV 20), however. That tomb can be reached from Deir el-Bahri by climbing over the mountains or through a long detour to the valley's entrance to the north. Most likely Hatshepsut was not the first king to be buried there, however. Originally she was interred together with her father, Thutmose I, but Thutmose III created another tomb made especially for him (KV 38) at a later time. The idea of detaching tomb from mortuary complex probably predated Hatshepsut. Amenhotep I may have had a mortuary temple at Deir el-Bahri, which Hatshepsut obliterated by building hers, and a tomb elsewhere. At least three locations have been suggested for that tomb, including one in the Valley of the Kings, but there is no certainty.

The tombs in the Valley of the Kings were descending sequences of chambers, connected with sets of stairs, leading to a burial chamber with side rooms for the mortuary equipment. The burial chamber, and after the 18th dynasty much of the passageways leading to it, were decorated with scenes that helped the dead king reach a new life in the hereafter. On the walls of the inner chamber mortuary texts were painted. The building and decoration of these tombs deep in the inhospitable desert required a specialist workforce that lived near the tombs' location. At Deir el-Medina a village appeared to house the workers and their families (which we will describe in more detail in Chapter 9). It is possible that Amenhotep I and his mother Ahmose-Nefertari founded the community as later residents honored the two as gods. The earliest evidence from Deir el-Medina dates to Thutmose I's reign, however. The workers would continue to dig and decorate the tombs of the Valleys of the Kings and of the Queens for almost 500 years, until the end of the New Kingdom.

New Kingdom bureaucracy

Also in western Thebes, separated from the Valley of the Kings, were hundreds of tombs of officials of the New Kingdom. Their decoration and inscriptions provide a rich source of information on the duties and powers of a large bureaucracy. The great wealth of the state and its expanded territory required the involvement of many individuals to take care of daily affairs. As always in ancient Egypt, the king was at the head of the entire system, and the strength of his personality may have been an important factor in guaranteeing that the administration functioned properly. But many kings were young when they came to the throne and all of them were regularly outside the country when on campaign. These absences do not seem to have created instability, which testifies to the strength of the administrative structure. Many of the offices passed on from father to son or to another family member, and it is clear that certain families dominated the administration for a couple of generations, thereby providing continuity. Political changes apparently did not cause a restructuring of the bureaucracy. Hatshepsut's administrators, for example, held on to their offices when Thutmose III became sole king.

Special Topic 7.1   *The tomb of Rekhmira*

Many of the hundreds of New Kingdom tombs of officials on the west bank of Thebes had elaborately painted decorations on their walls and ceilings, that include some religious scenes connected to the burial and the afterlife, and so-called scenes of daily life that give an idealized portrayal of the deceased's activities when alive to show that they merited offerings. The tomb of Rekhmira (its traditional scholarly designation is Theban Tomb [TT] 100) stands out because of the detail of its representations. It is also unusually large: behind its outer courtyard is a narrow transverse hall, some 65 feet (20 meters) across, and a deep narrow room with a unique rising ceiling, some 85 feet (26 meters) long. The whole tomb resembles an inverted T in plan. There is no tomb chamber, or one is yet to been found.

All the walls of the tomb – some 3,230 square feet (300 square meters) – contain images and texts that tell us much of Rekhmira's position in life. He was southern vizier in the middle decades of the 15th century, under Thutmose III as sole king and in the early years of Amenhotep II. There are three long texts regarding his office: a biography, an account of Rekhmira's installation by Thutmose III, and *The Duties of the Vizier*, also attested in other tombs.

In his biography Rekhmira portrays himself as very close to the king and as a protector of the weak in society, repeating a motif that goes back to Old Kingdom times (see Chapter 4):

> I defended the husbandless widow. I established the son and heir on the seat of his father. I gave bread to the hungry, water to the thirsty, meat and ointment and clothes to him who has nothing. I relieved the old man, giving him my staff, and causing the old woman to say: "What a good action!" I hated inequity, and wrought it not, causing false men to be fastened head downwards.[8]

The painted scenes on the transverse hall and outer half of the long room treat Rekhmira's activities in life. He receives tax payments and judges litigants and tax dodgers. He accepts tribute from foreign delegations from Punt, the Aegean, Nubia, and Syria, including enslaved women and children, and he ensures that temples are provided with agricultural products and craft goods. One section of the hall decoration shows him with his family, including his wife and children, and the families of his grandfather and uncle who preceded him as viziers.

In the outer part of the long room appear detailed depictions of craftsmen of the temple workshop at work: they include jewelers, leather workers, carpenters, and metal workers. Besides them unkempt Nubians and Syrians mold bricks and transport stones. Other scenes show the fabrication of monumental royal statues. On the opposite wall is a scene of a ritual banquet where musicians and dancers entertain Rekhmira and his wife.

The decoration of the second half of the long room is devoted to Rekhmira's passage into the afterlife. This involves many ritual scenes that are not fully clear to

Figure 7.5   Banquet scene from Rekhmira's tomb. akg-images/Erich Lessing

us, centered on gods of the dead such as Osiris and Anubis. A sequence of 50 episodes shows rites surrounding the statue of the deceased, the Opening of the Mouth ritual.

Rekhmira must have devoted much expense to the decoration of his tomb and he hired highly skilled artists. Image and text together announce his prominence in the court. At some point people turned against him, however, and effaced his name. Also the figure of an individual in the Mouth Opening ritual – probably his eldest son – was removed. Did Rekhmira fall in disgrace late in his career or did later ideological conflicts cause the rejection of his memory?

The New Kingdom administration was divided into two regions, with parallel offices for Upper and Lower Egypt. This division was formalized in many ways. Thebes, the home of the dynasty and the location of the most important temples of the period, was not the only capital. Memphis in the north was probably more important for administrative purposes, and the kings spent much time there. We know the Theban administrators better because more of their tombs have been uncovered, but those of Memphis may have been more significant. Many offices of the civil administration were divided into two, for the north and for the south.

The highest administrators were the viziers of the north and the south. The office represented royal interests in every aspect of the bureaucracy and supervised all official state activity. The viziers' recorded actions were mostly judicial in that they settled disputes, answered petitions, and authorized transfers of property. In four Theban tombs appears a long text we call *The Duties of the Vizier*, a standardized description of the man's wide ranging responsibilities. A staff of scribes (who were authorized to record on his behalf) and heralds (who were authorized to speak on his behalf) supported him and gave the vizier's office its regional influence. In the nomes, "mayors" were responsible for economic and governmental affairs and reported to the vizier.

Since the army had become larger and more professionalized with the New Kingdom expansion, a vast bureaucracy was attached to it as well, while military men acquired influence in other aspects of the state administration. Also temples flourished, especially those of Thebes, which benefited enormously from royal munificence: kings returning from campaigns offered part of the booty to the gods and many endowed temples with large areas of land. Bureaucrats and scribes accounted for all the resources, while the higher echelons of the priesthood acquired great influence at court.

Building activity in the early 18th dynasty

The conquests of the early 18th dynasty brought enormous wealth into Egypt, and it is no surprise that its kings used part of that wealth for building monuments, as kings of the past had done. The mortuary temples and tombs on the west bank of Thebes are just one type of construction that flourished. Kings also commissioned the renovation and enlargement of temples and they built grand palaces and residences for the court to live and work in, most likely throughout the land. The archaeological evidence available to us is very biased toward Thebes, where the greatest temples of Egypt stood and where numerous burials and mortuary complexes are preserved. The city of Memphis must have prospered equally in the New Kingdom, but its remains are buried underneath later deposits. Only relatively recently have archaeologists started to explore officials' tombs at Saqqara nearby (which are mainly from the later 18th and 19th dynasties). Other cities received royal attention as well, as the remains of residences, such as at Gurob, show. The succession of palaces at Avaris from the reigns of Thutmose I to Thutmose III and their elaborate Minoan-style frescoes show how construction was continuous and used up-to-date decoration.

Even in Thebes the record is very partial. The kings of the 18th dynasty had palaces on the east bank, but these were of mud brick and have disappeared.

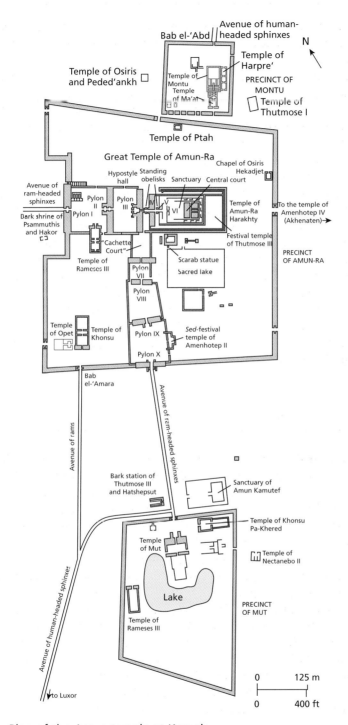

Figure 7.6 Plan of the Amun temple at Karnak

The Amun temple at Karnak in eastern Thebes was the grandest building project of Egypt after the Old Kingdom, one that started in the Middle Kingdom and continued into Ptolemaic times. The god Amun had merged with the sun god Ra and had become the chief god of Egypt in the Middle Kingdom. Kings of that period had initiated work at Karnak, but 18th-dynasty kings, starting with Thutmose I, expanded the temple enormously, often replacing Middle Kingdom structures with newer ones. In essence the temple was a dark shrine for the statue of the god, in front of which successive builders constructed complexes of rooms, courtyards, and massive gateways (we call those pylons) leading westward toward the Nile. The Karnak complex also grew in other directions after the early 18th dynasty to incorporate temples for Amun's wife Mut and his son Khonsu, and to connect it to the second major temple in Thebes at Luxor to the south (Figure 7.6). Embellishing Karnak was a source of great pride. On the walls of her mortuary temple at Deir el-Bahri Hatshepsut depicted how she had two obelisks carved at Aswan and then transported and erected at Karnak. One of them is still in place: it is 97 feet (29.5 meters) high and weighs 300 tons.

The early 18th dynasty thus initiated a period of new prosperity and grandeur for Egypt. The state was expansionist and eager to extract resources for its neighbors. It was in contact with distant cultures from which it received exotic gifts. The wealth generated enabled numerous state dependants in the civil, military, and religious branches of government to live in luxury and to expend many resources on their tombs. The kings at the center of this flourishing organization built grand palaces and temples and showed themselves as great warriors and devotees to the gods. In all these ways the early 18th dynasty established patterns of behavior that would remain in place for several more centuries in the rest of the New Kingdom Period.

Key Debate 7.1   *Hatshepsut's proscription*

Why did Thutmose III erase Hatshepsut's images or cover them up and destroy her statues? The practice is well documented and was so successful that for long modern historians did not know of the queen's existence. The ancient sources do not justify it, so scholars today have to find explanations, unless they accept it as "for unknown reasons" (Lipinska 2001). Originally they assumed that when Thutmose III finally gained the throne he turned against his "detested stepmother." He had used the years she was in charge to hone

his skills as warrior, and his military aggression in Asia, where Egypt had been put to shame by Hatshepsut's inaction, was an outlet for his frustrations (Hayes 1973: 318).

In the 1960s, however, scholars started to argue that close to 20 years into Thutmose III's sole reign Hatshepsut's images were still visible and untouched, and most Egyptologists now accept this idea, albeit not all (see the review by Meyer 1989). Another explanation for Hatshepsut's proscription was needed. The destruction of her remains was not random: it removed Hatshepsut's birth name, but not the names that included references to the gods Ra and Amun. It was a gradual process, starting with her name, which was usually replaced with that of one of her predecessors, and only later extending to smashing statues (Arnold 2005). Some suggest that male Egyptian elites could not suffer the idea that a powerful woman had ruled and removed all traces of it so that it would not happen again (Robins 1993: 152; Dorman 2005: 269). But other female rulers' representations, such as Sobekneferu at the end of the 12th dynasty, did not receive the same treatment.

Another suggestion is that Hatshepsut represented the line of Ahmose in the royal family, while Thutmose III represented that of Thutmose. Around the time the proscription started, Thutmose had selected Amenhotep II as his successor and the removal of Hatshepsut's memory may have been in order to weaken Ahmosid claims to the throne (Roth 2005). Some object that no Ahmosid pretender existed at the time (Dorman 2005).

A very simple explanation would be that the existence of two kings side-by-side (Hatshepsut and Thutmose III were sometimes represented as equals) was unacceptable. Hatshepsut's rule as king was always somewhat ambiguous (Baines, Wente & Dorman 2009), so it was easy to remove her representations as king and act as if Thutmose III had always been the man in charge. The question remains open.

NOTES

1. Translation after Breasted 1906, Vol. 2: 40.
2. Translation after Lichtheim 1976: 14.
3. Translation after Lichtheim 1976: 30–1.
4. Translation after Dziobek 1992: 54.
5. Translation after Breasted 1906, Vol. 2: 80.
6. Translation after Dorman 1988: 22, and Gillen 2005: 22.
7. Hayes 1973: 317.
8. Gardiner's translation from N. Davies 1943: 81. See also Blumenthal et al. (eds.) 1984: 424–5.

8

The Amarna Revolution and the Late 18th Dynasty (ca. 1390–1295)

The monotheistic revolution of Akhenaten was not only the first but also the most radical and violent eruption of a counter-religion in the history of humankind. (Assmann 1997: 25)

Akhenaten, whatever else he may have been, was no intellectual heavyweight. (Redford 1984: 233)

By 1400 BC, after 150 years of warfare and expansion, Egypt had secured in its international position and military activity abated. The empire rested on its laurels. For most of the 14th century only a few campaigns took place in Nubia, while in western Asia the royal house shifted its focus from hostile interactions to coexistence with its counterparts. Diplomacy dominates the record of Egypt's foreign relations in the late 18th dynasty. Our view is partly biased by the accidental discovery of an archive of international correspondence from this period, but the internationalism of the age is evident from other sources as well. In the 14th century Egypt's interactions with other countries in the eastern Mediterranean were intense, and until late in the century they were mostly peaceful. The country flourished under this policy: vast amounts of wealth flowed toward the royal court, which distributed it to the bureaucratic and priestly elites. This was a time of huge building projects on palaces and temples, while kings and courtiers received superbly decorated tombs packed with lavish goods. Whether or not the general population benefited as well is unknown. For the mass of the people this period may have been no different from others, but we have barely any information on them.

At the same time, the late 18th dynasty was an era of turmoil in the intellectual and religious life of Egypt. Kings Amenhotep III and Amenhotep IV, who changed his name to Akhenaten, upset traditional ideas about their own position in the universe and the hierarchy of gods. Both father and son expressed their new ideas with a frantic creation of buildings and other monuments made possible by the empire's wealth. Akhenaten's reforms in particular caused deep divisions within society. This most enigmatic king of Egyptian history promoted Aten, who previously had been an aspect of the sun god only, to a level of official worship that excluded other gods. If indeed his ideas were monotheistic, it would be the first example of such a religious outlook in world history. That many in Egypt resented the reforms is clear from the reactions after Akhenaten's death. Subsequent upheavals led to the end of the 18th dynasty and the destruction of Akhenaten's name and monuments.

Kings and courtiers of the late 18th dynasty left an enormous amount of remains, including some of the most famous of the entirety of Egyptian history. They include King Tutankhamun's tomb, whose discovery may be the most renowned archaeological feat of the 20th century. There exist numerous other tombs, hundreds of statues, extensive building remains, and less dazzling items such as inscribed jar sealings and pottery. Kings and events of the period have drawn the attention of many, not only within the field of Egyptology but also outsiders. Books on Akhenaten and his queen Nefertiti abound. Even Sigmund Freud studied the king's ideas to find the roots of a pure monotheism that set Jews apart from all others in history. With its mixture of wealth, grandeur, and innovation the late 18th dynasty is probably the most discussed era of Egyptian history.

Yet, Egyptologists struggle to reconstruct even the most basic facts of this period's history. Members of the royal family changed their names, and it is often unclear who is who. Did Nefertiti succeed her husband as king under a special throne name or did a man, and if so who was he and what was his relationship to the former ruler? Did the reigns of Amenhotep III and IV overlap and if so for how many years? The answers to these questions have major repercussions on the explanation of religious and other transformations. Modern accounts written closely together in time can present entirely different scenarios. No reconstruction is more than tentative.

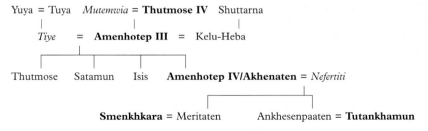

Tentative family tree of the late 18th dynasty (selected family members only)
Bold: kings; italics: queens; =: marriage

Summary of Dynastic History
Late 18th dynasty (ca. 1390–1295)

ca. 1390–1352	King Amenhotep III Initiates major construction activity in Thebes and throughout Egypt Marries two Mittanni princesses, Kelu-Heba and Tadu-Heba Celebrates three sed-festivals
ca. 1352–1336	King Amenhotep IV/Akhenaten Focuses all official attention on the Aten sun disk Moves his capital to Akhetaten Marries Nefertiti and raises her to a status equal to himself
?–?	King Neferneferuaten Identity much disputed. Probably two distinct persons, perhaps Nefertiti or Meritaten and Smenkhkara
ca. 1336–1327	King Tutankhamun Is forced to abandon Akhetaten for Memphis Restoration of traditional cults starts
ca. 1327–1323	King Ay Ascends throne as old man with government experience
ca. 1323–1295	King Horemheb Becomes king after career as commander-in-chief Dismantles Akhenaten's buildings in Karnak Starts erasing the memory of his predecessors

8.1 An International Age

When Amenhotep III built his massive mortuary temple in western Thebes – now almost fully taken apart – he expressed an unrealistic yet traditional Egyptian view of the world: Amenhotep III was the master of all other countries. On bases that originally held statues were carved images of bound prisoners with the names of the places they represented. The five preserved bases catalog the regions to Egypt's north in a wide geographical reach. One base lists great states: Babylonia, Mittanni, Carchemish, Aleppo, Hatti, Arzawa, and Assyria; a second lists minor states of Syria and Palestine, such as Damascus; a third, badly damaged, other Syro-Palestinian states; a fourth seemingly again great states of the north; and a fifth places in Greece and the Aegean. The 14 names on the fifth base have attracted much interest as they reveal the Egyptians' interest in that distant world. Scholars disagree about the exact readings of several names, but those seem to include Phaestos,

Knossos, Mycenae, Troy, and others, all places that are well known from Aegean archaeology.

The places named in the lists are not just distant locations about which the Egyptians barely knew anything, but they were partners with Egypt in an international world that stretched across the eastern Mediterranean. Contacts with some of these countries were probably rare and indirect, but none was outside Egypt's orbit. Even in the most distant ones in the Aegean Egyptian objects have been found, some of them inscribed. More objects with the names of Amenhotep III and his wife Tiye appear in the Aegean than for any other Egyptian. At the same time, goods from the Aegean found their way to Egypt and quite a few Mycenaean vessels have been excavated there.

Egypt's world domination was a fiction, however. Amenhotep III and his successors had to engage with countries in the eastern Mediterranean as equals. We know the real situation very well through a chance find from the late 18th dynasty: the Amarna archive. In the late 19th century AD local farmers discovered in the ruins of the capital that Amenhotep III's successor Akhenaten built, Akhetaten (see below), some 350 letters written to and from the Egyptian court. Because the letters are not dated, the chronology of the archive is uncertain. It covers at most 30 years, from 1360 to 1330, but may be from a shorter period of time – as little as 15 years, some scholars think. The Egyptian kings involved were Amenhotep III, Akhenaten, and two successors, probably Smenkhkara and Tutankhamun. The Amarna letters were not written in the Egyptian language and script but in the common format for international diplomatic correspondence of the era. They are clay tablets inscribed in the cuneiform script to render the Babylonian language (the Assyrian and Hurrian languages appear in one tablet each, and two letters are in Hittite), and most of the preserved ones were written to the Egyptian court. The Amarna letters are the only sizeable group of such letters recovered so far, but smaller finds from other Egyptian sites and cities in western Asia show that this format survived throughout the period of Egypt's New Kingdom. Courts addressed each other in Babylonian even if they had a lively scribal tradition of their own, as Egypt did. Local scribes learned the foreign language and script to translate missives to and from their masters. Amenhotep III's court had to participate in this system. When Amenhotep IV moved to a new capital he took some of his father's letters with him and his administration continued the correspondence. When some 15 years later Akhetaten was abandoned, letters that were no longer of use stayed behind, and this coincidence explains why 350 of them survived in the city's ruins until modern times.

The Club of the Great Powers

The Amarna letters fall into two groups: the larger involves Egypt's vassals in the Syro-Palestinian area and discusses matters of imperial control. The smaller group, some 40 letters, concerns states that were equal in status to Egypt at the time. Its rulers saw themselves as "brothers" and treated one another with respect. They formed an exclusive group that modern scholars have coined the "Club of the Great Powers," whose membership was jealously guarded. In the days of the Amarna archive the members included besides Egypt: Babylonia, the old state of southern Mesopotamia whose language was the language of diplomacy; Mittanni, the major power in northern Syria; the Hittites, who had recently united much of Anatolia and started to reach into northern Syria; Alashiya, a state on the island of Cyprus that was valued because of its copper mines; and Arzawa, a somewhat marginal old state in southern Anatolia. In the time span covered by the Amarna archive, Assyria from northern Mesopotamia forced its way into the club through its military successes, a move its neighbor Babylonia failed to block.

The Egyptian kings – and occasionally queens – corresponded with their colleagues in a formulaic language, inquiring at length about their wellbeing and that of wives, sons, soldiers, and horses. The actual messages were usually brief and did not involve issues of policy, but of courtesy. When the king of Babylon, for example, moved into a new palace, he invited his Egyptian colleague to the opening ceremony. It was unthinkable that the latter would make the protracted journey, but the invitation had to be extended. The men acted as if they were neighbors in a village. Most of the letters had a practical concern as well, however. They discussed exchanges of gifts between the courts. Each had access to valuable goods that the others desired and the kings traded these as if they were presents. In effect they created ties – a gift had to be reciprocated at a later point – and they moved luxury items throughout the region. In the same vein the kings exchanged brides. In both transactions Egypt had an unusual position, however.

As we have seen, with its conquest of Nubia Egypt gained access to rich gold deposits. The country had a monopoly on the metal, which other kings much desired. Thus many letters deal with gold, often griping about its quality and quantity. The Assyrian Assur-uballit wrote, for example: "Is such a present that of a great king? Gold in your country is like dust; one simply gathers it up. Why must it stay in your sight?"[1] The exchanges gave Egypt access to foreign luxuries such as lapis lazuli, copper, semi-precious stones, and craft products. There were other ways to acquire these as well – conquest and trade – but this system had the advantage of bolstering diplomatic ties at the same time.

Princesses were part of the exchange as well, but in this respect Egypt took a stance others much resented: no Egyptian princess went abroad although many foreign women came to Egypt. A group of letters deals with Amenhotep III's marriage to a Babylonian princess – her travel arrangements, the dowry she brought and the wedding gifts for her family in Babylon, which were both listed in detail. But Egypt did not reciprocate. Babylon's king complained bitterly that "from time immemorial no daughter of the king of Egypt is given to anyone," and he even suggested a ruse: "Send me a beautiful woman as if she were your daughter. Who could say, 'She is not the daughter of a king!'"[2] Egypt did not relent.

These activities exposed the Egyptian court to foreign emissaries, goods, and ideas, and kept it informed about what happened in distant countries. The exchanges made the Egyptians aware that despite the official rhetoric of world domination and the uniqueness of the pharaoh, others existed with a similar status and power.

The administration of Syria and Palestine

The bulk of the Amarna archive, some 310 letters, documents Egypt's interactions with its vassals in Syria and Palestine. Almost all of the letters were written to the Egyptian court in a Babylonian language that shows much influence from the vernaculars of the authors. They address Egypt's king as lord and master with formulae that equate him to the sun god. The content is very unlike that of the correspondence with equals in that vassals' letters discuss political issues: the relationship with Egypt and with other Egyptian subjects in the region. They show much quibbling and rivalry, and the local rulers beg for Egyptian support.

Egypt's control over the region was relatively loose. Local men continued to govern as kings at home, but as subjects to Egypt – the letters call them "mayors." Some 60 city-states survived under Egyptian supervision, which was enforced through small garrisons of troops. Egypt used the region as a buffer with its northern equals (Mittanni and the Hittites) and as a source of tribute, mainly agricultural goods. The letters show that Egypt had divided Syria-Palestine into three zones: Amurru on the northern coast, Apu in inland Syria and northern Palestine, and Canaan on the southern coast (Map 5). Each had a center from which an Egyptian commissioner administered the area. The commissioners may have been local men trained in Egypt and they traveled back and forth to the imperial court.

The letters show an annual pattern of contacts between Egypt and the local kingdoms. Sometime in the early spring the Egyptian court sent out letters to announce that a messenger with troops would come to collect tribute payments. Very few of these letters are preserved in the Egyptian archive. In the spring the Syro-Palestinian rulers replied to the instructions in the original Egyptian demand. Much of it consisted of stock phrases like "I will guard the city until the arrival of your messenger." The final letters, written in the late summer and collected by the Egyptian messenger, dealt with specific situations the vassals thought merited pharaoh's attention. They hoped the royal messenger would testify to the accuracy of the facts.

Local rulers used the correspondence to coax the Egyptian kings to support them in conflicts they had with neighbors or to reduce the amount of tribute. They always portrayed themselves as faithful vassals in a world of traitors and complained that pharaoh ignored them. The largest preserved group of Amarna letters derives from Rib-Adda, ruler of the important port city of Byblos. He accused the kings of the neighboring state of Amurru of threatening Byblos

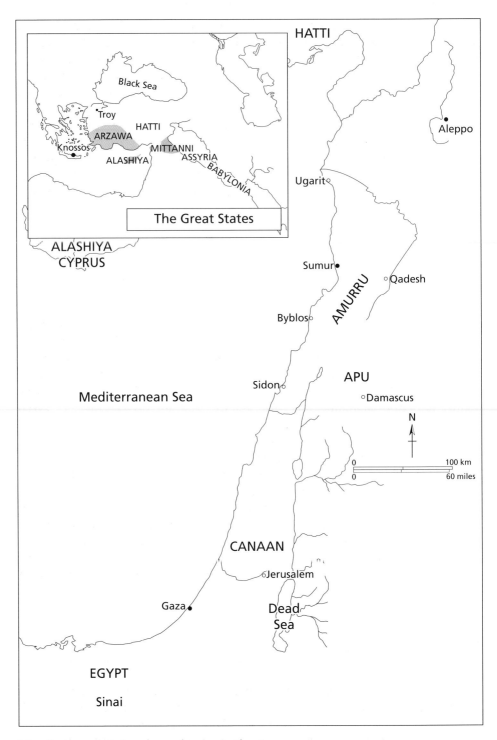

Map 5 Egypt's Syrian dependencies in the Amarna age

militarily, because Rib-Adda was such a good servant of the Egyptian king, while they supported the Hittites. Rib-Adda complained so much that Akhenaten sent a general to investigate, but he blamed Rib-Adda for the trouble. At some point, the king of Amurru was summoned to Egypt but was cleared. Somewhat later he would indeed betray Egypt and officially ally himself with the Hittites, however.

Scholars used to read the vassals' letters literally and saw them as evidence that under Akhenaten Egypt lost interest in its foreign territories. That is probably a mistake. Local rulers painted dire situations because they thought this would have an effect. But the Egyptian king was not interested in the day-to-day affairs of these rulers and tolerated their rivalries as long as his access to the region's resources was safe.

The rise of the Hittites

The Amarna letters and other evidence that derives mainly from outside Egypt indicate that the political situation in Syria was far from static. Under King Suppiluliuma I (the length of his rule is in doubt, but certainly included the years 1344–1322) the Hittites of central Anatolia rapidly expanded their territory. One of their victims was the state of Mittanni, whose rulers had become Egypt's allies during the reign of Thutmose IV, some 50 years earlier. King Tushratta, whose daughter was married to Akhenaten and who had asked Amenhotep III's queen Tiye to remind her son of the good relations between the two states, had been assassinated in his own palace, and in the ensuing civil war between two branches of the royal family both parties sought the support of the Hittite king. Ultimately Suppiluliuma annexed all Mittanni territories west of the Euphrates and made the Mittanni king his vassal. The Hittite control over northwestern Syria placed it in competition with Egypt, which claimed supremacy over the city-states there. Some vassal states switched allegiance to Hatti, for example, Qadesh and Amurru. In response the Egyptians may have mounted a campaign under King Tutankhamun, with little effect. The struggle over Syria would dominate Egyptian–Hittite relations for the next 60 years.

A failed marriage alliance

The hostilities were briefly interrupted by one of the strangest incidents in Egypt's international relations, an affair whose understanding is complicated, as we are not certain about the identity of the Egyptians involved. The episode shows, however, how closely foreign and internal affairs were related. Our only information comes from Hittite sources a generation after the event, which report that Suppiluliuma received a messenger from an Egyptian queen, recently widowed and childless. The text identifies her only as Dahamunzu, a Hittite rendering for the Egyptian term for "the king's wife." She pleaded:

> My husband has died, and I have no son. But you have many sons, they say. If you give me one of your sons, he will become my husband. Never would I take a servant of mine and make him my husband. I am afraid.[3]

Suppiluliuma rightly was suspicious of this highly unusual proposition and sent an envoy to check out the situation. When the envoy confirmed that the queen's request was genuine, a Hittite prince, Zannanza, went to Egypt where he was murdered soon afterwards. Most likely a faction of the Egyptian court did not want this marriage to take place. In revenge Suppiluliuma attacked Egyptian territories in Syria. The union would have created an alliance between the two major powers that competed over Syria at the time, and it involved a strange reversal of gender roles: the Hittite prince who went to Egypt to marry the queen was like earlier Mittanni princesses who married Egyptian kings.

Who was the queen of Egypt who made the request? The Hittite source calls her "the king's wife" and scholars debate whether she was Akhenaten's or Tutankhamun's widow who sought support in a court that had turned against her husband. The episode is crucial for our understanding of what happened at the end of Akhenaten's reforms, and the uncertainty is unlikely to disappear without entirely new evidence. This is just one example of the multiple questions that surround Egypt's internal turmoil in the late 18th dynasty, to which we turn now.

8.2 Amenhotep III: The Sun King

Amenhotep III was a young boy when he succeeded his father Thutmose IV around 1390, somewhere between the ages of two and twelve. He inherited a state that stretched from the northern Syrian coastline to deep into Sudan. An inscription from his first or second year, found in many copies, states that "his southern border is Karoy (upstream of the fourth cataract), his northern border is Naharina (northern Syria)."[4] Further expansion was not his concern. The official record mentions only two campaigns in Nubia, which were perhaps more ceremonial in character than to deal with rebellious groups, and were directed by military officers. In western Asia Amenhotep III followed his father's policy of peaceful relations with the Mittanni state. The era of aggressive militarism of the early 18th dynasty had ended. It had resulted in an enormous empire that brought much wealth into Egypt. The country's elites benefited economically and many expended part of their riches in building projects still visible today.

Amenhotep III's divinity and his building projects

King Amenhotep III sponsored more building activity than anyone else in his own time and for the rest of the New Kingdom. Only Rameses II, who ruled much longer (67 instead of 38 years), left behind more architectural remains and statuary, not least because he could usurp many of Amenhotep III's monuments. Numerous architectural remains of Amenhotep III had a monumentality unseen since Old Kingdom times, and he commissioned many statues that were colossal in size. The most famous of those are the so-called Colossi of Memnon (Figure 8.1). These are two massive monolithic statues of the seated king, 65

Figure 8.1 The southern colossus of Memnon

feet (20 meters) high and weighing 720 tons, which stood in front of his mortuary temple in western Thebes. Because one of them began to make a whistling
noise at dawn after an earthquake in 27 BC, Greeks in Egypt associated it with
the Homeric hero Memnon, the son of the goddess of dawn, Eos, to whom he
sang. The name "Colossi of Memnon" has survived into modern times, and
throughout the ages the statues have fascinated those who visited them. The
Roman emperor Septimius Severus repaired them in the 2nd century AD – and
stopped the whistling sound.

The architectural works Amenhotep III commissioned were connected to
changes in the king's relationship to the gods that become clear during his reign.
Amenhotep III took the idea of self-deification further than any previous
pharaoh and was the first to present himself as a divine being during his lifetime.
Some representations show him making offerings to his own image as a god.
He identified himself with the gods of Egypt, rather than with his royal ancestors. He was no longer just the "son of Ra," the sun god, but called himself
"the radiant solar disk." There was no difference between his cult and that of
the gods: he was venerated as the personification of other gods.

The king's main queen, Tiye, was very important in this ideological change.
Amenhotep III married her in his first or second year as king when he was still
a child. Tiye was the daughter of a military family and is the only Egyptian
queen whose parents we both know: Yuya and Tuya. Highly unusually that
couple was buried in the Valley of the Kings (KV 46). Many statues, one of
them colossal, represent Tiye at her husband's side and of equal size. No earlier
queen received so much official attention. In reliefs and private tomb paintings
as well Tiye appears as Amenhotep III's partner, and the names of the couple
are often paired in inscriptions. Many scholars believe she had great influence
over the king and was involved in the daily aspects of his rule (Plate 8). In the
program of royal deification Tiye took on the role of the cow-goddess Hathor,
who in her various aspects was the mother, sister, and daughter of Ra.

Amenhotep III commissioned the construction of two temples in Nubia
upstream of the second cataract for the couple's cult. The one at Soleb honored
the king as "Nebmaatra (Amenhotep's prenomen), lord of Nubia," and contained several open solar courtyards and offering scenes to the king as the sun
and the moon. In the smaller temple at Sedeinga, 10 miles (15 kilometers) to
the north, Tiye was worshipped as Hathor, companion of Ra. One of the courts
at Soleb contained representations of the sed-festival, the jubilee that renewed
kingship (see Chapter 2). Amenhotep III celebrated three such festivals in the
last decade of his life, the first after 30 years on the throne, the next two with
three-year intervals in his 34th and 37th years. It is likely that these celebrations
promoted the idea of royal deification. They were major events that involved
the entire empire, and administrative records show that numerous officials were
involved in the preparation. Amenhotep III built a massive palace city for the
ceremonies in western Thebes, at Malqata. The huge complex contained four
residential palaces – one seemingly reserved for Queen Tiye – a temple for
Amun, residential areas for personnel, and an artificial harbor. Sealings with

Figure 8.2 Scene from the Opet festival in the temple of Luxor. Werner Forman Archive

his name and title "the radiant solar disk" show that the complex was in use from his 29th or 30th year to his death in year 38.

Amenhotep III also devoted much attention to eastern Thebes, the religious center of Amun. He expanded the temple at Karnak, and connected it to Luxor, 2 miles (3 kilometers) to the south with a processional road. His work at Luxor was of special importance. He removed the existing temple and established the core of the temple as it is still visible today. Luxor's exact function is a puzzle, which scholars have tried to solve through study of the representations on its walls. Located on an unusual north–south axis along the Nile, the temple was crucial for the annual festival called Opet (Figure 8.2). The festival is first known from Queen Hatshepsut's reign, when it lasted 11 days. It grew in importance over time and by the end of the New Kingdom it went on for 27 days and involved a royal voyage through the country with many stages. Amenhotep III rebuilt Luxor to provide a monumental setting for Opet's crucial moment, the renewal of the king's divine birth.

During the festival the statues of the gods Amun, his companion Mut, and junior god Khonsu, left Karnak carried in boats and accompanied by the king and priests. A select group entered Luxor, where Amun's boat was placed in a special shrine. The king then entered the birth chamber to renew his special birth. Just as Hatshepsut had done in Deir el-Bahri (see Chapter 7), Amenhotep III portrayed himself as the offspring of the sexual union between his natural mother Mutemwia and the god Amun in the shape of his father Thutmose IV. The focus of the renewal was the king's *ka*. Each Egyptian had a *ka*, a vital force separate from the body. In the case of the king the *ka* contained his divine essence, fashioned at the same time as his human body. During the Opet festival the king united again with his *ka* in the Luxor temple and when he re-emerged his divine being was reaffirmed. Hence Amenhotep III called Luxor "his place of justification, in which he is rejuvenated, the palace from which he sets out in joy at the moment of his appearance, his transformation being visible to all."[5] Although Amenhotep III identified himself with the sun god Ra, it was the chief god Amun who assured his divinity.

Amenhotep III's other major project at Thebes was his mortuary temple in western Thebes, fronted by the two colossal statues discussed above. The most monumental mortuary temple in Egypt, it was dismantled in later years and, but for the colossi, only bases and fragments of statues remain. They still show how grand the building was. More statues stood in it than in any other religious complex from Egypt.

The buildings at Thebes and throughout Egypt and Nubia show the wealth Amenhotep III had at his disposal. We can only guess at the details of the expenditures for his massive projects at Thebes, but we have a record of the valuables used in a minor project to the north of the Karnak temple. They included:

electrum	31,485²⁄₃ *deben*
gold	25,182³⁄₄ *deben*
black copper	4,620²⁄₃ *deben*
lapis lazuli	6,406 *deben*
carnelian	1,731²⁄₃ *deben*
turquoise	1,075²⁄₃ *deben*
bronze	14,342 *deben*
pieces of copper	104,195³⁄₄[6]

Only the existence of the empire made such expenditures possible.

The king's family

A grand king like Amenhotep III required a large court, which he could easily support with the assets of the empire. The evidence for his entourage is abundant in Thebes as well as in other parts of Egypt. Many individuals left behind statues and other representations of themselves and some had lavish tombs.

Inscriptions narrate their careers and focus on their loyalty to the king. Courtiers resided primarily at Memphis, the administrative capital in the north, and at Thebes, the religious center.

The royal family is also well known. As we have seen, Amenhotep III's main queen Tiye was very important to him, including in her role as the divine spouse Hathor to the king as the god Ra. The couple had four daughters who also appeared in royal representations: Satamun, Henuttaneb, Isis, and Nebetah. In the last decade of Amenhotep's life Satamun became "great royal wife," perhaps because Tiye had been elevated to the status of a goddess at that time. They also had at least two sons, about whom we hear virtually nothing in Amenhotep III's lifetime. One, Thutmose, may have died before his father; the other, Amenhotep, became his successor.

Amenhotep III married many other women. He advertised his marriage to the Mittanni princess Kelu-Heba by distributing scarabs throughout the empire inscribed with this announcement:

> Marvel brought to his Majesty: the daughter of the Prince of Naharina, Shuttarna, princess Kelu-Heba and 317 women of her entourage.[7]

Correspondence shows that he also negotiated diplomatic marriages with another Mittanni princess (Tadu-Heba), two Babylonian ones, and one from the southern Anatolian state of Arzawa. Amenhotep III requested female personnel from his vassals as well. A letter to the king of Gezer in Palestine demanded on top of the tribute "40 female cupbearers, 40 shekels of silver being the price of a female cupbearer. Send extremely beautiful female cupbearers in whom there is no defect, so the king, your lord, will say to you: 'This is excellent, in accordance with the order I gave you'."[8]

The king's court

Multiple sources reveal the names and functions of officials from the last decade of Amenhotep III's reign. Many of them were engaged in the organization of the *sed*-festivals and used seals with their names to account for deliveries of goods. As was the case in other reigns, some officials became exceedingly influential, and in Amenhotep III's time such a person was Amenhotep son of Hapu. Although he never held the highest offices in the land, he yielded much influence by supervising Amenhotep III's building projects. He oversaw the quarrying, transport, and final positioning of many royal statues including the Colossi of Memnon. He also played a prominent role in the *sed*-festivals and was princess Satamun's steward. In return the king awarded him many honors and allowed him to set up many statues. Amenhotep son of Hapu died in Amenhotep III's 34th year at the age of 80. The king established a mortuary temple for him near his own, and set aside funds to pay for a workforce that

Figure 8.3   Detail of the decoration of Ramose's tomb. © 2010. Photo Scala, Florence

was still active 300 years later. This led to a veneration of Amenhotep son of Hapu like that of Imhotep of the Old Kingdom (see Chapter 3), with whom he became associated. In Greek times Amenhotep son of Hapu was honored as a healing god, and his name may be reflected in the later mortuary temple of Rameses III, to which Arabic tradition ascribed the designation Medinet Habu, that is, City of Habu.

Other officials too acquired so much wealth and royal favor that they could commission statuary and elaborate tombs. One of the most famous official's tombs in western Thebes belongs to a vizier of Amenhotep III who survived into Akhenaten's reign: Ramose (TT 55). Although left unfinished, the tomb is spectacular in the decoration of its large entrance hall. It displays an almost unique mixture of carved reliefs and painted scenes, all of the highest quality (Figure 8.3). Recent archaeological work has unearthed several tombs of Amenhotep III's officials at the northern capital of Memphis, near Djoser's complex in Saqqara. Those too show the enormous wealth available to the Egyptian elites. So little information is available about the general population, however, that we have no idea whether this wealth trickled down to them.

8.3   From Amenhotep III to Amenhotep IV/Akhenaten

Amenhotep III died in his 38th year of rule, still not that old as he had started his reign as a child. Many historians think that he was in poor health, although the evidence is very tangential. Some suggest that his mummy shows that he was a "fat, bald, old man, who had spent the last years of his life in luxury and indolence,"[9] but the identity of his mummy is uncertain.

The new king – named Amenhotep IV at first – was absent from the record until he ascended the throne but for one mention of his estate. There is much debate about when his rule started. Some suggest he was Amenhotep III's co-regent for up to 12 years; others think Amenhotep III died before his son took over. Art historians especially argue for co-regency because this would explain the mixture in artistic styles that is visible in certain monuments that seem to date to Amenhotep III's reign. Decoration in the tomb of the official Nefersekheru (TT 107), who clearly refers to Amenhotep III in his titles, already shows the artistic innovations that Amenhotep IV introduced. Because these innovations are so closely associated with the new king, their appearance in the reign of Amenhotep III suggests that the younger king had an influence. But other explanations for the mixture of styles are possible. Many representations of Amenhotep III and Tiye were excavated at the new city Amenhotep IV built from his fifth year onward, Akhetaten, which some scholars interpret as evidence that the royal pair dwelled there, while others see it as a sign of Amenhotep IV's devotion to his parents.

Proponents of the co-regency argue that the overlap allows us to relate events of Amenhotep III's last decade to those of Amenhotep IV's early years. For example, Amenhotep IV celebrated *sed*-festivals for the god Aten, including in his second or third year. One of these celebrations could have been the same event as Amenhotep III's *sed*-festival of year 34. Or, if the co-regency was only two years long, as some argue, the *sed*-festival for Aten would have been a continuation of the series Amenhotep III had initiated at the end of his reign with three-year intervals. Amenhotep IV's reforms, which promoted the sun disk Aten over all other gods of Egypt and which we will explore further below, could coincide with Amenhotep III's self-deification. The latter called himself "the radiant solar disk," that is, Aten (the Egyptian word for "solar disk" is Aten). In this interpretation, the son actively participated in the glorification of the father as sun god. Some scholars take this idea even further and suggest that Amenhotep IV's cult of Aten was a simple admiration for his father. They point out that the name Aten, which was pronounced *yāti*, sounded much like the Egyptian word for father, perhaps pronounced *yāta*, and in texts of the period the Aten is often connected to the idea of father.

Other scholars, especially those working with written sources, see no conclusive evidence for co-regency, certainly not one that lasted more than a couple years. All evidence adduced in favor of the theory can be explained otherwise. These scholars consider Amenhotep IV to have initiated his reforms independently from his father's and point out that the ideas were fundamentally different. Amenhotep III associated himself with many gods, especially the old and prominent gods Amun and Ra. Amenhotep IV promoted one god only, the sun disk, Aten. His father may have likened himself to the Aten, but he did not exclude other gods from the cult as Amenhotep IV would do. Whatever the answer – and I will follow those who see no co-regency – Amenhotep IV respected his parents greatly. He commissioned many representations of them, including at Soleb, where he is shown honoring his deified father, and at Akhetaten, where many representations of Queen Tiye were on display.

8.4 Akhenaten

The succession at the death of Amenhotep III seems to have been one of the least problematic of the 18th dynasty, as an adult son of the king and his main wife Tiye was alive and no one else claimed the throne. But those who try to write about the incumbent's reign face more unresolved questions than for any other king of Egypt's ancient history that range from basic facts, such as the identity of an individual, to the interpretation of a new religious ideology. King Amenhotep IV, who later became King Akhenaten, is probably the Egyptian who has elicited most modern fascination. His visual remains alone startle because of their unusual rendering of the human body, disregarding the canon of other periods of Egyptian art. The disorienting effect is much amplified by the abundance and the size of some of the works. People who visit Egyptian museum collections often find fragments of Akhenaten's buildings, colorful blocks with vivid reliefs, tens of thousands of which exist all over the world. Travelers to Cairo can see colossal statues of the king whose strange physique towers over them in massive proportions. These startling images are just the tip of the iceberg. A study of Akhenaten's history is filled with curious events and ideas.

The many unresolved questions make any reconstruction of Akhenaten's reign speculative, and specialists and others disagree vociferously on almost everything. Some basic facts are certain, however. Amenhotep IV or Akhenaten ruled for 17 years, he was married to Queen Nefertiti, and he instituted religious changes. We also know that whatever he did was later resented and that his successors tried to reverse his reforms. The details are much less clear; the following is one possible account.

Theban years (years 1 to 5)

When the new king ascended the throne, his official birth name (nomen, see Chapter 1) was Amenhotep, incorporating the name of the main Theban god Amun. From the start of his reign Amenhotep IV's main wife was Nefertiti,

Plate 1 Archetypical representation of a Nubian from the palace of Rameses III at Tell el-Yahudiyya. akg-images/Erich Lessing

Plate 2 Archetypical representation of a Syrian from the palace of Rameses III at Tell el-Yahudiyya. akg-images/Erich Lessing

Plate 3 Unidentified 1st-dynasty king with crown of Upper Egypt, wearing the *sed*-festival robe. Werner Forman Archive/British Museum, London

Plate 4 Official Hesira shown here with the tools of a scribe hanging over his shoulders.
Werner Forman Archive/Egyptian Museum, Cairo

Plate 5 Stone head of King Amenemhat III. Werner Forman Archive/Ny Carlsberg Glyptotek, Copenhagen

Plate 6 Mummy mask from Mirgissa near the second cataract. Louvre, Paris/The Bridgeman Art Library

Plate 7 Hatshepsut in the form of Osiris. Werner Forman Archive/Egyptian Museum, Cairo

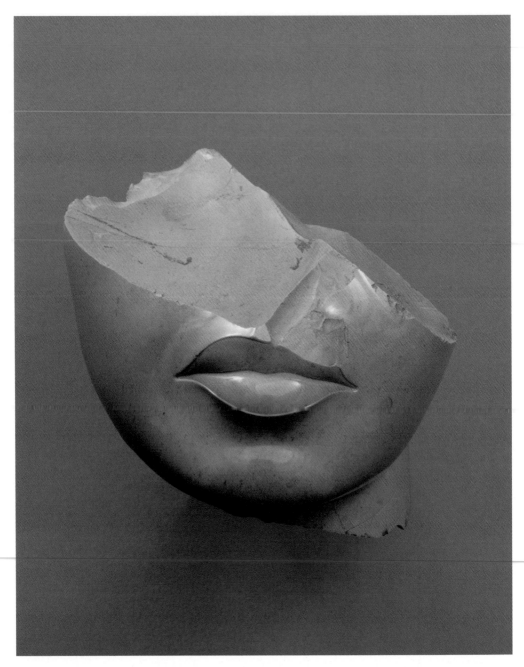

Plate 8 Fragment of the face of a woman, possibly Queen Tiye. Metropolitan Museum of Art, New York. Purchase, Edward S. Harkness Gift, 1926. Acc.n.: 26.7.1396. Photo: Bruce White. © 2010. Image copyright The Metropolitan Museum of Art/Art Resource/Scala, Florence

Plate 9   Golden death mask of Khaemwaset, son of Rameses II. akg-images/Erich Lessing

Plate 10 Golden mask of Psusennes I. Werner Forman Archive/Egyptian Museum, Cairo

Plate 11 Head of Wesirwer, Priest of the God Montu during the 30th dynasty. Brooklyn Museum of Art, New York/Charles Edwin Wilbour Fund/The Bridgeman Art Library

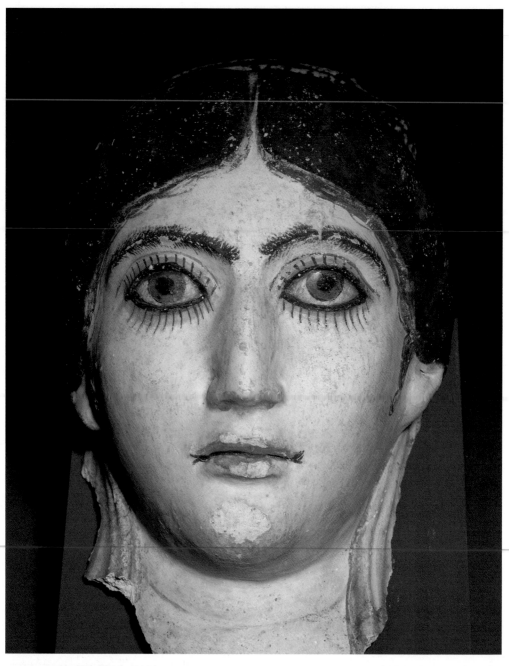

Plate 12 The waning of Egyptian culture? Mummy mask in Greco-Roman style from the 2nd century AD. Akg-images/Erich Lessing

whose family is unknown. Amenhotep IV's mother Tiye had been very prominent in public life, but her status was still secondary to her husband's. Nefertiti
seems to have achieved full equal status to her husband and the two are shown
together in various official contexts (on parade, interacting with officials, etc.).
Images of the couple suggest (in our eyes at least) remarkable intimacy. They
appear kissing each other, a royal image unprecedented in Egyptian art. There
are many family scenes that portray the couple with an increasing number of
children, all of them girls. In total they would have six daughters. Because of
Nefertiti's prominence in public images, we tend to assume that she was closely
involved with her husband's ideological reforms, but no explicit evidence for
that exists.

Although Amenhotep IV and Nefertiti treated Thebes as the religious center
of Egypt early on in the reign, they had an unusual attitude toward the god
Amun, who had been so central to Amenhotep III's royal ideology. Outside the
reference in the king's birth name, the god did not appear in the royal titulary.
The king commissioned a building to the east of Amun's temple at Karnak
devoted to another god: Aten, who was Ra-Harakhty in the visible form of the
solar disk. Amenhotep III had equated himself with the sun disk; Amenhotep
IV elevated it to a status above Amun. The cult of Aten would define the latter's reign, during which ideas about Aten constantly developed. Already in
Thebes Aten was special. The god's name and titles uniquely appeared in two
cartouches indicating that he was king, and in his second or third year Amenhotep
IV celebrated a *sed*-festival for the god and himself. Queen Nefertiti placed
Neferneferuaten, which means something like "The most perfect is Aten,"
before her name, and an area in Aten's temple in Karnak was devoted to her
alone. Aten was still a traditional god in some respects, however. Early representations show him as a falcon-headed man with a sun disk on his head.

The royal couple demanded the fast construction of new buildings, and
to accommodate this a new technique was introduced. Instead of massive
blocks of stone whose transport and setting in place was cumbersome and time-
consuming, the builders used smaller blocks. Today we call them *talatat* from
the Arabic word "three," a term modern Egyptian workmen invented based on
their length of three hand spans. The blocs measure 20.5 by 10 by 9.4 inches
(52 by 26 by 24 centimeters) and weigh about 110 pounds (50 kilograms).
Builders handled them more easily and could construct walls rapidly by lining
mud-brick cores on both sides with *talatats*. Sculptors afterwards carved reliefs
in the walls, which painters decorated with bright colors (Figure 8.4). Tens
of thousands of *talatats* are preserved, because later Egyptians took apart
Amenhotep IV's constructions and recycled the blocks, turning the painted
sides to the center and thus protecting the colors. Most of the *talatats* recovered
from Karnak were reused in massive pylons (the 2nd, 9th, and 10th) built under
King Horemheb.

In his third to fifth years Amenhotep IV's religious changes became more
intense. The representations of the god Aten became unique for ancient Egypt,
no longer a falcon-headed human but only a sun disk with the rays ending in

Figure 8.4 *Talatat* showing King Akhenaten sacrificing a duck. Metropolitan Museum of Art, New York. Gift of Norbert Schimmel, 1985. Acc.n.: 1985.328.2 © 2010. Image copyright The Metropolitan Museum of Art/Art Resource/Scala, Florence

little hands. The changes affected every aspect of life: religion, art, language, and the economy. The temples of traditional gods were closed and their priesthood re-schooled in the new ideology. These reforms cannot have been unopposed as they upset powerful lobbies, and we think Amenhotep IV relied on the army to carry them out. Only this sector of society had the political weight and the necessary labor force to undertake the building and other activities. This was a period of little military activity (only one campaign in Nubia is recorded), but Amenhotep IV emphasized the army's importance in Egyptian life and – unusually – represented soldiers in many scenes of life at Amarna.

Akhetaten (years 5 to 12)

In his fifth year Amenhotep IV changed his birth name to Akhenaten, which can be translated in various ways, including "Beneficial to Aten," "Whom Aten uses," "Radiance of Aten," or "effective spirit of the Aten." In any case, Amun disappeared from the king's name and titles. The king also abandoned Thebes as the religious capital and founded an entirely new city to its north at a previously uninhabited site, called Amarna today. By locating the new city halfway between the two traditional centers of power, Thebes and Memphis, the king distanced himself from the elites who had previously run the state. Akhenaten named the city Akhetaten, "Horizon of Aten" and inscriptions on steles set up at its boundaries proclaimed that he planned it personally with advice from the god. The city was large and laid out as a monument for the celebration of god and king. We have to see it as a huge example of conspicuous display of wealth, which was only possible because of the empire's existence. Although built with *talatats* and mud brick it still represents a vast architectural achievement accomplished in a few years.

In the center of town was a great temple to Aten, in form unlike most other Egyptian temples because it was devoted to a solar deity. Because Aten had no statues and was the sun disk, the temple had no roof but a large courtyard with an altar in the open. The city was also the showcase for the king. He paraded from his residential palace in the northern sector to the center, where he fulfilled his public duties. Images show him, Nefertiti, and their daughters at the "Window of Appearances," a balcony from which they showered gifts onto officials. The images appear in these very officials' tombs, proclaiming how the royal family was the source of their happiness and wealth. Also there we find versions of the most important written statement about the new religion, "The Great Hymn to Aten" (Sources in Translation 8.1). It and other texts from Amarna represent an innovation in Egyptian cultural history: the language used was not the classical Middle Egyptian of earlier literature, but the vernacular of the time. The hymn presents Aten as the sole force of order and prosperity. When the sun is down fear and chaos rule the world, but at dawn Aten chases away the dangers and makes life possible. He is the creator of humans, animals, and the entire world: Egypt, Syria, and Nubia all depend on Aten.

With the move to Akhetaten, Akhenaten no longer just ignored the other gods of Egypt, but started to persecute them, especially Amun, whose name and images he had removed. This even affected the way people wrote. Instead of using ideograms that represented a divine name, such as Mut, the scribes spelled the consonants phonetically. Aten was not just the most important god; he was the only god. Was this monotheism? The answer depends on one's interpretation of that religious concept, but Akhenaten's ideas certainly stressed the idea of a god with "no other beside him." Aten did not even have a female companion or opponents. How this affected the general population of Egypt is unclear. Akhenaten always showed himself and his family alone as honoring the god, and court officials as benefiting from the Aten through the mediation of the royal family. There is evidence, however, that individuals of different social classes could communicate with the god directly. Yet, many people continued their previous religious practices in private, although no official cults but Aten's were tolerated.

Akhenaten's frantic building activity also had a revolutionary impact on representation in Egyptian art, which is visible from the start of his reign. From the Early Dynastic Period on Egyptian art had been characterized by rigorous schematization. Akhenaten discarded many of the conventions and introduced new stylistic features, which according to a graffito of the chief sculptor Bak "his Majesty himself taught."[10] Amarna art, as we call it today, startles in its representation of the human body, especially that of the members of the royal family. The faces are elongated, the lips thick, the neck long, the belly protruding, and the hips wide. Gender distinctions were partly eliminated, and many see in

Sources in Translation 8.1
Hymn to Aten

The Great Hymn to Aten honors that god as the creator of the universe and as the most important force in nature. It portrays the daily cycle of the sun as a sequence of times of chaos at night and of order and happiness during the daytime. The language vividly contrasts the two situations in this passage from the start of the hymn.

> When you set in the western horizon,
> Earth is in darkness as if in death;
> One sleeps in chambers, heads covered,
> One eye does not see another.
> Were they robbed of their goods
> That were under their heads,
> People would not notice it.
> Every lion comes out from its den,
> All the snakes bite;
> Darkness hovers, and earth is silent;
> As the one who created all things rests in the horizon.
>
> Earth brightens when you dawn in the horizon
> When you shine as Aten of daytime:
> As you dispel darkness,
> As you cast your rays,
> The Two Lands are in festivity.
> Awake and stand on their feet,
> As you have roused them.
> Bodies are cleansed and dressed,
> Their arms held high in adoration of your appearance.
> The entire land set out to work.
> All beasts browse on their pastures,
> Trees and vegetation are sprouting;
> Birds fly from their nests,
> Their wings greeting your *ka*;
> All flocks frisk on their feet,
> And all who fly up and alight,
> They live when you dawn for them.
> Ships sail downstream and upstream,
> The roads lie open when you rise;
> The fish in the river leap before you,
> And your rays are in the midst of the sea.[11]

An important aspect of the composition is its connection to King Akhenaten. The text ends with the statement that only he knows Aten and in return asks the god to give him counsel. This statement has led some Egyptologists to believe that Akhenaten himself composed the hymn, something we can only conjecture.

Special Topic 8.1   *The city of Akhetaten*

Akhetaten is the only city in ancient Egypt for which we know the entire layout. Akhenaten planned It early in his reign, and no subsequent occupation covered up the ruins when the city was abandoned some 20 years later. Although all stone buildings were dismantled, we can still reconstruct their plans on the basis of the remains of mud-brick walls and foundations.

Akhetaten covered a large area of about 10 by 8 miles (16 by 13 kilometers). Much of the area on the Nile's west bank was intended for agriculture and the fields there could support an estimated 45,000 people. The urban core was located on the east bank. It was a four-mile- (six-kilometer-) long stretch of official buildings and residential districts for the king's courtiers and support staff connected by a 100-feet- (30-meter-) wide royal road that ran parallel to the Nile. The king's residence was situated on the northern edge of the city by the riverbank. When he traveled to his working quarters in the city center he passed through a residential area (the so-called North Suburb) and a sacred zone with ceremonial palaces and the great Aten temple. Depictions of the journey show it as a procession with people lining the road to honor the king. His destination was the town center where – according to depictions – the royal family handed out gifts to the state officials from the "Window of Appearances," probably in a building called "The King's House." The royal north-to-south journey coincided with the sun's movement from east to west, reaching the high point of the day over the town center, where Aten's temple was located. King and god acted as one at that moment. At the end of the day they both retired and their beneficent powers receded.

The southern part of the city included a zone for relaxation with gardens. On the eastern edge of the town the tombs of officials were located and farther away in the eastern mountains the king's tomb. The eastern location breaks with the predominant tradition to place tombs on the west bank in the direction of the sunset. Akhenaten placed them where the sun rose, perhaps so that the dead could benefit from Aten's presence throughout the day.

The city's construction must have continued throughout Akhenaten's reign, and many houses in town belonged to craftsmen active in the project. They and officials of state lived in residences that ideally stood alone surrounded by a wall. The house plans were standardized, and distinctions in wealth were indicated by the size of the houses. Many houses contained silos for grain and a place where one could keep small livestock. There was no clear distinction in wealth from neighborhood to neighborhood: large and small houses were mixed. In the east of the city, however, was a workers' village that was very clearly planned and surrounded by a wall. Some 70 houses of the same size and layout were laid out along five north–south streets. In one of the corners was a larger house, which probably belonged to the overseer.

Akhenaten's statues and reliefs an effeminate body. Art historians and others have debated the intent of these depictions at length. Did Akhenaten and his family truly look like this, and if so why (numerous theories of Akhenaten's exotic illnesses circulate), or do we see representations that are as conventional and artificial as the traditional form in Egyptian art? Amarna art is truly innovative in some of the scenes it depicts. In no other period do we see such intimacy among royal family members and scenes of daily life are much more vivid now than in other periods. The sculptors of Egypt had to learn the new style quickly to produce an enormous output, and archaeologists have found several models with details of the human body, including images of hands in various postures. Most famous today is the model head of Nefertiti, discovered in the house of sculptor Thutmose and now in Berlin's Egyptian Museum.

The focus on religion should not make us forget that Akhetaten was an imperial capital. The center contained buildings with offices of various government departments, including the "Bureau of the correspondence of Pharaoh," that is, the place where the king's international correspondence on clay tablets was written and archived. The court's move to Akhetaten probably caused sweeping changes in the country's bureaucracy. The old families from Thebes and Memphis that had provided bureaucrats in the past seem to have been sidelined, while the king reaffirmed his grip on the administration. He was the source of all power and wealth, and in the houses at Amarna people kept little shrines in his honor. Akhenaten was not a weak king; on the contrary he must have been very confident in order to implement his reforms.

Turmoil (years 12 to 17)

The last official inscribed monuments of Akhenaten's reign are reports of a minor military campaign in Nubia and tribute lists from the 12th year. The remaining five years were a time of turmoil and there is much confusion about events, as it seems that individuals changed names and new people with political influence arose (see Key Debate 8.1). A few elements are certain: Nefertiti, who had been the king's equal partner with great religious importance, disappeared from the record and Akhenaten had a new female partner. There is no sign that he abandoned his beliefs, and although he stayed in Akhetaten until his death he seems not to have been buried near his capital. Many scholars believe his mummy was placed in a tomb in the Kings' Valley at Thebes (KV 55), although this remains contested.

Akhenaten's successors

Matters do not become clearer with Akhenaten's successors. First a person named Neferneferuaten became king, perhaps originally as co-regent. The feminine form of her throne name (Ankhetkheperura) shows she was a woman, but who exactly she was scholars much debate. A man with the same throne name (Ankhkheperura) succeeded her; his second cartouche contained the name Smenkhkara. He was probably the husband of Akhenaten's eldest daughter, Meritaten, who thus legitimized his rule. Aten's cult still had royal support, and the king continued to reside at Akhetaten.

The next king was one of ancient Egypt's most famous, not for anything he did in life, but for his tomb: Tutankhamun. He was a young boy when he became king, at most ten years old, and already married to Akhenaten's daughter Ankhesenpaaten. He started his career as Tutankhaten, but his reign marks the return to primacy of the god Amun. Soon the king's name became Tutankhamun and he left Akhetaten for the old administrative capital of Memphis. A stele found at Karnak declared the restoration of traditional cults like Amun's and promised the king's continued support (see Sources in Translation 8.2).

The powers behind Tutankhamun's throne were old officials: Ay, whose wife had been Queen Nefertiti's wet-nurse, and Horemheb, a military commander. The latter started a lavish tomb in Saqqara during Tutankhamun's reign. His skills were needed as at this time the Hittite threat in Syria increased and Egypt had to reassert its authority there. Tutankhamun died young, after ten years of rule. His burial has made him known to anyone with even the slightest interest in ancient Egypt. His small tomb in the Valley of the Kings – some say it was not even intended as a royal tomb – was packed with grave goods including vast amounts of gold, other metals, and semi-precious stones, fashioned into the most exquisite works of craftsmanship and art (Figure 8.5). Tutankhamun's tomb was surely not exceptional in the amount of goods the king received; its uniqueness comes from the fact that looters did not find its treasures, which remained untouched until the early 20th century AD.

Tutankhamun's death led to a power struggle at court. It may have been his widow Ankhesenpaaten, renamed Ankhesenamun, who sought an alliance with the Hittite King Suppiluliuma through marriage. Tutankhamun's first successor, Ay, was already an old man when he became king. He may have taken advantage of Horemheb's absence in Syria to lead Tutankhamun's funeral and claim the throne. He ruled four years at most.

General Horemheb, whom Tutankhamun had designated his second-in-command, succeeded Ay and expressed his displeasure at having been upstaged by removing the latter's name from monuments. He completed the closing stages of the Amarna revolution. Although the Aten cult survived, it was just one of many and Amun's prominence was restored. Horemheb revived the Opet festival to emphasize how Amun had selected him as king, and may have married Nefertiti's sister to legitimize his rule. Thus he was still connected to the royal family that made up the 18th dynasty, albeit it in a tenuous way. Horemheb started the process of removing the Amarna kings – from Akhenaten to Ay – from memory. In the succeeding 19th dynasty the idea developed that no legitimate king had existed between Amenhotep III and Horemheb. Records

Sources in Translation 8.2

The Restoration Stele of Tutankhamun

In Tutankhamun's reign the court restored the traditional cults of Egypt and announced this policy on steles set up throughout the land. One such stele was erected in the temple of Amun at Karnak, and its creators gave much care to the physical appearance of the inscription. The stone was red granite and the hieroglyphs originally were inlaid with blue paste, traces of which survive. Not that much later Horemheb usurped the inscription substituting his name wherever Tutankhamun's appeared, because by then the latter was seen as a participant in the Amarna revolution. The text compares the sorry situation of Egypt and its temples under Akhenaten to the new situation in Tutankhamun's reign, when the king devoted more resources to the gods' statues than ever before.

> When his Majesty appeared as king, the temples and the cities of the gods and goddesses, starting from Elephantine and down to the Delta marshes ... had fallen into decay, and their shrines were in ruin, becoming mounds of rubble, overgrown with weeds. Their sanctuaries were like something that had not existed and their temples were a footpath – for the land was wrecked and ruined. The gods ignored this land. If an army was sent to Djahy (= Syria) to widen the boundaries of Egypt, no success occurred. If one prayed to a god to ask something, he did not come at all; and if one implored any goddess in the same way, she did not come at all. Their hearts were weak because of their bodies, and they destroyed what was made.
>
> But after time passed his Majesty appeared upon the throne of his father and he ruled over the shores of Horus (= Egypt). The Black Land (= Nile Valley) and the Red Land (= desert) were under his supervision, and every land was bowing to his might.
>
> When his Majesty was in his palace, which is in the domain of Aakheperkara (= Thutmose I), like the god Ra in heaven, his Majesty was governing the land and managing the daily affairs of the two shores. Then, his Majesty took counsel with his heart, investigating every excellent deed, seeking benefactions for his father, the god Amun, and fashioning his noble image out of genuine electrum. He gave more than what had been done before: he fashioned an image of his father, the god Amun, to be upon thirteen carrying-poles, his sacred image being of electrum, lapis-lazuli, turquoise, and every precious stone. Now, the Majesty of this noble god had formerly been upon only eleven carrying-poles.[12]

Figure 8.5 Alabaster vessel from Tutankhamun's tomb. akg-images/Erich Lessing

of that time use dates suggesting that Horemheb succeeded Amenhotep III directly.

Horemheb selected as heir his vizier, Paramesu, who succeeded him after a reign about which we have little information; we do not know its exact length. Paramesu ascended the throne as Rameses I, the first king of a new dynasty. He and his descendants saw Horemheb as the start of a new era and they continued the long struggle over Akhenaten's memory.

8.5 Akhenaten's Memory

Horemheb had started the removal of Akhenaten's name from inscriptions and began to use his many buildings as stone quarries for his own projects. In Karnak he filled several pylons of the Amun temple with *talatats* recovered from Akhenaten's Aten temple. Later kings continued the practice, and the stone of Akhetaten was especially useful to Rameses II, who commissioned massive building projects in Hermopolis nearby. The 19th-dynasty kings ignored Akhenaten and his three successors in their king lists: when Sety I depicted himself making offerings to a long list of earlier rulers of Egypt, he jumped from Amenhotep III to Horemheb.

Yet, Akhenaten had promoted his ideas long and forcefully enough that they could not be fully erased. The use of Late Egyptian as the language of literature rather than classical Middle Egyptian persisted. Although Akhenaten disappeared from the official record, except with the soubriquet "evil one of Akhetaten," his memory did not totally vanish. The third-century-BC historian Manetho listed four kings between Amenhotep III and Horemheb. Akhenaten seems to have appeared as Akherres or Akhenkheres. The first-century-AD historian Josephus quoted other passages from Manetho, which many Egyptologists think refer to Akhenaten as well, albeit in a very garbled way. Josephus carried on Manetho's tales about the Hyksos (see Chapter 6) with an account of King Amenophis whose advisor Amenophis, son of Papis, told him to banish all of Egypt's lepers to Avaris. The lepers organized under a priest Osarsiph, who forbade them to worship ancient gods, and invited the Hyksos back to Egypt, chasing King Amenophis south. Together they ruled Egypt for 13 years before Amenophis and his son Rhampses liberated the country. According to Josephus Osarsiph renamed himself Moses. The king and counselor called Amenophis must refer to Amenhotep III and his advisor Amenhotep, son of Hapu, well known in Manetho's time. Consequently, Osarsiph could be Akhenaten or a man close to him. Osarsiph's rejection of Egyptian gods may refer to Akhenaten's religious ideas and the story of a 13-year period of mismanagement of Egypt to that king's reign. Scholars have different opinions about exactly what historical events Josephus's account recalls, but many see a lingering memory of Akhenaten and his unpopular rule in the tale.

Be this as it may, the link between Akhenaten and the biblical Moses has turned the king into a crucial figure in the history of world religions, as the possible inspiration of Mosaic monotheism. Some Egyptologists have emphasized the exclusionary character of the worship of Aten and have compared the way Akhenaten presented him to the depiction of God in the Hebrew Bible. Unique among Egyptian gods Aten was not represented as a human or animal; the biblical God could not be shown at all. The great hymn to Aten resembles in some ways Psalm 104, which honors the biblical God. Other elements can be adduced. So some – Egyptologists and others – suggest that Akhenaten inspired Moses and that he was at the basis of pure monotheism. Sigmund Freud's last published work, *Moses and Monotheism*, saw Moses as a member of Akhenaten's court who elaborated the religious ideas after his master's downfall. In this investigation of the roots of anti-Semitism he compared the rejection of Aten's worship to modern rejections of Jewish monotheism.

But others as well, often with radically opposing ideologies, have chosen Akhenaten as their idol in scholarly and non-scholarly writings, music, art and popular culture. Akhenaten has been portrayed as a pacifist, a great black African ruler, the first individual in history, a freak with physical deformities, a sexual deviant, and in many other forms. He intrigues because he is mysterious. We read in him our own ideas on religion, revolution, idiosyncrasy, and other concerns. He deserves the fascination he elicits, but we have to remain aware of the fact that our preconceptions dictate what he means to each one of us.

Key Debate 8.1   *The end of the Amarna Period*

If there are many questions about events in the beginning of Akhenaten's reign, they become even more numerous in the later part and in the years immediately following his death. A few facts seem clear. Nefertiti, who had been consistently at his side, disappeared from the record after Akhenaten's 12th year. Akhenaten lived for another five years and probably died in his 17th year of rule. One or two rulers late in his life and afterward held the throne name Neferneferuaten, and the birth names of two of his successors were Smenkhkara and Tutankhamun. Numerous other names appear in the record, however, and there is much confusion about what happened in the decade or so from Akhenaten's 12th year to Tutankhamun's death (Vandersleyen 1995: 449–57; Gabolde 1998; Eaton-Krauss & Krauss 2001).

What happened to Nefertiti? Since there is no evidence that she died before Akhenaten (Krauss 1997), most scholars believe she lost her status to another wife called Kiya whom Akhenaten had married before (Hornung 1999c: 107–8), probably in the hope of fathering a son after Nefertiti bore him daughters only (Allen 2009). Several scholars think Kiya was the princess Tadu-Heba, one of the Mittanni women Amenhotep III had brought to Egypt (Gabolde 1998: 279; 2001: 20). Others believe, however, that Nefertiti became Akhenaten's co-regent under the throne name Neferneferuaten, a name she held before as epithet (Harris 1973). This had to be a woman because it appeared with the feminine term Ankhetkheprura (Vandersleyen 1995: 452–3). But Nefertiti's burial goods do not refer to her as pharaoh, only as king's wife (Allen 2009), so other women have been suggested as

Akhenaten's late co-regent Neferneferuaten. His daughter Meritaten is a likely candidate (Gabolde 1998: 183–5; 2001: 27–8). Akhenaten had a daughter who was called Neferneferuaten from birth, however, and why would she not have been his co-regent late in life (Allen 2009)?

The highest attested date for Neferneferuaten is year 3, which means that she was Akhenaten's co-regent for a maximum period of three years or succeeded him for at most that long. Another person, however, male this time, used the name Neferneferuaten as well, and many scholars believe that was Smenkhkara (Schneider 1994: 260), Meritaten's husband who succeeded his father-in-law (Clayton 1994: 124). Some scholars argue that Meritaten was the widow who asked for a Hittite prince in marriage, and that Smenkhkara was Zannanza, who would not have been assassinated as the Hittites reported (Gabolde 1998: 221–4).

Smenkhkara's successor was the boy-king Tutankhamun, who was married to another daughter of Akhenaten, Ankhesenpaaten (Clayton 1994: 126). Because he appeared once with the title king's son, some scholars argue that he was the son of Akhenaten and Nefertiti (Gabolde 1998: 279), but a son-in-law could hold that title as well (Franke 1986: 1033), and there is no need to imagine that the royal couple managed to produce a son late in life. Many historians think that it was Tutankhamun's widow who contacted the Hittite king for a husband (Clayton 1994: 135) and that the aged bureaucrat Ay or general Horemheb foiled her plans and by seizing kingship ended the Amarna age. After this happened at least the question of who held kingship became clearer.

NOTES

1. Moran 1992: 39 (EA 16).
2. Moran 1992: 9 (EA 4).
3. Translation after Güterbock 1956: 94.
4. Translation after Blankenberg-Van Delden 1969: 16.
5. Kemp 2006: 272; see also L. Bell 1985: 254.
6. B. Davies 1992: 10. A *deben* weighs approximately 90 grams.
7. Translation after Blankenberg-Van Delden 1969: 18.
8. Moran 1992: 366 (EA 369).
9. Redford 1984: 52.
10. See Aldred 1988: 93–4.
11. Translation after Lichtheim 1976: 97.
12. Translation after Murnane 1995: 213.

9

The Ramessid Empire
(ca. 1295–1203)

Steady, steady your hearts, my soldiers!
See me victorious, me alone –
For the god Amun is my helper, his hand is with me.
How faint are your hearts, my charioteers!
None among you is worthy of trust!
(Rameses II to his soldiers)[1]

In the list of famous pharaohs Rameses II has a special place. Many regard him as the greatest warrior of Egypt's history, an impression he himself much promoted. Gigantic battle scenes grace the walls of his monuments, which are among the most impressive of Egyptian antiquity. We speak of the Ramessid Period after New Kingdom Egypt recovered from the confusion of the Amarna revolution, the period of the 19th and 20th dynasties. Many kings were called Rameses between 1295 and 1069, but it is Rameses II who gave the era its name. The nine successors who adopted the name, Rameses III through XI of the 20th dynasty, did so as a sign of admiration.

Was Rameses II really "Egypt's greatest pharaoh" as some have written? He stands out because of the length of his reign – 67 years – but in other cases (with Pepy II) this is seen as a negative rather than a positive element. His military exploits were impressive, but they did not surpass those of Thutmose III, for example. Rameses's self-presentation is what explains his fame. In texts and images he portrayed himself as a great warrior, who single-handedly gained victories. As the quote above asserts, his army did not help; on the contrary the king saved his cowardly soldiers. Rameses especially proclaimed this idea in his descriptions of one battle – the battle of Qadesh in 1275. He commissioned accounts of it in many places with detailed images and texts of high literary value. Qadesh has become one of the famous battles of the ancient world, and Rameses's declaration of victory is hard to ignore. But was this truly its real

Summary of dynastic history
Early 19th dynasty (ca. 1295–1203)

ca. 1295–1294	King Rameses I Crowned king after career in army and administration
ca. 1294–1279	King Sety I Campaigns in Syria, western desert, and Nubia Initiates much building activity Involves crown-prince Rameses in royal functions from year 7 on
ca. 1279–1213	King Rameses II Commissions massive building activity throughout Egypt and Nubia Fights Hittites in battle of Qadesh, 1275 Concludes peace treaty with Hittites, 1259 Marries Hittite princess, 1246 Receives cult as god while alive

significance? It may be more important to see Qadesh as an indication of a changing eastern Mediterranean world, one in which Rameses was perhaps more successful as diplomat and architect of a new imperial structure than as warrior.

In any case, Rameses's reign and the period around it represent the final phase of success for the Egyptian empire. The Ramessid Period indicated a full recovery from the confusion the Amarna revolution caused. Its kings returned the country to its former glory. For about a century, most of it under Rameses II's rule, Egypt continued to benefit from its empire. A large number of monuments and other sources from the period survive. Not only the king but also other members of the court and many officials commissioned numerous statues, steles, and other remains. They convey an image of great wealth and success.

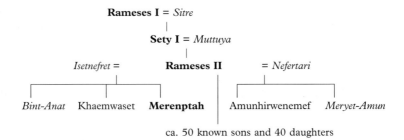

Tentative family tree of the early 19th dynasty (selected family members only)
Bold: kings; italics: queens; =: marriage

9.1   Domestic Policy: Restoration and Renewal

Horemheb's appointed successor, Rameses I, was not of royal blood but had made his career in the army and in the administration. When he ascended the throne the family connection with the 18th dynasty was broken completely and he initiated a new dynasty – the 19th in Manetho's count. He had little time to make an impression, however, dying after little more than a year of rule. For more than four decades at this point the political situation in Egypt had been unsettled. This ended with the next king, Sety I. Although his reign was relatively short at a probable 11 years, he was able to restore Egypt to its former glory.

Sety I

Sety started an enormous building program that was to last through the reign of his son Rameses II, who as crown prince already assisted his father. Many sculptors and builders were engaged in the restoration of temples that had suffered disrepair since Akhenaten's days. But Sety I also initiated projects that would set the standard for the future. The temple at Abydos was one of his most ambitious. At the main cult site of the god Osiris, Sety constructed a massive sanctuary that served as his mortuary temple but also contained six shrines for the main gods of Egypt. A seventh shrine was for the cult of the deceased king, who was buried in the Valley of the Kings at Thebes. The temple was thus in part a cenotaph to assure the king's place near Osiris (see Chapter 5). Behind it was the Osireion, a dummy tomb shaped like a royal tomb of the 18th dynasty. The entire temple at Abydos was a center for the cult of Osiris, and soon became a place of pilgrimage.

In the decoration of his Abydos temple Sety stressed his connection to the earlier kings of Egypt. In a corridor he depicted himself and crown prince Rameses making offerings to 75 earlier rulers represented by their cartouches. The list started with Menes, the legendary founder of the Egyptian state, and ended with Rameses I (Figure 9.1). It was not complete, however. Certain recent kings were omitted because they were considered to have been illegitimate: Hatshepsut and the four Amarna rulers. For earlier periods the rulers of the intermediate periods were also dropped and the focus was on the earliest kings of Egypt. The list contains 56 names from Menes to the end of the 8th dynasty. Sety's reign was a renaissance of Egypt's early grandeur.

With Sety I the god Amun's pre-eminence was fully reinstated, so the city of Thebes received much attention as well. The king expanded Amun's sanctuary at Karnak by constructing the hypostyle hall in front of the third pylon. He filled a massive area (large enough to fit Notre Dame of Paris) with rows of columns that supported a stone roof. The two rows of six columns of the central nave are 70 feet (21 meters) high and their tops in the form of open papyrus

Figure 9.1 King Sety I and crown prince Rameses offering to the earlier kings of Egypt. akg-images/Erich Lessing

plants have a diameter of 18 feet (5.4 meters). One hundred and twenty-two columns, that are 40 feet (12 meters) high and have closed-bud papyrus plants as capitals, flank the central rows.

One of Sety's most impressive architectural achievements was his tomb in the Kings' Valley (KV 17). This represented an important innovation in royal tombs. Earlier tombs had been decorated only in the main areas, but Sety's was the first in which all surfaces were covered with painted reliefs. The longest tomb of the valley, it was covered with two types of depictions: the king praying or offering before a god, and excerpts from various "books of the netherworld." Those were intended to aid the king in his dangerous travels to join the sun god Ra, whose daily cycle is a rebirth. The gods Ra and Osiris became fully interchangeable and joined as one in the netherworld.

Rameses II

Rameses II completed several projects of his father Sety, including the works at Abydos and Karnak, and he carried on massive building activity of his own There is virtually no site in Egypt and Nubia where he was not active. He left behind more monuments than any other Egyptian king. In order to achieve this he usurped works of earlier rulers and he used Akhenaten's buildings as stone quarries. Many of Akhetaten's *talatats* ended up in Rameses's constructions at Abydos and other sites in Middle Egypt. His most famous monument today is the temple at Abu Simbel, north of the second cataract in Lower Nubia. In order to cut its rooms 60 meters deep into the cliff of the Nile Valley architects must have explored the rock carefully in advance to see that there were no fault-lines. The innermost sanctuary contains the statues of the gods Ra-Harakhty, Amun-Ra, and Ptah, as well as King Rameses as god, and wall reliefs show the king and his queen, Nefertari, making offerings to these four. Rameses was thus a living god. He was not the first Egyptian king who claimed this status – Amenhotep III had identified himself with the divine solar disk (see Chapter 8) – but is perhaps the one for whom most evidence is preserved. All his temples in Lower Nubia express his self-proclamation as a god, and some monuments in Egypt itself – albeit fewer – indicate a cult for the living king. The idea arose after several years of rule, seemingly not before his eighth year. Work on the Abu Simbel temple started early in his reign and the first reliefs honor existing gods alone. At some point these were re-carved to show the king as a god. The smaller temple at Abu Simbel extends the deification to Queen Nefertari, who was identified there as the goddess Hathor (as had been the case with Amenhotep III's wife, Tiye).

Abu Simbel's popular fame derives from its facade with its four 69-feet- (21-meter-) high statues of the seated king. At his feet stand much smaller statues of his mother Muttuya, his queen Nefertari, and several sons and daughters, still larger than life size. The facade of the smaller temple in honor of Nefertari shows two statues of the queen each standing between two 33-feet- (10-meter-) high statues of the king. Any ship that passed this point on the Nile could not fail to see these grand monuments (Figure 9.2).

Rameses II's most elaborate project was probably the creation of a new capital in the eastern Delta, Piramesse or "House of Rameses." His father had already built a summer palace there, but Rameses created a giant city of some 1,000 hectares. When he did so he integrated in its confines earlier cities including Avaris, the capital of the Hyksos. Piramesse's current location beneath agricultural fields has made archaeological exploration difficult, and only some sectors are known. Moreover, when the city lost access to the river due to the shifting of its branches, 21st-dynasty kings moved farther northeast to Tanis and used the stones of Piramesse for their buildings. Little but foundations is left, and it is hard to reconstruct the glory of the city from them. We know about Piramesse from some written descriptions, however, and these contain much praise:

> I have arrived at Piramesse-beloved-of-Amun and found it in extremely good condition. It is a fine district, whose like does not exist, having the layout of Thebes. It was the god Ra himself who founded it. The residence is pleasant to live in – its countryside is full of everything good, and it has food and provisions

Figure 9.2 Rameses II's temple at Abu Simbel

every day. Its ponds have fishes; its pools have birds. … Its granaries are full of barley and emmer. … Its ships sail forth and moor so that foods and provisions are in it every day. Joy dwells in it, and no one says, "I wish I had" in it.[2]

As the working capital it contained a large palace and the find of a cuneiform tablet shows that the international correspondence of the time still used the same format as in the Amarna Period. Many temples stood in Piramesse. Another text states:

> Its west is the estate of the god Amun, the south is the estate of the god Seth, the goddess Astarte is in its east, and the goddess Wadjet is in its north.[3]

The mixture of deities is of interest: Amun, Seth, and Wadjet were traditional Egyptian gods, whereas Astarte was a goddess from Syria, attested in Egypt before but not with such prominence.

Another structure may surprise. In the northern part of town archaeologists found the remains of a garrison with a workshop to make and repair chariots and other equipment. The occupants were not Egyptians, however. Archaeologists found molds to make bronze shields shaped for the Hittite variety of that weapon, not the Egyptian. They also found evidence for glassmaking at the site, mostly crucibles, which show that this imported technology from Asia had become fully established in Egypt by the 19th dynasty.

Piramesse's buildings thus demonstrate close contacts with western Asia, as does its location in the eastern Delta. Although situated inland, it was Egypt's main sea harbor connected to the Mediterranean through river channels. Nineteenth-dynasty Egypt faced a different world in the north from before, as the Hittites had gained much ground in Syria. Rameses may have moved the capital nearer to Asia to face the challenge. Conversely, the Hittite presence in the city and further evidence of Asiatics and other foreigners show that people from the outside world played a great role in Egypt. International relations are the key to understanding what happened.

9.2 International Relations: Reforming the Empire

Wars in Syria

As we have seen, from the start of the New Kingdom Egyptian armies had campaigned often in the Levant as far north as northern Syria. By Amenhotep III's time this effort had paid off, and in his reign and that of Akhenaten Egypt's hold over the region was secure and required no military action. But by late in Akhenaten's time problems emerged. The Hittites under King Suppiluliuma gained influence after they established a secure foothold in northern Syria by annexing Mittanni territory. During the confusion after Akhenaten's death a queen, probably Tutankhamun's widow, tried to organize a diplomatic marriage between her and a Hittite prince, but the man was assassinated (see Chapter 8). Possibly in revenge Suppiluliuma intensified his Syrian campaigns, and Egyptian armies had to react. Suppiluliuma's successor Mursili II (ruled 1321–1295) continued his father's policy and asserted Hittite dominance as far south as Qadesh. This city had great strategic value as it controlled the crossing of two highways of northern Syria: the only inland road that ran from north to south along the Orontes River, and the west–east road from the northern Lebanese coast to the interior. Sety I came to the throne around the same time as the Hittite Muwatalli (ruled ca. 1295–1272), and both kings were intent on bolstering their presence in northern Syria. Muwatalli may even have moved his capital to southern Anatolia to serve as a base of operations – a move Rameses II imitated by founding Piramesse in the eastern Delta.

Sety I's reliefs depict him fighting several wars in Syria against Hittites and against the kings of Amurru and Qadesh. Many scholars see this as a disruption of the status quo, which counted the regions of Amurru and Qadesh as part of the Hittite zone of influence. Naturally Muwatalli reacted, and these kingdoms bore the major brunt of the competition, being forced to switch sides repeatedly. It is unlikely that the armies of the great kings confronted each other directly, however: Sety's reference to a battle against the Hittites is very vague and did not mention the Hittite ruler.

The conflict escalated under Rameses II. In his fourth year the Egyptian army marched along the Lebanese coast at least as far north as Byblos, but no details are known about what happened. The campaign of the next year has become the major military episode of Rameses's reign in modern imagination: it led to the battle of Qadesh of 1275. Rameses described and depicted the event numerous times. Two narratives exist, a poetic description found in eight places and a prose version repeated seven times. Moreover, large pictorial renderings were carved on five monuments as well. The details of the battle are well known, at least from the Egyptian point of view. The Hittites were mostly silent about it; in a later account of Muwatalli's reign his brother merely stated that the Hittites defeated the Egyptians.

Rameses described his army as made up of four divisions, each composed of infantry and chariotry and named after a god: Amun, Ra, Ptah, and Seth. As the king, at the head of the leading Amun division, approached Qadesh he met two Hittite soldiers who claimed to be deserters and gave the false information that the Hittites were near Aleppo, some 120 miles to the north. Rameses led his troops to the high ground northwest of Qadesh and set up camp to wait for the other divisions. His soldiers captured Hittite scouts who, after being beaten, revealed that the Hittite army was hiding behind Qadesh. Rameses sent a message to the rest of his troops to hurry up, but Hittite chariotry attacked the Ra division, still in marching formation, from the side. The Egyptians panicked and fled to Rameses's camp with Hittites in pursuit. When the king heard the news that Hittite chariots surrounded his camp, he broke out, singlehandedly killing vast numbers of enemies from his chariot. The description becomes fanciful in its praise of Rameses:

> Then, his Majesty advanced in a gallop, and he charged the forces of the enemies from Hatti, being alone by himself, none other with him. His Majesty proceeded to look around him. He found 2,500 chariots encircling him on his way out, the fast troops of the enemy from Hatti and the many countries who were with them – Arzawa, Masa, Pidasa, Keshkesh, Irun, Kizuwatna, Aleppo, Ugarit, Qadesh and Lukka, three men to a chariot acting together.

> No officer was with me, no charioteer
> No soldier of the army, no shield bearer;
> My infantry, my chariotry yielded before them,
> Not one of them stood firm to fight with them.
> His Majesty spoke: "What is this, my father Amun?
> Is it right for a father to ignore his son?
> ...
> What are these Asiatics to you, O Amun,
> These wretched ones, ignorant of god?
> Have I not made for you many great monuments,

Filling your temple with my plunder?
...

I sacrificed to you thousands of cattle,
And all kinds of sweet-scented herbs."
...

Now, though I prayed in the distant land,
My voice reached to Southern On (= Thebes)
I found that the god Amun came when I called him.
He gave me his hand and I rejoiced!
He called from behind as if near by:
"I am with you,
I am your father and my hand is with you.
I prevail over 100,000 men
I am lord of victory who loves courage!"
...

One called out to the other saying:
"No man is he who is among us,
It is the god Seth, Great-of-Strength, Baal himself.
The deeds of man are not his doing,
They are of the one who is unique,
Who fights hundreds of thousands without his army and chariotry!
Come quick, flee before him,
To seek life and breathe air . ...."[4]

Students of the battle think that it is more likely that auxiliary troops, depicted in the reliefs but not mentioned in the text, came to Rameses's aid. They also point out that the Hittites started to loot the camp before the battle was over to explain their rout. Rameses's account goes on to relate how the pharaoh continued to fight until the king of Hatti sent a letter suing for peace.

Most historians regard Rameses's claims of a great victory with some skepticism and argue that the battle was a draw at best. His later campaigns in Syria-Palestine only reached points farther south, and Egyptian influence over Amurru and Qadesh seems to have been lost forever.

How special was the battle of Qadesh? Perhaps it is only the amount of attention that Rameses paid to it that sets it apart, which scholars interpret in various ways. Some say the king wanted to discredit the army in a power struggle at home and showed the soldiers as cowards whom he personally saved. Others think the king really changed the course of battle and wanted to explain the army's safe return. He certainly seems to have believed the story. In a later letter to the Hittite King Hattusili III he repeats the ideas that he was cheated and that he single-handedly gained victory (See Sources in Translation 9.1). More important, however, is the fact that it was the first major battle where the armies of great kings fought each other directly. Moreover, the Hittites broke several rules of war: they did not issue a challenge nor attack frontally. Normally attackers and defenders played set roles, but the Hittites reversed those. They used attack as the best defense. The battle of Qadesh was a sign of a breakdown in the expected diplomatic and military behavior of the time.

Sources in Translation 9.1
Rameses defends his account of the battle of Qadesh

In the correspondence between Egyptian and Hittite courts after the peace treaty of 1259, Rameses II did not shy away from bringing up the hostilities of the past. In a letter regarding the fugitive Hittite ruler, Urhi-Teshub, he mentioned the battle of Qadesh to the new Hittite king Hattusili III. The terms he used show that he was convinced of the fact that he had single-handedly crushed the enemy, as his official inscriptions so vividly state.

And when the leading division of the Great King, King of Egypt, reached the city Shabtuna, two warriors from the army of Hatti came to the king and told him: "The king of Hatti is in the area of Aleppo." Three divisions were still marching and had not yet reached the place where the king was. The king sat on his throne on the western side of the Orontes River and the leading division was in the camp he had set up. While the king knew that Muwatalli, king of Hatti, had left the area of Aleppo, the king did not know where he was. And the king of Hatti attacked him with his army and all the countries that sided with him. But the king of Egypt defeated him on his own, although my army was not with me, although my horses were not with me. And I took the enemies from Hatti to Egypt in full view of the people of Egypt and the people of Hatti. So if you say about my army: "Was there really no army, were there really no horses?" I say, "Look. One of my divisions was in Amurru, one was in [ ], and one was in Taminta. That is the truth!"[5]

Egyptian–Hittite peace

Some three years after the battle of Qadesh Muwatalli died and the Hittite state saw a conflict over the throne between Muwatalli's son, Urhi-Teshub, and brother, Hattusili. The latter prevailed after a number of years and Urhi-Teshub fled to Egypt. Rameses II did not take advantage of the situation to expand in Syria. We hear of no military action after his tenth year. Then suddenly in his twenty-first year the two great powers concluded a peace treaty and defensive alliance. The treaty was special to both parties, and each formulated a version that was engraved on a silver tablet. The Egyptian record was sent to the Hittite capital, where it has survived in the Babylonian language on several damaged clay tablets. The Hittite version, sent to Egypt, was translated into Egyptian and carved unto the walls of the Amun temple at Karnak and of the Ramesseum. The primary concerns of the treaty are clear. The royal houses wanted peace forever and promised to help each other whenever threatened. Should an outsider attack one party, the other party had to send military support, and they pledged mutual assistance in the case of local rebellions. Hattusili included a special clause that demanded that Rameses would support his designated successor; as a usurper he knew how easily young kings could fall.

Rameses II, his queen Nefertari, and one of their sons started a correspondence with their counterparts in the Hittite court, and a set of cuneiform letters written in the Babylonian and Hittite languages was found in the capital's archives there. Several letters deal with arranging a diplomatic marriage, which finally took place in Rameses's 34th year (1246). He honored the occasion in several inscriptions, including one at Abu Simbel. The accompanying representation shows Hattusili respectfully delivering his daughter to Rameses, which we know that king did not do. Officially Rameses showed himself as the leading character in the alliance, but in reality the kings were equal. Hattusili's wife had demanded that her daughter became Rameses's "Chief wife," and the Egyptian king had agreed.

The promise of mutual support in the treaty was not purely rhetorical. Hittite charioteers were stationed in Piramesse, and Egyptian soldiers may have traveled to Hatti in return. That country was eager to obtain Egyptian support because it felt threatened on its eastern side by an expansionist Assyria. What compulsion Rameses felt is less clear to us.

A new imperial structure

Egypt's administration of its Syro-Palestinian territories had been relatively loose during the 18th dynasty. Local vassals were responsible for carrying out imperial orders and only a few Egyptian administrators were involved. After the conquest phase Egyptian military presence was also limited. That system ended in the Ramessid Period. Instead the Egyptians intensified their presence in the region, building officials' residences and military garrisons, and transforming strategically located towns into fortresses. The amount of Egyptian remains increased dramatically, with more architecture, including temples to Egyptian deities, royal and private statuary, steles, inscriptions, and pottery. It also seems that local people accepted Egyptian cultural influence more readily and in archaeological remains the local traditions grow fainter. The strengthened presence suggests that the Egyptians annexed the region and occupied it militarily. But the reach of Egypt's control was much smaller than before; it limited itself to Palestine and southern Syria seems to have been left alone.

The policy was replicated in Lower Nubia. Earlier New Kingdom rulers had focused their building activity south of the second cataract, and before Rameses II few Egyptian monuments existed between the first and second cataracts. Rameses changed this. He constructed seven temples in the region, six of them rock-cut temples like those at Abu Simbel. Their purpose is somewhat of a mystery. Few people inhabited Lower Nubia and those who did already knew that the Egyptian king was powerful. In the only case where archaeologists investigated the surrounding area (es-Sebua) there was a small indigenous settlement nearby. It was separated from the houses and cemetery for the priesthood in charge of the cult. Rameses's self-promotion was certainly a concern. The temples honored him as god, as we have discussed before.

In addition to the rock-cut temples Rameses also developed existing settlements, especially around the second cataract. In this he followed a policy his father had established. Sety I had founded two new fortified towns on either side of the cataract; Aksha nearby in the north and Amara West at a distance in the south. They were relatively small towns intended to replace the former administrative centers of Lower and Upper Nubia. Sety I founded them, Rameses II embellished them with large stone temples. Both kings were concerned with the exploitation of gold mines in that area and boasted of the wells they dug to provide water to miners and others. Sety seems to have failed but graffiti left by individuals near Rameses's wells attest to the fact that his projects were a success. South of Amara West Rameses's building activity was limited and often the work of high officials. The southernmost remains are at Gebel Barkal, the large Amun sanctuary near the fourth cataract. There was relatively little military activity in the region, probably because Nubia had been securely in Egypt's hand for more than 200 years by this time, and only nomadic groups in the desert posed a threat. Rameses II paid keen attention to Lower Nubia, however. His actions there may indicate he intended to secure the southern border.

A new area of concern for Egypt was the western desert. Sparsely inhabited by nomadic groups, it had been the setting for military activity from the beginning of the Egyptian state, but it does not seem that it was considered a great danger. To refer to the people of the region in general the Egyptians used the term Tjehenu or, from the late Old Kingdom on, the variant Tjemhu (see Chapter 5). After an almost complete silence about the west in the 18th dynasty, Sety I was the first to report military activity there. Rameses II mentioned clashes in the region more often in his inscriptions, but especially his building activity shows that he saw its inhabitants as a threat. He laid out a string of fortresses along the western edge of the Delta and the Mediterranean coast for at least 200 miles (300 kilometers) west of the Delta. These were intended to monitor the movement of herdsmen from areas farther to the west into the Delta, where they sought pastures for their flocks. That region had been mostly deserted it seems, but Rameses settled people in it as a defense against these Libyan incursions.

It seems thus that Rameses strengthened all the borders of Egypt with architectural structures that confirmed Egyptian presence and dominance. The area he could control in that way was more restricted in size than what the empire had previously dominated through less direct means. After the peace treaty with the Hittites these defenses were not needed to counter a great state. They were intended for less organized opponents, people of the regions surrounding Egypt who saw the Nile kingdom as a place to start a new and better life.

Foreigners in Egypt

The early Ramessids may thus have had a siege mentality, surrounding Egypt with border fences where they could control entry into the country. But as all governments who adopt this policy find out, it is virtually impossible to close off land where others want to settle. Egypt's wealth and domestic stability must have appealed to outsiders who would try to immigrate. Moreover, Egyptian policy itself throughout the New Kingdom promoted the influx of foreigners, and it is no surprise that they influenced the society in many ways. This was not a new phenomenon. From Old Kingdom times on, if not before, foreign groups entered Egypt and gained positions as mercenaries, as we saw, for example, with Nubians in the 6th dynasty (see Chapter 4).

In official rhetoric the king of Egypt depicted foreigners as inferior beings devoid of culture and manly attributes. They were "vile," "wicked," and "cowards." This explained why they always lost in war. Rameses's heroism in the account of the battle of Qadesh, for example, did not derive from the fact that he defeated worthy opponents; enemy soldiers gained strength from their great numbers alone. From the early New Kingdom on, victorious kings had captured people as part of their booty and taken them to Egypt. Battle accounts boast of the numbers of prisoners taken. This continued into the Ramessid Period and it is likely that certain campaigns were organized primarily for the capture of new people. The huge building projects required a labor force, and who better than foreign workers to provide that? Although we do not know the actual numbers of people who were moved, we can use the term deportation. Foreigners were sent to places where they were needed. Hence an inscription at Abu Simbel states about Rameses:

> The good god who slays the nine bows (= enemies of Egypt)
> … who carries off the land of Nubia to the northern land (= Delta) and the Asiatics to Nubia. He has placed the Shasu (= Asiatic nomads) in the western land and has settled the Libyans on the ridges of the east Delta. The strongholds he built are filled with the plunder of his strong arm.[6]

As earlier in history, New Kingdom Egyptians were eager to take advantage of foreign skills, especially in the military. Thus the army recruited people they had fought before. Rameses II mentioned that he campaigned against people called Sherden in the west. Soon afterwards they appeared as mercenaries in the Egyptian army.

Also upper-class foreigners entered Egypt as a result of royal initiatives. Marriages with foreign princesses have been mentioned several times before. Rameses II married at least two Hittite women and one Babylonian one. They came to Egypt with large trains of attendants. Sons of vassals and allies lived in the Egyptian court as hostages, and political refugees found a home there as well. When Urhi-Teshub was deposed from the Hittite throne, he fled to Rameses.

The arrival of foreign people had many repercussions for Egypt. Naturally, the population became more diverse and it seems that ethnic neighborhoods developed. Memphis had a "field of the Hittites," for example. The Hittite soldiers who came to Piramesse after the peace treaty between Rameses II and Hattusili III lived together in a garrison and left behind such typical remains that archaeologists could recognize them easily.

Many households and certainly large institutions like temples had foreign servants. Although these people seem at first to have been restricted to menial tasks, their skills enabled them to rise to high positions, including ones at court. A remarkable aspect of the Ramessid court is that many of the "butlers" were men of Asiatic descent. They bore Egyptian names of a type habitually given to foreigners in which they honored the king, such as, "Rameses is valiant." Their original names make their foreign roots even clearer. Butler Rameses-em-per-Ra, "Rameses is in the house of Ra," had the Semitic name Ben-azen, and his own inscription tells us that he came from northern Jordan. Butlers needed to be trustworthy men as they had direct access to the king and could influence decisions at court. In the late 19th dynasty one of them, Bay, became the real power behind the throne (see Chapter 10).

The presence of foreigners in all levels of society had a profound effect on the Egyptian language in the New Kingdom. Hundreds of Semitic words, for example, appear in the records of the period, transcribed into a special syllabic form of the Egyptian script. Military terms make up the largest group, which shows the importance of Asiatic soldiers and technology in the Egyptian army. Other terms deal with crafts, objects, food, and the like.

The immigrants had their own gods and religious beliefs. In the New Kingdom the cults of several Asiatic gods entered Egypt, often with royal support. The Syrian god Reshep and goddess Astarte received official backing as gods of the war chariot when that equipment arrived in Egypt. The leading Syrian storm god, Baal, entered the official Egyptian cult in the 19th dynasty. Although of foreign origin, these gods were integrated into the Egyptian pantheon and were often closely connected to existing Egyptian gods. Anat and Astarte figured as the partners of the god Seth, and Astarte as the daughter of Ptah. Baal as principal god of Syria was associated with the Egyptian Seth, god of the desert and the foreign Asiatics, and could take on a whole array of Seth's attributes. Thus, although the gods remained recognizably Syrian through their names, they became hybrid creatures with Syrian and Egyptian attributes. That duality is reflected in the iconography. The gods Baal and Reshep, for example, were shown in the regular poses of Syrian warrior gods, brandishing axes or maces, but they wore Egyptian royal crowns. Although these gods started out with minor roles in the cult and pantheon, over time they gained prominence. When Rameses II constructed Piramesse, the main temple in the eastern quarter was for Astarte's cult. His oldest daughter's name referred to the goddess Anat. The name was fully Semitic: Bint-Anat, "daughter of Anat." Only Syrian gods seem to have gained a foothold in Egypt. No Nubian deities received official support and few if any Libyan ones.

Egyptian elites especially were exposed to foreigners and their cultures because they not only met immigrants but also dealt with foreign traders and bought foreign goods. In all countries of the eastern Mediterranean it was fashionable for elites to show off their special status through the acquisition and display of exotic goods. Artists used expensive materials – ivory, gold, silver, etc. – to create objects that merged foreign motifs into a unique mixture. Egyptian iconography combined with images and motifs from Syria, the Aegean, and other parts of the eastern Mediterranean. Some art historians do not single out a specific place of creation, but see an international style that aimed at pleasing elites in many countries.

The merging of cultures extended to the non-material as well. Evidence of Babylonian literature in the Amarna archive shows that scribes there at least knew some tales from that foreign culture. Because of the introduction of Syrian gods into the Egyptian pantheon, some stories about them entered Egyptian literature, for example, a myth about the goddess Astarte, involving the battle between gods and the sea. The pantheon represented was multicultural. The sea was an important force in Syrian mythology, as was Astarte, who appears in the myth as the daughter of the Egyptian god Ptah. The sea's opponent is the Egyptian god Seth, identified with Syrian Baal. Some scholars regard the composition as a translation of a Syrian myth, but it was clearly adapted to an Egyptian context. Similarly, Egyptian magical papyri contained Syrian spells.

Egypt in the New Kingdom in general, and certainly in the Ramessid Period, was not a monolithic culture adhering to local traditions alone. The empire brought in people, goods, and ideas from conquered territories and beyond, and at the same time Egyptians who traveled abroad as soldiers, imperial administrators, and traders came back home with foreign ideas. The New Kingdom was a cosmopolitan age, not only because of political interactions but also in cultural terms.

9.3 Rameses's Court

Officials

An empire as large and centralized as Rameses II's required a massive bureaucracy. In Egyptian ideology officials received their appointment from the king in person, so – at least in theory – Rameses II handed out posts to numerous individuals over his 67 years of rule. As high positions came with big rewards, the holders were able to build themselves lavish tombs and commission statues, steles, and other objects, which were regularly inscribed. Some 70 tombs in western Thebes are of southern officials of Rameses II, and excavations in Saqqara continue to reveal elaborate tombs from officials who worked in the north of Egypt. Hundreds of inscribed objects from bureaucrats, priests, army commanders, and others of the period are preserved.

The genre of an official's biography was long established by New Kingdom times – we have seen examples from the Old Kingdom (Chapter 3). Many such texts from the Ramessid Period refer to the moment that the king appointed the official. The high priest of Amun, Nebwenenef, wrote, for example:

> Nebwenenef, the justified, was ushered into the presence of his Majesty
>   (= Rameses II).
> Now, he was the high priest of the god Onuris,
> High priest of the goddess Hathor, Lady-of-Dendera,
> And overseer of priests of all the gods
> To his south, as far as Heriheramun (= probably western Thebes);
> And to his north, as far as Thinis.
> Then, his Majesty said to him:
> "You are now high priest of the god Amun;
> His treasuries and his granary are under your seal.
> You are chief spokesman for his temple;
> And all his endowments are under your authority."[7]

The structure of Rameses II's government continued earlier New Kingdom practices. It consisted of three major units: the internal government of Egypt, the (relatively powerless) administration of the dynasty, and the important government of conquests. The internal government had four sectors: the administration of the royal domains, which were vast at the time; the army; the religious government, in control of enormous resources; and the civil government. The latter supervised agricultural production, collected taxes, provided justice, and maintained order through a police force. The civil government had northern and southern divisions because of the size of the country and the high level of economic activity. Its crucial challenge was to coordinate interactions between the central administration and villages, which relied on a communal organization of justice and other matters. While local affairs were usually handled internally, individuals tried to subvert the course of justice by appealing directly to government officials. Accusations of corruption were thus not uncommon. But Egypt had a legal system at the time that relied on written documentation as well as oral testimony and could involve long-running litigation. This aspect of Egyptian society is poorly documented, but some remarkable sources are available (see Special Topic 9.1).

Special Topic 9.1   *Litigation over real estate*

Ancient Egyptian law is relatively poorly known. No law codes have been preserved, although they seem to have existed in antiquity and there are some royal edicts, such as Horemheb's against corruption. We have to reconstruct legal concepts from documents of practice, which are more common in the New Kingdom than earlier in Egyptian history. These also show how legal disputes were settled. One of the most interesting such records derives from a tomb near Memphis. On its walls the owner, Mose, inscribed an account of a dispute he won over the tenure of a plot of agricultural land. Uniquely he also showed a picture of himself standing before the judges while making his case.

Mose lived in the reign of Rameses II, but it was Ahmose, the first king of the 18th dynasty, who had granted the area in dispute to his ancestor Neshi. Neshi's descendants were absentee landlords and had kept the area in common, sharing the income while one of them managed it. In the reign of Horemheb, Mose's grandmother, Werel, went to court and obtained the right to administer the estate on behalf of five other heirs. Her sister, Takhuru, successfully contested the decision, but Werel and her son Huy somehow regained the right. Mose was Huy's son. When Huy died a man called Khay argued before the vizier that Huy's wife Nubnofret and son Mose had no claim over the land, as they were not related to the original owner Neshi. He succeeded initially because the land registers did not list Nubnofret or her heirs. When Mose became an adult he went once more to court and on the basis of testimonies by a dozen members of the community showed that Huy had legally managed the fields and that he was a legitimate descendant of Neshi.

In order to investigate the matter the vizier turned to records that listed the owners of lands.

> Nubnofret said to the vizier, "Have the land register of the Treasury and of the Office of the Granary of Pharaoh be brought for me!" The vizier said to her, "What you have said is perfectly good." We were taken north to Piramesse and entered the Treasury of Pharaoh and also the Office of the Granary of Pharaoh. The two registers were brought before the vizier in the Great Law-Court. Then, the vizier said to Nubnofret, "Who is your heir among the heirs who are listed on the two registers in our hands?" Nubnofret said, "No heir of mine is among them." "Then you are in the wrong," said the vizier to her.

But Khay seems to have introduced false documentation into the case, which had convinced the vizier in his favor. To overturn the decision Mose turned to witnesses. Several villagers testified that Huy was the descendant of Neshi and had legitimately cultivated the land.

Statement by Hori, Beekeeper of the Treasury of Pharaoh:

"As the god Amun endures and as the ruler endures! Should I speak falsely, then cut off my nose and my ears and have me exiled to Kush! As for the scribe Huy, he was the son of Werel. And as for Werel, she was the descendant of Neshi."[8]

Mose was clearly very proud of this victory and recounted it in detail on the walls of his tomb. The record also shows us that women had equal rights to men in these matters and that they could manage landed property.

The royal family

As a man with a long life and many wives, Rameses II had an enormous number of offspring of whom he was very proud: some 50 sons and more than 40 daughters are known. He mentioned children in many inscriptions, regularly representing processions of them on his major monuments. For more than a millennium it had been highly exceptional to show male royal children prominently on monuments; Rameses II changed that trend. Some of their mothers are especially well known, above all Nefertari, one of his "queens" from before he became king to her death in his 24th year. The attention devoted to her in her tomb and other monuments have made her one of the most famous queens of ancient Egypt (Figure 9.3). She was indeed of special importance to the king. The pair of sanctuaries at Abu Simbel was devoted to the royal couple as a divine couple: the great temple for Rameses as god, the smaller one for Nefertari as the goddess Hathor. Nefertari appeared in many representations beside the king, often at a much smaller scale as was very common for women in Egyptian art, but sometimes of equal size. She observed him when he defeated enemies, offered to the gods and rewarded officials with him. She was not as close to her husband as Nefertiti was to Akhenaten, it seems, but she did involve herself in his work. When Egyptians and Hittites had formed their alliance, Nefertari corresponded as actively with the Hittite court as did Rameses. Her tomb (QV 66) is the most magnificent in the Valley of the Queens, elaborately decorated and of substantial size.

Nefertari was not Rameses's only "queen" even in her own lifetime. From the very beginning, before Rameses became king, she had a colleague Isetnefret. The latter never appeared next to her husband in sculptures in the round although she was the mother of Rameses's thirteenth son and successor, Merenptah, as well as of Rameses's oldest daughter and of his famous son Khaemwaset (see below). The first generation of "queens" overlapped partly in time with the second, which was made up mostly of Rameses's own daughters. Isetnefret gave birth to Bint-Anat, Nefertari to Meryet Amun, and unknown women to Nebet-tawi and Henut-mi-Ra. The first two became queens when

Figure 9.3 Queen Nefertari making an offering, from the tomb of Nefertari. Valley of the Queens, Thebes/The Bridgeman Art Library

their mothers were still alive, and Rameses had several colossal statues with one of them at his side in smaller size. We do not know whether they bore their father children. All these women, except for Isetnefret, had tombs in the Valley of the Queens.

Rameses's seventh queen was Hittite. When Hattusili III's wife Puduhepa arranged for her daughter to marry the king, she insisted the girl would receive that status. We do not know her original name, but in Egypt she became Maat-Hor-Neferura, "Neferura-is-the-one-who-beholds-the-Falcon." Rameses made much of the marriage in official inscriptions, boasting that it was a sign of the Hittite king's submission to him. He did seem to like his Hittite wife, if we can believe the description of her arrival: "And so, she was beautiful in the opinion of His Majesty, and he loved her to distraction."[9] In official monuments he sometimes showed her beside him, and they had at least one daughter. Her actual status may have declined over the years. When she was middle-aged Rameses housed her in a secondary residence away from the capital, and she did not receive a tomb in the Valley of the Queens.

The king's large offspring came from other women as well. He showed his children without prejudice irrespective of their mothers' status. On the facade of Abu Simbel's main temple, for example, appear his oldest son with Nefertari, his second son with Isetnefret, the oldest daughter with Isetnefret, a daughter of Nefertari, and two daughters of unknown mothers. An early relief from the rock-cut temple at Beit el-Wali shows his two oldest sons, Amunhirwenemef of Nefertari, and Khaemwaset of Isetnefret, side by side fighting a battle with him.

Only one of Rameses's children left a substantial number of monuments of his own, his fourth son Khaemwaset, who predeceased him (Plate 9). He was the high priest of the god Ptah in Memphis. In inscriptions on six Old Kingdom pyramids he claimed to have restored the monuments and recorded the owners' names on them.

> Now, his name was not found on his pyramid. The priest and king's son Khaemwaset wished very much to restore the monuments of the kings of Upper and Lower Egypt, because of what they had made, which was falling into ruin.[10]

Khaemwaset is sometimes described as an early archaeologist or the "first Egyptologist," but some scholars think that he used the massive structures as stone quarries for his father's building projects and left the inscriptions to ensure that the original owners remained known. Khaemwaset's name lived on in Egyptian culture as a great magician. Demotic papyri of the Greco-Roman Period contain a cycle of stories about Setne Khaemwaset, a corruption of one of his priestly titles. In one story he enters the tomb of an ancient magician to take his magic book and encounters the ghost of the deceased's wife, who tells their life story and how her husband obtained the book. He challenges the dead to a board game, which he loses several times. Only magic can save him, and he steals the book on his way out of the tomb. It seems that later Egyptians admired Khaemwaset because he was able to read old inscriptions, but at the same time thought him reckless as he entered tombs. They honored him as a wise man – as they did with men like Imhotep or Amenhotep, son of Hapu – but never made him a god. Other stories of the cycle show Khaemwaset as a magician in Rameses II's court, but it is less clear why the events described were connected to him (see Chapter 13).

Rameses's special attention to his children, many of whom predeceased him, is perhaps most visible in a highly unusual tomb in the Valley of the Kings (KV 5), whose true nature has only recently become known. Instead of one burial chamber the tomb contains a warren of tunnels and chambers. Still under excavation, archaeologists have already found 121 of them, some beneath others. So far they have identified burials for six sons of Rameses, and since more than 20 are represented in the tomb's decoration that number of sons may have been interred there.

9.4 A Community of Tomb Builders

Royal tombs are among the most impressive remains of the Ramessid Period and of the New Kingdom in general. We have mentioned those of Tutankhamun, Sety I, Rameses II's sons, and Nefertari, and there are many more of the 18th through 20th dynasties. The effort invested in them was considerable. The mortuary temples on the edge of the agricultural zone of western Thebes were the visible parts of the burial complexes and were often massive and intended to impress. The tombs were to be secluded places where the buried bodies would be safely hidden, but that did not mean they were plain and simple. They were deep shafts into the rock and, especially from Sety I on, the decoration was elaborate and covered every surface. We know the craftsmen who built these tombs because the village where they lived was excavated in western Thebes in between the farming area and the valleys of kings and queens. The desert location led to an especially good preservation of the remains and they provide the best available source of a village community in ancient Egypt. Scholars refer to the place as Deir el-Medina after a later monastery built nearby.

The Deir el-Medina community was unusual. Made up of specialist workers and their families, its inhabitants were exceptionally literate and artistic because they decorated tombs with writing and art. They were probably relatively well-off also, as their income was guaranteed in bad and in good agricultural years. We cannot see them as typical Egyptian villagers then, but they are the closest we get to such people for the moment.

The settlement included living quarters and cemeteries. At its height (probably under Rameses II) it contained a walled sector with some 70 houses and another 40 to 50 houses outside the walls (Figure 9.4). The houses were packed closely together along a main street that transected the village from north to south and two perpendicular streets. All houses were quite small. Most of those whose plans are clear contain four areas in a straight line, with the kitchen at the back. Stairs led to the roof, where people probably slept when it was hot. The village had a number of shrines, including for King Amenhotep I and his mother Ahmose-Nefertari, who may have founded the village of Deir el-Medina or its community of artisans.

The written remains are extraordinarily well preserved, counting more than 10,000 texts in hieratic script. Most of them were written on pieces of pottery or limestone (ostraca), fewer on papyrus. They include letters, lists, accounts, reports on work and deliveries, legal records, and an amazing array of literary and magical texts. They provide a unique insight in the inhabitants' lives.

Figure 9.4 The village of Deir el-Medina. Werner Forman Archive/E. Strouhal

Because the village was located away from agricultural fields the people relied to a great extent on outsiders to provide food. The state distributed much of what they needed – grain, meat, fish, vegetables, water, and firewood – and provided the service personnel to feed, clothe, and keep them healthy. The village men had little time to farm, as their job was to build the tombs of kings and queens. These were located too far from the village for a daily commute, so the workmen may have stayed in camps near the work site for eight days per Egyptian 10-day week. They could take days off for illness, family emergencies, and religious holidays, such as the Opet festival.

The number of workers varied according to how grand a king intended his tomb to be, but usually there were between 40 and 70. Registers divide them into teams of the right and of the left on the model of a ship's crew, each under a supervisor and responsible for one side of the tomb. The workers first cut the tomb entrance and chambers, which was relatively easy, as the stone was soft but for veins of flint. Then they plastered the walls. Scribes and artists drew the decorations on the plaster and sculptors and painters executed the final work. As sunlight did not reach deep into the shafts they worked mostly with the help of burning linen wicks, soaked in oil and fat and with salt added to reduce smoke. Several tasks took place simultaneously, but the entire tomb was planned from the beginning as the decoration needed to be organized in a system covering all the rooms. Guard posts watched over the area where the men lived and worked, and policemen, who did not live in the village, kept out unwanted visitors. The vizier of Upper Egypt monitored all activity, and a scribe of the tomb reported deliveries, absences, and other daily events in the so-called Journal of the Tomb.

Work on tombs started early in the kings' reigns and no one knew how much time would be available. All of them are unfinished. When the king died, workers theoretically had only 70 days to prepare for the burial, which took place when mummification was complete. Other workshops made the tomb furniture (some was recycled from earlier tombs, however). From the start of the 19th dynasty on the queens' burials received equal attention, and the community of workmen had to expand. Queens' tombs were less elaborate than those for kings and required less time, but they demanded the same level of skill and attention.

Still, on their days off they built their own tombs, and the Deir el-Medina cemeteries contain some elaborate examples with superstructures that include a small pyramid. The artisans also did contract work for others, making sarcophagi and the like, which provided a source of income alongside the state wages and enabled them to acquire goods (see Key Debate 9.1). They recorded such transactions in writing as documentation in cases of dispute, which were settled in front of a court made up of other villagers. Such courts were probably normal practice in New Kingdom Egypt and took care of most local problems. At Deir el-Medina the vizier intervened only when the issue at hand was very important. The highest local voice of authority was the god's oracle. A case was presented in front of the divine statue, whose bearers moved it in a way that indicated what party the god supported.

The unusual degree of literacy of Deir el-Medina villagers is illustrated in the person of Qenherkhopshef, a chief scribe. His career certainly encompassed the period from Rameses II's 40th year (1240) to the first year of Saptah (1194) at the end of the 19th dynasty, and probably started earlier. Qenherkhopshef apprenticed with his predecessor, the scribe Ramose. He reported about the progress on tombs to high officials, including the vizier, regularly complaining about the lack of materials. Other workers wrote to him, sometimes accusing him of poor treatment (see Sources in Translation 9.2, no. 3). There are clear indications that he abused his position; records indicate that workers were absent from their official jobs because he had forced them to work for him personally, and he accepted bribes to keep silent about their petty crimes.

Qenherkhopshef seems to have liked to wander through the mountains behind the village and left many graffiti behind on rock surfaces. He was unusually interested in earlier kings. Among his belongings was an offering table onto which were inscribed the cartouches of all kings of the 18th dynasty – except for the disgraced Hatshepsut and Amarna kings – and two of their wives, the kings of the 19th up to Rameses II, three kings of the 17th dynasty, and

Sources in Translation 9.2
Letters from Deir el-Medina

The inhabitants of Deir el-Medina have left us more written remains than any other community of ancient Egypt. The people noted down numerous transactions of their daily lives and communicated about their work on the royal tombs with people from outside the village, providing rare insights on the interactions of ordinary people. Some examples are:

1. The mayor of the west of the City (= Thebes), Ramose, communicates to the foremen of the crew, ... namely to the foreman Nebnefer and to the foreman Kaha and to the crew, likewise. To wit:

   Now, the city prefect and vizier Paser has written to me, saying: "Please have the wages delivered to the necropolis crew consisting of vegetables, fish, firewood, pottery, small cattle, and milk. Do not let any of these remain outstanding. Do not make me treat any part of their wages as balance due. Attend to it and pay heed!"

2. Addressed by the scribe Pabaki to the father of the draftsman Maaninakhtef: I have heard what you told me: "Let Ib work with you!" Look, he spends his entire day bringing a jug of water – there is no other task charged to him, each and every day. He has not heard your plan to ask of him: "What have you accomplished today?" Look, the sun has set, and he is still far off with the jug of water.

3. The draftsman Prehotep sends greetings to his superior, the scribe of the necropolis Qenherkhepeshef: In life, prosperity, and health!

   What is the meaning of your negative attitude towards me? I am like a donkey to you. If there is work – bring the donkey! And if there is food – bring the ox! If there is beer, you never ask for me; but when there is work to be done, you ask for me. Upon my head, if I am someone who is bad under the influence of beer, don't ask for me. It is good for you to take notice in the estate of Amun-Ra, King-of-the-Gods! (Postscript) I am a man who lacks beer in his house and I am seeking to fill my stomach by writing to you.

4. Addressed by the scribe Nebnetjeru, to the scribe Ramose: In life, prosperity and health! Saying the following:

   Now, I call upon the gods Amun, Ptah, and Min to keep you alive, and to keep you in the favor of Pharaoh, my good lord. Please be attentive and fetch me some ink because my superior has told me the good ink has gone bad.[11]

Figure 9.5 Drawing on an ostracon from Deir el-Medina. Louvre, Paris © 2010. White Images/Scala, Florence

Mentuhotep II of the 11th. On ostraca he wrote out the names of Rameses II's sons and of the 18th dynasty kings. He owned a library with literary materials, including a copy of the Egyptian Dream book – an interpretation of dreams – and the praise of ancient scribes quoted in Chapter 5. He liked to use blank spaces on the papyri for his own writings. He copied the start of the poetic account of the battle of Qadesh twice on one papyrus, possibly directly from the walls of the nearby Ramesseum, where they were carved about 60 years earlier. In Qenherkhopshef we find thus a man of relatively low social status who was able to acquire a high level of literacy and familiarity with many aspects of Egyptian written culture.

The draughtsmen were equally creative. They used ostraca to copy images from royal monuments, it seems (such as the queen of Punt from Hatshepsut's temple, see Chapter 7). They practiced drawing and often showed a freedom of expression absent in official art (Figure 9.5). One papyrus, now in the Egyptian Museum of Turin, contains detailed drawings of erotic poses and satirical images of animals in court scenes.

The village's history was closely connected to that of the royal house in the New Kingdom. Probably founded by Amenhotep I, the community depended on royal commissions, which ceased in the reign of Akhenaten. Under Horemheb's restoration of the old system it revived. The village flourished with the kings of the 19th dynasty and its population increased. But later

Key Debate 9.1 *Markets in ancient Egypt*

The royal imagery of Egypt shows the king as the sole source of people's wealth and we know that the state was very important in the feeding and care of the population. Egypt had a redistributive economy in which government bureaus collected agricultural resources and handed them out to numerous people in the form of food and clothing rations as reward for their service. This organization does not preclude the existence of a parallel system in which people produced goods and traded them for profit. Many records calculate the value of items in amounts of silver, copper, or grain, which could conceivably indicate that people sold them for payments in these commodities. Even in a community like Deir el-Medina, which worked full time for the state and received rations of all its needs in return, sale documents for foodstuff, livestock, and manufactured objects abound (Černý 1953–4; Janssen 1975a). There also exist some tomb paintings – including at Deir el-Medina – that show people displaying goods for others to acquire (Kemp 2006: 325).

Do these pieces of evidence indicate that there was a market economy in ancient Egypt? All scholars agree that such transactions took place without coinage, which was unknown in Egypt until the 4th century BC and even then was limited in use to the payment of foreign mercenaries. But a system that evaluates items with amounts of standardized goods (silver, copper, grain) permits barter, which could be inspired by the desire to make a profit. Some scholars argue that the ancient Egyptians were driven by the same economic motives as we find in modern societies, taking advantage of supply and demand to set as high a price as possible and hoping to collect as much as possible (Silver 2004).

Many reject this idea, however, and see basic differences between the economic attitudes of the ancient Egyptians and ourselves. They argue that barter has a fundamentally different attitude toward profit than selling: it aims at parity rather than gain (Bleiberg 1995: 1376–7). The social cohesion of ancient Egyptian communities was such that people sought to help each other rather than make a profit. Moreover, barter activity was of little economic value when compared to what the state distributed, and it mostly provided a means of access to resources that were not crucial to one's survival or to fill gaps in state allocations (Altenmüller 1980). The ancient economic mindset was entirely unlike ours (Janssen 1975b; somewhat differently S. Morenz 1969). Yet other scholars see a mixture of practices in which the state played a crucial role but could not provide everything to everyone, and where markets were important (Kemp 1983: 81; 2006: 319–26; Altenmüller 2001).

The debate is part of a much wider discussion on the nature of ancient economies and our ability to comprehend and study them. Often it is not an exchange of ideas but a repetition of evidence that best fits one side of the argument: ancient governmental records and public announcements stress the importance of the state, notices of private transactions show wheeling and dealing and a role of private enterprise in the economy. How we interpret the records depends to a great extent on our modern ideological stances. Just as we cannot agree on how the modern economy should be organized, we should not expect to share the same opinion when interpreting ancient economic data (Van De Mieroop 2004).

in that dynasty trouble appeared on the horizon. Events in Deir el-Medina after the reign of Rameses II show how the breakdown of the empire had an effect on the daily lives of all Egyptians. These events are the subject of the next chapter.

NOTES

1. Translation after Lichtheim 1976: 67.
2. Translation after Caminos 1954: 73–4.
3. Translation after Burkard & Thissen 2008: 160.
4. Translation after Lichtheim 1976: 64–8.
5. Translation after Edel 1994: 58–61 lines 21'–33'.
6. Translation after Kitchen 1996a: 67.
7. Translation after Frood 2007: 36.
8. Translation after Kitchen 2000: 308–9.
9. Kitchen 1996a: 96.
10. Translation after Kitchen 1996a: 567.
11. Translations after Wente 1990: nos. 160, 167, 204, and 221.

10

The End of Empire
(ca. 1213–1070)

> They arrested me and imprisoned me in the office of the Mayor of Thebes. I took the 20 *deben* of gold that had fallen to me as my share and I gave them to Khaemope, the District-Scribe of the Landing-Quay of Thebes. He released me. (Testimony of stonemason Hapiwer)[1]

When Rameses II died of old age in 1213, the country he left behind seems to have been in good shape. Egypt was secure in its fortified borders, it was at peace with other great states, and economically it was strong. One hundred and forty years later, if not earlier, it was in ruins. Foreign rulers no longer treated it with respect and politically the country was divided. One hundred and forty years is a long time, of course, and it is no surprise that conditions varied dramatically between the beginning and the end of this period. The numerous problems Egypt confronted are remarkable, however. Even if there were moments of recovery, crises erupted frequently. They included civil wars, robberies of tombs and temples, embezzlement of state resources, and other crimes. Many of these are reported in records of investigations by the state as it tried to restore order – the quote above derives from such a record – but the royal house could not prevent its loss of control. Perhaps we should be amazed that the New Kingdom state survived for so long.

We will look at events of this period, taking what happened to the villagers of Deir el-Medina as a starting point. These people were closer to the court than the average Egyptian, because their livelihoods depended entirely on royal commissions and rewards, but still their village can be seen as a microcosm of the country in general. The problems the villagers faced reflect what happened all over. Their internal struggles for power resembled court intrigues and succession crises. Their lack of food was a result of the state's economic downturn. The rise in crime, including the robbing of tombs that their ancestors had built, was possible because of the collapse of royal authority, and the final abandonment of the village around 1100 was due to the pressure of foreigners who raided the countryside. Royal inscriptions and documents discuss many of these events, but Deir el-Medina evidence tells us what happened on the ground.

Summary of dynastic history
Late 19th and 20th dynasties (ca. 1213–1070)

Late 19th dynasty

ca. 1213–1203	King Merenptah
	Claims victory over invading Libyans and Sea Peoples, 1209
ca. 1203–1194	Kings Sety II and Amenmessu
	Civil war for 2 to 3 years
ca. 1194–1188	King Saptah
	Placed on the throne by butler Bay
	Executes Bay in year 5, 1190
ca. 1188–1186	Queen Tausret
	Wife of Sety II who ascended throne after her regency in Saptah's reign

20th dynasty

ca. 1186–1184	King Sethnakht
	Takes throne as non-royal and seeks to restore order
ca. 1184–1153	King Rameses III
	Builds mortuary temple at Medinet Habu
	Claims victories over invading Libyans, 1180 and 1174
	Claims victory over Sea Peoples, 1177
	Grants huge tracts of land to temples
	Strikes of the Deir el-Medina workforce
	Harem conspiracy
ca. 1153–1099	Kings Rameses IV–X
	Mostly brief and poorly documented reigns of middle-aged men
	Tomb robberies
	Successive strikes by Deir el-Medina workers
ca. 1099–1069	King Rameses XI
	Temple robberies
	Civil war in Thebes
	Proclaims "Era of restoration" starting in year 19, 1081
	High priest of Amun becomes independent

Historians seek to explain why things happened. It is always difficult to interpret chaos and weigh the importance of various factors. It is clear that the end of the New Kingdom had internal and external causes, feeding on each other. Egypt was not alone in its troubles: the entire eastern Mediterranean system that had shaped the lives of people over a wide area for centuries collapsed at this time. Egypt had been at the center of its rise; it was also central in its fall.

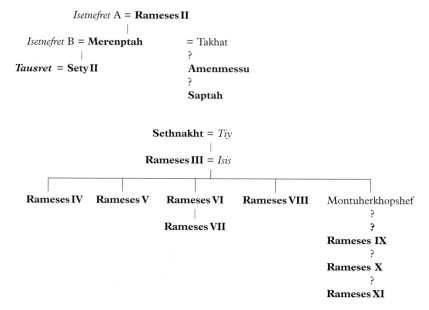

Tentative family tree of the late 19th and 20th dynasties (selected family members only)
Bold: kings; italics: queens; =: marriage; ?: possible descent

10.1 Problems at Court

A papyrus of the late 19th or early 20th dynasty describes the accusations Amennakhte brought against Paneb; both of them were workmen in the village at Deir el-Medina. The case involved the position of foreman of the right side of the crew, which had been in the same family for several generations. Paneb had inherited it from his adoptive father, Neferhotep. The accuser, Neferhotep's brother, wanted the post himself and claimed Paneb had obtained it illegitimately. According to him, after an unidentified enemy had killed Neferhotep, Paneb had bribed the vizier and gained the position even though his father had disowned him. He also accused Paneb of rape, adultery, tomb robbery, and the dishonest use of workers for his private affairs. If the accusations were true, Paneb was a despicable man. The document seems not to have been presented to a court, so we do not know what the verdict was, but Paneb disappeared from the record afterwards. Whether or not this was coincidence is unclear.

Sety II and Amenmessu

Amennakhte's accusations depict a distressing situation: viziers accepted bribes, people abused their positions, and tomb robberies were an acknowledged fact.

The vizier who heard the accusations worked under Sety II, the grandson of Rameses II and son of Merenptah. The confusion over who was foreman of the workers was partly a result of events at court. Paneb had received his office from the vizier in the midst of a civil war between two contenders to the throne: Sety II and Amenmessu. Merenptah had chosen Sety as his heir, but Amenmessu, a son by another wife or perhaps even an adult son of Sety, had established a power base in Nubia, where he left several monuments. Amenmessu captured Thebes, and most scholars think he was the enemy who killed Neferhotep and whose vizier gave Paneb his position. For two to three years their reigns overlapped, but finally Sety II regained Thebes, where he took over the tomb intended for Amenmessu (KV 10) and erased all records of his name.

Saptah and Tausret

Many elements in the above account are uncertain, and scholars differ in their interpretation of events, but it is clear that in the late 19th dynasty succession to the throne had many problems that did not end with Sety II's victory. The reconstruction presented here is just one possibility. When Sety died, a young boy called Saptah became king. His father is unknown, and scholars have suggested both Sety II and his rival Amenmessu as possibilities. The latter seems possible as later accounts connect Saptah to Amenmessu. Saptah's mother bore the name Shoteraya, which is of Canaanite origin.

While the presence of foreign women in the court was not new and sons of foreign women may have held kingship in the past, Saptah's dependence on Asiatic support seems to have been greater than before. The real kingmaker was a man called Bay, who was butler in Sety II's court. As we saw in Chapter 9, many butlers were of Syrian origin. When they took up their post they assumed Egyptian names; Bay's Egyptian name was Rameses-khaemnetjeru ("Rameses-risen-with-the-gods"). His inscriptions claim that he placed Saptah on the throne, something normally only gods asserted, and probably at that time he became "chief treasurer of the entire land," a title that was unique to him in the New Kingdom. Bay did not hide his power. In official representations of Saptah he regularly appeared alongside the king and on the same scale, and he openly participated in foreign affairs. He was the author of a letter addressed to the king of Ugarit in northern Syria, in which he identified himself as Bay "the head of the bodyguard of the great king, king of Egypt." Bay started to build a tomb for himself in the Valley of the Kings (KV 13), one of the few non-royal tombs of the 19th dynasty there. His success was short-lived, however, as the unfinished state of the tomb shows. In his fifth year Saptah gave the order to execute Bay. The workmen at Deir el-Medina received this message: "On this day, the scribe of the tomb Paser came announcing, 'Pharaoh has killed the great enemy Bay'."[2] They stopped building the tomb.

Saptah died soon afterward, probably without producing a male heir. Thus Queen Tausret, widow of Sety II who had remained "queen" during Saptah's reign and probably had been regent, assumed the kingship. She ignored her predecessor's reign and dated her documents as if she had succeeded her husband directly. Her royal ambitions were not new, it seems. Already under her husband, she had started one of the largest tombs in the Kings' Valley (KV 14), something no queen since Hatshepsut had done. Saptah had supported the work, but after he died Tausret had the inscriptions of his name replaced with those of Sety II. She suffered a similar fate, however. The next ruler, Sethnakht, usurped her tomb for himself.

Sethnakht

Tausret may have been the final actor in a power struggle between two lines of descendents of Rameses II, Sety II's and Amenmessu's. The result of the competition was chaos, and an entirely new party stepped in to restore order. A man of unknown ancestry called Sethnakht became king and started the 20th dynasty. In an inscription he claimed that the god Ra had chosen him "out of millions, setting aside the hundreds of thousands who were in front of him."[3] Later texts depict a dire situation when he ascended the throne, as does a stele Sethnakht set up in Elephantine, in which he accused earlier kings of having given away gold and silver to Asiatics. A papyrus, composed in the reign of Rameses IV but written in the name of Rameses III, stated:

> A certain Syrian, Yarsu, was their chief. He made the entire land tributary to him. One would gather his companions and steal their property. They treated the gods just like men. No one made offerings in the temples.[4]

Most scholars equate the Syrian Yarsu – a name that probably means "self-made man" – with Bay, but some argue that the reference is to Saptah, Bay's puppet. Sethnakht restored the Egyptians' hold over the country, harking back to the good times of Rameses II, something his entire dynasty stressed by assuming the throne name Rameses. After Sethnakht, Rameses III through XI ruled in succession.

Too many interest groups seem to have made up the royal court, however. Rameses III himself was the victim of a conspiracy planned in his own household, the so-called harem conspiracy. A secondary wife, Tiy, wanted her son to become heir in preference to Amunherkhopshef, whom Rameses had chosen. She enlisted the help of several men and women in Rameses's inner circle, according to the record of the punishments imposed on them from the reign of Rameses IV. The accused included a chief of the chamber, a butler, an agent of the retinue, and an overseer of the treasury, and during the investigation it emerged that some of the judges had consorted with the plotters.

The record does not identify most of the accused with their real names, but makes up pseudonyms that denigrate them. The chief of chamber is called Pai-bak-kamen, "that blind slave," for example. Was this to protect leading families from embarrassment? The sentences imposed were severe. Seventeen men and women were executed; eight – including the prince who was to be made king – were forced to commit suicide; three had their ears and noses cut off, but one was released. The conspiracy failed. The situation was not unprecedented – we know of such a conspiracy in the 6th dynasty as well – but it did exacerbate the weakening of a court already under pressure.

After Rameses III documentation becomes scarce and we are not well informed about events at court. The next eight kings all used Rameses alongside their birth name (nomen) when they ascended the throne. Rameses IV, V, VI, and VIII seem to have been Rameses III's sons, and Rameses VII was probably the son of Rameses VI. The last three kings of the dynasty seem to have been descendents of Rameses III through a prince Montuherkhopshef whose son became Rameses IX. Perhaps brothers kept on fighting each other over the throne, and there is some indication that Rameses VI seized power when his brother was in charge. Most of the reigns were short – from two to seven years – but Rameses IX ruled 17 or 18 years and brought back some stability.

10.2 Breakdown of Order

The disruption of lawful practices in royal succession found parallels in communities outside the palace, where an increase in crime and economic volatility is visible. The village at Deir el-Medina, with its rich textual record, provides detailed evidence on this with papyri that report tomb robberies and workers' strikes provoked by lack of pay.

Tomb robberies

The grave goods deposited in tombs naturally invited attempts at looting, especially the tombs of royalty and rich state officials. From prehistoric times on tombs had been robbed, sometimes quite soon after the dead were buried in them. Builders tried to prevent this by devising massive defenses – in the pyramids, for example – or by burying in inaccessible places, as was the case in the desert valleys of western Thebes. Yet, robberies happened, especially in times when the government was weak. Under the 20th dynasty they became a big problem, and an entire dossier of papyri contains investigations of accusations and actual occurrences of tomb robberies. The tombs involved were located all over the west bank and included those at Dra Abu el-Naga belonging to royalty of the 17th dynasty and those in the extremely rich Valleys of the Kings and Queens.

The textual record on these robberies dates primarily from the reign of Rameses IX (ruled 1126–1108) and was triggered by a power struggle between two Theban officials: Paser, the mayor of the east bank, and Pawerao, the mayor of the west bank, whose responsibilities included the protection of tombs. Paser alleged that various royal and private tombs in western Thebes had been robbed. An investigative team of high court officials found that most of them were intact, although they discovered evidence of attempts to enter several tombs, and a few tombs indeed had been looted. Pawerao's hands were far from clean, however, and it seems that he was complicit in the activity.

Other papyri attest to the reality of robberies. A manuscript from Rameses IX's sixteenth year contains the testimony of a stonemason, Amun-panufer, who described in detail how he and seven accomplices robbed the tomb of the 17th-dynasty king Sobekemsaf II and his queen.

> We collected the gold that we found on the mummy of this august god, together with his amulets and jewels that were at his neck, and on the coffin in which he reposed. We found the queen in exactly the same state. And we collected all we found on her likewise and then set fire to their coffins. We took their funerary equipment, which we found with them, namely vessels of gold, silver, and bronze, and we divided them up amongst ourselves.[5]

Perhaps a still clearer indication of the breakdown of order was Hapiwer's confession – quoted at the start of the chapter – that he bribed his way out of prison with 20 *deben* (ca. 1.8 kilograms) of gold after he was arrested, and that he received compensation from his accomplices. The papyri report on several additional investigations, some based on false testimonies and others on real evidence, and they show how the practice of robberies was a real and constant problem.

Because robberies became more numerous in the late 20th dynasty and started to involve tombs of kings and queens of the New Kingdom, the high priests of Thebes took precautions. Especially under the 21st dynasty, they removed mummies and hid them in small and inconspicuous tombs to safeguard the physical remains of ancient rulers. For example, they placed the mummies of Thutmose III, Sety I, Rameses I and II, a number of queens, princes, and lesser people in the shaft of the tomb of the 17th-dynasty queen Inhapy. They tagged these mummies with hieratic dockets that gave their names, and thus ensured that we have the physical remains of numerous kings and queens of the New Kingdom. Moreover, they seem to have removed the grave goods, which obviously reduced the appeal of the tombs to robbers. Emptying tombs also provided the priests with access to luxuries that no longer came into Egypt as booty and tribute. They were inclined to take them as the disappearance of the empire made it difficult to keep up some of the usual practices of temple embellishment and the like.

Workers' strikes

Economic necessity may also have inspired the original robberies. Many communities in Thebes depended on the state for their survival as they worked on public projects and were paid rations in return. Records from Deir el-Medina show that there were severe problems with payments going back to early in the 20th dynasty, in the reign of Rameses III. In his twenty-ninth year the workers from Deir el-Medina protested that they had not received their rations for two months. They assembled near the mortuary temple of Thutmose III, and refused to leave even when officials promised them in the name of the king that they would be paid. On the third day they entered the Ramesseum, Rameses II's mortuary temple, where the grain reserves were kept, and finally they received one month's back pay. Only after eight days did they receive the second month's pay. Two weeks later their rations did not arrive once more, so they demonstrated again, now accusing the supervisors of embezzlement. We do not know what the result of that accusation was, but two months later the vizier feared to cross the river when visiting Thebes, and only sent a convoluted message that he understood his duty as provider and would give them whatever he could find:

> Now, as for your saying, "Do not take away our ration!" Am I the vizier who was promoted in order to take away? Have I not given you what someone in my position would have accomplished? It so happens that there is nothing in the granaries. I will give you what I have found.[6]

Eleven days later the workmen stopped working again. The mayor of Thebes provided them with 50 sacks of grain from the temple granaries, but this led to an accusation by the high priest of Amun that he was using the temple offerings. All this information comes from entries on a papyrus that end at this point. Forty years later under Rameses IX a record by a paymaster indicates that rations were again 90 days in arrears, and four years later the workmen complained to an official, "'We are weak and hungry, for we have not been given the dues which Pharaoh gave for us.' And the Vizier, the High Priest, the Butler, and the Chief Treasurer of Pharaoh said: 'The men of the necropolis gang are right!'"[7] Under Rameses X we find them again complaining to the mayor of Thebes.

10.3 The Decline of Royal Power

The inability of the state to provide for its dependents must have done major harm to the royal image. In ideology the king was the source of all wealth for the people, and for close to 400 years the success of the New Kingdom had guaranteed that he could spread prosperity. When in the 20th dynasty he was

Figure 10.1   The mortuary temple of Rameses III at Medinet Habu. akg-images/James Morris

no longer able to do so, even for the treasured workers who built the tombs, the sense of order vanished. The provider state had failed.

The reasons for the state's economic failure were probably multiple and the result of various challenges that fed upon one another. As we saw, the problems started no later than the reign of Rameses III. He was still able to build one of the largest mortuary temples of western Thebes, at the now-called Medinet Habu. In plan it closely resembled Rameses II's nearby temple, and Rameses III certainly hoped to imitate his great predecessor (Figure 10.1). But, unlike Rameses II, he built few other major monuments. The loss of Egypt's foreign territories (see below) was one cause of the economic decline. Corruption may have aggravated the situation. As we have seen, bribery was common, and officials and others embezzled state assets. Legal papyri show that people stole temple property and one record documents how a ship's captain over ten years pilfered close to 6,000 sacks of the grain he was to transport on behalf of the state.

Perhaps one of the major causes of the state's economic decline was a shift of power from secular to religious authorities accompanied by a transfer of resources. A long papyrus of the reign of Rameses IV (ruled 1156–1150) reaffirms the donations his father, Rameses III had made to temples, especially the temple of Amun at Thebes (Papyrus Harris I) (Figure 10.2). The royal benefac-

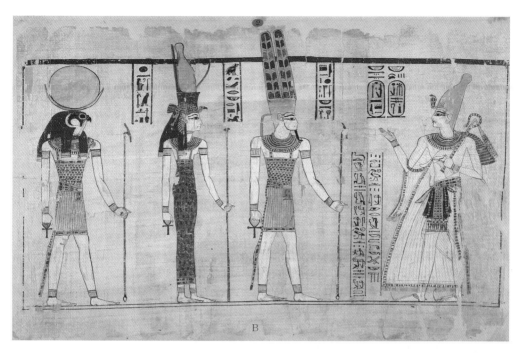

Figure 10.2 Vignette from the Harris Papyrus; King Rameses III provides for the gods of Thebes: Amun, Mut, and Khonsu. © The Trustees of the British Museum

tions were truly staggering. Rameses III donated 2,954 square kilometers of agricultural land, possibly 15 percent of all that was available in the country. Moreover, he gave 107,615 male servants, which may have been 3 percent of the entire population. If women and children accompanied these men, they would have made up half a million people. More than 80 percent of the donations went to temples in Thebes. These are amazing figures, and many scholars therefore believe that afterwards temples owned one-third of all the land of Egypt.

What prompted Rameses III's generosity? As the son of the founder of a new dynasty who had no royal blood, Sethnakht, he may have wanted to bolster his position by seeking priestly support. We know from the harem conspiracy, discussed above, that his hold on power was contested and that other factions even within the royal house pushed their own interests. If indeed he sought priestly support, it came with a high price. The loss of agricultural properties and manpower severely weakened the king's ability to commission and pay for public projects.

There are other indications of the rise of the gods' status at the expense of the king, and among these gods especially Amun of Thebes, who was also the chief recipient of Rameses III's donations. This trend predated the late New Kingdom and may have been a reaction to the Amarna revolution, which had tried to eliminate the power of the Amun priesthood. After the failure of Akhenaten's reforms that priesthood may have had a major resurgence, and we see a new way in which they interfered in official life: the oracle. The gods of Egypt had communicated in oracles earlier in the New Kingdom. Amun had proclaimed Hatshepsut king this way, for example (see Chapter 7). Oracles were rare, however, until the 19th dynasty when they involved the gods' statues carried in barques upon the shoulders of priests. The statues replied to questions with movements triggered by the priests. Amun in particular was consulted on major decisions. Rameses II, for example, asked him to determine who should be high priest in Thebes. The extent of direct involvement by the god was a novelty in Egyptian thought. Earlier on the gods were seen as creators who left humans to run things; now they kept on managing affairs. The idea reached all levels of society, and villagers at Deir el-Medina consulted oracles to settle legal disputes (see Chapter 9). This trend continued in subsequent periods of Egyptian history. In the Third Intermediate Period the god Amun, communicating via the oracle, became so important that he was declared king in Thebes.

The loss of the king's status in society was thus acute and explains why there was such a breakdown of order in the late New Kingdom. The kings of the 20th dynasty seem to have been incapable of doing much about this: they were mostly middle-aged men, who ruled a few years only and had no chance to reassert their power.

10.4 Pressures from Abroad

Despite shortages of rations and repeated protests, the community of workers at Deir el-Medina continued to build tombs up to the very end of the 20th dynasty. They dug most of the tomb intended for the final ruler, Rameses XI (ruled 1099–1069), but barely started its decoration, applying plaster to some walls and sketching the images to be carved. The work had to be stopped, because groups of Libyans roamed the countryside and made it too dangerous for the workmen to leave their village. Those Libyans were not part of the usual pattern of immigration into Egypt in which foreigners were allowed to enter the country under supervision of the state. From the 19th dynasty on the pressure of outside groups had grown to such an extent that the official record portrayed it as a real danger. The evidence is bewildering, however.

Libyans and Sea Peoples

We have seen how Rameses II surrounded Egypt with fortified borders, possibly in response to mounting attempts of nomadic groups to settle in Egypt. He did not report any wars against such groups, however. That became an issue in the inscriptions of two of his successors, Merenptah (ruled 1213–1203) and Rameses III (ruled 1184–1153), who reported major difficulties with Libyans and the so-called Sea Peoples. The record is difficult to interpret and it seems contradictory.

In his fifth year (1209) Merenptah reported a great invasion of people led by Mereye, chief of the Libyans, and including a coalition of people he said came from the countries of the sea in the north: Ekwesh, Teresh, Lukka, Sherden, and Shekelesh. Merenptah's pride in defeating them was so great that he announced his victory on the temple walls of Karnak. Three decades later, Rameses III reported similar events, for his fifth (1180) and eleventh (1174) years and most elaborately for his eighth year (1177). Once again the attackers included Libyans and a variety of people of the sea. The record is very explicit in its description of the latter's attack:

> The foreign countries conspired in their islands. All at once the lands were removed and scattered in the fray. No land could resist their arms, from Hatti, Kode, Carchemish, Arzawa, and Alashiya on – being cut off at one time. A camp was set up in Amurru. They desolated its people, and its land was like that which had never existed. They were coming forward toward Egypt, while the flame was prepared for them. Their confederation was the Peleset, Tjeker, Shekelesh, Denen, and Weshesh, lands united. They laid their hands upon the lands as far as the circuit of the earth, their hearts were confident and trusting: "Our plans will succeed!"[8]

Once again Rameses III celebrated a great victory with long inscriptions and massive relief sculptures that depicted battles on land and on water (Figure 10.3). Scholars continue to analyze the record to determine what exactly happened. They seek to connect the Sea Peoples to groups found throughout the eastern Mediterranean in second- and first-millennium contexts, both textual and archaeological, to determine where the Sea Peoples came from and where they ended up (see Key Debate 10.1). Peleset, for example, may have become the Philistines, people who resided in the southwest of Palestine in the early first millennium. From evidence, such as the *Tale of Wenamun* (see Special Topic 10.1) it appears that some of the Sea Peoples – Tjeker in Wenamun's case – settled in areas of Syria-Palestine, but the exact locations where most of these groups would have ended up remain unclear and the search for their origins is highly problematic.

Another problem is the nature of the attacks. Both Merenptah and Rameses III present them as sudden events, unforeseen and with massive numbers of people involved. Rameses III's reliefs even show carts loaded with women, children, and household goods, as if a population movement was involved. His account of the Sea Peoples' appearance in the north of the eastern Mediterranean suggests that it was unexpected, very sudden, and highly destructive. But Merenptah had reported occurrences of the same type 30 years earlier. Nor

Figure 10.3   Depiction of the naval battle against the Sea Peoples. akg-images/Erich Lessing

were the names of the members of the Sea Peoples new in the Egyptian record. Several of them appeared decades earlier, for example as mercenaries in Rameses II's account of the battle of Qadesh in 1275, serving both Egyptian and Hittite armies. Likewise, it seems that Rameses III integrated many Libyans in his army after their purported attack. In the western Delta appeared colonies of Libyans who were allowed to settle with their families. Their inhabitants would later on, in the Third Intermediate Period, gain enormous political influence. If there had been a defeat of invading Libyans and Sea Peoples, their intent to enter Egypt was certainly not thwarted.

The record is thus problematic and opaque in itself. It is also hard to connect it with certainty to events we can observe in the archaeological and textual record of the eastern Mediterranean of the period. Rameses III claimed "no land could stand before their arms," and his list of obliterated states included Alashiya on the island of Cyprus, which actually flourished at the time. It is clear, however, that this was a very eventful period in the region, and several cities and states did indeed disappear. The Hittites abandoned their capital Hattusa and seem to have retreated to the southern part

Special Topic 10.1   *The Tale of Wenamun*

The late Egyptian *Tale of Wenamun*, set in the New Kingdom's final years, provides the only narrative we have of Egypt's interactions with the Levant at the time and may reveal much about the political situation in Egypt. It is a work of literary fiction, however, written perhaps a hundred years after the events it describes. The only manuscript preserved probably dates to around 950. Some scholars think it is a copy of the actual report Wenamun submitted around 1060, but that is unproven.

Wenamun's story presents an interesting perspective on the end of the New Kingdom. It describes how a servant of Herihor, the high priest of Amun, set off to Lebanon to obtain cedar wood for Amun's boat in the fifth year of the "era of restoration," that is, Rameses XI's year 23 or 24. When Wenamun's ship docked in the Palestinian harbor of Dor, identified as a town inhabited by Tjeker (a group of Sea Peoples), a member of his crew ran off with the gold and silver he had brought as payment. Because the thief was one of Wenamun's own men, the local lord was not obliged to compensate the victim. Instead, Wenamun confiscated goods from a Tjeker ship in the harbor and sailed on.

When Wenamun reached Byblos, the ruler there, Zakar-Baal, at first refused to see him, a diplomatic rebuff that would have been unthinkable in earlier times. When they finally met, Wenamun requested the wood with the attitude that Amun's greatness would make a positive reply obvious. But Zakar-Baal did not agree. He wanted payment up front, and Wenamun had to appeal to Smendes of Tanis to obtain some valuables before the wood was delivered to him.

Wenamun's troubles were not over. Tjeker boats sailed into Byblos to capture him, but Zakar-Baal prevented them from doing so on his own territory. Instead he arranged for Wenamun to flee before the Tjeker could pursue him on the open sea. Wenamun landed in Alashiya on Cyprus, where the population tried to kill him. He fought his way to the local princess, Hatiba, and sought her protection. The final part of the story is not preserved.

The world depicted in this tale is very different from that of the eastern Mediterranean system in earlier New Kingdom times. Power in Egypt was in the hands of the high priest of Amun and a non-royal ruler at Tanis (neither one of them has royal titles in the tale). The legitimate king, Rameses XI, is not mentioned at all. The traveler ran great risks that suggest an unstable world. Wenamun was robbed, himself stole, men seeking revenge pursued him, and the population of Alashiya hounded him. Egypt's status in the Levant was that of a common trading partner, not that of a great power. No other narrative reveals the weakness of Egypt at the end of the New Kingdom so clearly.

of their state. The rich harbor city of Ugarit ceased to exist. The 12th century was one of major changes throughout the eastern Mediterranean, and the accounts of the Sea Peoples' attacks reflect Egyptian reactions to them. They could envision threats to their territory only in terms of major armies attacking them. Hence, pressure from people trying to enter Egypt from Libya and the north may have been portrayed as military invasions. The Egyptians were also unsure about what happened beyond their borders. They imagined total mayhem in the north, even if in reality the situation was much more complex.

Sources in Translation 10.1

The "Israel Stele" of Merenptah

The most discussed inscription of Merenptah is on a more than 10-feet- (3-meter-) high stele he set up to celebrate his victory over Libyans in his fifth year of rule (1209), clearly connected to his accounts of battles against Libyans and Sea Peoples in that year (Figure 10.4). A fragmentary copy of it was found at Karnak as well. The text is a hymn in praise of the king, who utterly destroyed the enemy and brought peace and happiness to the people of Egypt. The end summarizes Merenptah's accomplishments as follows:

> The princes prostrate themselves, saying "Peace!"
> Not one of the Nine Bows dares raise his head;
> Tjemhu is plundered while Hatti is peaceful,
> Canaan is seized by every evil,
> Ashkelon is carried off and Gezer is seized,
> Yenoam is made as that which never existed,
> Israel is wasted without seed,
> Khor is made a widow of Egypt,
> All the lands are at peace.
> Everyone who travels has been subdued
> By the King of Upper and Lower Egypt, Baenra Meryamun,
> Son of the god Ra, Merenptah, Contented-with-Truth,
> Given life like the god Ra every day.[9]

The victory over the Libyans brought peace to Hatti, Egypt's Hittite ally, and ensured Egypt's hold over Syria and Palestine, Khor and Canaan. The text identifies three cities as centers of opposition in Canaan: Ashkelon, Gezer, and Yenoam. Unlike these places the term Israel appears in the text with the hieroglyphic determinative for a people, not for a country or a city. This is the earliest evidence of the name Israel in any source and three centuries older than any other one. The reference precedes the existence of the state by that name by at least 200 years. It is thus very difficult to interpret. Does it show that a people with the name Israel moved through the Syro-Palestinian region at the time – is it a reference to the biblical story of the Exodus? Where did these people come from and why are there no other references to them? These questions are of special importance to students of biblical history, and will remain contentious and unanswerable until further evidence emerges.

Figure 10.4 Victory stele of Merenptah (ca. 1236–1217 BC) known as the Israel Stele, from the Mortuary Temple of Merenptah, Thebes. Egyptian National Museum, Cairo/Giraudon/The Bridgeman Art Library

The end of the international system

Egypt's ignorance of what happened in the north was due in large part to the collapse of the international system that had existed for centuries. The usual flow of information was interrupted when diplomatic contacts between the great courts stopped because partners like the Hittite state disappeared around the year 1200. The system had supported the status of the Egyptian elites both at home and abroad. The Egyptian king had been able to obtain luxury items from his colleagues through gift exchanges (see Chapter 8), but now that international diplomacy had come to a halt, these goods no longer came into Egypt.

Egypt depended on the south of the Syro-Palestinian area for mineral resources. For its entire history mines in the Sinai Desert had provided access to copper and semi-precious stone, such as turquoise. Expeditions for this purpose continued after 1200, but none is known from after the reign of Rameses VI (1143–1136). Somewhat later, Egypt lost control over its Nubian territories, whose viceroy became an independent actor. It was his intervention in Egypt itself that marked the close of the New Kingdom.

10.5   End of the New Kingdom

Throughout the 20th dynasty problems mounted for the Egyptian kings. Their hold on power weakened because of the brevity of many reigns and the loss of status to the benefit of the god Amun and his priesthood. Foreign territories slipped out of control and the state economy was in decline. Those trends culminated in the reign of Rameses XI (1099–1069), which was relatively long at 29 years, but saw the political fragmentation of the country. In the final decade Rameses XI was merely a feeble figurehead and other men held power in various parts of the country. The reconstruction of events is very difficult and scholars have proposed two divergent narratives. What is presented here is one possibility.

Early in Rameses XI's reign the volatility of the situation around Thebes reached new levels: the countryside was insecure, tomb robberies increased, and there may have been a famine, remembered later as "the year of the hyenas, when one was hungry." Several papyri detail investigations of systematic thefts from Rameses II and III's mortuary temples and even the Amun temple at Karnak. Perhaps in an attempt to bring order, the viceroy of Kush, Panehsy, marched Nubian troops into the city. His seizure of the main granary roused the reaction of the high priest of Amun, Amenhotep, and conflict erupted between the two. Some time between Rameses XI's 17th and 19th years, Panehsy laid siege to Rameses III's mortuary temple complex at Medinet Habu where the high priest and his supporters had sought refuge, workers of Deir el-Medina amongst them. Rameses XI sent his general Herihor to relieve the high priest and a civil war ensued. Herihor chased Panehsy into Nubia and took over his titles. He also declared himself vizier and, after the high priest Amenhotep's death, seized the high priesthood of Amun. His assumption of all these military, religious, and civilian offices made him de facto ruler of the south of Egypt. At this time the region adopted a new time-reckoning system, instead of continuing to count Rameses XI's regnal years. An "era of restoration" began in Rameses XI's nineteenth year, and for the next 12 years Thebans dated records according to this system. It suggested that order had been restored after a period of chaos, more a wish than a reality.

Sources in Translation 10.2
Disregard for the king

Quite a number of letters written in the late 20th dynasty are preserved and they provide unofficial insights into the political and social conditions of Egypt. Letters are often very difficult to understand as they are terse in their wording and assume knowledge by the recipient that we today lack, but they are important historical sources. A group of three letters from the tenth year of the "era of restoration," that is, Rameses XI's year 28, deals with the punishment of two policemen. The author of the three letters was a general, almost certainly Piankh who was in Nubia at the time, fighting the viceroy Panehsy. This Piankh would become Herihors' successor as high priest in Thebes. He wrote the letters to three different people in that city, including to the scribe of the workmen of the necropolis, Thutmose with the nickname Tjaroy, who by then had set up house in the temple of Medinet Habu. The second part of the letter is surprising, as Piankh, nominally still in the service of the king, accuses Rameses XI of weakness and incompetence.

> The general of Pharaoh, to the scribe of the necropolis, Tjaroy, saying: "I have taken note of all matters you wrote me about. As for the mention you made of this matter of these two policemen, saying, 'They made these charges,' join up with Nodjme and Payshuweben, and they will send word and have these two policemen brought to my house and get to the bottom of their charges quickly. If they determine that they are true, put them in two baskets and they shall be thrown into the water at night – but do not let anybody in the land find out!
> Another matter: As for Pharaoh, how will he ever reach this land (Nubia)? And as for Pharaoh, whose superior is he after all? Moreover, these three full months, although I sent a boat, you have not sent me a *deben* of gold or a *deben* of silver. That is all right. Do not worry about what he has done.
> As soon as my letter reaches you, you should supply a *deben* of gold or a *deben* of silver and send it to me by boat.
> Address: The general's agent Payshuweben from the general's scribe Kenykhnum."[10]

Herihor commissioned some building and restoration works in the temples of Thebes, which had been ignored for decades. At first he acknowledged the existence of Rameses XI, but soon he paid no attention to the king. Herihor's successors as high priest and highest military officer had full control over the southern part of Egypt, ruling from Thebes. When Rameses XI died, a man called Smendes, perhaps the son of Herihor, started the 21st dynasty in the north with its capital at Tanis in the eastern Delta. The border between the two territories was some 60 miles south of Memphis. The division of power between Tanis and Thebes would characterize the early Third Intermediate Period, which started in 1069.

Key Debate 10.1 *The Sea Peoples*

One factor in the decline of the New Kingdom that has received disproportionate attention in Egyptological scholarship and beyond is the role of the Sea Peoples, a group of attackers identified in inscriptions of Merenptah and Rameses III as "of the countries of the sea." The term only appears in Egyptian texts, but the people and their actions are almost universally connected to the upheavals that beset the eastern Mediterranean at the end of the Bronze Age. They could have been a catalyst in the fundamental changes that occurred in the region around 1200 BC and that led to a new world order in the first millennium, in which the ancient Greeks, Judeans, and Israelites, that is, the ancestors to the much later west, became prominent. Classicists, biblical scholars, Egyptologists, and others have investigated these Sea Peoples in great detail.

The documentary basis from which we can work is very limited, although it is remarkable in the specificity with which it names and depicts the members of the Sea Peoples. In the relief sculptures warriors wear particular headdresses (feathered caps, horned crowns, etc.; Figure 10.5) and carry distinct weaponry. The inscriptions provide explicit lists of names. Merenptah says he fought Sherden, Lukka, Ekwesh, Teresh, and Shekelesh, while 25 years later Rameses III repeats the names Shekelesh, Sherden, and Teresh, drops the two others but adds Tjeker, Denen, Peleset, and Weshesh. Since we only know the names from Egyptian writings that do not indicate vowels, other readings appear in scholarship as well: Shardana, Denyen, etc. From the moment of the decipherment of hieroglyphs the names' similarity to those of otherwise known people

Figure 10.5 Member of the Sea Peoples, whose headdress identifies him as a Peleset. akg-images/Erich Lessing

was recognized. Already Champollion equated the Peleset with the biblical Philistines (1836). In 1867 the first attempt to connect Sea Peoples as a group to later populations of the Mediterranean appeared: Mysians, Lycians, Dardanians, Achaeans, Tyrrhenians, Sicilians, and Sardinians (Rougé 1867). The exercise has continued ever since and seeks to find both the places of origin and the destinations of the groups. For example, the name Denen sounds like the Danuna mentioned in an Amarna letter (i.e., before the invasions; Moran 1992: 238) as well in later first-millennium inscriptions from northern Syria. The Danuna seem to reside on the Mediterranean coast of southern Turkey and even today a city called Adana is located there. The name Denen also sounds like the Greek term Danaoi, used by Homer and other Greek poets to identify "Greeks" (Barnett 1975: 365). But the name also sounds like the biblical tribe of Dan (Sandars 1985: 161–4). The search for the origins of the Sea Peoples and their destinations does not subside (cf. Cline & O'Connor 2003), but many scholars have become increasingly skeptical about the entire exercise, although the identification of Peleset with later Palestine seems hard to give up (Bard 2008: 216). One study urged us to forget about equating peoples across distant times (Bunnens 1990), while another pointed out the methodological slackness in the investigations so far (Cline & O'Connor 2003).

One can wonder why the Sea Peoples have engendered so much passion. Many consider them Indo-Europeans from the Northern Mediterranean – although the Egyptian information that they were circumcised causes awkwardness in this respect – and the idea that they were the agents of crucial change at the end of the Bronze Age had great appeal to imperialist European circles of the 19th and 20th centuries AD (Silberman 1998). Why they still appear in every textbook on world history remains to be explained.

NOTES

1. Peden 1994a: 251.
2. Grandet 2000.
3. Peden 1994a: 3.
4. Papyrus Harris I; translation after Peden 1994a: 213.
5. Peden 1994a: 251.
6. Translation after Edgerton 1951: 140–1, and Frandsen 1990: 188–9.
7. Wilson 1956: 278.
8. Translation after Wilson in Pritchard 1969: 262.
9. Translation after B. Davies 1997: 185–7.
10. Translation after Wente 1990: no. 301.

11

The Third Intermediate Period (ca. 1069–715)

Amun-is-the-king

The names modern scholars use to designate periods in the long history of ancient Egypt have a great impact on how we perceive them (see Chapter 1). This is perhaps especially true for the centuries that followed the New Kingdom, after Egypt was an empire and at the height of its strength. One prominent German Egyptologist entitled the chapters treating Egypt's history from the end of the New Kingdom to when the Greeks ruled as if it were a battle of survival against foreign influences. He used "Collapse of the state" for the centuries right after the New Kingdom ended, "Egypt as the theater of foreign quarrels" for the subsequent period of Nubian dominance, "Restoration" for the brief reunification under an indigenous dynasty, and "Egyptian nationalism and Persia" for the final centuries before Alexander's conquest of Egypt.[1] In this view outsiders determined what happened, while Egyptians resisted and at times reasserted their vanishing culture. More neutral labels still designate what followed the New Kingdom as an epilogue: first the Third Intermediate Period – in parallel with earlier times when power was fragmented – then the Late Period – a term that suggests the final act of a long history ending in 332 BC when foreigners from the northern Mediterranean took over the country's rule.

For a long time the period between the end of the New Kingdom and Alexander's conquest of Egypt received relatively little scholarly attention, because the purity of Egyptian culture was thought to have disappeared. It would be foolish to see seven centuries as a mere epilogue of Egyptian history, however. These were times of fundamental change in the country, and the homogeneity of earlier times – something we may stress too much – did disappear. Non-Egyptians most often dominated political life and although they adopted the trappings of earlier Egyptian kingship and culture, they did not hide their foreign origin. At times, Egypt indeed seems to have been the plaything caught in the midst of struggling alien powers. Still, Egyptian customs usually influenced the behavior of these foreign powers fundamentally. Culture showed a great deal of hybridity, combining elements from Egypt's past with those the newcomers introduced. These "Late Periods" were as much a part of Egypt's ancient civilization as any of the preceding periods, and we have to take them into account to appreciate the country's history fully.

In this chapter we will discuss the so-called Third Intermediate Period, which is not an easy period to grasp. The concept of royal dynasties continued, but in reality various bases of power coexisted and kingship itself was perceived differently from before. We call it an intermediate period because Egypt was politically fragmented, but the official record shows no resentment of that situation – unlike in earlier Intermediate Periods. It may have been hard for a traditional Egyptian to understand what happened at the time, and it is difficult for us as well. We know the names of many rulers – with such titles as king, chief, and high priest – but rather than representing opposing camps in a struggle for dominance, they often were closely related by blood, and they agreed on a division of power. Moreover, all saw the god Amun as the supreme authority who determined everything. One of the first kings of the era was called Amun-is-the-king, Amenemnisu, to express that thought. The Third Intermediate Period presents a significant era in Egypt's history because of its mixture of drastic changes and adherence to the country's past. It was not a period of chaos – as the term might Intermediate suggest – or a pale imitation of earlier situations. With its duration of some 350 years (compared to 135 years for the First Intermediate Period and 100 for the second) it constitutes an important stage in the country's evolution, when traditional indigenous and fresh foreign elements formed a new society.

11.1 Sources and Chronology

Compared to the New Kingdom and especially the Ramessid Period, the source material for the Third Intermediate Period is limited. This is true for all levels of society. The village of Deir el-Medina ceased to produce the abundant documents of daily life, and only dispersed finds illustrate how people outside temples and palaces lived during this time. The upper levels of society also left fewer records and royal inscriptions are relatively few. The shortage of evidence partly results from the location of the political capitals in the Delta, where more humid conditions caused the decay of many remains. In Upper Egypt building activity declined and was mostly limited to reuse of materials from earlier periods. Although this was possibly a sign of respect for earlier times, the lack of new construction indicates a failure of rulers and others to finance large projects. As the major religious center of the country, Thebes still stands out as the place with the most monuments, and the names of many pharaohs, high priests, and other officials are often only known from there. Some private individuals do seem to have been affluent, and left behind majestic tombs in Thebes and commissioned statues to be placed in temples.

Although Egypt's interactions with the outside world decreased substantially in the Third Intermediate Period, the country did not exist in isolation and it encountered other cultures that left historical records. Near Eastern accounts are of two types. From the 9th century on, the Assyrians from northern Mesopotamia campaigned almost continuously in the Syro-Palestinian area and reached increasingly farther south and closer to Egypt. Before 715 they never threatened Egypt, but Egyptians supported Syro-Palestinian resistance to the Assyrians, and in some battle accounts the latter mentioned Egyptian troops. The accounts provided very little detail, however. The other source that mentions Egypt regularly is the Hebrew Bible. Located just beyond the Egyptian border, the inhabitants of the states of Israel and Judah naturally were in contact with this important neighbor. The historical usefulness of the Bible is controversial, however. It is likely that most accounts were composed many centuries after the Third Intermediate Period, and their accuracy even in the narrative of Israel's history is questionable. For example, the Bible describes a large united kingdom under Solomon, who was so powerful that he married an Egyptian princess. Many scholars use this passage to illustrate Egypt's weakness in the 10th century – never before was an Egyptian princess sent abroad – but one can also read it as a later invention to underscore Solomon's greatness – he was the only foreign man ever to marry an Egyptian princess. The biblical material is hard to use in the reconstruction of Egyptian history.

At the end of the Third Intermediate Period Egypt was in close contact with Nubia to its south. Rulers from that region left some records of their actions in Egypt, one of which, Piy's victory stele (Sources in Translation 11.2), is the most informative account of the political situation in Egypt at the time.

The chronology of the Third Intermediate Period is also not secure. No king list exists except for Manetho's 3rd-century-BC compilation. He took only Delta rulers into account and our modern designation Third Intermediate Period comprises four or five of his dynasties. All scholars include in the period dynasties 21 through 24, whose capitals Manetho placed at Tanis, Bubastis, and Sais, all Delta cities. Alongside them existed other centers of power, at first under high priests of Amun and Libyan chiefs, later ruled by men who claimed royal titles as well. Some scholars include Manetho's entire 25th dynasty, when Nubians ruled Egypt, in the Third Intermediate Period, others see it as part of the Late Period. Others still, myself included, consider the beginning of the 25th dynasty until 715 to be a continuation of the political fragmentation characteristic of the Third Intermediate Period. With the Nubian conquest of the whole of Egypt the Late Period started.

The absolute chronology of the Late Period, which follows the Third Intermediate Period, is very secure because at that time the Assyrians and Persians invaded Egypt in years that are firmly established. Counting backwards from these firm dates and using the lengths of reigns Manetho and other sources provide allows for the approximate dating of Third Intermediate Period kings. There is the usual confusion of overlapping reigns in Intermediate Periods, and it is also clear that Manetho regularly underestimated lengths of reigns.

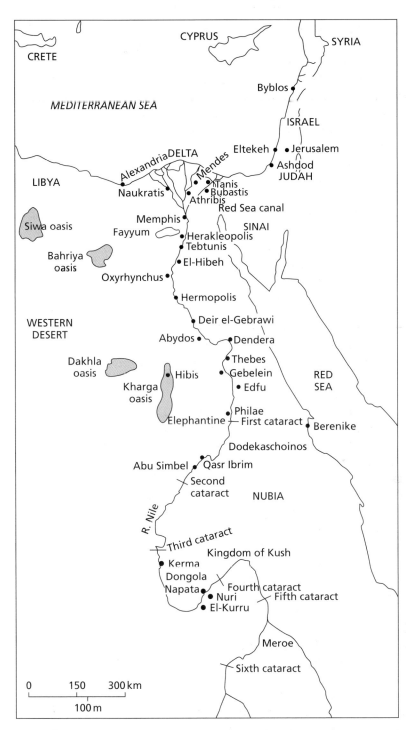

CRETE

CYPRUS

SYRIA

MEDITERRANEAN SEA

Byblos

ISRAEL

LIBYA

Alexandria DELTA
Mendes
Eltekeh   Jerusalem
Ashdod
JUDAH
Naukratis   Tanis
Athribis   Bubastis
Red Sea canal

Siwa oasis

Memphis
Fayyum   SINAI
Herakleopolis
Tebtunis
El-Hibeh

Bahriya
oasis

Oxyrhynchus

Hermopolis

WESTERN
DESERT

Deir el-Gebrawi

Abydos   Dendera

Dakhla
oasis

Thebes
Hibis   Gebelein   RED
SEA
Edfu

Kharga
oasis

Philae
Elephantine   First cataract   Berenike

Dodekaschoinos

Abu Simbel   Qasr Ibrim

Second
cataract   NUBIA

R. Nile

Third cataract

Kingdom of Kush

Kerma
Dongola
Napata   Fourth cataract
Nuri   Fifth cataract
El-Kurru

Meroe

Sixth cataract

0   150   300 km

100 m

Map 6   Late Period Egypt

Summary of dynastic history
21st–early 25th dynasties (ca. 1069–715)

ca. 1069–945	**21st dynasty** Royal dynasty of Tanis shares power with High Priests of Amun at Thebes High Priests hide New Kingdom royal mummies in caches Tanis developed as counterpart to Thebes in the Delta
ca. 945–715	**22nd dynasty** Kings in Tanis acknowledge Libyan background overtly King Sheshonq I concentrates power in Tanis and raids Palestine Increased fragmentation of power between families related by blood and marriage, ca. 850
ca. 818–715	**23rd dynasty** Grouping of rulers from multiple centers in parallel to Manetho's 22nd to early 25th dynasties Office of God's Wife of Amun gains great importance
ca. 727–715	**24th dynasty** Two Libyan kings at Sais King Tefnakht seeks hegemony over northern Egypt
ca. 750–715	**Early 25th dynasty** King Kashta places daughter Amenirdis as God's Wife in Thebes, ca. 750 King Piy raids throughout Egypt, 728

Moreover, many people have relied excessively on biblical chronology, which is not as firm as they would like. A thorough study of the chronology of the period demands a "ca." before every date. For simplicity's sake I will mostly omit that caveat.

11.2 Twin Cities: Thebes and Tanis (the 21st dynasty, 1069–945)

Wenamun's tale (see Chapter 10) depicts a divided Egypt where two men held the reins of power: Wenamun's superior, the high priest of Amun at

Thebes Herihor, and the secular leader Smendes in his residence at Tanis. The "real" pharaoh, Rameses XI, was still alive but Wenamun did not bother to visit him or even mention him. *The Tale of Wenamun* may be pure fiction, but we know that, after Rameses XI's death in 1069, Thebes and Tanis functioned as independent centers of power. They were the seats of parallel dynasties – hence we speak of the Third Intermediate Period. But matters were not that straightforward. The official characterization of government in the two places was distinct – religious in Thebes and secular in Tanis – and the holders of power were related by blood and marriage and most often worked in unison in a system they both accepted. Scholars have likened the arrangement to a concordat, the division of power between popes and kings in European history. The parallel is quite apt. Before we study the nature of the interactions we will look at Thebes and Tanis individually to clarify the character of government there.

Thebes

When Tutankhamun was forced to leave Akhetaten after the Amarna revolution failed, the court did not return to Thebes but went to Memphis near the Delta where the later New Kingdom capitals were located. Thebes flourished during the remainder of the New Kingdom, however, as the center of Amun's cult, and that god's role continued to increase. The priesthood was powerful and wealthy. A report of Rameses III's gifts to the Amun temple suggests that it controlled a vast part of all agricultural land in Egypt (see Chapter 10). The priesthood's influence was limited to the cult and administration, however. That changed at the very end of the New Kingdom when the high priest of Amun also became the highest military commander. High Priest Herihor was the first to combine these powers, perhaps because Rameses XI commissioned him to remove the viceroy of Kush, Panehsy, from Thebes. This unprecedented accumulation of offices remained in practice throughout the Third Intermediate Period. The high priest of Amun was also "supreme commander of the army," or "Generalissimo" as many scholars translate his title. One could say that this control over all sectors of government made him like a king and most high priests of Amun used royal titles, but only as local kings and they did not date records with their regnal years. The god Amun was the real king in Theban ideology. His name regularly appeared in cartouches and the priests were merely his temporary representatives and appointees. Thebes was thus a theocracy: the god ruled.

This ideology finds expression in a long hymn to Amun that focuses on the god's solar character and his role as primordial god and creator. The hymn ends with these lines:

King of Upper and Lower Egypt, Amun-Ra, King-of-the-Gods,
Lord of heaven and earth,
Of the waters and the mountains,
Who created the land through his incarnation.
He is greater and more sublime
Than all the gods of primordial times.[2]

The god made decisions of state in actual practice. A regular Festival of the Divine Audience took place at Karnak when the god's statue communicated through oracles, by nodding assent when he agreed. Divine oracles had become important in the 18th dynasty; in the Third Intermediate Period they formed the basis of governmental practice. Some decisions that were considered to be of great importance were recorded in writing. For example, around the year 990 the high priest of Amun Menkheperra wanted to permit the return of people banished previously for unstated crimes. The inscription commemorating the event describes the interactions between high priest and god:

> Then the High Priest of Amun Menkheperra spoke to him, saying: "My good lord, is there a matter about which one should speak before you?" The Great God agreed very strongly. Then, he (Menkheperra) went again before the Great God and said: "My good lord, is it the matter of the rebellious servants with whom you were angry and who are now in the oasis where they were banished?" The Great God agreed very strongly, while the general whose hands were lifted in praise, honored his lord as a father speaks to his own son.[3]

Under further questioning Amun empowered Menkheperra to allow the exiles to return home. The god agreed with Menkheperra's suggestions. Although priests manipulated the statue, the ideology is clear: Amun decided.

As the god's representatives, the high priests of Thebes took charge of what had been royal duties. They commissioned work in temples at Thebes, almost always reusing existing monuments. High Priest Pinudjem I set up a double line of sphinxes from the facade of Karnak to the river, some 100 in total. He reused sphinxes carved in the 18th dynasty for the Luxor temple, adding his name to the existing inscriptions. More ambitious were the fortifications the high priests built at the northern frontier of the territory they controlled. Near the city of Herakleopolis they constructed fortresses of mud brick, including at the modern site of el-Hibeh, whose ancient name became Teudjoi, which means "their walls." It was the residence of the "Commander of Upper Egypt," that is, the south. High priests of Amun Pinudjem I and Menkheperra left bricks stamped with their names in the fortifications (see Key Debate 11.1). They mentioned their wives' names as well, both called Istemkheb, something earlier builders rarely did.

The high priests were preoccupied with their own burials and the preservation of the mummies of New Kingdom kings, endangered by tomb robbers. They disinterred the latter, tagged them, and hid them in secret places, in the cliffs above Deir el-Bahri or in the Valley of the Kings (Figure 11.1). Records

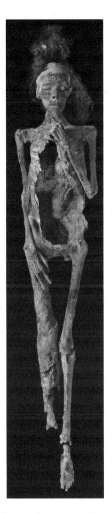

Figure 11.1 Mummy found in the cache in KV35, the tomb of Amenhotep II. akg-images/De Agostini Pict.Li

show that several priests of the 21st and 22nd dynasties moved the mummies repeatedly and regularly wrapped them in new linen. They also used the secret places as their own family crypts, to be used for themselves, and their wives and daughters. Some scholars refer to the crypts as mass graves; in one cache 36 mummies were interred.

Tanis

Unlike Thebes, which was an ancient city with a millennium-long history by the end of the New Kingdom, Tanis was a brand new city. No archaeological evidence from it pre-dates the reign of Psusennes I (ruled 1039–991), but many scholars think it originated in the late New Kingdom. Tanis's creation was probably due to the silting up of the Nile branch that ran by Piramesse, which forced people to seek another area with access to water. Tanis is only some 16 miles (25 kilometers) northeast of Piramesse and its builders used stones and statues taken from that site. The first explorers thought it was a creation of Rameses II as so many of his inscriptions appear there. Now it is clear that his dismantled buildings were the building blocks of Tanis.

The layout of Tanis was not innovative. When King Psusennes I decided to build a temple for Amun, he copied the layout of that god's temple at Thebes albeit on a somewhat less grand scale. The remains constructed by him and several of his successors show many parallels with the Karnak temple: a west–east orientation, a massive enclosure wall, a sacred lake, obelisks, courts and monumental gates, and subsidiary temples for Amun's spouse, Mut, and son, Khonsu, as well as a southern temple parallel to the temple of Luxor for the Opet festival. The inscriptions in the temple honor the gods as Theban deities and mention place names from that location rather than from the north. It is no surprise then that later on Tanis also became known as Thebes of Lower Egypt.

Tanis's role as the seat of the dynasty is clear from the location of royal tombs there. But there was a major difference from Theban and all earlier practices in the character of the royal burials. Instead of being located in inaccessible mountains, the tombs of 21st-dynasty kings were within the temple complex beneath a mastaba-like structure. The tomb of King Psusennes I was a major archaeological surprise. Unlike other tombs at the site, looters had not disturbed it and the original grave goods were preserved intact. They were stunning: the king was buried in three sarcophagi, the outer one of red granite (reused from Merenptah), the middle one of black granite (also reused from the Valley of the Kings), and the innermost one of solid silver (Figure 11.2). That metal was not available in pure form in Egypt and was imported from the Levant. It may have been more costly than gold. The king's face was covered with a gold mask (Plate 10) – similar to Tutankhamun's – and he wore a massive amount of gold jewelry. Egypt may have lost its international clout at the time, but the king was still able to command great wealth in death. Another novelty of the burials was that several dead individuals were entombed in the same complex. In Psusennes's tomb were chambers for his wife and two army generals.

The kings at Tanis saw themselves as the legitimate successors on the throne of Upper and Lower Egypt. They used traditional titles and displayed their royalty in building work, although that was insignificant when compared to activity at the height of the New Kingdom. Manetho portrayed the Tanite dynasty as the only ruling power in Egypt. People of the time of the 21st dynasty did recognize these royal claims, not only in the north of the country but in Thebes as well. For example, nine officials in Thebes referred to Amenemope

Figure 11.2 Silver sarcophagus of King Psusennes I. Werner Forman Archive/Egyptian Museum, Cairo

of Tanis (ruled 993–984) as king in their tomb inscriptions, while they acknowledged Pinudjem II as their high priest. This is one sign of the coexistence of the two centers of power.

The concordat

In previous Intermediate Periods the dynasties that governed Egypt simultaneously were in competition with each other: Thebes and Herakleopolis in the First Intermediate Period (Chapter 4) and Thebes and the Hyksos in the

Second (Chapter 6). We may exaggerate the degree of antagonism in these periods, but the official rhetoric saw times with more than one ruler as anathema. This feeling was not expressed in the Third Intermediate Period. Kings at Tanis and high priests at Thebes recognized each other's existence without rancor. They regularly helped each other and acted jointly. For example, King Smendes sent assistance to Thebes when a flood threatened the Luxor temple, and High Priest Pinudjem I helped King Psusennes I when he built the Amun temple at Tanis. The two left joint inscriptions. The relationship between the two houses was very personal. The founder of the dynasty, Smendes, may have been the son of High Priest Herihor, and his daughter married High Priest Pinudjem I. Their son married the daughter of the third king, Psusennes I. The last high priest under the 21st dynasty, Psusennes, probably became the last king of the dynasty as well, the second Psusennes of the royal line. Close family members thus shared power in the country. They coexisted under an agreement that can be likened to the concordat between church and state in European history: secular and religious powers accepted each other's areas of influence. In 21st-dynasty Egypt the northern royal house nominally ruled the entire country, but in reality allowed another branch of the family to run the south on the basis of its priestly office.

The official power-sharing actually hides a greater fragmentation of Egypt in the 21st dynasty, one that would become much more visible in the 22nd dynasty. Alongside Thebes and Tanis existed at least one other powerful family with its seat in Bubastis, a Delta town south of Tanis. The title used to refer to its leader was "Great chief of the Meshwesh" or abbreviated "of the Ma," that is, Libyans. They descended from people who had migrated from the western desert into the Delta during the later New Kingdom and who had mainly stayed in northern Egypt. The Libyan influence most likely explains why the coexistence of different centers of power was tolerated. Libyans seemingly had an ideology where leaders could rule in parallel, and were able to introduce that idea of kingship into Third Intermediate Period Egypt. It is probable that the kings and high priests of the 21st dynasty were Libyans themselves, although they used Egyptian names. If so, they merely continued practices that were common in their society but unacceptable to earlier Egyptians. The strong reliance on the god Amun may have been their way to make these changes palatable.

The political power of Libyan-Egyptians increased over time and the end of the 21st dynasty was the result of their nonviolent take-over. According to an inscription he left behind, the Great Chief of the Ma Sheshonq, in the presence of King Psusennes II, asked the oracle of Amun in Thebes for permission to set up a statue of his father Nimlot at Abydos. Amun approved and also permitted Sheshonq to be associated with the king in all the great festivals. He thus became Psusennes's official heir (Sources in Translation 11.1). The transfer of the throne from one family to another was made official when Psusennes's daughter married Sheshonq's son, Osorkon, and the 22nd dynasty began when Psusennes died in 945.

Sources in Translation 11.1

Sheshonq I's accession to power

The transfer of power from the 21st to the 22nd dynasties was a diplomatic decision. Sheshonq I, a member of a long line of Chiefs of the Meshwesh or Ma from Bubastis, obtained the status of heir apparent to Psusennes II of Tanis, who was also high priest of Amun. The god Amun had to endorse the arrangement and did so through his oracle. Sheshonq commemorated the event in an inscription on a stele he left at Abydos, the religious center of Osiris. The occasion he commemorated was the setting up of a statue of his deceased father Nimlot there, which entailed large donations, which are listed in detail. But the text starts out with the request that Amun allows Sheshonq to participate in all royal festivals.

> Will you let the great prince of princes, Sheshonq the justified, and his child dwell in the Seat of the Blessed (= Abydos) near his father (= Nimlot)? Will you let him magnify his beauty in the city of Tjawwer (near Abydos) in front of the Healthy-Wakeful-One (= Osiris)? Will you let him be revered more than the one who attained old age, his son continuing thereafter? Will you let him participate in the festivals of his Majesty (Psusennes II), receiving joint victory?" This Great God agreed very plainly. Then, his Majesty spoke again in the presence of this Great God: "My good lord, will you slay the officer of the army, the sergeant, the scribe, the inspector, any messenger, anyone sent on an errand in the countryside, who will seize property belonging to this statue of the god Osiris, the Great Chief of the Meshwesh, Nimlot the justified, son of Mehetemweskhet, which is in Abydos; and any people who will take from its sacred offerings, its land, its people, its cattle, its garden, any of its oblations, and any endowments belonging to it? Will you exercise your great and mighty power against them and against their wives and their children?" This Great God agreed. Then his Majesty kissed the ground before him and his Majesty said: "You are justified, O Sheshonq the justified, you Great Chief of the Meshwesh, prince of princes, my great one, together with all your supporters and your army likewise, inasmuch as Amun-Ra, King-of-the-Gods favors you because of all you have done for your father. You shall attain old age, dwelling upon earth, your heirs being upon your throne forever.[4]

The passage illustrates the political situation in the Third Intermediate Period well. Rulers from northern Egypt continued to use southern Egyptian cult centers and supported them with donations. The king was willing to share power with someone not related to him and clearly a son of another family. But ultimately the god Amun had to give his approval, because he ruled the world.

11.3   Libyan Rule (22nd to 24th Dynasties, 945–715)

Centralization and diffusion of power

The god Amun had ratified that kingship could pass to a new family, that of Chiefs of the Ma who for a century or more had had their power base in Bubastis, a city in the central Delta. The first king, Sheshonq I (ruled 945–924), moved to Tanis to take the throne and started a period of overt Libyan rule that would last more than 200 years. He and the kings that succeeded him used their Libyan names openly. Some scholars argue that this was the only clear difference with the previous dynasty whose kings, with one exception (Osorkon I), had Egyptian names. They think these names belonged to men of Libyan descent as well, and point out that many high priests of Amun bore Libyan names. Whatever was the case, the plain use of Libyan royal names shows that this population group had become fully accepted in Egyptian society.

Libyan concepts of rule allowed for the parallel existence of leaders who were related by marriage and blood. Sheshonq and his immediate successors used that practice to consolidate their grasp on all of Egypt. Whereas in the 21st dynasty in essence two families linked by marriage ties formed ruling dynasties in Tanis and Thebes, Sheshonq terminated the hereditary succession of the high priesthood of Amun. Instead he and his successors appointed men to the position, most often their own sons, a practice that lasted for a century. The supremacy of Tanis was thus clear. At the same time the kings gave their daughters in marriage to other priests and high officials in Thebes and elsewhere, thereby creating a closely linked ruling elite throughout Egypt.

The consolidation of power in the kings' hands seems to have provided them with the ability to take initiatives we expect from Egyptian rulers: building monuments and fighting wars. Sheshonq I was the first king in a long time to add substantial monuments to the Karnak temple at Thebes. He constructed a court in front of the second pylon – then the facade of the complex – with colonnades on the sides. In one corner, between the second pylon and a small temple Ramesses III had built, he erected a gate, which is now called the Bubastite portal after the home city of the dynasty. The decoration contains inscriptions of various 22nd-dynasty kings. Nearby Sheshonq I carved a report of campaigns in Nubia and Palestine, with a detailed list of conquests in Palestine. This is the first military action outside Egypt formally commemorated for several centuries.

Sheshonq's representation and account are summary. The text contains Amun's praise of Sheshonq:

> My heart is very glad when I see your victories, my son, Sheshonq Meryamun, my beloved, the one who came forth from me to be my champion.[5]

The relief shows Amun and the goddess of Thebes Waset leading a total of 156 bound prisoners to the king, whose image was later erased. In traditional

Figure 11.3 List of conquered cities in Palestine on the Bubastite portal. akg-images/Erich Lessing

Egyptian fashion, the prisoners' bodies are ovals in which the names of their cities and localities are written out: some 75 names are preserved (Figure 11.3). Because of a possible biblical connection, this account has occupied many scholars of Egypt and the Hebrew Bible. Two biblical passages (I Kings 14:15 and II Chronicles 12:1–10) state that an Egyptian king, Shishak, sacked Jerusalem and looted its temple and palace in the fifth year of King Rehoboam of Judah, Solomon's son. He looted the mythical wealth of King Solomon. The names Shishak and Sheshonq are so close that a connection between the two accounts seems obvious. But there are problems in their correlation: Sheshonq's Karnak list does not include Jerusalem – his biggest prize according to the Bible. His list focuses on places either north or south of Judah, as if he did not raid the center. The fundamental problem facing historians is establishing the aims of the two accounts and linking up the information in them. Sheshonq carved his Karnak relief soon after the events to commemorate a great military victory. The list of places he raided could be an accurate reflection of where his troops went, but some scholars think it copies earlier New Kingdom materials and has no historical value. The biblical authors, whose version of events as known to us postdate them by many centuries, saw the invasion as a punishment by their god and a reason for the end of Jerusalem's former greatness. To see in their words more than a vague memory of a past Egyptian campaign is problematic. Even more awkward is the fact that the records disagree on where Sheshonq campaigned, so it is difficult to correlate them. Most likely we can conclude that Sheshonq conducted military actions abroad, but their exact reach is hard to evaluate.

Sheshonq's campaign had no lasting effect, and building activity at Thebes stopped when he died. His successors initially maintained their grasp on Egypt's political life by placing family members into central positions everywhere, but a century or so into the dynasty the control loosened when these appointees claimed greater autonomy. Fathers passed offices on to sons and local dynasties emerged with varied titles. At Memphis the high priests of Ptah were paramount, at Herakleopolis governors, elsewhere Great Chiefs of the Ma, and so on. The country became divided among numerous local rulers, many of whom claimed the title King of Upper and Lower Egypt. The 22nd dynasty survived in Tanis until 715, but for more than a hundred years it coexisted with kings outside its control – we call them the 23rd and 24th dynasties, and there were several more royal houses. Reports from outsiders expose the conditions. When the Nubian King Piy raided Egypt in his 20th year (728) he did not face unified opposition but defeated a series of local potentates. His commemorative stele shows a scene where eight kings, princes, and chiefs prostrate themselves before him, and the inscription lists additional names. An Assyrian account from the mid-7th century groups numerous leaders – chiefs, kings, high priests, etc. – under the title "kings," and the Greek historian Herodotus in the 5th century stated that there were 12 kings who, united by intermarriage, governed in mutual friendliness (Book 2.147). The situation was not considered to be chaotic or unacceptable. Piy's stele represents various men with royal symbols, including names in cartouches, or as chiefs of the Ma with the appropriate signs of their office.

The division of Lower Egypt was more acute than it was in Upper Egypt, where Thebans maintained greater authority. It is likely that a royal dynasty established itself in Thebes whose kings controlled the area up to the traditional border with northern Egypt at el-Hibeh. Although there is some evidence of conflict between various Egyptians and certain accounts describe brutal oppression of rebellions, it is insufficient to imply constant strife and upheaval. Local leaders coexisted in a system that tolerated the division of power.

The God's Wife of Amun

The sharing of authority was not limited to men, and some women attained unprecedented influence. The powers of existing offices were reformulated to fit the new political situation. In general women remained of secondary importance, as was the case throughout Egyptian history, but some women of the Third Intermediate Period acquired remarkable titles. The wife of the 21st-dynasty high priest of Amun Pinudjem II, Nesikhons, was "overseer of the southern foreign lands" and "King's son of Kush." As Thebes probably had no effective control south of the first cataract these titles were merely honorific and a guarantee of income from estates in Egypt itself, but they show a perception that women could hold high military and administrative offices.

The true power of at least one woman at a time in the Third Intermediate Period and the succeeding 25th and 26th dynasties appears in the office of God's Wife of Amun. This priestly office already existed in the 18th dynasty, when queens, starting with Ahmose-Nefertari wife of Ahmose, held it. Hatshepsut was God's Wife of Amun until she took the title of king. Most of the 18th-dynasty women were married and had children, and they were mainly involved in religious rituals. The office came with an income generated on sizeable agricultural estates. Its importance in the New Kingdom varied, but it continued to exist and, from Rameses VI on, a princess rather than a queen occupied it. It seems that from that time on the holder had to remain celibate and adopted her successor. The king decided who that woman should be.

When multiple kings ruled that aspect of the office gained an important political connotation. Whichever ruler was most powerful could place his daughter in the position, which gave him access to influence in the affairs of Thebes. We only know a few of the God's Wives of Amun of the early Third Intermediate Period. They include one daughter of Psusennes I of the 21st dynasty from Tanis and one daughter of the Theban high priest of Amun Menkheperra soon afterward. For the end of the period and in the subsequent 25th and 26th dynasties the sequence of God's wives is clear, and their ancestry shows who was most able to enforce a claim. Many of these women lived to a remarkable old age. The sequence started with Shepenwepet, daughter of King Osorkon III from Thebes. She lived until around 700, but already around 750 she was forced to adopt Amenirdis, daughter of the Nubian King Kashta as her successor (Figure 11.4). Two later Nubian princesses succeeded her, a result of the Nubian occupation of Egypt. The end of that occupation was signaled by the adoption of a princess from northern Egypt, Nitiqret, daughter of King Psamtek I of the 26th dynasty. The account to commemorate Nitiqret's adoption is the longest of her father's preserved inscriptions and shows how much wealth was connected to the position. Psamtek states that he convinced the existing Nubian God's Wife to adopt his daughter. Nitiqret received massive assets including domains in seven Upper Egyptian and four Lower Egyptian nomes, a total of some 2224 acres (900 hectares). Moreover various priests had to provide her daily with 420 pounds (190 kilograms) of bread and with cereals, herbs, and milk, and monthly with oxen, geese, and other foodstuffs. The king contributed thus to her wealth, but the priests of Amun also had to support her. Later 26th-dynasty princesses continued to hold the office and merged it with that of First Prophet of Amun, the foremost priesthood in Thebes. When the Persians conquered Egypt in 525 they abolished the office.

The political importance of these women was very great and publicly acknowledged. They often acted as regents for their fathers or brothers in the Theban area, adopting royal attributes there. Like a king they used multiple throne names and wrote them in cartouches. Their burials were inside the west-bank temple of Medinet Habu, which contained Rameses III's mortuary temple and

Figure 11.4 Statuette of Amenirdis, God's Wife of Amun and daughter of Kashta. © 2010. Photo Scala, Florence

also a small temple to Amun. Near the latter temple stood mortuary chapels for the God's Wives, in a parallel arrangement to the royal tombs of the 21st and 22nd dynasties at Tanis.

11.4 The End of the Third Intermediate Period

Nubian resurgence

The adoption of Amenirdis I, daughter of the Nubian King Kashta, shows that the southern kingdom had acquired unmatched influence in Egypt. To understand how this came about we have to look at the historical evolution in Nubia after the New Kingdom. Starting from the late 20th dynasty written and archaeological documentation becomes very scarce there, and there is scholarly disagreement over the facts. The cemetery at Hillat el-Arab near Gebel Barkal shows some continuity. It continued in use from the New Kingdom into the Third Intermediate Period to serve local people, who may at first have served the Egyptians, but when independent retained the same burial customs. A unique inscription of Queen Katimala carved on the facade of a temple Thutmose III had built at Semna on the southern side of the second cataract, is especially controversial. Some see it as evidence of Nubian state formation at the time of the 21st dynasty, others as an indication of Egyptian influence that far south. There is little Egyptian information for influence over Lower Nubia. Theban sources mention viceroys of Kush until around 750, for example the high priest's wife Nesikhons mentioned above. Did they just occupy a ceremonial office with no actual powers beyond the first cataract, where they regularly left inscriptions in the temple of Khnum at Elephantine? Some scholars believe that Lower Nubia between the first and second cataracts was depopulated for centuries and that the great temples of Rameses II and other New Kingdom kings were abandoned. Others think that some population remained and that the viceroys administered the surviving temple towns.

Politically the area south of the second cataract had reverted to a fragmentation of power with multiple chiefs over small districts. In the mid-9th century one chiefdom grew larger and more powerful in the fertile region known as the Dongola reach, between the fourth and third cataracts. Its background and gradual increase in power is clear from the cemetery at el-Kurru, some 10 miles (16 kilometers) downriver from Gebel Barkal where New Kingdom Egyptians previously had a religious and administrative center. The cemetery contains a set of monumental burials that were clearly intended for special individuals; hieroglyphic inscriptions attest that the latest ones were for the kings of the 25th dynasty and we can assume that earlier tombs belonged to chiefs and early kings whose names we do not know. The tombs' layout changed over time. The earliest were tumulus-mounds of pebbles and rubble over an underground chamber, with a stone wall encircling the mound. These developed into mastaba-like structures on top of which stood a small pyramid, and the final stage was a full pyramid. The famous Old Kingdom pyramids of northern Egypt may have been the inspiration, but the Nubian constructions usually had a much steeper angle and were much smaller, like non-royal pyramids in Thebes. The goods within these tombs became increasingly more Egyptian in character over time, however, and show a desire to express special social status through the display of goods, often of foreign origin. The tombs' evolution indicates that select people with local Nubian cultural traditions acquired greater wealth and the ability to create impressive mortuary monuments. No absolute dates can be assigned to the start of the process, as the time-span of the cemetery cannot be established with certainty, but by 850 it was well underway.

The source of the tomb owners' wealth seems to have been trade: Nubians acquired Egyptian objects while sub-Saharan African products re-emerged in

Egypt in this period. Egypt used Nubian items in its interactions with states in the Near East. In the mid-9th century the Assyrians recorded that they received a hippopotamus, a rhinoceros, elephants, and monkeys from Egypt, which must have been of Nubian origin. The Nubians seem to have traded directly with Assyria as well, probably using Red Sea ports. From around 730 on, Assyrian palace accounts record the presence of Nubian horses, which seem to have been the preferred breed for cavalries at the time. Near Eastern ivory production flourished in this period, as many finds in Assyrian palaces attest. Since Syrian elephants were already extinct then, it is likely that the material was imported from Africa. If that was indeed the case, the organization of this trade may explain the renewed wealth of Upper Nubia.

The earliest occupants of the el-Kurru tombs lived in a non-literate society. No writing appears in Upper Nubia until the mid-8th century, when kings started to use Egyptian hieroglyphs for their inscriptions. We are thus uninformed about the names and actions of early rulers. Later Nubian kings honored a man called Alara as the founder of the dynasty, but details of his reign are very scarce. Some scholars think that he is to be equated with a King Ary, the husband of Katimala who left an inscription at Semna, but that is doubtful. Alara's successor, Kashta, is somewhat better known and by his reign Upper Nubia had grown into a true kingdom with political and military influence as far north as Egypt. Kashta left behind a stele in the Khnum temple at Elephantine on the first cataract in which he called himself King of Upper and Lower Egypt, and had he sufficient influence in Thebes to have his daughter Amenirdis adopted as God's Wife of Amun.

The religious center of the Nubian state was Napata, at a strategic location close to the fourth cataract, controlling the overland route that cut straight from the fifth to the third cataract avoiding the long river meander. At the foot of a 250-foot (74-meter) rock outcrop – the Gebel Barkal – the New Kingdom Egyptians had built a temple to Amun, who they thought dwelled in the mountain. The early Nubian king Alara restored the temple and used it as the ideological center of their state. The god Amun granted kingship, and just as Tanis was the parallel of Thebes in the north, Napata was its parallel in the Nubian south.

Saite expansion

At the same time that the Nubians extended their influence into Thebes, a ruler from northern Egypt tried to unify the Delta and was so successful that modern scholarship made him the founder of a brief, two-ruler, dynasty, the 24th of Sais. The Libyan chief Tefnakht seized control in that western Delta city some time after 750 and made it the base of the dominant power in northern Egypt, forcing other rulers into alliances. Those included Nimlot, king of Hermopolis, a city south of the traditional boundary between Theban and northern zones of influence.

Sources in Translation 11.2

Piy's victory stele

After his successful campaign through Egypt in his 20th year (728) the Nubian king Piy set up a large stele at Napata, 5.9 by 6.03 feet (1.80 by 1.84 meters) in size and almost fully inscribed with the longest preserved royal inscription from ancient Egypt. He probably erected similar steles in other locations, but they are now lost. The text has 159 lines and is almost twice as long as the *Poem* on the battle of Qadesh. It is a masterpiece of Egyptian literature whose author must have been very skilled and educated in ancient literature, which he exploited in composing his text. The style is vivid and relies on speeches to liven up the narrative. Some scholars call it "Piy's epic."

The top of the stele contains a relief scene that shows Piy (whose figure was scratched out at a later date) before Amun and Mut receiving the submission of northern Egyptian rulers. Nimlot of Hermopolis and his wife head the group. They are standing up and lead a horse. Below them three men lie prostrate, and on the left side of the scene five more do the same. All men are clearly identified by name and with their symbols of rule, be they kings or chiefs.

The text alternates narrative with speeches and omits the lengthy praises that usually take up most space in royal inscriptions. At the start reports of Tefnakht's advance on cities in Upper Egypt reached the king:

> The Chief of the West, count and grand one in Netjer, Tefnakht ... has conquered the entire West from the coastal marshes to Itj-tawy, sailing southward with a large army, with the Two Lands united behind him, and the counts and rulers of domains like dogs at his feet.

At first Piy sent troops already stationed in Upper Egypt to confront the advance, insisting that they observe ritual purity. Although they claimed to be successful, Piy was not satisfied.

Figure 11.5 King's Piy's victory stele

His Majesty raged about it like a panther: "Have they left a remnant of
Lower Egypt's army, to let some of them escape and report the campaign,
instead of killing and destroying the last of them?"

In detail the text describes the sequence of sieges and battles that ensued.
Inserted in the descriptions are lists of the names and titles of Piy's opponents,
which show how politically fragmented Lower Egypt was. Many adversaries sur-
rendered immediately, but others resisted. Memphis in particular put up a fight.
Its own warriors were artisans, builders, and sailors, but Tefnakht sent his choice
troops to aid them. Piy's victory was decisive.

Then, Memphis was seized as if by a cloudburst. Many people were slain
in it or brought as captives to where his Majesty was.

Finally Tefnakht sent a messenger to announce his submission.

"Be gracious! I cannot see your face in the days of shame; I cannot stand
before your flame; I dread your grandeur!
...
Have mercy! Dread of you is in my body; fear of you is in my bones!"

Piy accepted the surrender through an intermediary and returned back home.
The Nubian appears in the text as the true Egyptian. He observed proper rituals
and especially honored the rules of purity, which others habitually broke. The
text states that when four enemies came to submit only one could enter the
palace as the others were uncircumcised and ate fish.

The text shows that Piy respected Nubian customs as well. When he entered
Nimlot's stables in Hermopolis, he was appalled by the treatment of the horses.

His Majesty proceeded to the house of King Nimlot. He went through all
the rooms of the palace, his treasury and storehouse. Nimlot presented the
royal wives and daughters to him. They saluted his Majesty in the manner
of women, while his Majesty did not direct his gaze at them.
His Majesty proceeded to the stable of the horses and the quarters of
the foals. When he saw that they had been left to starve he said: "I swear,
as the god Ra loves me, as my nose is refreshed by life: that my horses
were starving pains me more than any other crime you committed in your
recklessness!"

Piy's love of horses set him apart as a Nubian, an origin he did not want to
conceal. The Egyptian character of this text is obvious, however. Only someone
who was fully steeped in Egyptian literary culture could have created it.[6]

These actions incited a response by the new Nubian ruler Piy, who had succeeded Kashta around 747. Piy resided in Napata as a king fully aware of Egyptian customs who credited his appointment to the god Amun. In his choice of five royal names he paid homage to Thutmose III, whose stele still stood in Napata, where Piy extended the Amun temple. His control over Upper Egypt was assured. Early in his reign he visited Thebes, where his sister was firmly established as God's Wife. Nubian officials and soldiers assisted her. Piy described his reaction to Tefnakht's advance in detail in a stele inscription he set up in his 21st year at Napata (Sources in Translation 11.2). The events happened in the previous year (728). Initially Piy sent the troops that were stationed in Thebes, but then he personally led an army against the northern opponents. He captured several fortified towns in succession, often receiving surrender without a fight. After he defeated Memphis, Piy accepted the submission of all northern rulers. The text lists them in detail, including King Osorkon of Manetho's 22nd dynasty and Iuput of the 23rd. Several chiefs of the Ma appear as well. Finally, Tefnakht sent an emissary to capitulate but did not come personally to Memphis. Although Piy claimed to have gained full control over Egypt, he did not stay there but returned to Napata. He was not interested in changing the political situation of the country; instead he restored the status quo that Tefnakht had sought to alter. At Napata he decorated the Amun temple with reliefs depicting the submission of Egyptian rulers, and his celebration of the *sed*-festival, the traditional Egyptian festival of royal renewal. His Nubian origins show in his mortuary complex: besides graves for several wives, he had one for four of his horses – a complete chariot team – buried standing up and facing east. His successors would continue this practice.

Piy's campaign in Egypt did not mean the end of the Third Intermediate Period, as he did not reunify the country. That happened only ten years later when his successor, Shabaqo, annexed Egypt to Nubia. The reasons for doing so related to the new international situation of the time. The greater Near East had entered an age of empires, and Egypt's fate depended on the actions of others.

Key Debate 11.1 *Fortresses in Middle Egypt*

Although Egypt was politically fragmented during the Third Intermediate Period, most scholars agree that the division was generally amicable and befitted an ideology where various members of the same family shared power. It is thus surprising that the center of Egypt was heavily fortified at the time. Mud bricks with the names of the 11th-century high priests of Amun Pinudjem I and Menkheperra were discovered at several sites just south of Herakleopolis (Wainwright 1927). The remains at el-Hibeh are especially impressive; 12.60-meter-thick walls are preserved up to 10 meters high (Foster 2001: 557). The site was the residence of the commander of Upper Egypt, and the northernmost part of Thebes' territory in the 21st dynasty. Some scholars think it was older, however. Because the papyrus manuscript of Wenamun's tale (see Chapter 10) may have been found at el-Hibeh, those who believe it is an actual report argue that the fortress already existed in the last days of the New Kingdom (Kitchen 1996b: 248 note 32). It is possible that the construction was even earlier: 20th-dynasty textual evidence mentions five fortresses in the region settled by Sherden. In the 21st dynasty Libyan mercenaries took over el-Hibeh, although the fortress was in Theban territory (Jansen-Winkeln 2001: 170–1). We know of these troops from an archive of letters, which was acquired on the antiquities market and was said to be from el-Hibeh. They mention high priests of Amun and Libyan troops (Černý 1975: 653; Wente 1990: 205–9).

At the time of the 22nd dynasty the fortress of el-Hibeh seems to have been part of the Lower Egyptian sphere of influence, however. King Sheshonq I built a temple to Amun there (http://neareastern.berkeley.edu/hibeh/01_report_temple.htm), and it was the base of a prince of the Tanis dynasty whose story is complicated. Late in life Osorkon left an inscription on the Bubastite portal at Thebes where he narrated how as crown prince he sailed down from el-Hibeh to subdue a rebellion in Thebes, which started a civil war for close to a decade (Caminos 1958; Kitchen 1996b: 330–1). He held

the position of high priest of Amun, and some scholars believe that when he was passed over as king in Tanis, he assumed kingship in Thebes (http://neareastern.berkeley.edu/hibeh/references_finds.htm). About a century later the fortress appeared as an opponent to the Nubian king Piy, who described it as a stronghold of the Lower Egyptian Tefnakht in his victory stele.

If the division of power was agreed upon, why was the center of Egypt so heavily fortified? Many historians say it was to protect the Theban region from Libyans. Even if relations with Tanis were good, there were other Libyans in Lower Egypt, especially around Herakleopolis, who threatened the south (Wainwright 1927: 81; Černý 1975: 653; Edwards 1982: 535; Foster 2001: 556–7). But somehow the fortress became part of the northern, Libyan, sphere of influence and was used as a base to control Thebes. Some say it was to prevent to the south from becoming fully independent (Edwards 1982: 543). Others see Thebes as the center of traditionalism and the driving force behind efforts at reunification of the country. The Libyans would have used el-Hibeh to thwart such efforts (Jansen-Winkeln 1992: 171). Whatever one believes, it seems that the situation in the Third Intermediate Period was less peaceful than is sometimes thought.

NOTES

1 Helck 1968.
2. Translation after Assmann 2002: 306.
3. Translation after von Beckerath 1968: 12.
4. Translation after Blackman 1941: 84.
5. Translation after Breasted 1906, Vol. 4: 356.
6. Translations after Lichtheim 1980: 68–79. See Assmann 2002: 322–34 for an interesting discussion of this text.

12

Egypt in the Age of Empires (ca. 715–332)

> The Great Chief of all foreign lands, Cambyses came to Egypt, and the people from every foreign land were with him. When he had conquered this entire land, they established themselves in it, and he was the great ruler of Egypt and great chief of all foreign lands. His Majesty assigned to me the office of chief physician. He made me live at his side as "companion" and "administrator of the palace." I composed his titles as King of Upper and Lower Egypt, Mesutira. (Udjahorresnet)[1]

The final phase of the history of "Egypt of the Pharaohs," from the end of the country's officially tolerated political fragmentation in the Third Intermediate Period to its conquest by Alexander of Macedon, lasted about four centuries. Since the lands of Upper and Lower Egypt were united once more, modern historians call it the Late Period, that is, not an Intermediate Period. But they also see the situation not as comparable to the kingdom periods attested before (Old, Middle, and New). Egypt was still a formidable country; yet it existed in a world where its neighbors' military were frequently stronger. Egypt was mostly too powerless for expansionism and had to fight for its independence. The eastern Mediterranean was home to a series of increasingly large empires, whose rulers saw Egypt's wealth and cultural heritage as a coveted prize. For about half of the period, Egypt was the subject of a foreign ruler; in the other half Egyptian dynasts governed the country, but they oftentimes only managed to keep their independence by relying on hired outside military experts.

No foreign ruler remained unaffected by the country, however. Emperors readily adopted Egyptian royal titles, participated in Egyptian cults, and had themselves depicted as Egyptian pharaohs. Their officials likewise adopted the trappings of Egyptian elites. They did not abandon their own traditions, but in Egypt fashioned a hybrid culture: they were both foreign and native. In the quote above the Egyptian physician Udjahorresnet boasted how he helped in the process. After the Persian Cambyses had conquered Egypt, Udjahorresnet advised him on the throne name he should take, Mesutira, "Offspring of Ra." Perhaps in an effort to understand better what was truly Egyptian in a world where foreign influences were so powerful, interest in the past peaked at this time. Artists revived imagery that was sometimes 2,000 years old and scholars copied texts that were just as ancient – or composed new ones to read like old texts. Egypt's glorious past was admired by all people, both Egyptian and foreign, but it was not slavishly copied. The ability to engage with past models creatively shows that Egyptian culture was still very much alive.

12.1 Sources and Chronology

The political situation of Egypt in the Late Period is reflected in the source material: both Egyptian and foreign sources are important. Kings continued to publicize their accomplishments in monumental inscriptions with hieroglyphic writing, and wealthy officials commissioned inscribed statues or monuments in which they told what public services they provided. The number of such inscriptions is not that great, but they provide additional information on kings recorded in Manetho's king list.

In the Late Period, the Demotic script and form of the Egyptian language gradually became the administrative norm throughout Egypt, displacing so-called Abnormal Hieratic by 550. Demotic script was a product of northern Egypt and more cursive than the Hieratic script that had been in use in the Third Intermediate Period. There was a great increase in documents of legal transactions in the Late Period, which may have been a result of governmental reform or due to the accident of preservation. Groups of related contracts on papyri and ostraca are attested throughout the era, and became even more numerous in Greek, Roman, and early Arab times. Although Demotic was an offshoot of earlier Egyptian language and writing, it lost the connections to Hieratic in the Ptolemaic Period, when it was very widely used, including for non-administrative texts. The study of this language and script has grown into a specialized discipline in Egyptology, and its sources remain relatively untapped for historical research on the Late periods as well as for Ptolemaic times, from which much more Demotic survived.

The international character of Egyptian society in this period is clear from written sources in non-Egyptian languages and scripts, including Aramaic, Phoenician, Greek, Cypriote, Lycian, and Carian. Speakers of these languages living in Egypt used them for legal records, letters, and some inscriptions. They include, for example, Aramaic papyri written by Jewish mercenaries living at the southern border of Egypt in Elephantine in the

Persian Period. Also recovered is a bag of 18 or 19 letters written in Aramaic on parchment from high-ranking Persian bureaucrats to their representatives in Egypt.

The non-Egyptian sources that have done most to shape our ideas of Late Period Egypt are the narratives of Assyrian, biblical, and Greek authors. The Assyrians provide the only information available on their conquest of the country. Their earlier encounters with Egyptian armies in Syria-Palestine are described in less detail, but the biblical text, written by the people over whose lands they fought, complete the picture. The two groups of sources sometimes disagree, however, and scholars spend much time in finding explanations for these divergences.

The most influential narrative source for the Late Period is a new one in the reconstruction of Egyptian history: classical authors, especially the Greek Herodotus of the 5th century BC. We have mentioned him several times before when discussing posthumous traditions about Egyptians and his description of mummification. His work on the 5th-century wars between Greece and Persia investigates the histories of the parties involved, and Egypt as part of the Persian empire received much of his attention because Herodotus was fascinated with the country. His historical description becomes detailed from the start of the 26th dynasty, some 200 years before he wrote his work. Herodotus claims to have visited Egypt, to have seen its monuments and talked to its priests, who read ancient sources and recounted traditions to him. Most scholars accept this claim, although they acknowledge that he made some blatant errors. It is clear that he knew a lot about Egypt, its history, and its customs and that he found it a very strange place. He portrayed Egypt as the opposite of his home country, Greece. Herodotus writes:

> For instance, women attend market and are employed in trade, while men stay at home and do the weaving. In weaving the normal way is to work the threads of the weft upwards, but the Egyptians work them downwards. Men in Egypt carry loads on their heads, women on their shoulders; women pass water standing up, men sitting down. To ease themselves they go indoors, but eat outside in the streets, on the theory that what is unseemly but necessary should be done in private, and what is not unseemly should be done openly.[2]

Herodotus's topics range from the first king of Egypt to the Persian rulers of his own time. Modern historians tend to see his statements on earlier periods as fantastic and unreliable, but credit those on the Late Period with great historical value. The account appeals because of the detail he provides and also because of the format he uses, the narrative. As the "father of history" in western tradition Herodotus provides the model of how we still write history today. While for earlier periods of Egyptian history we have to compose our own narratives on the basis of data extracted from varied sources, with

Herodotus we have an ancient narrative whose outline we can follow. His impact is enormous: The highly authoritative *Cambridge Ancient History* states in its chapter on Egypt in the Persian empire, "His (Herodotus's) account is so important that, whatever his faults, all modern histories of the period are essentially a commentary on him."[3]

And indeed analyses of Egyptian and other sources have shown that Herodotus's account contains much factual truth or statements that can be harmonized with events we know otherwise. Still, the exciting details he provides, which make the ancient Egyptians so much more human than in other sources at hand, are impossible to verify. Was the rebel Amasis truly such a colorful character that he broke wind in reply to a demand to appear before the king (Book 2.162)? We will never know, but modern historians like the human element and allow it to influence the way in which they portray the end of the 26th dynasty. Herodotus's account of the Late Period is a great asset, but like any other ancient historical source, it requires careful scrutiny.

The chronology of the Late Period is well established. We even know the exact day on which certain events occurred according to the Julian calendar, for example, that King Psamtek II died on February 9, 589 BC. Such accuracy is the result of astronomical information, primarily in non-Egyptian sources but in some Egyptian sources as well. There are still some uncertainties about the lengths of reigns in the Nubian 25th dynasty, but on the whole our chronological knowledge is far superior to that for earlier periods of Egyptian history.

12.2   The Eastern Mediterranean in the First Millennium

Egypt's history needs to be considered within the wider world that surrounded it. Up to the first millennium the country was always independent from neighboring powers. Foreign rulers may have controlled parts of Egypt in the Second Intermediate Period, but the country was never subject to a state that had its center elsewhere. This changed radically with the Nubian conquest in the first millennium, the first time that Egypt became incorporated into a foreign empire. Increasingly large empires dominated the eastern Mediterranean region in the first millennium BC. Their centers were located in various places – never in Egypt, however – and their ruling elites always established their dominance through military means. Egypt was a desirable target to all of them. In materialistic terms its huge agricultural resources and accumulated treasure made any emperor wish he could control them. In less materialistic terms, the enormous antiquity of the country's traditions and its status as a center of culture whose great kings of the past were still remembered through their monuments appealed as well. Many of the new empires had little recorded history of their own and grew up on the margins of ancient states: Nubia next to Egypt, Persia next to

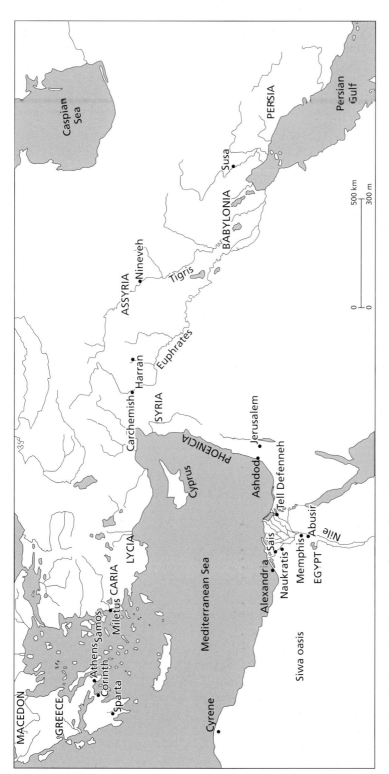

Map 7 The Eastern Mediterranean in the first millennium

Babylonia, and Macedon next to Greece. Becoming part of the long sequence of Egyptian kings must have been a great temptation. Egypt was oftentimes unable to resist these powers. It adhered to outdated military technology, it seems, and its army was no match for the seasoned warriors that attacked it. For about half of the Late Period the country kept its independence, but that was often due to a reliance on foreign mercenaries who had adopted the new methods.

The reason Egyptians faced different adversaries was due to events beyond their control; when they tried to influence the situation they failed. The crucial struggles for regional supremacy happened to its north, in western Asia. In the time of the Third Intermediate Period the Assyrians of northern Mesopotamia had gradually annexed the entirety of that area. By the late 8th century they reached the Egyptian border and their subsequent invasions were a natural continuation of their expansion. In 610, Assyria fell to its southern neighbor Babylonia, despite a desperate Egyptian attempt to support its former overlord. The Babylonians continued Assyrian policies in most respects, extending the hold over the Syro-Palestinian lands, but they never succeeded in conquering Egypt. In 539 they fell victim to the Persians of southwestern Iran, who in a very short time captured a vast territory from the Indus Valley to the Mediterranean Sea. The annexation of Egypt in 525 was only to be expected. The repeated Persian attempts to conquer Greece – the subject of Herodotus's history – failed, and more than a century later, in the 330s, Greece's new ruler, Alexander of the kingdom of Macedon to its north, defeated the empire and occupied its territories. Egypt was one of the crown jewels. The sequence of empires does not end there: the subsequent ones – Ptolemaic and Roman – will be treated in the next chapter.

Also in non-military terms the Mediterranean world, starting in the 8th century, was much more integrated than earlier. The Phoenicians of the Lebanese coast and the Greeks were enterprising seafaring merchants and competed to establish colonies throughout the Mediterranean. Both groups found in Egypt a market for products like wine and olive oil and a source of agricultural goods. The overseas trade contacts were not new, but seem more intense than before, and Egypt promoted them by upgrading its own navy. Greeks also entered Egypt as mercenaries. They seem to have been so superior in their military skills that access to them was the key to success. Besides men from the Greek mainland, soldiers from Anatolian regions and from the former kingdom of Judah also sold their services. Inscriptions and other texts attest to the presence of Lycians and Carians in Egypt, while a Jewish mercenary colony guarded the southern border of the country at Elephantine. There were also travelers, students, and artisans who visited or settled in Egypt. The same was true in other parts of the eastern Mediterranean. Everywhere people with varied skills searched for opportunities outside their place of birth. Enhanced sea travel and the existence of vast empires that imposed a uniform political system over much of the eastern Mediterranean facilitated mobility. These were very cosmopolitan times.

Summary of dynastic history
Late Period

715–656	**Later 25th dynasty**
715–702	King Shabaqo
	Unites Nubia and Egypt, ca. 711
	Develops Memphis as his northern capital
702–690	King Shabitqo
	Confronts Assyria at Eltekeh in Palestine, 701
690–664	King Taharqo
	Embellishes monuments throughout Egypt and Nubia
	Flees Memphis under Assyrian pressure, 671
	Recaptures northern Egypt, 669
	Chased from Egypt by Assurbanipal, who raids Thebes and
	deposes vassal rulers, except Nekau and Psamtek of Sais, 667–666
664–656	King Tanutamani
	Recaptures Egypt, 664
	Is permanently removed from Egypt by Assurbanipal who
	reinstates Psamtek as his primary vassal, 663
664–525	**26th dynasty**
664–610	King Psamtek I [Greek Psammetichos]
	Proclaims himself King of Upper and Lower Egypt, 657–656
610–595	King Nekau II [Greek Necho]
	Fails to save last Assyrian king in Harran, 610
	Loses battle of Carchemish against Babylonians, 605
595–589	King Psamtek II [Greek Psammetichos]
	Invades Nubia, 593
	Invades Palestine, 591
	Erases memory of 25th-dynasty rulers
589–570	King Haaibra [Greek Apries]
	Fails to annex Cyrene
570–526	King Ahmose II [Greek Amasis]
	Regularizes Greek presence at Naukratis
526–525	King Psamtek III [Greek Psammetichos]
	Suffers defeat by Persian Cambyses a few months into his reign
525–404	**27th dynasty**
	First period of Persian occupation
525–522	King Cambyses
	Conquers Egypt, but fails in his attempts to extend empire to
	Cyrene, the Egyptian oases, and Nubia

522–486	King Darius I
	Orders the collection of Egyptian laws
	Develops temple in Kharga oasis and builds Red Sea canal

404–399	**28th dynasty**
404–399	King Amyrtaios
	Ruler from the Delta whose authority reached southern Egypt only in 400

399–380	**29th dynasty**
399–393	King Nepherites I
	Ruler from Mendes who replaced 28th dynasty
393–380	King Hakor [Greek Achoris]
	Wins out against two other claimants to the throne
	Organizes military campaign to Cyprus

380–343	**30th dynasty**
380–362	King Nectanebo I
	Seizes throne as military commander
	Commissions much building activity
	Prevents Artaxerxes II from retaking Egypt, 374/3
362–360	King Teos [Greek Tachos]
	Invades Syria
360–343	King Nectanebo II
	Usurps throne

343–332	**31st dynasty**
	Second period of Persian occupation
343–338	King Artaxerxes III Ochus
	Institutes oppressive regime upon reconquest of Egypt
336–332	King Darius III Codoman
	Loses empire to Alexander of Macedon

12.3   Egypt, Kush, and Assyria (ca. 715–656)

Military incidents

Most empires of the first millennium developed in western Asia before they incorporated Egypt, but the country's earliest foreign master was its own former subject to the south, Nubia. From the mid-8th century the Kingdom of Kush had controlled the political situation in Egypt, as we saw in the previous chapter. King Piy's campaign in 728 reaffirmed the division of power between local lords, all of whom acknowledged the Nubian as the highest authority. Piy resided in Napata outside Egypt and left the country at least nominally independent. In Manetho's system the most important Egyptian ruler was from Sais, Tefnakht's son Bakenrenef (referred to in Greek sources as Bocchoris), who by himself made up the 24th dynasty. Modern scholars include the father as a member of the dynasty.

Sometime between 711 and 709 the new ruler of Kush, Shabaqo, changed the policy toward Egypt and his army asserted full Nubian control. No victory stele like Piy's is preserved, so we do not know the details of the campaign, but Manetho claimed that Shabaqo seized Bakenrenef and burned him alive. For an Egyptian this was a terrible fate as no body was available for mummification and burial. The severity of Shabaqo's actions leads modern scholars to assume that Bakenrenef triggered the campaign by attempting to broaden Sais's influence as his father had done earlier. But this is conjecture. Shabaqo may have been inspired by events beyond Egypt's borders in Syria-Palestine, where Assyria gradually extended its territory southward. It seemed clear to Kushites as well as Egyptians that Assyria posed a threat, and for decades they had supported anti-Assyrian coalitions. Shabaqo may have taken Egypt in order to pre-empt an Assyrian onslaught.

Unlike in the days of Piy, the Nubian campaign led to the annexation of Egypt, and Shabaqo set himself up as king in Memphis. Hence Manetho called him the founder of the 25th dynasty, which ruled a unified Egypt for about 50 years, and we will consider him as the king who ended the Third Intermediate Period (many scholars use the start of the 26th dynasty as the marker of that moment). At the same time the kings ruled Kush, which they still considered their home. Three rulers of the 25th dynasty were buried in the ancestral cemetery at el-Kurru (see Chapter 11), while the fourth, Taharqo, built a large pyramid nearer to Napata at Nuri, which would become the burial ground for many later Nubian kings. The extent of the combined kingdoms was enormous: Napata and Memphis are some 1,000 miles (1,600 kilometers) apart by river. It is impossible to determine how the Kushite rulers divided their time between Egypt and Nubia, but it is clear that they used Memphis as a residence. Whenever the Assyrians attacked northern Egypt they mentioned the king of Kush as personally in command of the army.

It was indeed the competition between Nubia and Assyria that dominated events in Egypt for about a decade in the 7th century and that ultimately led to the eviction of both from the country. For the first 25 years of the Kushite dynasty its rulers kept Assyria at bay through military action and diplomacy. At times they tried to appease the enemy. In 712, Yamani, king of Ashdod in Palestine, escaped to Egypt after a failed rebellion against Assyria and initially found asylum there. In or before 706, however, the Kushites sent him back in shackles. At other times the Nubians sent troops into Palestine to help anti-Assyrian coalitions. In 701, Egyptians and Nubians participated in a battle at Eltekeh in support of Judah. Assyria's King Sennacherib claimed victory, but the coalition prevented him from capturing Jerusalem.

Twenty-five years later the wars were fought on Egyptian soil. Taharqo (ruled 690–664) resisted the Assyrians in 674, but three years later (671) King

Figure 12.1 Stele of King Esarhaddon of Assyria, found in northern Syria. The relief depicts the Nubian king Taharqo (or his son), held by a leash, and the king of Tyre as supplicants to the Assyrian king. Vorderasiatisches Museum, Berlin. Photo: Jürgen Liepe © 2010. Photo Scala, Florence/BPK, Bildagentur für Kunst, Kultur und Geschichte, Berlin

Esarhaddon managed to conquer Memphis. Taharqo fled south, leaving behind his heir and several other family members whose capture Esarhaddon celebrated (Figure 12.1). The Assyrian king did not stay in Egypt, nor did he leave behind an army to hold the country, which gave Taharqo the opening to retake Memphis. In 669 Esarhaddon again advanced toward Egypt, but he died on the way. Upon asserting power at home, his successor Assurbanipal almost immediately dealt with the situation. In the years 667 and 666 he sent out an army that pursued Taharqo from Memphis to Thebes, which it also raided. The Nubian ruler escaped, however, and his successor Tanutamani returned to Egypt in 664. On a stele he set up in Napata the new Nubian king recounted how Amun in a dream inspired him to do so.

His Majesty saw a dream at night with two serpents; one on his right, the other on his left. His Majesty woke up but could not understand it. His Majesty said, "Why has this happened to me?" The response to him was as follows: "The southern land is yours, seize for yourself the northern land. The Two Ladies (= vulture-goddess Nekhbet and cobra-goddess Wadjet) appear on your head, and the land in its full length and width shall be given to you, as no one shall share it with you."[4]

The Assyrians reacted almost immediately to Tanutamani's capture of Memphis. Assurbanipal's troops seized Memphis and Thebes and carried off a large booty of treasure that had accumulated in the city for centuries.

The Egyptians were stuck in the middle between these two competing powers and must have borne the brunt of the devastation that went with the wars. They were not passive, however, and the Assyrians in particular needed them. Assyrian policy was to control distant regions by putting locals in charge of the administration and forcing them to pay tribute. This saved the trouble of organizing an enormous central bureaucracy for the vast empire. The policy relied on the army to restore order whenever the appointed locals rebelled. In Egypt the Assyrians turned to the old families that had ruled the country in the Third Intermediate Period to serve them. In the account of his first campaign there Assurbanipal listed 20 of them as vassal kings, whom his father Esarhaddon had installed in various cities. He could not govern Egypt without them, as is clear from the treatment of rulers from Sais. Esarhaddon had given Memphis to Nekau of Sais. But Nekau and his colleagues betrayed Assyria and switched sides upon Taharqo's return to the country, which naturally displeased the Assyrian. Assurbanipal described in detail how he had all rebels from Egypt brought to his capital Nineveh for punishment. He showed mercy to Nekau, however. Not only did he reinstate him, but he also gave Nekau presents of gold, chariots, horses, and mules, and made his son Psamtek (to whom Assurbanipal gave the Assyrian name Nabu-shezibanni) ruler of the Delta city Athribis. After the final removal of Tanutamani from Egypt Assurbanipal bestowed all powers of the deceased Nekau – possibly killed during the Nubian reoccupation – on Psamtek.

Psamtek took advantage of the power invested in him by the Assyrian invaders in 663. With Nubia fully out of the way he was the strongest ruler in Egypt and secured control over the entire country. According to Herodotus he relied on mercenaries to subdue his colleagues – a subject we will discuss later in the chapter. It is clear, however, that the Assyrians had promoted Psamtek as their chief vassal in Egypt, and when they disappeared he was able to proclaim himself King of Upper and Lower Egypt, which he did in the year 657/6.

The half-century between 712 and 657 was thus an unsettling time for the Egyptians. The armies of two outside powers marched through the country many times and, even if Egyptians were not directly involved in battle, they suffered. The Assyrians put entire populations to death when their lords rebelled. Neither power, however, did away with the existing political organization and the change of rulers did not lead to a wholesale shake-up of the administration. Local lords stayed in place and some of them flourished.

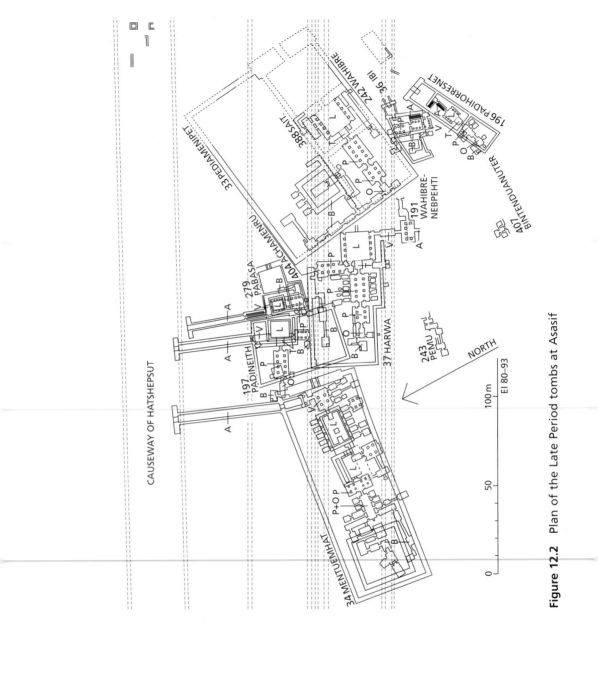

Figure 12.2 Plan of the Late Period tombs at Asasif

The prime example of a man who survived the period is Mentuemhat, the fourth prophet of Amun, mayor of Thebes, and governor of Upper Egypt. His priestly title was relatively modest, but he was certainly the chief civil authority of the Theban area and probably the most powerful priest as well. The Assyrians called him king of Thebes. Mentuemhat inherited the office of mayor from his father around 700. He married three women, including a Nubian princess, Udjarenes. His powers became especially clear after the first Assyrian sack of Thebes, when he took charge of the restoration. In a relief in the Mut temple at Karnak he appears behind Taharqo below a row of statues that he repaired or replaced, and the accompanying inscription describes his works in detail. His status enabled him to commission statues of himself for display in the temple and a magnificent burial (TT 34) at Asasif. This site near Deir el-Bahri contains the first truly monumental tombs in Thebes since the New Kingdom and Mentuemhat's is the grandest (Figure 12.2). It is a massive edifice with a large entrance gate, numerous subterranean chambers, and a sunken courtyard dug open to the sky. Its reliefs are of the highest quality and show the craftsmanship of Egypt's best artists (Figure 12.3).

The official notification of Psamtek's control of Upper Egypt came when the king established his daughter Nitiqret as God's Wife of Amun at Thebes in 656, an event commemorated in the so-called Adoption Stele (see Chapter 11). It is no surprise that Mentuemhat was present at the event. He probably had governed the Theban region on his own after the Assyrians had left Egypt, and the Adoption Stele mentions him as the first official who pledged to support the new God's Wife. In return Psamtek kept Mentuemhat on as mayor of Thebes and the latter died shortly before 648 after a glorious career.

12.4 Egypt, Greeks, and Babylonians (656–525)

Greek–Egyptian relations

Herodotus tells a story about the rise of Psamtek of Sais, whom he calls Psammetichos, that is quite different from the one recounted here. He ignores the Assyrian role and instead focuses on other foreigners, the Greeks. According to him (Book 2.151–7) the Egyptians decided to divide the country into 12 regions under a king each. These were related by marriage and had friendly relations, which matches our perception of the Third Intermediate Period. An oracle had predicted – Herodotus continues – that the one who would make a libation with a bronze cup would become the sole ruler. On one occasion only 11 golden cups were available and Psammetichos used his bronze helmet for the libation. The others realized his unintended mistake and exiled Psammetichos, something he resented bitterly. An oracle told him that he would take revenge with the help of bronze men, an allusion he understood when he saw sea-raiders

Figure 12.3 Relief of a woman with child reaching for a sycamore fig, from the tomb of Mentuemhat at Asasif, western Thebes. Brooklyn Museum of Art, New York/The Bridgeman Art Library

from Anatolia in bronze armor unknown to Egyptians. He engaged their services and captured all of Egypt. Herodotus writes:

> They were the first foreigners to live in Egypt, and after their original settlement there, the Greeks began regular intercourse with the Egyptians, so that we have knowledge of Egyptian history from the time of Psammetichos onward.[5]

With the rise of the 26th dynasty of Sais, the Egyptian focus shifted radically from the south to the north. The Mediterranean Sea connected the country not only to the Syro-Palestinian coast, but also to Greece and western Anatolia. These intensified contacts had a great impact on Egypt.

In the 8th century several cities on the Greek mainland and the Anatolian coast, whose surrounding countryside was incapable to feed the expanding populations, had started to establish colonies along the Mediterranean. These were built on the Greek model and life in them was much like that in the mother cities. They were mostly located in regions without strong states, and Egypt with its entrenched bureaucracy was not a typical setting for a colony. But it was a country with much desired products, and after the expulsion of the Assyrians and Nubians the Greeks established themselves in an existing harbor city, Naukratis, situated close to the new capital Sais. The first Greek evidence in the form of decorated pottery from the site dates to around 620, that is, within the reign of Psamtek I, and it confirms Herodotus's statement that Greeks started to visit Egypt at that time. His subsequent statement that it was only King Ahmose II (ruled 570–526) who made Naukratis the commercial head-quarters for any Greek who wanted to settle in the country (Book 2.178) may refer to a greater degree of formalization of Greek–Egyptian trade relations.

The excavations of Naukratis were difficult because of the site's location in the Delta, with its destructive groundwater, and the fact that local farmers used its mud brick to fertilize fields. Archaeologists of the late 19th century could merely record the traces of buildings being destroyed and pick up pottery and other remains. Today much of the site lies beneath a lake. Its overall charac-teristics are clear, however, and show the unique quality of Naukratis as a Greek colony. The city contained several sanctuaries to Greek gods, Apollo, Hera, Aphrodite, and others. Large amounts of decorated pottery show contacts with several Greek cities, such as Miletus on the Anatolian coast, and Corinth and Athens in mainland Greece. Most other colonies were the foundation of one mother city; it seems that in Naukratis Greeks from various cities lived side-by-side. They wanted grain, which Egypt could produce in large amounts, to feed their home populations. Herodotus claims that Egypt flourished in this period: "It is said that the reign of Amasis (Ahmose) was a time of unexampled material prosperity for Egypt; the river gave its riches to the earth and the earth to the people. The total number of inhabited towns, they say, was twenty thou-sand."[6] The Greeks also imported papyrus, which spread as a tool for writing throughout the eastern Mediterranean at this time, and linen, but cereals were what they wanted the most. In return they shipped wine and olive oil to Egypt, and often they used silver to pay. Many hoards of Greek coins and un-minted silver appear in Egypt from that time on.

The kings of the 26th dynasty promoted trade with audacious projects. According to Herodotus, Nekau II (ruled 610–595) started the digging of a canal from the eastern Nile Delta to the Red Sea, a scheme he abandoned after 120,000 workers died but that the Persian king Darius completed. Nekau also sponsored an expedition by Phoenician sailors to circumnavigate Africa, which took three years. Many historians are suspicious of the claim that they suc-ceeded, but the statement that they saw the sun on their right in the north – which Herodotus himself did not believe (Book 4.42) – seems to confirm that they rounded the southern tip of Africa. Commercial interests inspired such an enterprise. As the trade brought them substantial wealth, Egyptian rulers pro-moted good relations with the Greek city-states. Herodotus reports that King Amasis (Ahmose) made a huge financial contribution to the restoration of the burned-down temple at Delphi and he sent other cities gifts including gold-plated statues and fancy textiles. We can compare those to the diplomatic exchanges of the Amarna Period (see Chapter 8).

Not only traders visited Egypt. The country's antiquity and long traditions drew scholars – Herodotus is one example. Tales about famous Greeks, such as the poet Homer, lawgiver Solon, and mathematician Pythagoras, state that they found inspiration in Egypt, which is most likely false but shows the respect the country's culture inspired. Egypt also had a great impact on cultural developments in archaic Greece, especially visible in the visual arts. Some examples are the construction of monumental walls with fully dressed masonry and the depiction of the human body in statuary.

The most important impact of Greeks and others from the northern Mediterranean on Egypt may have been in the military. Herodotus's tale of Psamtek I's rise quoted above credits the king's success to his use of western Anatolian warriors in bronze armor. References in Assyrian accounts indicate that King Gyges of the Anatolian state Lydia sent troops to Egypt, probably to help Psamtek in the unification campaign. The importance of mercenaries seems to have increased during the 26th dynasty. When at its end Egyptians faced the Persian king Cambyses they fielded Greek and Carian mercenaries. In fact, a former mercenary betrayed them. Herodotus relates that a Phanes of Halicarnassus deserted to Cambyses and advised an attack through the desert with the help of Arabs. When the battle lines were drawn Phanes's former colleagues in the Egyptian army cut his sons' throats in his sight and drank the blood mixed with wine. The Persians prevailed, however.

The mercenaries were hardened by the internecine wars of the Greek city-states, where they learned to fight in well-organized battle lines. They may also have used superior weaponry. The Greek settlement at Naukratis provides the earliest evidence for iron smelting in Egypt, which suggests that mercenaries introduced the technology – although other sources of inspiration are possible. Greek technology also seems to have revolutionized the Egyptian navy, a subject of much scholarly debate. Herodotus claims that Nekau ordered the building of Greek triremes, the fastest ship in the world at that time and equipped to engage in sea battles. Although the navy had always been a crucial part of the Egyptian military, it served for troop transport, while triremes provided a strike force. Records of the 26th dynasty document an increased number of naval officers, such as harbormasters, which confirms a growing importance of the navy, but these men were also active with merchant-vessels.

Archaeology shows that the Egyptians stationed mercenaries in forts at the borders. Several lines of fortresses controlled access to the Delta both from the east and the west: sites such as Tell el-Kedua, Tell Defenneh, Tell el-Maskhuta, and Marea have massive mud-brick enclosures. Pottery shows the presence of Greeks in these forts. They were joined by Jewish soldiers, who fled their country under Babylonian rule and settled in various places in Egypt. Jewish mercenaries occupied a military colony at Elephantine on the southern border; the evidence for them is much richer in the Persian Period.

The presence of foreign mercenaries gets much attention in the Greek sources and in modern discussions of the 26th dynasty. Egyptians did not entrust the defense of their country to hired foreigners, however, nor did they leave them unsupervised. When a mixed army of Egyptians and foreign mercenaries passed by Abu Simbel, one Greek left this graffito on one of the legs of the colossal statues:

> When King Psammetichos had come to Elephantine, this was written by those who sailed with Psammetichos, son of Theokles, who went as far as they could – above Kerkis. Potasimto led the foreigners and Amasis the Egyptians. This was written by Archon son of Amoibichos and Pelekos son of Eudamos.[7]

Potasimto, the leader of the foreigners, was an Egyptian. He is known as Pedismatawy in several inscriptions, including on his sarcophagus, where he has such titles as "overseer of the foreigners," and "overseer of the Greeks." The presence of separate generals for Egyptians and foreigners may indicate that Potasimto had to communicate in Greek to his troops, at least one of whom seems to have been very literate as he left the long graffito. The fact that the overall commander mentioned had an Egyptian name, Psammetichos, but was the son of a Greek, Theokles, suggests that the mercenaries integrated themselves in their host society.

The importance of Greeks in the Egyptian army seems to have led to resentment among Egyptians and in one case to an overthrow of the king. According to Herodotus, King Apries (Haaibra) sent Egyptian troops to annex the Greek colony of Cyrene in northern Libya, a campaign that failed utterly. The troops rebelled and Apries sent Amasis (Ahmose) to reason with them; he joined the rebels, however, and they crushed the mercenary troops Apries fielded. Whatever the truth of this story, the events did not disrupt Egypt's relations with Greece. Ahmose was one of the most philhellenic kings on record.

Military activity

Attention to the military was needed to protect Egypt from outsiders. From the very beginning of the 26th dynasty its rulers realized that the Babylonians presented a worse threat than the Assyrians who had put them in power. Psamtek I and Nekau II sent several armies in support of Assyria when it was under Babylonian attack. In 610 they failed to relieve the last Assyrian ruler holding out in the north Syrian city of Harran. Egypt took advantage of the temporary power vacuum in western Syria and Palestine with the political changes in Mesopotamia, but in 605 Babylonian troops routed Nekau's army at Carchemish on the Euphrates. Over the next decade the Babylonians captured all former Assyrian provinces in the west, repeatedly clashing with Egyptians. Their king Nebuchadnezzar famously went on to conquer Jerusalem and annex regions up to the Egyptian border into his empire. There are indications that he tried to invade Egypt several times, once in support of King Haaibra (Apries), whom Ahmose (Amasis) had deposed. The multiple lines of fortifications in the eastern Delta also indicate that the threat from Babylonia was real. Classical sources state that the Egyptian navy captured Cyprus in this period, but these are unconfirmed reports.

Fortresses also guarded the southern Egyptian border, because Nubia's retreat from the country had not reduced that state to insignificance. On the contrary, the Nubian dynasty flourished and continued its building activity and artistic production, heavily influenced by Egyptian traditions, while gradually developing along different lines. It is likely that the two states maintained close trade contacts, but relations soured in the reign of Psamtek II (595–589). In 593 he invaded Nubia – using mercenaries like Archon who left his graffito at Abu Simbel – and reached the capital Napata. Why he did so is unclear, although many scholars suspect Nubian aggression as the trigger. In Egypt itself Psamtek II turned against Nubian remains and ordered the systematic removal of the names of 25th dynasty kings. This may have been an act of frustration: unable to defeat the Nubians in person he desecrated their names in territory he controlled. The consequences of Psamtek's campaign caused Nubians to shift their focus from the north to the south, and also caused a decline of Egyptian influences.

Egypt's fortified borders failed to keep the enemy out. In 525 the Persians dodged the first line of defense in the eastern Delta by using desert routes and prevailed in a major battle. Herodotus mentions that he could still see the skeletons of the slain soldiers – Egyptians and Persians – in the desert sand a century later. Egypt became part of the Persian empire.

12.5 Recollections of the Past under the Kings of Kush and Sais

The reunification of Egypt that ended the Third Intermediate Period brought a new era of prosperity despite the devastations caused by military raids. If we can believe Herodotus, under the 26th dynasty Egypt flourished economically on an unprecedented scale. Archaeological remains show that, starting with the 25th dynasty, kings and the elites were able to commission building projects and artwork on a scale not seen since New Kingdom times. The Nubian kings embellished existing temples at Memphis, Thebes, and elsewhere, and Saite rulers built in the Delta –much of which has disappeared. Leading figures in the royal families, such as the God's Wives of Amun, were also active. The art of statuary prospered, with beautiful works in hard stones recalling examples from earlier kingdom periods.

The kings of Kush used artists with the same skills in Egypt and in Nubia, as is shown by a remarkable set of royal statues archaeologists excavated at Doukki Gel near Kerma in 2003. The kings represented include rulers both of Nubia and Egypt, Taharqo and Tanutamani, and later ones who did not control

Figure 12.4 King Taharqo represented as a sphinx. The general figure and the lion's mane are Egyptian in style, but the face and double *uraeus* are typically Nubian. © The Trustees of the British Museum

Egypt, Senkamanisken, Anlamani, and Aspelta. The quality did not diminish after the Nubians left Egypt, which shows that local artists had fully absorbed Egyptian styles and iconography. Ironically these statues were preserved because of Egyptian aggression. When Psamtek II's troops raided Kerma, they broke them into pieces. Local people picked up the fragments and buried them together in caches, which remained intact until the recent excavations.

Although the works kings and other Nubians commissioned were fully Egyptian in style, they had important iconographic details unique to the 25th dynasty (Figure 12.4). Nubian kings wore a double *uraeus* with two cobra-snakes sometimes bearing the red and white crowns (see Chapter 2) and representing Upper and Lower Egypt. They also wore ram's-headed amulets around the neck or as earrings in a way not found in earlier Egyptian art, and fancy footwear. The artists found inspiration in the past but modified their work to take new ideas into account. When Psamtek II turned against Nubian remains in Egypt and removed the royal names from them, he also had one of the *uraei* and the amulets cut out.

Active engagement with the past is also visible in the monuments of private individuals in Egypt, who were able to commission enormous tombs and numerous statues. We have mentioned Mentuemhat's tomb at Asasif before. It is not only remarkable in its gigantic size, but also for its lavish decorations of the highest artistic quality. The reliefs display texts and imagery that had disappeared in tombs after the New Kingdom: vignettes from the Book of the Dead and scenes of the deceased sitting behind an offering table and of daily life, including butchering and fishing. Such images had last appeared in 18th-dynasty tombs, which served as models for the artists. They took scenes from the tomb of Rekhmira (see Chapter 7), for example, but did not copy them slavishly. They carved the scenes, which had only been painted, in stone and adapted the human figures to the tastes of the Late Period, emphasizing the musculature.

Other officials' tombs in the area display the same features. Near Mentuemhat was buried Pediamenipet, whose enormous tomb (TT 33) was decorated with a veritable library of Egyptian underworld books. It contained extracts of Old Kingdom Pyramid Texts, Middle Kingdom Coffin Texts, and a full range of the mortuary texts of the New Kingdom. People searched all over Egypt to find ancient tombs whose decorations and inscriptions could serve as models for their own. A Theban official under King Psamtek I called Ibi knew of the tomb of a man with the same name from the 6th dynasty at Deir el-Gebrawi in Middle Egypt. He made artists copy out parts of the inscriptions, with minor adjustments:

> Deir el-Gebrawi, 6th dynasty
> Overseeing all work in the workshop of the craftsmen, in the hands of every crafts-man inside or outside; assessing the activity of every craftsman by the scribes of his funerary estate; making a plan for every kind of work ... governor of the mansion, Lower Egyptian seal-bearer, true sole companion revered under Mati, the well-disposed, Ibi.

> Thebes (TT 36), 26th dynasty
> Overseeing all work in the workshop of the craftsmen, in the hands of every crafts-man inside or outside; assessing the activity of every craftsman by the scribe of his funerary estate; making a plan for every kind of work the Chief steward of the God's Wife, Ibi.[8]

The scribe changed the grammar and spelling appropriately to adjust for the small variations with the original text. Meanwhile, the artists who decorated the later tomb found inspiration in the scenes of the earlier one. The two Ibis oversee six rows of the same craftsmen at work, who have identical personal names. Various other examples of the reuse of older models are preserved.

The interest in the past is also visible in written sources. An intriguing object from the time of King Shabaqo is a basalt slab with an inscription that praises

Figure 12.5 The Shabaqo stone. The damage is the result of the stone's use as a millstone. © The Trustees of the British Museum

the city of Memphis and recounts a creation story in which its god Ptah is the original creator, the so-called *Memphite Theology* (Figure 12.5). In it, the god engenders other deities through thought and speech. In the introduction to the text King Shabaqo states that it is a copy of a worm-eaten original and the language used is archaic. Scholars for long argued that the original dated to the Old Kingdom or even before, but today we know that it cannot predate the 19th dynasty. The fact that Shabaqo ordered such an archaic-looking text copied or perhaps even composed, shows that writings of the past were thought to have great authority, and that scholars of the Late Period could write in an archaic form of the Egyptian language that was long dead.

Archaism is a primary characteristic of Egyptian culture of the 25th and 26th dynasties. The past, whose remains were visible everywhere, fascinated and inspired scribes and artists who actively engaged with it; they did not just copy but modified what they saw to fit their own conditions. Why were they so interested? The pressure of foreign influences in politics and culture may have led to a nativist reaction and a wish to uphold what was "truly" Egyptian. In our consideration of this issue we have to keep in mind that the Kushites – foreigners themselves and willing to admit the fact – were supporters of this cultural policy. The desire was more likely to emulate the grandeur of the past, not because it was Egyptian, but because it was grand.

12.6   Egypt and Persia (525–332)

Early in his reign King Ahmose II had successfully resisted the Babylonian king Nebuchadnezzar's invasion of Egypt, and afterwards the western Asiatic power no longer posed a threat. But the political situation in that region evolved rapidly, and in the last two decades of Ahmose's reign an opponent emerged more formidable than Egypt had ever encountered: the Persian empire. Around 550, Cyrus from the southwest of Iran started the conquest of a vast landmass, which by his death in 529 stretched from the Indus Valley to the Mediterranean Sea. The inclusion of Babylonia with its territories west of the Euphrates placed Persia on the Egyptian border. Ahmose's philhellene behavior (see pp. 297–8) may have been a diplomatic strategy to contain Persia in the west. This was to no avail, however, especially when some powerful allies like Polycrates, the Greek ruler of Samos, switched sides. With the help of a mercenary leader who had betrayed Egypt, Cyrus's son and successor Cambyses marched into the country in 525 and deposed the last Saite king, Psamtek III.

Persia's desire for expansion did not end with the conquest of Egypt. Cambyses tried to annex regions farther west along the Mediterranean coast of Africa, Egyptian oases, and Nubia in the south, but failed. In the next two centuries the Persians mounted several campaigns into Central Asia and Europe, also with limited success. Their repeated clashes with the city-states of Greece are the best documented by far. Greek authors portrayed it as a struggle between tyranny and democracy, east and west, a dichotomy that still affects modern western thought. By the mere fact that the Egyptians resisted Persian rule for almost two centuries the Greek authors showed them as victims of an oppressive regime. We have to be conscious of this bias when writing Egypt's history in this period.

One fact is clear: Persia was a political structure very different from anything Egypt had ever dealt with before. It was enormous in size and the first empire in western Eurasia whose ruler saw himself as master of distinct populations and cultures. The Persian king readily acknowledged the diversity of his subjects and did not want to erase it. He inserted himself in existing ideologies and power structures. In Babylonia he was a Babylonian king; in Egypt he was a pharaoh; and so on. Still, the Persian ruler could not be present everywhere and his main capitals were in western Iran, a long distance from Egypt. Supposedly no Persian king after Darius I set foot in Egypt, although people continued to honor them as pharaohs. Governors – we call them satraps after the Greek rendering of the Persian title *khshathrapavan* – were in charge of day-to-day affairs in the provinces – satrapies – of the empire. They were Persian noblemen, often related to the king but also closely monitored by him. The relationship between the foreign ruling class and local Egyptians was not simple and over 200 years it never settled down. In order to evaluate Persia's rule over Egypt we need to survey the political and cultural interactions between the two.

Domination and resistance

Egypt was part of the Persian empire from 525 to 332, but it was never fully pacified. Numerous rebellions occurred, including one so successful that it gave the country independence for 60 years, from 404 to 343. Egypt's distance from the core of the empire may explain why it was so difficult to control, but we should also keep in mind that the abundant information on rebellions derives from Greek authors who liked to underscore Persia's setbacks. Moreover, Greeks almost always played a role in Egyptian struggles as mercenaries or allies. Both Athens and Sparta received substantial payments to help the Egyptian cause.

When Cambyses conquered Egypt in 525 he maintained the existing governmental structure but integrated Persians into it. No fundamental changes are visible. In *The Petition of Petiese* the conflict between the petitioner's family and the priesthood in their native town continued irrespective of the change in government, and the parties used the same techniques to gain advantage (see Sources in Translation 12.1). Likewise the Jewish mercenaries quartered at Elephantine on the southern border switched allegiance from the indigenous Egyptian king to Cambyses without disruption. The empire installed Persians to oversee affairs at the highest levels, however. The chief administrator was the satrap with an official residence in Memphis. All the men who held the office were Persian nobles and they had close ties with the king. One of them, Achemenes, was the brother of King Xerxes (ruled 486–465). Also provincial governors and administrators with even more limited regional powers could be Persians.

Many Egyptians remained in government service, however. One famous example is Udjahorresnet who left behind a statue inscribed with his autobiography. He was a naval officer under kings Ahmose II and Psamtek III of the 26th dynasty, whom Cambyses selected as chief physician and personal advisor. He spent time in Persia until Darius sent him back to Egypt, where he was buried in a massive shaft grave at Abusir. The Persians had a need for administrators who knew the Egyptian language and scripts, as most local affairs were conducted in Demotic. Throughout the empire the administration used Aramaic, a Semitic language recorded in alphabetic script, alongside local languages and scripts. The Aramaic material from Egypt is mostly letters of Persian officials and records of foreign communities like the Jews in Elephantine. Some administrative records in the language appear as well, sometimes mixed with Demotic material.

As they did elsewhere in the empire, the Persians encouraged economic development in Egypt and their access to enormous manpower and technological

Sources in Translation 12.1

The Petition of Petiese

A group of nine papyri, said to be from the site of el-Hibeh in Middle Egypt includes a long scroll with a 25-column draft of a complaint sent to the finance minister of Egypt under the Persian king Darius in 513 BC. The papyri record legal transactions of a priestly family in the years 644 to 513, and this Demotic text, called *The Petition of Petiese* traces the family history for some 150 years.

The writer, Petiese, accuses the priests of Amun at Teudjoi (the ancient name of el-Hibeh) of embezzling the temple's assets, which had been organized by Petiese's great-great-grandfather, also called Petiese. They refused to pay the family the stipends it had been awarded for services, and forced members to flee the town, destroying their house and dumping statues into the river. This abuse continued irrespective of what government was in charge in Egypt. Now Petiese again had to seek refuge in Memphis.

Petiese gives every detail of the conflict that spread over six generations. For example, the two sons of his great-grandfather's sister were killed when they went to claim the stipend from the Amun temple in 634 BC.

> In the year 31 (of the reign of Psamtek I), third month of the growing season (*peret*), they brought the grain for the offering to the god Amun of Teudjoi and poured it out in the temple. The priests gathered in the temple and said: "Say, by the god Ra, shall he still take a fifth of the offering? This coward of a southlander is in our hands!"
>
> They ordered a few young scoundrels: "Come with your sticks in the evening. Lie down on this grain and bury your sticks in it until the morning!"
>
> Now, it so happened that Horwedja, son of Paiftjauawibastet, had two strong young sons. The next morning the priests came to the temple to distribute the grain to the phyles (= groups of priests). The two young sons of Horwedja, son of Paiftjauawibastet, came to the temple and said: "Let a fifth be measured!"
>
> The young priests got their sticks out of the grain, surrounded the two boys of Horwedja and beat them. They ran up to the sanctuary and they ran after them. At the entrance of the chapel of the god Amun they caught up with them and killed them. They threw them into a storeroom of the chapel of the platform of stone.[9]

The papyrus ends with several pleas to Amun to avenge the family.

While the narrative sounds much like a true story, many scholars think it is literary and fictional in character. It fits the literary motif of corrupt officials and the search for justice from the pharaoh, in this case a Persian king.

expertise enabled them to accomplish projects that had failed before. King Darius I (ruled 522–486) revived the idea of digging a canal from the eastern Delta to the Red Sea that Nekau II had abandoned (see above). This time the project was successful. To commemorate the event he erected along the canal's course stone steles – now badly damaged – inscribed with Egyptian hieroglyphs on one side and Old Persian cuneiform on the other. The latter text states:

> King Darius proclaims: I am a Persian; from Persia, I seized Egypt. I ordered this canal to be dug, from a river called Nile, which flows in Egypt, to the sea, which goes to Persia. So this canal was dug as I had ordered, and ships went from Egypt through this canal to Persia, as was my desire.[10]

The manpower required in this thinly populated region ran into the tens of thousands. Not only did the workers have to dig the canal but they also had to keep it free from silt and windblown sand, which is pervasive in that area. The canal connected Egypt directly to the core of the empire, as ships could sail from Memphis across the Red Sea and Persian Gulf to Iranian coastal harbors near the capitals. Scholars debate its actual utility, however. Some see it as a symbolic link that could only operate when the Nile flooded and was intended to show the empire's ability to collect Egypt's wealth. Others believe that its practical purpose was important. The canal did away with the need for overland transport through Egypt's formidable eastern desert. Access to the Red Sea was more important now than it had been before because it connected Egypt to the eastern empire and its massive resources.

On the opposite side of the Nile the Persians promoted settlement in the oases of the western desert. In the 5th century there appeared in Egypt an entirely new system of water supply, the *qanat*. It consisted of underground tunnels that channeled groundwater from aquifers over long distances and enabled the irrigation of large areas of land. *Qanats* as an irrigation technology are typical for central Iran and the likelihood that Persians introduced them into Egypt is great. The Egyptian tunnels remained in use into Roman times. Twenty-two of them have been excavated in the Kharga oasis where they supported several small villages. Demotic ostraca discovered in a temple attest to the villages' existence from the late 26th to early 30th dynasties. The texts – still unpublished – often record transactions with water. Farmers bought the right to have water flow into their fields for a number of days and promised part of their yields in return. The contracts are dated in the traditional Egyptian way according to the regnal years of kings. They include both Persians and those who ruled when Egypt was independent from the empire. The changes in government did not affect how the records were kept.

Trade flourished in the Persian Period. Despite the wars with the Greeks the eastern Mediterranean was mostly safe, and ships from Anatolia and Syria could travel back and forth to Egypt. The empire collected taxes on this activity. A unique papyrus found at Elephantine contains a record of the inspection, regulation, and taxation of ships entering Egypt in the 11th year of a Persian king, either Xerxes (which would date the record to 475) or Artaxerxes I (which would date the record to 454). Originally the papyrus was 24.6 feet (7.5 meters) long, more than 12 inches (30 centimeters) high, and contained 64 columns of text. At a later point in the 5th century someone erased the papyrus to reuse it, but much of the account is still visible, albeit faintly. A sample entry reads:

> On the 15th of Pakhons (= August 31) they inspected for Egypt 1 ship of X son of Ergilos, Ionian, ... 1 large ship is in accordance with its measurements. The oil that was found in it is 50 jars. The duty that was collected from it and transferred to the house of the king: gold, 12 staters for gold, which is 1 karsh and 6 hallurs (= 85.5 grams); wooden support, 1; empty jars, 30, of which are not coated, 10.[11]

The ships brought primarily oil and wine, but also wood, metals, wool, and a type of clay, and they originated in Greece and probably Phoenicia. Tax rates depended on the origin and size of the ships: Greek ships had to pay amounts of silver and gold and a share of the cargo, Phoenician ships one-tenth of everything transported. There were also taxes in silver on the men of the boats as well as payments on the goods exported, mostly natron, which was used in textile production. These dues added up to substantial amounts that entered the royal treasury. This is one record only of an unidentified harbor, and many more such sources of income for the empire must have existed.

Another important economic resource in Egypt was temple property and the Persians wanted to control that as well. The abuse of temples was a favorite subject for anti-Persian rhetoric and doubtless overstated. The idea that the Persians ransacked temples upon Cambyses's conquest was probably a wild exaggeration, if not untrue. Yet there is evidence that the empire confiscated temple property, and over time this policy may have become harsher in reaction to Egyptian rebellions. Thus, the report of Greek historians that Artaxerxes III Ochus plundered temples and carried off vast quantities of gold and silver upon recapturing the country after its spell of independence in 343, is likely to be true.

Not all Persian imperial acts concerned the economy. Darius organized the legal system by ordering scholars to collect all the laws of Egypt down to the reign of Ahmose II (570–526). They labored on the project for 10 years and produced Demotic and Aramaic versions of the collection. These volumes are lost, but the enterprise earned Darius the title of one of the great lawgivers of Egypt. He and the other Persian kings were intent on making Egypt an integral part of the empire.

The Egyptians were defiant subjects, however, especially those of the Delta. Throughout the period they rebelled whenever the Persians showed weakness due to internal dissent or military setbacks. Greek authors, who cherished Persian troubles, are often our only source on these revolts. Egyptian data are mostly quiet as the men who claimed kingship had limited territorial success and survived only briefly. But rebellions were certainly real and confirmation appears for some of them. The ostraca from the Kharga oasis (see above), for example, include one that is dated in the second year of Inaros, "the rebel prince." We had only Greek testimonies of his existence before. These report that he seized parts of the Delta when Xerxes of Persia was assassinated in 465 and that he relied on Libyans and Greeks to accomplish this.

Egyptian opposition was not well organized or coordinated, even when it was successful. In the period from 404 to 343 the country was independent from Persia, but the three dynasties that Manetho lists were a set of rival families that regularly fought one another. Amyrtaios from Sais took advantage of a palace revolt in Persia to claim kingship of Egypt in 404. Until 400, people from Elephantine in the south continued to recognize the Persian Artaxerxes II, however. Amyrtaios was the sole ruler of Manetho's 28th dynasty. A family from the Delta city Mendes replaced him as the 29th dynasty. When its founder, Nepherites I, died in 393 three men claimed the throne. The winner, Hakor, did have a stable reign for 13 years and even supported anti-Persian activity in Cyprus. His successor, however, was soon overthrown by Nectanebo I, probably his commander, who founded the 30th dynasty in 380.

The second member of the 30th dynasty, Teos (ruled 362–60), felt secure enough to invade Syria with the help of Spartan soldiers. While he was abroad his nephew snatched the throne, although part of the population supported another pretender. Various factions in the court and people with different regional support had conflicting interests. In essence the fragmentation of Egyptian power that characterized the Third Intermediate Period continued in this brief period of independence. Still Artaxerxes II failed to retake Egypt in 374/3. In 343, his son Artaxerxes III Ochus succeeded because he had a massive army – according to Greek sources – and some Greek mercenaries switched sides. The last Egyptian king, Nectanebo II, fled to Nubia. Even afterwards an enigmatic rebel with the non-Egyptian name Khababash fought the Persians, but the Egyptians had to wait until the Macedonian Alexander crushed Persian forces in Asia for the overthrow of that regime. In 332 Alexander entered the country with little resistance.

Why did the Egyptians fight Persian rule so much? Many historians have written that these struggles were "nationalist movements" inspired by a dislike of the foreigner, xenophobia even. They regularly point to an incident in the Jewish mercenary community at Elephantine to substantiate this notion: papyri found there show that in 410 the Egyptian priests of Khnum destroyed the temple of the Jews. All information on the event derives from the Jewish community. In letters to Memphis they accused the local governor Vidranga – a man with a Persian name – of having supported the attack. The initial complaints were without result, but three years later a letter to the Persian satrap in Jerusalem led to permission to rebuild the temple. There is no indication that the Egyptians' action was inspired by xenophobia, however. A property dispute instigated the move as an Egyptian sanctuary abutted the Jewish one. Both Egyptians and Jews depended on Persians to settle their disagreements. We cannot say that the mercenaries symbolized Persia to the people of

Elephantine. When Amyrtaios gained independence, his government kept the mercenaries on.

Several concerns probably inspired the revolts, but it is likely that the upper classes that had governed Egypt in the Third Intermediate and Late Periods instigated them. Deprived of their offices by the arrival of a Persian administration, some assimilated themselves into the Persian ranks but others were probably denied that opportunity. Many of them had Libyan ancestry and may have maintained close connections with that area. Some scholars even suggest that it was not Egyptians but people from the west who directed the revolts. They may have found support because the Persians imposed oppressive duties on Egyptians. The Persians saw the country as a source of imperial income and used its population for projects that may have received little Egyptian backing. The construction of the Red Sea canal, abandoned previously, was completed perhaps with a loss of many Egyptian lives. Egyptians had to fight in Persian armies for causes that had no benefit to them. Many of the Egyptian revolts seem to have been opportunistic attempts of various families to gain control. We cannot say that they represented popular countrywide anti-Persian uprisings, however, or that the Persian kings were loathed as foreigners.

Mixing cultures

The Persians did try to integrate themselves within the existing Egyptian ideologies and religious structures and certainly did not spurn the country's culture. Elsewhere in the empire they also accepted and promoted local traditions and their attitude toward Egypt was not unique in this respect. This is especially well documented in the early part of the occupation. King Cambyses chose an Egyptian throne name, Mesutira, that is, "Offspring of Ra," and supported important Egyptian cults, such as that of the Apis bull (see Special Topic 12.1). Darius commissioned the decoration of Amun's temple at Hibis in the Kharga oasis, a temple the Saites had founded. The decoration follows classical Egyptian styles and includes numerous reliefs that show the Persian king as an Egyptian pharaoh with gods and goddesses. He refurbished other temples throughout Egypt and buried the Apis bull with full honors. Later Persian kings do not seem to have encouraged major constructions, but a small group of short hieroglyphic inscriptions that contain their names in cartouches confirm their status as pharaohs.

The Persians did not try to hide their origins. Darius's bilingual steles along the Red Sea canal (see above) show that he was willing to combine Egyptian and non-Egyptian traditions and styles of representation on the same monument. Other eloquent examples of this fusion existed in the core of the empire. In the capital Susa in modern western Iran stood a larger-than-life-size granite statue of Darius that displays a mixture of Egyptian and Persian elements. It is the only free-standing royal statue found in Persia so far and shows the king in

Special Topic 12.1   *The Apis bull and other animal cults*

Herodotus told the story of Cambyses's murder of the Apis bull at Memphis as proof of that king's madness and his disregard of Egyptian religious feelings. The cults of gods in animal form indeed boomed in the Late Period and continued to do so in Greek and Roman times. Very prominent among them was the cult of the bull, an animal connected to the king from the Early Dynastic Period onward. Various cities had bull cults. At Memphis the animal was called Apis and associated with the god Ptah in life; in death it became the Osiris Apis, a name rendered Sarapis in classical sources (Figure 12.6). From at least New Kingdom times on the dead Apis was mummified and buried near Djoser's step pyramid at Saqqara. Rameses II's son Khaemwaset (see Chapter 9) started the digging of subterranean tunnels for the purpose. Psamtek I of the 26th dynasty extended them substantially, and the complex grew into the Roman Period. The bulls were interred in massive stone sarcophagi placed in vaults along the tunnels. In classical times the mausoleum acquired the name Serapeum;

Figure 12.6   30th-dynasty statue of the Apis bull from Memphis. Louvre, Paris © 2010. White Images/Scala, Florence

some 7,000 dedicatory inscriptions in hieroglyphs and demotic were discovered in it. They include royal and non-royal steles that indicate the dates of birth, death, and burial of the bulls and allow us to reconstruct the sequence of these sacred animals and the rituals surrounding them.

It was only after a bull died that a new Apis could be selected – two of them never coexisted. This involved a search throughout Egypt for the right animal. Herodotus claims it had to be black with a white triangle on its forehead, an eagle on its side (that is, the Egyptian vulture), and a scarab beneath its tongue (whatever that may mean). The chosen animal was called Apis henceforth and was only distinguished from the other bulls through the names of its mother, who also became the object of a cult. The Apis was installed in the Ptah temple at Memphis and resided there for its entire life. It was used for breeding and its calves were venerated as well. In these sheltered conditions bulls usually lived some 20 years or more. When they died the entire country went into mourning and the body was mummified like that of a king with special rituals in an embalming house at Saqqara. After the ritual period of 70 days the dead Apis was interred. Successive dynasties embellished the processional road to the Serapeum: 30th-dynasty kings lined the ways with sphinxes, and Ptolemies placed statues of 11 Greek philosophers and poets near the complex.

Many other animal necropolises existed in Saqqara. The mothers of the Apis were buried in one, others contained mummies of baboons, cats, ibises, and falcons. The mass mummification of a species of animals was a Late Period innovation. Farms attached to temples bred thousands of these animals to sell their mummies to pilgrims. At some point, annually almost 10,000 ibises were deposited in the cemetery. Demotic texts reveal that the priests involved could cheat. Several of the jars that were supposed to contain a mummified bird only held some sticks and feathers wrapped in linen.

Egyptian pose, with the left foot forward on a pedestal that contains the age-old symbol of the unification of Upper and Lower Egypt. On the sides of the base appear the names of imperial territories in hieroglyphs inside the Egyptian symbol of conquered peoples. The hieroglyphic inscriptions on the pedestal and parts of the statue describe Darius as a wholly Egyptian pharaoh, King of Upper and Lower Egypt. For example:

> The good god, who rejoices in truth, whom the god Atum, Lord-of-Heliopolis, has chosen to be master of all that the sun encircles, because he knows that he is his son and caretaker. He has ordered him to conquer both of the Two Lands, and the goddess Neith gave him the bow she holds, to throw back all his enemies, acting as she did on behalf of her son, the god Ra, on the first occasion (= creation), so that he may be effective in repelling those who rebel against him, to reduce those who rebel against him in the Two Lands.[12]

The statue is also Persian, however. Darius wears a Persian robe and dagger and there are cuneiform inscriptions as well, in three languages – Old Persian, Akkadian, and Elamite – that state, for example:

A great god is Ahuramazda, who created this earth, who created yonder sky, who created man, who created happiness for man, who made Darius king.[13]

Also non-royal imperial administrators in Egypt adapted to the country's culture. Some used Egyptian names in addition to their Persian ones. Others had mortuary steles carved with their image in Persian dress but in an Egyptian setting. These immigrants did not remain aloof from the ancient culture that surrounded them.

Egyptians were willing to accept the Persians as proper Egyptian rulers. The small and crudely carved stele of a man called Pediosiripra shows him worshiping Darius as the falcon-god Horus. Egyptians adopted Persian customs, especially if they wanted to be integrated into the imperial administration. Udjahorresnet, already mentioned, represented himself wearing a Persian dress, and boasted of his service to Cambyses and Darius. He was not the only one who moved from an Egyptian administration to a Persian one. An official of the 30th dynasty, who died in the Ptolemaic Period, Somtutefnakht, survived the reconquest of Egypt by Artaxerxes III unscathed. He wrote on his mortuary stele:

> When you (the god Herishef) turned your back on Egypt,
> You put love of me in the heart of the ruler of Asia.[14]

When Herodotus told the story of how Cambyses went mad and killed the Apis bull in Saqqara, he repeated a lie (see Key Debate 12.1). We know that the king buried this sacred animal with all the usual honors and that he supported other Egyptian cults, as did his successors. Persians were portrayed as vandals because it strengthened the idea that the Greeks were the guardians of civilization. When we look at the material from Egypt itself, we see how the Persians continued and reinforced cultural practices that the Saites had fostered. Examples are animal cults in religion, the use of Demotic in administration, and styles of representing human beings in art.

When in 404 – after 120 years of Persian rule – Amyrtaios started a 60-year-long period of Egyptian independence from Persia, all the elements were still in place to carry on the cultural practices of the 26th Saite dynasty. The 30th-dynasty kings especially supported temple construction throughout Egypt and the artwork produced at the time displays the stunning abilities of sculptors to work in stone (Plate 11). The Persians must have promoted the training and support of such artists. Creativity remained high and was rooted in old Egyptian traditions. Under Nectanebo I a new architectural feature started to be added to temples, the birth house that Egyptologists call *mammisi*, a term the decipherer of hieroglyphs, Jean-François Champollion, invented on the basis of the ancient Egyptian *pr-mst*. The shrine promoted the idea that the divine king was born in the temple and spent his first weeks in a chapel under the protection of the gods. This and other innovations of the Late Period flourished in the Ptolemaic Period when a new group of foreigners, the Greeks, came to rule Egypt.

Key Debate 12.1   *King Cambyses and the Apis bull*

Herodotus's account of the Persian invasion of Egypt in 525 is a sad tale: Cambyses treated the Egyptians with cruelty and disdained their customs, among other things burning the corpse of the Egyptian king Amasis. His madness reached its height when he killed the Apis bull in a fit of jealousy after he saw how the Egyptians celebrated the animal's appearance (cf. Kuhrt 2007: 129–31). Although Herodotus's credibility as historian was contested from antiquity on, no one really doubted the Apis murder story, but when in the mid-19th century the Serapeum at Saqqara was excavated, evidence of a very different nature appeared. A stele set beside a mummified bull records that an Apis was buried in the middle of Cambyses's sixth year (that is, between October 28 and November 26, 524). The king appears on the stele giving the animal full honors and he also donated a fine sarcophagus (cf. Kuhrt 2007: 122–4). These contemporary sources seem more convincing than a tale written close to a century later. Most scholars accept that Herodotus concocted or repeated anti-Persian propaganda (Bresciani 1985: 504; Ray 1988: 260; Briant 2002: 55–7; Asheri et al. 2007: 427–8). The tale is one example of a long literary tradition depicting Persian conquerors in a negative light – Artaxerxes III Ochus received the same treatment (Schwartz 1948).

But support for Herodotus's veracity continues, as the events documented in the Egyptian sources are highly unusual and there was great confusion at the time. By rule no two Apis bulls could be alive at the same time and the successor to the one Cambyses buried was born on May 29, 525. Cambyses's bull remained thus unburied for at least one year and a half, while usually only 70 days passed between death and burial, but this could have been due to the chaos of the conquest (Posener 1936: 172–3). That bull also seems not to be the one Herodotus describes. Herodotus speaks of a young animal, while the one Cambyses buried was 20 years old. Thus, some scholars suggest that another animal was involved. After the bull of the Cambyses stele died another animal was selected. It was his installation that enraged the king, who killed it and buried it in a secret place. The remains of that animal are unknown. A third bull was born in 525 and the earliest Apis – left unburied so far – was interred with full honors when the king was away on campaign elsewhere (Depuydt 1995; somewhat different and more cautious Devauchelle 1995: 70). Or, some suggest, the bull found in the Serapeum had nothing to do with Cambyses. The date on the Louvre stele refers to a time after Cambyses's own death, when the entire Persian empire was in chaos (Devauchelle 1998). These attempts to salvage Herodotus as a reliable historical source seem much too complicated to be convincing, but they are not likely to end.

NOTES

1. Translation after Lichtheim 1980: 37–8.
2. *Histories* Book 2.35, de Sélincourt 1972: 142–3.
3. Ray 1988: 285.
4. Translation after Eide et al. 1994: 196–7.
5. Book 2.154, de Sélincourt 1972: 191–2.
6. Book 2.177, de Sélincourt 1972: 199.
7. Boardman 1999: 116.
8. Translation after der Manuelian 1994: 25–7.

9. Translation after Hoffmann & Quack 2007: 35–6.
10. Translation Kuhrt 2007: 486.
11. Translation after Kuhrt 2007: 686.
12. Translation after Kuhrt 2007: 478.
13. Translation Kuhrt 2007: 478.
14. Translation after Lichtheim 1980: 42.

13

Greek and Roman Egypt (332 BC–AD 395)

Cleopatra's nose, had it been shorter, the whole face of the world would have been changed. (Pascal, *Pensées*)

Alexander, the young king of Macedonia to the north of Greece, truly was a world-historical figure whose actions had a profound impact on many people of his own time and long afterwards. Hence, he deserves the soubriquet "the Great" in the eyes of many. His efficient army annexed the Persian empire and neighboring regions in one swoop and in less than a decade unified a territory of an unprecedented size. Only his men's fatigue seems to have prevented Alexander from going even farther east. As a part of the Persian empire, Egypt came under his dominion as well. In the fall of 332 the army of Macedonians and Greeks entered the country unopposed. Classical sources present them as liberators from the oppressive Persians.

The conquest started the final period of ancient Egyptian history, one that in many respects was very different from what preceded it. Henceforth Egypt's ruling classes were unabashedly foreign and had no qualms about being distinct from the majority of the population. Most of them did not speak Egyptian but Greek. For the first 300 years the royal dynasty – the Ptolemies – resided in Egypt, albeit in a city on its margins, and for the next four centuries the country was a province of Roman emperors, who lived far away and rarely visited. The Greeks and Romans who governed imposed many customs and practices that were entirely foreign to Egyptians. They introduced changes in all aspects of life: agriculture, administration, finance, the military, religion, architecture, the arts, literature, scholarship, and much more. But Egyptian culture did not fade into oblivion rapidly. Its roots in deep antiquity and its accomplishments were so obvious everywhere that it could not be ignored. Moreover, like the foreigners who had held Egypt in the past, Greeks and Romans found much that appealed to them. History is a constant interaction between continuity and change, and Ptolemaic and Roman Egypt (sometimes called "Egypt after the Pharaohs") shows these two forces at work. Often the disciplinary background of historians determines what aspect receives most attention in their work. Those working with Egyptian language materials – mostly Demoticists – focus on continuity; those trained in Greek and in classical history emphasize change.

Similar processes occurred in other parts of the Mediterranean world, especially in the Near East. Old traditions merged with those the conquerors introduced. Egypt was first part of a large Hellenistic world, a fusion of Greek (Hellenic) and Near Eastern traditions; then it was integrated into the Roman empire with its even larger extent and multiple traditions. These contexts determined many developments in the country's political, cultural, and economic history. The 700-year-long period from Alexander's conquest in 332 BC to the time when Egypt became part of the Byzantine empire in AD 395 is well documented in sources from Egypt itself and from outsiders. It is filled with individuals the memory of whom was never lost because the ancients were so enthralled by them. Thus could the 17th-century Frenchman Blaise Pascal muse about Cleopatra's nose long before the decipherment of hieroglyphs. We can only provide broad outlines here of a history that is extremely rich in detail. In this chapter we will focus on the encounter of cultures, tracing the interactions that caused ancient Egypt to evolve into something drastically new.

13.1 Sources and Chronology

Historians of Egypt who study the Ptolemaic and Roman periods have an abundance of documentation available to them when compared to earlier periods of the country's history. Masses of papyri have been discovered and the work to read them is far from finished. Some finds number into the tens of thousands of items. They derive from relatively few sites, however, and do not provide coverage of the entirety of Egypt. Many are from the Fayyum region, while the Delta is virtually undocumented. The preservation of papyri in the Ptolemaic Period is often due to the fact that they were used in the cartonnage of mummies that were buried in the desert (see Chapter 1). This method of producing coffins ended in Roman times, but from that period derive several village dumps with enormous numbers of papyri at sites such as Karanis and Tebtunis in the Fayyum region, and Oxyrhynchus in the Nile Valley, some 45 miles (70 kilometers) farther south. Some of these dumps continued in use into the early Muslim Period. The reconstruction of the papyri is often a painstaking piecing together of fragments dug up in a rushed manner and distributed over various museum collections, and research centers around the world are engaged in the task.

The papyri contain a mixture of documents, mostly from the government, which was the largest consumer of the writing material. Private legal contracts and letters are also preserved, while the Oxyrhynchus collection is one of the most important sources of early manuscripts of Greek literature. Scribes of the Ptolemaic Period wrote both in Greek and Demotic, albeit different types of texts in each language. The Romans ended the use of Demotic as a language of bureaucracy and it soon had little relevance in people's daily lives, although it remained a language of temple literature for another 250 years. In the 4th century AD, Coptic became a commonly used language in writing. Latin appears rarely in Egypt.

The hieroglyphic tradition continued with numerous inscriptions, especially in temples. Ptolemaic kings and Roman emperors commissioned inscriptions that portrayed them as rulers in the Egyptian tradition. Also the Egyptian elites of the Ptolemaic Period could order mortuary steles and the like with hieroglyphic texts. But in Roman times these people were sidelined and non-royal documentation became rare. Still, in the 2nd century AD the town of

Summary of dynastic history
Greco-Roman Period

332–30 BC	**Ptolemaic Period**
332	Alexander of Macedon conquers Egypt
331	Foundation of Alexandria
305	Ptolemy I Soter declares himself "King of Egypt"
217	Ptolemy IV Philopater wins battle of Raphia against the Seleucid Antiochus III
168	Romans force Seleucids to withdraw from Alexandria
130	Rebel Harsiese is last Egyptian called pharaoh
51–30	Reign of Cleopatra VII
30 BC–AD 395	**Roman Period**
30 BC	Egypt becomes a Roman province
30 BC–AD 14	Emperor Augustus commissions much monumental construction
24 BC	Meroites sack Aswan
AD 130–131	Emperor Hadrian makes state visit to Egypt
AD 270–272	Syrian Queen Zenobia briefly occupies Egypt
ca. AD 350	Axumite kingdom destroys Meroe
AD 391	Emperor Theodosius closes down Egyptian temples
AD 395	Egypt becomes part of the Eastern Roman (Byzantine) empire

Oxyrhynchus employed five hieroglyph carvers. The last known inscription in that script, carved at Philae, dates to AD 394.

The narrative of the period's history derives from non-Egyptian sources, however: the Greek and Roman historians who included information on the country in their discussions of the Hellenistic and Roman worlds in general. Authors like Polybius (2nd c. BC), Diodorus of Sicily (1st c. BC), Plutarch, Arrian (1st–2nd c. AD), and others usually did not write about events of their own lifetimes, but used earlier sources now lost. Roman generals like Julius Caesar did describe their own actions in Egypt. These sources can be very detailed, with stories of palace intrigues and the like, and inspired later ideas of Egypt as a country of great wealth and decadence.

The chronology of this period is very secure and we can regularly date events to the day.

13.2   Alexandria and Philae

Alexandria

At opposite ends of Egypt two places experienced enormous growth in the Greco-Roman Period and they serve as ideal examples of the new mixture of cultures that characterized the country at the time. Alexandria on the Mediterranean Sea coast was a fully Greek city with little Egyptian influence; Philae on the first Nile cataract in the south was an Egyptian temple complex with few recognizable Greco-Roman traces. Both places received extensive royal patronage, however. Kings who commissioned Greek buildings in Alexandria also had traditional shrines to Egyptian gods constructed at Philae.

As its name indicates, Alexandria was a creation of Alexander the Great who, according to tradition, was told to found the city in a dream in 331 BC. It arose on the location of a small Egyptian town, Rhakotis, but was a departure from Egyptian practices in every respect. It was the first major Egyptian sea harbor located on the strip of land that separates Lake Mareotis from the Mediterranean. Over the previous centuries the commercial center of Egypt had shifted north because of Mediterranean contacts, but harbors like Naukratis (see Chapter 12) were located in the Delta in Lower Egypt. Alexandria was first a Mediterranean city, second a part of Egypt. The inland lakes behind it, Mareotis and Abukir, separated it from the country, and the Romans saw the city as distinct from Egypt. The official who governed the country on the emperor's behalf was "prefect of Alexandria and Egypt."

The city's appearance was thoroughly Greek. Today few remains of buildings exist and we rely on ancient descriptions and subterranean structures to imagine how it looked. These leave no doubt about the un-Egyptian character of Alexandria. The streets were laid out on a Greek Hippodamian grid-plan along an east–west axis, and were lined with Greek buildings: a theater, a

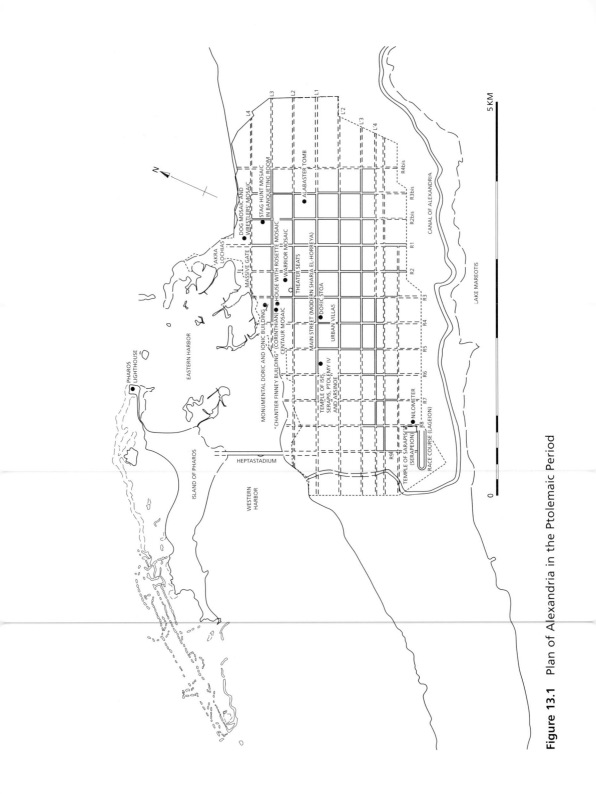

Figure 13.1 Plan of Alexandria in the Ptolemaic Period

hippodrome, the famous library of Alexandria, the Museum (that is, "shrine of the Muses"), Greek temples, and an agora. So many buildings were of marble – rather than the traditional Egyptian limestone – that Arab conquerors in AD 642 allegedly had to shield their eyes against the sun reflected from them. The preserved traces of residential structures are Greek in style, not Egyptian (Figure 13.1).

Also in non-physical terms the city was Greek. Only some of its inhabitants were free citizens, and for centuries that status was reserved for Greek immigrants and their descendants. Egyptians only qualified under the Roman empire when rules on citizenship changed everywhere. Alexandria was the center of intellectual life in the Hellenistic world and Greek was the language of discourse. At its height the famed library held half a million papyrus scrolls, many with more than one work, all in Greek. Some of them were translations of writing in other languages – most importantly the translation of the Hebrew Bible, the Septuagint, according to tradition commissioned by Ptolemy II Philadelphus (ruled 285–246 BC) – but the focus certainly was on Greek literature and learning. Resident scholars collected manuscripts with the aim of reconstructing the original texts for interpretation. They also created their own works, and Alexandrian poetry was especially famous. Until the mid-2nd century BC the city was the preferred residence for scholars from all over the Hellenistic world.

Alexandria was also one of the most important commercial centers of the Mediterranean world, with two harbors and a lighthouse at Pharos that counted among the wonders of the ancient world. A canal connected the city to the Nile and beyond. Egypt was a major producer of grain and in the Roman Period served as the breadbasket for the empire's core. The Nile River connected Alexandria to Africa, whose products appealed greatly to Mediterranean elites. Greek and Roman rulers developed harbors on the Red Sea shores, connected to the Nile by overland routes and the Persian canal. These gave access to countries as far as India, a source for highly desired pepper and other luxuries. Alexandria was the transit point for all these products.

As a result of long-distance trade the city's population was very diverse with people from distant and nearby regions flocking to it. In the mid-1st century BC it possibly housed half a million residents. Egyptians must have formed a sizeable part of them and seemingly they resided primarily in the western part of town. Their traditions did influence the culture of Alexandria, partly because the Ptolemaic kings wanted to show off their special status within the Hellenistic world and used Egyptian elements to give themselves an exotic tinge. They happily set up massive statues in which they appeared as pharaohs in traditional Egyptian dress. They also took older monuments from other parts of the country to adorn Alexandria. Several temples to Egyptian deities existed in Alexandria. The gods so honored were the ones that Greeks and Romans preferred: Isis and Sarapis, that is, the Apis bull as Osiris (see Chapter 12). The temple to the latter seems to have been fully Greek in architecture, however. Not surprisingly Egyptian influence was strongest in the burials. Underground

Figure 13.2 Fresco with mortuary scene on the interior of the Alexandria Catacombs (1st–2nd century AD). akg-images/De Agostini Pict.Li

chambers display Greek and Roman architectural styles, in the columns for example, but also contain such Egyptian elements as embalming scenes involving Egyptian gods (Figure 13.2). The ancient culture was not fully denied but it was certainly not dominant.

Alexandria's fortunes had their ups and downs. The city flourished especially in Ptolemaic times when it was the capital of a large state and the primary royal residence. When the Romans annexed Egypt as a province its status declined. Imperial repression of rebellions – Alexandrians were notoriously unruly and violent – and a sequence of earthquakes did much damage to the city. An earthquake in AD 635 caused part of it to sink into the sea. The city lost its foremost status in Egypt only when the Arab conquerors returned to the Memphis area to build a new capital at the later Cairo.

Philae

A visitor to Philae born and raised in Alexandria entered an alien world. The architecture on the small island at the first cataract was traditional Egyptian in style and decoration. Philae's main temple belonged to the goddess Isis and

Figure 13.3 Second pylon of the Isis temple at Philae; King Ptolemy XII Neos Dionysos offers to Isis and Horus

was located near the Abaton, the local tomb of Osiris on the neighboring island of Biga. Kings no later than the 26th dynasty had built on Philae, but only with the Ptolemies did the entire island grow into a magnificent religious complex. Because of the building of the Aswan dam in the 1960s, modern tourists admire the splendid remains as reconstructed on the island of Agilkiya. The complex is not large but contains all the standard elements of traditional Egyptian temples: an inner sanctuary, pylons, and courtyards. A birth house or *mammisi*, subsidiary temples – including one for Imhotep, Djoser's architect – and some other structures surround the Isis temple. The abundant decoration shows traditional scenes of Greek and Roman rulers as Egyptian kings honoring Egyptian gods (Figure 13.3), and scenes involving Isis, Osiris, and their son Horus. Numerous hieroglyphic inscriptions accompany the images. The Ptolemies built most of the structures, but Roman emperors continued to work on the island. Trajan (ruled AD 98–117), for example, commissioned a beautiful kiosk with 14 elaborate columns.

Philae was a stronghold of Egyptian culture for more than seven centuries after the Greeks conquered the country. But just as Alexandria was not purely

Greek, Philae was not purely Egyptian. Even during the very beginning of the Ptolemaic development of the temple, kings also left inscriptions in Greek on the monuments. There are relatively few building inscriptions that commemorate construction, somewhat more dedications on steles and other monuments. The majority of Greek texts are graffiti left by visitors. The same practices continued in the Roman Period. A stele commissioned by Gaius Cornelius Gallus, Roman prefect from 30 to 26 BC, commemorates his suppression of a revolt at Thebes in three languages. The Latin and Greek versions closely resemble each other; the Egyptian hieroglyphic version is very poorly preserved. In much later centuries Christian churches appeared alongside the Isis temple showing the displacement of traditional Egyptian ideas.

The Egyptian character of Philae gained much support from people from the south. Nubians and inhabitants of the eastern desert considered the complex an important religious center and pilgrimage site. Shrines devoted to their gods appeared in front of Isis's temple. One belonged to Arensnuphis, a Nubian deity whose name means "the perfect companion"; the other was probably devoted to Mandulis, a prominent Nubian god associated with Horus. Philae's importance to these people actually prolonged the complex's existence beyond that of other temples when Christian Roman emperors suppressed Egyptian religion. Theodosius's decree in AD 391 that closed down Egyptian temples had no effect in Philae, and as late as the mid-5th century Byzantine emperors gave the Nubians access to take the Isis statue on a sacred journey southward. It is no coincidence that the last known hieroglyphic inscription is found on Philae within a Nubian context, inscribed next to an image of Mandulis. It dates to August 24, AD 394 and reads:

> Before Mandulis son of Horus, by the hand of Nesmeterakhem, son of Nesmeter, the second priest of Isis, for all time and eternity. Words spoken by Mandulis, Lord of Abaton, great god.

Below it is a related Demotic inscription:

> I, Nesmeterakhem, the scribe of the House of Writings(?) of Isis, son of Nesmeterpanakhet the second priest of Isis, and his mother Eseweret, I performed work on this figure of Mandulis for all time, because he is fair of face toward me. Today, the Birthday of Osiris, his dedication feast, year 110.[1]

Christianity ultimately gained the upper hand. The Byzantine Emperor Justinian (ruled AD 527–565) forbade Nubian worship – it took 40 years before the prohibition became fully effective – and turned the Isis temple into a church of St. Stephen.

Alexandria and Philae show the sometimes awkward coexistence of traditional Egyptian and more recently developed Hellenistic cultures. Both could express themselves fully in Egypt, but they did not remain unaffected by one another. The same relationship showed in other aspects of life, which we will explore next.

13.3 Kings, Queens, and Emperors

When Alexander started to form his enormous empire by the might of his sword he was a king from a backward region whose father Philip II had only recently gained fame and authority by imposing dominance over Greece. Alexander's Greek and Macedonian soldiers encountered cultures with royal traditions that were millennia old and of an entirely different nature from anything they had experienced before. To rule his empire Alexander had to slide into the shoes of his Persian predecessors, who had faced similar challenges when they united the Near East. In Egypt, Alexander found a concept of kingship with very close ties to the gods and he had no qualms about inserting himself into that tradition. He visited the then famous oracle of Amun in the Siwa oasis and learned there that he was that god's son; tradition has that he then went to Memphis to be crowned pharaoh. His building work in the center of the Luxor temple strengthened his legitimacy as local king.

Alexander's realm was vast and he did not stay long in Egypt. His capital was at Babylon in the Near East where he died in 323 aged only 32 years old. Under the dynastic idea his heirs succeeded him as rulers of the entire empire, but they were mere figureheads with little power over the generals who had been appointed administrators of the provinces. These people started to assert independence, and by 305 Ptolemy was "king of Egypt." His state was substantial in size: outside the customary Egyptian borders it included Cyprus, the southern part of Syria-Palestine, sections of the Aegean, and Cyrene to the west along the North African coast. But the borders of the kingdom were never secure. Throughout the next three centuries the Hellenistic kings fought wars, which preserved the military's role as a crucial player in their societies. Egypt mostly competed with the Seleucid kingdom of Mesopotamia over the control of Syria and many battles occurred. Some of them, such as the battle of Raphia near Gaza in 217, were encounters of massive armies with tens of thousands of men and dozens of war elephants. Egypt won that battle and secured its control over the Syrian coast, but its success was short-lived and the Seleucids reclaimed the region in 200.

The Ptolemies

Ptolemy I Soter initiated a dynasty that was to rule Egypt for almost 300 years. The family faced a special challenge in its search for legitimacy: albeit of foreign origin and proud of that fact, it was an Egyptian royal house. Nubians, Assyrians, and Persians had annexed the country to their existing domains; the Ptolemies had no other home. They were both Egyptian kings and of Macedonian origin. To strengthen the latter connection, Ptolemy I claimed that Philip of Macedon had impregnated his mother before she married his father Lagus. But at the same time, numerous images represented the Ptolemies as Egyptian kings in traditional garb and settings, offering to the gods and so on. The Ptolemies built upon the idea of the king's proximity to the divine world and created an invented tradition of the ruler cult, which involved kings and queens. From Ptolemy II Philadelphus (ruled 285–246) on, both were considered to be living gods and the beneficiaries of active cults, with priests, offerings, temples, and statues. Ptolemy II's second wife, Arsinoe II, was the first member of the dynasty to have a temple devoted to her and later kings and queens received similar attention. Ptolemy II and Arsinoe were also the first full siblings to be married in a new practice that continued throughout the dynasty's existence. The marriage was not exclusive and kings were still polygamous, but the primary queens were most often full sisters of the kings. The inspiration for this practice could have been Egyptian –the goddess Isis, whose popularity escalated in this period, was the sister of Osiris – but also Greek mythology had many sibling marriages among the gods (Zeus and Hera, for example).

The Ptolemaic dynasty's complicated family relations were part of its downfall. After about a century of strength and success at home and abroad, central power started to unravel in the late 2nd century BC. Infighting in court was vicious and murderous, and siblings were not spared. Regularly the Alexandrians acted as executioners. Classical authors recount numerous intrigues full of twists and turns. In 145, for example, Ptolemy VIII Euergetes II inherited the throne from his elder brother Ptolemy VI Philometor, with whom he had fought for several decades. He married Cleopatra II, his brother's widow and the sister of both men, and assassinated her younger son. Soon he also married the daughter of Cleopatra II and Ptolemy VI, his niece Cleopatra III. The two women started a civil war, and in 131 Ptolemy VIII and Cleopatra III fled to Cyprus. When they returned in 130 they forced Cleopatra II to seek refuge in Syria and took bloody revenge on the citizens of Alexandria. In 124 the parties were reconciled after the loss of many lives.

The strains on the central power caused by these struggles provided opportunities to native Egyptians to seek independence, whose confidence was bolstered after the battle of Raphia in 217 where Egyptian troops played a major role. From 207 to 186 most of the Theban area had seceded from the Ptolemaic state. During the conflict in Ptolemy VIII's time the last Egyptian to claim the title pharaoh, Harsiese, briefly ruled Thebes. Also other Hellenistic rulers, especially the Seleucids from Syria and Mesopotamia, took advantage of the power struggles in Egypt. They picked off the Ptolemies' non-Egyptian territories and at times threatened the country itself. During the sixth Syrian war (170/169–168) the Seleucid Antiochus IV Epiphanes – the uncle of Egypt's king – was about to capture Alexandria and it was only Roman intervention that saved the city. During the last 150 years of Ptolemaic Egypt's existence this new powerhouse from the western Mediterranean increasingly influenced affairs and soon Roman senators determined which member of the royal house ruled Egypt. It is no surprise that the country became a province of the Roman empire in the year 30 BC.

Figure 13.4 Stele with Greek inscription showing Cleopatra VII making an offering to Isis breastfeeding her son. Louvre, Paris/Lauros/Giraudon/The Bridgeman Art Library

Queen Cleopatra VII

More famous than any other Egyptian perhaps, and one of the few whose memory was never lost, was the last member of the Ptolemaic dynasty, Queen Cleopatra, the seventh with that name (Figure 13.4). She managed to revive Egypt's fortunes briefly, but saw the kingdom lose its independence to Rome. The momentous events in the reign, and especially the queen's tumultuous personal relationships with the generals who changed Rome from a republic to an empire, have made her the object of fascination from ancient times onward. In officially approved Roman accounts she was a predatory temptress who lived in the lap of luxury, and this image has stuck in European tradition. It is impossible to uncover the true Cleopatra from the ancient and later sources. Her fate was so closely tied to that of the Roman contenders for power that we cannot really recognize her own accomplishments. Some traditions show her in a different light: she is said to have been the only Ptolemaic ruler who learned to speak Egyptian, and later Muslim writers saw her as a scholar and sage.

In 51 BC, upon the death of her father (Ptolemy XII Auletes), Cleopatra came to the throne of Egypt at the age of 18 together with her full brother – and perhaps husband – the 10-year-old Ptolemy XIII. Soon exiled from Egypt, she sought the support of the Roman general Julius Caesar and with his help besieged Alexandria. The fleeing Ptolemy XIII drowned in the Nile. Cleopatra married another brother, Ptolemy XIV, but when in 47 BC she gave birth to a son, she called him Ptolemy Caesarion (popularly known as "little Caesar"), and claimed that he was the Roman general's son, which cannot be verified. When Julius Caesar was assassinated in 44 BC, she was on a visit in Rome, and soon she became drawn into the struggle over his succession. Now married to her own three-year-old son Ptolemy XV Caesarion, she dazzled Mark Antony with theatrics – presenting herself as the goddess Isis – and (perhaps) beauty. She bore the Roman general twin boys and a daughter, and in 32 BC Antony divorced his Roman wife, Octavian's sister Octavia. Antony granted Cleopatra and her family members large territories in the eastern Mediterranean from southern Turkey to Cyrene in North Africa as dominions. In return she financed Antony's eastern campaigns. In Rome, Octavian, who prided himself on his disdain of "oriental" luxury, convinced the people that Antony was giving away Roman lands to her, and on September 2, 31 BC, he crushed the armies of Antony and Cleopatra at Actium in Greece. The two fled to Alexandria and soon thereafter committed suicide. Octavian stated succinctly "I added Egypt to the empire of the Roman people." Egypt's independence came to an end.

Roman Egypt

Upon his defeat of Antony and Cleopatra, Octavian – soon afterwards called Augustus – made Egypt his personal province to be governed by a prefect. The country's agricultural resources were too valuable to be left in the hands of a senator, and Roman senators were even banned from visiting the country without the emperor's authorization. The province was relatively docile and required little effort in its pacification. Augustus left three legions of 6,000 men each in it; in later centuries the number went down to one legion, although some rebellions occurred. Several emperors and their family members visited the country for its tourist attractions. Hadrian (ruled AD 117–138) spent close to 10 months there. He participated in a lion hunt in the Libyan

Desert and heard the colossi of Memnon in western Thebes sing, an event reported in a Greek inscription on the foot of one of them. Disaster struck when his lover Antinous drowned in the Nile. Hadrian founded the city Antinoopolis in his memory, the center of a cult of Antinous as a god. He made it a center of trade as well by building a road connecting it to the Red Sea port of Berenike.

The 3rd century AD was a difficult period for Rome, and Egypt suffered as well. At one point in 270–272 Syrians from Palmyra conquered it, and documents acknowledge their Queen Zenobia as empress of Egypt. In later times her memory became conflated with that of Cleopatra VII. The strains of keeping the vast Roman empire together became too great in the 4th century and by its end east and west separated. Egypt became part of the Byzantine empire with its capital at Constantinople in modern Turkey, and the country continued its role as the imperial breadbasket. At the same time the religious transformation of the Mediterranean world with the rise of Christianity affected Egypt deeply and ultimately led to the end of its ancient culture. The transfer of power over Egypt from Rome to Constantinople in AD 395 is a convenient point to end its ancient history.

13.4 Greeks, Romans, and Egyptians

Administration

How did the non-Egyptians in political control and the Egyptians interact? Did they have parallel lives – the Egyptians in the villages, the immigrants in towns and cities – with little contact and exchange, or did they mingle and merge into a single population? Scholars have very different opinions on this question, and the situation certainly changed over the centuries (see Key Debate 13.1). The immigrants themselves were a mixed lot. Alexander's army included Macedonians and Greeks, and some Macedonian traditions, like the month names, became official practice. All spoke Greek, however. They encountered an alien culture and people who communicated in a language totally unlike their own. The Egyptians had seen the arrival of foreigners before and had integrated them within their society. The upper classes had to work together: the new foreign elites could not run the country alone; even though they occupied the highest offices, Egyptians had to assist them. The autobiography of a priest called Somtutefnakht shows how certain men had no qualms about allying themselves with whoever was in power. The priest started his career under the last native Egyptian dynasty (the 30th) and served under the Persians, participating in a battle against Alexander on their side (see Chapter 12). Then the god told him in a dream to return to Alexander's Egypt, and by the time of his death he held a string of priestly and secular offices.

In order to be accepted by the population the foreign rulers needed the ideo-logical support of the priesthood, which was made up of native Egyptians. The temples also continued to play a crucial role in the administration of the coun-try's resources, as they had done in earlier times. The Ptolemies sponsored massive building programs throughout Egypt, and the best-preserved temples today (at Dendera, Edfu, and Philae) are mostly their work. The dynasty's reliance on cult to legitimize its rule gave the priesthood a hold over it. Several decrees are preserved in which councils of priests declared their support for the dynasts but expected rewards. An early example was issued in the city of Canopus in the Delta near Alexandria in the year 238. The priests awarded King Ptolemy III Euergetes I and his wife Berenike the title Benefactor Gods (Euergetes in Greek). In return the royal couple:

> constantly confer many great benefactions on the temples throughout the land and increase more and more the honors of the gods and show constant care for Apis and Mnevis and all the other famous sacred animals in the country at great expense and outlay.[2]

The decree was to be distributed throughout the land in three languages and scripts: Middle Egyptian (written in hieroglyphs), Demotic, and Greek. Some 40 years later the famous Rosetta Stone – the key monument in the decipher-ment of Egyptian hieroglyphs – recorded a similar arrangement. The priests, assembled for the coronation of Ptolemy V Epiphanes (ruled 204–180), prom-ised that temples throughout Egypt would honor the king and his statue. In return, however, Ptolemy pledged to increase royal contributions to temples and to alleviate the tax burden (see Sources in Translation 13.1). Over time certain Egyptian members of the priesthood acquired many secular duties as well and administered areas of Egypt on behalf of the royal house living in Alexandria. The division of the country into nomes continued; indeed it is only for this period that we know all the nomes of Lower Egypt.

At least some Egyptians chose a Greek name alongside their Egyptian one, but it is hard to tell how common this practice was. It even occurred on the village level. In the later 2nd century BC, the secretary of the village Kerkeosiris, for example, mostly used his Egyptian name, Menches, but he was known with the Greek name Asklepiades as well (see Special Topic 13.1). Peoples' names do not indicate whether they were of Egyptian or Greek birth, or of mixed origin. We know of families where some brothers have Egyptian names, others Greek ones. Greeks and Egyptians intermarried, and over time the distinction between the two must have blurred.

When the Romans conquered Egypt, the court no longer resided in the country. The emperors continued to rule from Alexandria out, but broke down the powers of regional administrators and instead appointed men who came from the outside and served for a short term only. Also officials who had remained in the same place for their entire careers were replaced with private citizens who were forced to conduct state business for a brief period without compensation.

Sources in Translation 13.1

The Rosetta Stone

The key monument in the decipherment of Egyptian hieroglyphs was a stele Napoleon's troops found during the French campaign in Egypt in the late 18th century. It contains an edict from 196 BC issued on behalf of the 13-year-old King Ptolemy V Epiphanes in Memphis, and recorded in three languages and scripts: from top to bottom, Middle Egyptian hieroglyphic, Demotic, and Greek. The decree is also known from fragmentary other versions, one for each of the three languages. It makes the king a "manifest god" (Epiphanes in Greek), but in return abolishes new taxes and dues, frees prisoners, and allows rebels to return home. The following passage deals with such affairs.

The arrears which were due to the King from the people who are in Egypt and all those who are subject to his kingship, and which amounted to a large total, he renounced; the people who were in prison and those against whom there had been charges for a long time, he released; he ordered concerning the endowments of the gods, and the money and the grain that are given as allowances to their temples each year, and the shares that belong to the gods from the vineyards, the orchards, and all the rest of the property which they possessed under his father, that they should remain in their possession; moreover, he ordered concerning the priests that they should not pay their tax on becoming priests above what they used to pay up to the Year 1 under his father; he released the people who hold the offices of the temples from the voyage they used to make to the Residence of Alexander each year; he ordered that no rower should be impressed into service; he renounced the two-thirds share of the fine linen that used to be made in the temples for the Treasury, he bringing into its correct state everything that had abandoned its proper condition for a long time, and taking care to have done in a correct manner what is customarily done for the gods, likewise causing justice to be done for the people in accordance with what Thoth the Twice-great did; moreover, he ordered concerning those who will return home from the fighting men and the rest of the people who had gone astray in the disturbance that had occurred in Egypt that they should be returned to their homes, and their possessions should be restored to them.[3]

Special Topic 13.1 *The archive of Menches, village scribe*

In AD 1900, excavators at the Fayyum site of Tebtunis stumbled upon a necropolis with thousands of mummified crocodiles, some of which were wrapped in large sheets of discarded papyrus. They contained records from the village Kerkeosiris, many of them the work of Menches, son of Petesouchos, who also used the Greek name Asklepiades. Some 150 of his papyri are in Greek, only one in Demotic. On behalf of the crown, Menches recorded taxes and crops and surveyed agricultural land between the years 120 and 110 BC. The state was concerned to receive all the income due to it, and requested the surveyors' assessments of the size and productivity of fields. Menches registered those in accounts that could contain hundreds of entries. He also reported villagers' complaints to the authorities, regularly including accusations of assaults and robberies. This record alleges that Greek soldiers broke into a house and robbed its valuables on August 23, 113 BC:

> To Menches village clerk of Kerkeosiris, from Harmiysis son of Sarapion, a crown-land farmer of the said village. On the 8th of Mesore of year 4 my house was invaded by Pyrrhichos son of Dionysios, one of the cavalry colonists, and Herakleios son of Poseidippos, of the said village, together with very many others armed with swords. Forcing their way in they broke the lock of my mother's room and carried off the objects listed below, although I had done absolutely nothing to offend them. I therefore submit this complaint to you in order that you may add your signature regarding the details and forward a copy of the complaint to the authorities concerned, so that I may recover my property and they suffer the appropriate punishment. Farewell.
>   A woman's robe worth 1 talent 4,000 drachmas.
>   A woman's sleeved tunic worth 4,000 drachmas.
>   A jar containing 1,600 copper drachmas.[4]

Archives of this nature are the accidental remnants of what must have been an enormous bureaucracy. They give an insight into the daily lives of Egyptians rarely available before the Ptolemaic Period and permit the study of social history in a way unparalleled for the rest of the Hellenistic and Roman worlds.

Culture and religion

It is easiest for us to study the cultural interactions between the literate people, however small a part of the population they were. It seems that initially at least more Egyptians learned Greek than the other way around. Supposedly, no Ptolemaic ruler before Cleopatra knew the language of the mass of the population. Conversely, the Egyptian priest Manetho in the early 3rd century BC wrote a history of his country in Greek (see Special Topic 13.2). A (relatively small) number of multilingual texts exist. Most celebrated is the Rosetta Stone with its inscriptions in hieroglyphic Middle Egyptian, Demotic, and Greek, all three of which are written expertly. A rare inclusion of Latin appears on the stele Gaius Cornelius Gallus set up at Philae in Greek, Latin, and hieroglyphic Egyptian (see above).

Special Topic 13.2 *Manetho's History of Egypt*

The most foundational ancient source for our reconstruction of Egypt's history is a work from the Ptolemaic Period: the *Aegyptiaca* of Manetho of the 3rd century BC. The long list of kings and its division into dynasties provides the structure that all modern scholarship still follows (see Chapter 1). Manetho's work is an eloquent product of the cultural interactions between Greeks and Egyptians: it uses the Egyptian tradition of king lists as the basic framework and inserts narratives within it in the Greek historical tradition.

Almost everything about the author and his work is a mystery, however. Manetho is the Greek rendering of an Egyptian name; which one is unclear, however. Suggestions include the Egyptian for "Gift of Thoth," "Lover of Neith," "Groom," and "Temple Guardian." Even the Greek and Latin sources on Manetho spell his name in various ways. Some events in his life are connected to the rulers Ptolemy I and II, that is, the first half of the 3rd century BC, but there is no evidence that these kings commissioned his work. He wrote several books, none of which is fully preserved. Only for *The History of Egypt* do we have an idea of the contents and structure of the work. The length of three papyrus scrolls, it gave a survey of the dynasties in chronological order, starting with divine rulers and ending with the Persians. The 3rd-century work itself is lost. In the 1st century AD, Josephus made use of it – or of an edited version – for his defense of Jewish antiquity (see Chapter 6). At the same time another version of Manetho's work already existed, which was the source for later excerpts: one by Sextus Julius Africanus in the 3rd century AD, known from a 9th-century edition by the monk Syncellus, and a 4th-century-AD one by Eusebius, preserved in a Latin translation by Jerome (4th–5th centuries), an Armenian translation of the 6th to 8th centuries, and an edition by Syncellus. All these are very fragmentary renderings of Manetho's text.

The versions we have often disagree in the number of years assigned to a ruler or in their order within a dynasty. It is a challenge to match Manetho's information with the ancient Egyptian material. He renders names in ways that are not always easy to connect to what we know from monuments or other king lists, and his excerpters give different forms. For example, Manetho's Khebros (Africanus) or Khebron (Eusebius) derives from Thutmose II's throne name, A'a-kheper-en-Ra, using only the middle part.

This simplified example for the 18th dynasty illustrates the challenges in using Manetho's information.

Royal name		years of rule		royal name
Manetho	Africanus	Eusebius		modern
Amosis		25		Ahmose
Khebros	13	13		Thutmose II
Amenophtis	24	21		Amenhotep I
Amensis	22			Hatshepsut
Misaphris	13	12		Thutmose III
Misphragmuthosis	26	26		Thutmose III
Tuthmosis	9	9		Thutmose IV
Amenophis	31	31		Amenhotep II
Oros	37	28/36/38		Amenhotep III
Akherres	32	16/12		Akhenaten
Rathos	6	39		Smenkhkara
Akherres	12	12		Ay
Khebres	12	15		Tutankhamun?
Armesis	5	5		Horemheb
Ramesses	1	68		Rameses II
Amenophath	19	40		Merenptah

The list mistakenly includes 19th-dynasty kings. What makes it fascinating for the modern scholar is that it acknowledges the existence of Hatshepsut and the four Amarna kings, removed from memory in other king lists. One wonders where Manetho obtained the evidence for their placement in the 18th dynasty. Sources unavailable to us must have been at his disposal.

Despite the obvious difficulty in connecting Manetho's information to that from other sources, his aim for completeness has made this a crucial task in the reconstruction of Egyptian history. Jean-François Champollion, the decipherer of hieroglyphs, started it. We cannot envision this history without Manetho's structure; we should be careful, however, not to use it uncritically.

In the Roman era the Greek language was pre-eminent for records of daily use – as was the case throughout the eastern empire – and the government discontinued Demotic Egyptian in administration. Greek fundamentally affected the final stage of ancient Egyptian writing. After occasional use of the Greek alphabet to write Egyptian, a system was developed in the 1st centuries AD to write traditional magical texts, setting the stage for recording Christian and other materials with a new script in the late 3rd century AD: Coptic. It used Greek characters with some additional letters to render sounds unknown to Greek. For the first time in Egyptian writing the script also recorded vowels. The script rendered a phase of the ancient Egyptian language that began to incorporate Greek vocabulary. Coptic and Christianity became closely connected in Egypt, and the script and language survive in the liturgy used today. Various dialects of Coptic coexisted throughout Egypt, which shows that the majority of people spoke the language.

The contacts between the Egyptian and Greek and Latin languages and traditions had an effect on the literatures of both peoples. The Greco-Roman Period shows the final stage of ancient Egyptian literature with a vast new corpus of material written in Demotic. Many of the preserved manuscripts date to the first two centuries AD and seem to indicate a flowering of creativity at that time. The authors reached back into earlier Egyptian history for characters in their stories. A number of tales center on the figure of Setne Khaemwaset, son of Rameses II (see Chapter 9). They involve magic, including a competition between a Nubian sorcerer and Setne's son, Siosire, a re-born magician whom Osiris allowed to return to earth. The tales include a tour through the netherworld where Siosire guides his father. He declares on the fate of the dead:

> Take it to your heart, my father Setne, that to the one who is good on earth, they will be good in the netherworld. And to the one who is wicked, they will be wicked. That is determined and will never change.[5]

Many scholars see Greco-Roman influence in this description of the netherworld. They also suspect such inspiration in another cycle of stories about Pedubastis – a name used by several Late Period kings – and the hero Inaros, seemingly the rebel leader against Persia (see Chapter 12). The stories include a battle over the armor of Inaros and a campaign against a land with an army of women. Heroes engage in single combat, as is the case in Homer's *Iliad*. Some scholars see this as a sign that Greek literature had a great impact on the authors of Demotic tales, others stress the similarities with earlier Egyptian writings and consider the Greek influence to be minimal.

By contrast, however, the influence of Egyptian ideas on Greek literature is clear, especially in poems in honor of Egyptian deities. The goddess Isis (the Greek rendering of the Egyptian name Ese) received much attention. Poets in Egypt and abroad composed texts in her honor, and her cult prospered greatly in Greek and Roman times. In Egypt itself she received numerous major temples – including the one at Philae – and she absorbed the attributes of various other goddesses. She became the "queen of all the gods" and a deity revered by the entire universe. A Greek hymn, carved in an Egyptian temple during the 1st century BC, states:

> All mortals who live in the boundless earth,
> Thracians, Greeks, and Barbarians,
> Express your fair name, a name greatly honored among all,
> But each speaks in his own language, in his own land.
> The Syrians call you: Astarte, Artemis, Nanaia,
> The Lycian tribes call you: Leto, the lady.
> The Thracians also name you as Mother of the gods,
> And the Greeks call you Hera of the Great Throne, Aphrodite,
> Hestia the goodly, Rhea and Demeter.
> But the Egyptians call you Thiouis (= the one) because they know that you, being
>   one, are all other goddesses invoked by the races of men.[6]

Isis's cult spread throughout the Mediterranean and she had a temple in the city of Rome decades before the Roman conquest of Egypt. The Romans took her cult wherever they went in the empire, and temples and cult objects to her have been excavated from northern England to Afghanistan. Latin literature celebrated the goddess as well. In the 2nd century AD novel by Apuleius, *The Golden Ass*, Isis as queen of heaven restores the hero, Lucius, to his human form and he is initiated in her priesthood.

At the end of *The Golden Ass* Isis promises Lucius that he will also serve her divine husband Osiris. The tale of the divine couple was the basis of a Greek study of Egyptian religion in the late 1st–early 2nd centuries AD. Plutarch's *On Isis and Osiris* is a long analysis of Egyptian religious ideas, evaluated in relation to multiple Hellenistic philosophical notions. The book narrates parts of the continuous battles between Osiris and his brother Seth and shows Isis as her husband's loyal supporter, as she was in earlier Egyptian sources. Plutarch refers only briefly to another deity, whose cult surpassed that of Osiris in importance during Ptolemaic times: Sarapis. The Ptolemies created this god by merging Osiris and the Apis bull (see Chapter 12), and connected his cult to that of the dynasty. They associated Isis with the queen, Sarapis with the king. Sarapis's original sanctuary was at Saqqara, but the Ptolemies founded the most important Serapeum in Alexandria. Sarapis took over Osiris's role as god of the underworld and fertility, and also was a healing deity. His representations were Greek in style to appeal to a Greek audience: a bearded man seated on a throne with his right hand resting on the three-headed guard dog of the netherworld in Greek religion, Cerberus. The Romans honored Sarapis as well. When Egyptian legions selected Vespasian as emperor in AD 69, he sought approval of the god in the Serapeum of Alexandria and received the power to heal the blind and the lame in return. Sarapis became increasingly associated with the gods Zeus and Helios, and throughout the Roman empire cult places to him existed.

Egyptian gods and religious ideas possessed a mysterious character that had a great appeal to foreigners, as it still does today. It was natural that they spread so broadly when Egypt became more integrated into the wider Mediterranean. Through Greek and Roman intermediaries Egyptian culture remained known, albeit in very corrupted form, in later European traditions as a highly esoteric one.

13.5 Economic Developments: Agriculture, Finance, and Trade

Egypt's economy flourished in the Ptolemaic and Roman eras. The states promoted projects, but perhaps more importantly they encouraged private initiatives that developed the country's resources. The basis of the economy was, as always in antiquity, agriculture, and Greeks and Romans expanded initiatives that had been started by the Persians if not earlier. The Ptolemies' key accomplishment in this area was the reclamation of land in the Fayyum. They augmented the agricultural zone substantially by regulating the water flow into the lake at its center and founded many villages. The region became a separate nome around the town of Arsinoe (Crocodilopolis), which was renamed after the wife of Ptolemy II Philadelphus. They also developed other regions in Middle Egypt. Ptolemies and Romans introduced new irrigation technologies such as the Archimedian screw and animal-powered waterwheel, which were primarily used in horticulture. Wine production became a major enterprise, especially in the western oases.

Although coins had been in use in Egypt since the start of the Late Period, their use had been limited. This changed starting with the Ptolemies who collected at least some of the taxes in money rather than in kind. Scholars disagree over the extent of the impact of coinage on the general population. Some think small coin permitted market transactions in cash, while others argue that by far most exchange was transacted in produce. In any case, the state guaranteed the value of coins, and there is some evidence for inflation. Ptolemy II Philadelphus (ruled 285–246) established banks to collect taxes in coin, partly on imported goods. Banks also managed deposits from individuals, and exchanged currency at officially determined rates. Throughout the Greco-Roman Period Egyptian coinage could not be exported and foreign coins had to be exchanged when entering the country.

The massive grain production of Egypt – now focused on durum wheat, which is much easier to process than the emmer wheat previously grown in Egypt – made it a supplier for other parts of the Mediterranean world. In the Roman empire, the populace of the city of Rome depended on grain distributions shipped in with privately owned boats from Alexandria. The ships returned with cargoes of wine, olive oil, and craft products. The market for Egyptian grain seemingly was unlimited, and the mostly peaceful conditions under the empire provided a safe environment for that trade.

Egypt was also the nexus of the Roman empire's trade connections with regions to the east. Arabia, India, and East Africa were sources of luxury goods such as perfumes, precious stones, ivory, hardwood, and textiles, including Chinese silk. Oriental spices were in much demand, especially pepper, which functioned as a condiment, preservative, and medicine. In the 1st century AD, the author Pliny the Elder griped that Romans wasted millions of gold coins on the spice. A travel account in Greek, probably from the same century, describes sea voyages along the coasts of Arabia, India, and East Africa (perhaps as far south as Madagascar), and archaeology shows the presence of Roman traders in India. Conversely, writings and languages from South Asia and southern Arabia appear on objects found along the Red Sea and in graffiti from the eastern desert. The Romans especially developed Red Sea harbors and turned them into substantial towns, despite the great difficulties of provisioning them with fresh water and food. The southernmost Egyptian port was Berenike, founded by Ptolemy II Philadelphus but much expanded by the Romans. Because of coral reefs in the Red Sea and the threats of Arabian pirates, they preferred to load and unload ships in southern harbors and had camel caravans carry the cargo through the eastern desert. Although the camel had been domesticated in the Near East since the early 1st millennium BC, in Egypt it became a beast of burden only under the Romans. They developed the desert routes providing water sources and rest places. These routes also gave access to quarries for stones such as porphyry, an imperial stone.

The prosperity allowed for an increased Egyptian population, probably the largest it ever was in pre-modern times. Estimates of the number of inhabitants are difficult, however. The 1st-century-AD historian Josephus claimed that there were 7.5 million people outside Alexandria, which many scholars see as an exaggeration. Be this as it may, numerous villages and several urban centers originated in the period in the Nile Valley and Delta as well as in the oases, which experienced unprecedented growth. A recently discovered cemetery in the Bahriya oasis may contain 10,000 mummies, which shows a population level never known before in that area.

13.6   The African Hinterland

After 593 BC, when Psamtek II raided Napata (see Chapter 12), Egypt and Nubia existed side-by-side. The southern kingdom seems to have known great stability. This did not change fundamentally when Greeks and Romans ruled Egypt, and contacts intensified. By 300 BC the core of the Nubian kingdom shifted farther south to the fertile area between the fifth and sixth cataracts around Meroe. The city was strategically located on the crossroads of several trade routes: there was a direct overland road from Napata bypassing the long northward bend in the Nile, and other routes connected Meroe to the Red Sea in the east and the sub-Saharan region in the west. The Nile gave access to central Africa. The rulers of Meroe constructed a city with several monumental temples and located the royal cemeteries to its east. Some 120 pyramids of kings and family members stand there, stretching in time from ca. 300 BC to AD 360, and surrounded by other tombs. They have the same shape as earlier Nubian pyramids (see Chapter 11): they are smaller and have a steeper angle than those in Egypt, and they have mortuary temples with pylons at their base (Figure 13.5).

Meroitic culture shows much Egyptian influence, always mixed with local ideas. Many temples housed cults to Egyptian gods like Amun (called Amani) and Isis, but indigenous deities received royal patronage as well. A very prominent Nubian god was the lion-deity Apedemak, a god of war whose popularity increased substantially in this period. Local gods were often associated with Egyptian ones: in Lower Nubia Mandulis, for example, was considered to be Horus's son.

Hybridity is also visible in the arts and in royal ideology. For example, kings of Meroe were represented in monumental images on temples in Egyptian fashion but with local elements, such as garments, crowns, and weapons. An eloquent example stands at Naqa on the eastern desert route where several

Figure 13.5   Royal pyramid at Meroe. Werner Forman Archive

temples were constructed using an Egyptian-style ground plan. One of the temples from the 1st century AD, devoted to Apedemak, shows on its pylon King Natakamani in the traditional Egyptian pose of subduing a throng of enemies that he holds by the hair, beneath the image of a winged falcon god. Non-Egyptian, however, is the mirror image on the other side of the gate showing Queen Amanitore in the same posture beneath a vulture goddess. The representation of the queen shows a local idea of beauty: unlike the ideal Egyptian woman, who is slim, she is corpulent (Figure 13.6).

In the 2nd century BC, Meroites started to write their spoken language in newly developed scripts that derived from the Egyptian. Two versions were in use: a monumental one for temple and tomb inscriptions, based on hieroglyphs, but with 23 signs only; and a cursive script for daily records and mortuary steles, whose sign-forms to an extent originated in the Demotic script. We can read the signs but do not understand the language they render except for some standard formulae and Egyptian loanwords.

Meroe flourished from ca. 300 BC to AD 100, as is clear from building activity, artwork, and craft production. Its success depended on trade with its northern neighbors. The Ptolemies and Romans wanted African goods such as

Figure 13.6   Queen Amanitore defeating enemies, represented on the Lion Temple at Naga. Werner Forman Archive

hardwoods, ivory, other exotica, and animals including elephants. Those animals had become important in warfare in the Mediterranean after Alexander had encountered them in his eastern campaigns, and all Hellenistic armies included an elephant division. The relations between Egypt and Meroe were mostly peaceful. The Ptolemies considered the area south of Aswan as a border territory they controlled. They called it Dodekaschoinos (which literally means "twelve miles"), a region of ca. 120 kilometers along the Nile, and wanted to be in charge of it because it gave them access to the gold mines in the eastern desert. Both Ptolemies and Meroitic rulers sponsored construction in several temples of the region, which may show peaceful cooperation between the two kingdoms in places sacred to both (some scholars think it demonstrates that power switched back and forth, however). After the Romans annexed Egypt, Meroe sacked Aswan in 24 BC and the Roman army retaliated and seemingly reached Napata. They fortified a site north of the second cataract, called Qasr Ibrim today, to defend the border. But trade was so beneficial to both countries that they preferred peace. Around AD 200 the Romans made the kingdom of Axum in Ethiopia, which used a Red Sea harbor, their preferred African trading partner, and this switch caused a steady decline of Meroe.

People from Nubia in a sense held on to Egyptian traditions longer than the Egyptians themselves. As pointed out above, its inhabitants continued to use Philae as a religious center after the Roman emperor had closed down Egyptian temples in Egypt. Christianity ultimately prevailed in the south as well: around AD 350 the Christian king of Axum destroyed what remained of Meroe, and the tribal people who resided in the region, as far north as Aswan, gradually converted to the new religion as well.

13.7 The Christianization of Egypt

Ancient Egyptian culture ceased to exist during the Roman empire. It had survived numerous political changes and cultural influences of peoples from Africa, Asia, and Europe in the more than 3,000 years of Egyptian history, but in the first few centuries AD its institutions and other means of expression vanished. The processes involved were very complex, and scholars focus on many aspects of Egyptian culture to seek explanations (Plate 12). The edict of Emperor Theodosius in AD 391 that closed down temples and forbade the teaching of hieroglyphic writing probably was the final step in a long decline of Egypt's ancient traditions. Its importance cannot be denied, however, as it took away the last support for the official articulation of ancient Egyptian culture. Even if individuals and groups like Nubian tribes continued to adhere to cults and other ideas, they were no longer surrounded by massive state-sponsored endorsements of the same beliefs.

Political and administrative changes since the Roman conquest had weakened crucial aspects of Egypt's ancient ideology. The Roman emperor as king no longer resided in the country nor did he participate in its festivals and public events. Even if traditional temples were constructed, they did not benefit from royal visits. The economic crisis that hit the empire in the 3rd century AD greatly reduced state support for such projects in any case. The Roman administration also took away the raison d'être of much Egyptian writing. It enforced the use of Greek for legal and administrative purposes, relegating the writing of Demotic to literature and religious materials. It also promoted foreigners in government at the expense of indigenous elites, who lost the means to sponsor traditional expressions of Egyptian ideas. Some scholars see these developments as the main causes of the decline of Egyptian culture.

The rise of Christianity – which affected the entire Roman empire and beyond in the first centuries AD – may have had a more decisive impact on Egypt's culture. The early Roman empire was a religious melting pot that incorporated numerous influences, including Egyptian ones. As pointed out above, the cult of Isis, for example, reached the outer margins of the empire. Within this enormous diversity, the monotheistic ideas of a small religious sect from Palestine gained a special appeal to the urban middle classes. In the first centuries of its existence the elaboration of Christian creed and its fusion with Greek philosophical concepts, especially Neo-Platonic ideas, occupied many thinkers, and Egypt's Alexandria as a center of intellectual activity played a major role in these developments. Various schools of thought existed and Christianity competed with other new religions, such as Gnosticism, Manichaeism, and Zoroastrianism, while it also suffered official and unofficial persecutions. It survived, however, and in the 3rd century its popularity in

Key Debate 13.1 *Greeks and Egyptians in Ptolemaic Egypt*

The Greeks and Macedonians who came to Egypt with Alexander or in his footsteps in later centuries were conquerors and colonizers. They saw themselves as distinct from the indigenous population and found their own culture superior to the Egyptian even if they admired aspects of the latter. How did the two communities interact? Many immigrants stayed in newly founded Greek cities, but others moved into the countryside where they could not avoid contact with Egyptians. Scholars disagree on the extent to which the communities interacted with each other and opinions have changed over time. When the concept of Hellenism was developed in the 19th century, its proponents saw the creation of a new world that molded Greek and eastern traditions into one. But 20th-century historians, perhaps less optimistic about the modern colonial experience with its parallel situations, were more skeptical and stated that there was little interaction. The Greeks saw Egyptians and other peoples of the east as barbarian, and the Egyptians did not want to share their culture, which was deeply imbued with ancient religious ideas, with outsiders (Préaux 1977: 545–65; Chauveau 2000: 170–1). Scholars who work with both the Greek and Demotic evidence argue that the idea of isolation is false, however (Clarysse 1992).

A prominent case study of this integration derives from an archive from the town Pathyris (modern Gebelein, 20 miles [29 kilometers] south of Thebes) from the second century BC (see http://www.trismegistos.org/arch/archives/pdf/74.pdf). It shows how a cavalry officer with the Greek name Dryton married an Egyptian woman as his second wife. She had a double name: in Greek she was Apollonia, "the one of the god Apollo," in Egyptian, Senmonthis, "daughter of the god Montu." We know that the Greek Apollo was equated with Egyptian Montu in the cult (Vandorpe 2002b: 326). The couple had five daughters, all of whom had double names. When her father died the oldest – Apollonia, whose Egyptian name was Senmouthis – became owner of the archive, which contains both Greek and Demotic documents (Vandorpe 2002a: 12). Most scholars see the archive as evidence that Greeks became increasingly Egyptian: Dryton married an Egyptian woman and started to use Demotic as well as Greek (Lewis 1986a: 87-103; Ritner 1984). There is sometimes surprise that he married someone of a lesser social status – Apollonia's father was an infantry soldier (Chauveau 2000: 160–4). But that is a male-oriented view. When we see the marriage from Apollonia's perspective, the initiative is reversed. She came from a family that had immigrated into Egypt from the North African Greek settlement of Cyrene and that had taken on Egyptian habits over two or three generations. Apollonia tried to reverse that trend, accepting fewer legal rights as a Greek woman than she had as an Egyptian. But she became a successful businesswoman. In the end her attempt to become Greek again failed, however, as all her daughters married Egyptian men (Vandorpe 2002b). We can thus see how the cultural preferences of families could go either way.

Egypt extended to the lower classes as well. After Emperor Constantine (ruled AD 306–337) converted in the early 4th century, the church became increasingly an instrument of imperial government.

The early history of Christianity is too multifaceted a subject to discuss here even within the Egyptian context alone. Although some ancient Egyptian concepts influenced the characteristics of Christianity in the country, many of the core ideas of the two cultures were incompatible. The exclusivity of the sole Christian god could not tolerate Egypt's vast pantheon, its sacred animals, and the like. The original Christian values of a simple and modest lifestyle clashed with Egypt's massive temples and festivals. We cannot determine how fast conversion to Christianity happened in Egypt. The end of persecutions in the early 4th century accelerated the process and increasingly large numbers of people gave their children names with Christian references in them. By the end of the 4th century signs of non-Christian religious observance almost fully disappeared. A new and different era in the country's history began.

NOTES

1. Translations Parkinson 2005: 19.
2. Translation Bowman 1986: 169.
3. Translation R. S. Simpson in Parkinson 2005: 57–8; quoted by permission of the author.
4. Translation Lewis 1986a: 121.
5. Translation after Hoffmann & Quack 2007: 123.
6. Translation Assmann 1997: 49.

Epilogue

Cultures never fully vanish. Even if people no longer express themselves with the methods and habits of their ancestors, influences linger in overt and subconscious ways. This was certainly true for ancient Egyptian culture, which had flourished for more than 3,000 years. Its impact had not been limited to inhabitants of Egypt, and over the centuries neighboring peoples had assimilated its inspiration. Egypt's influence on Nubia had been prolonged and deep and the southern people expressed Egyptian-style ideas openly long after they had been officially banned in the north. In the 1st millennium BC the emerging cultures of Southern Europe – Greece and Rome – absorbed Egyptian ideas as did the Near Eastern world where the biblical tradition developed. In recent decades, Egypt's impact on the classical European traditions has been the topic of often heated debate. Afrocentric research has sought to identify Egyptian traces in Greek and Roman cultures, and by stressing Egypt's African background it hopes to establish roots of western culture in that continent. Likewise – and this effort is a primary reason why Egyptology developed as a discipline in the 19th century AD – many highlight Egyptian influence on the biblical text. Especially King Akhenaten's religious ideas, which many regard as monotheistic, are seen as an inspiration of Abrahamic religions. But when it comes to pinpointing exact traces of Egyptian thought in classical European and biblical traditions, matters are not that simple. How much did Greek philosophers know of ancient Egyptian ideas? How would the author of a biblical psalm have encountered Akhenaten's hymn to the sun disk?

The search for Egyptian influences on the foundations of European tradition has much value, in that it corrects the mistaken perception that no culture existed before the so-called Classical Greek miracle of the mid-1st millennium BC. Ironically, however, it gives European culture pre-eminence as it grants importance to ancient Egypt *because* it was an ancestor to the west. When almost all scholars of Egyptology were of European background this might have made sense, as they explored the deep roots of their culture, but in today's more diverse cultural setting this is no longer the case.

In a land filled with monuments the Egyptians of the Middle Ages and later could not disregard the past. To say that ancient Egypt was rediscovered in the 19th century is Eurocentric. Egyptians lived with their past throughout the ages, and scholars writing in Arabic discussed monuments like the pyramids and the sphinx, speculated about ancient Egyptian writing and thought, and remembered figures like Imhotep and Cleopatra. Just like their European counterparts, Egyptians after antiquity focused on the mysterious aspects of a culture they did not share. They did not ignore their country's ancient remains, nor systematically destroy them as some claim. They could not comprehend the writings of ancient Egypt although they saw them all around them. So they fantasized in ways that show fascination and respect, not disdain. In the 13th century AD the geographer Al-Idrisi wrote a lengthy description of the pyramids, in which he rendered in Arabic verse the text of a hieroglyphic royal inscription purportedly found in the 9th century. Al-Idrisi sums up why people in his own time could not fail to admire the ancient Egyptians:

> I am the owner of all the pyramids in Egypt,
> And the first builder of its temples.
> I left in them signs of my efficiency and wisdom
> Which shall never decay or disappear.[1]

Still today we wonder at these signs, which, we hope, will indeed never disappear.

NOTE

1. El Daly 2005: 43.

Guide to Further Reading

This guide can only present a very small part of the mass of literature that exists on ancient Egypt. In my selection I have focused on books and articles that are easily accessible and in English. Whenever I found works in French or German very useful for a chapter I have included them as well. I list a small selection of websites; I have highlighted the ones with abundant images.

Chapter 1

Surveys of ancient Egyptian history are available in all European languages in various forms and with different degrees of detail. Recent reliable and accessible ones, include in English: Baines & Malek 2000 (brief), Baines, Wente, & Dorman 2009 and Bowman & Samuel 2009 (brief), Grimal 1992 (detailed), Hornung 1999a (brief), Shaw ed. 2000 (multi-authored and detailed), Trigger, Kemp, O'Connor, & Lloyd 1983 (detailed); in French: Vandersleyen 1995 and Vercoutter 1992 (detailed, only up to ca. 1200 BC); in German: Helck 1968 (detailed up to 332 BC).

A large number of encyclopedias, dictionaries, and other works with short articles on many aspects of ancient Egypt have appeared, which can be very useful for introductory information and bibliography. They include Redford ed. 2001 (available online, www.oxford-ancientegypt.com), Sasson ed. 1995, and Shaw & Nicholson 1995. The seven-volume work, Helck, Otto, & Westendorf eds. 1975–92 is a massive reliable resource with articles in English, French, and German. The website www.uee.ucla.edu is building up an expanding set of articles of ancient Egypt in English.

For good maps, see Baines & Malek 2000 and Manley 1996.

The parameters of ancient Egyptian history are rarely discussed explicitly. For a discussion of who the ancient Egyptians were, see Kemp 2006, chapter 1, with whose conclusions I agree. O'Connor & Reid eds. 2003 contains useful papers on Egypt's African context. Baines 1996 studies representations of foreigners in Egyptian sources.

Kemp 2006, chapter 2, provides an excellent survey of the Egyptian king lists. A long study of them is Redford 1986. For annals, see Baines 2008. Hornung

1992: 147–64 presents the idea that every king ritually re-enacted aspects of royal behavior.

On papyri, see Parkinson & Quirke 1995 for Pharaonic times, and Bagnall 1995 for the Greco-Roman period. A survey of the written sources available from the various periods of Egyptian history before 1972 is provided in Institut Français d'archéologie orientale du Caire 1972, Volume II.

For historical methodology as it affects Egyptian sources, see Björkman 1964 and Van De Mieroop 1997.

The volume edited by Hornung, Krauss, & Warburton (2006) represents the latest ideas on Egyptian chronology, both relative and absolute.

For Egyptian prehistory and the Early Dynastic period, see Midant-Reynes 2000 and 2003 (more up-to-date, in French) and Wengrow 2006.

The handiest guide to ancient and modern Egyptian place names is Baines & Malek 2000.

Websites

Views of environment and sites: Old photographs are available online at http://oi.uchicago.edu/museum/collections/pa/egypt/ and www.flickr.com/photos/ brooklyn_museum/sets/72157605038624179/. For recent photographs, see www. museumphotography.com.
General information on Egypt is available at these sites:
www.ancient-egypt.co.uk
www.digitalegypt.ucl.ac.uk
www.globalegyptianmuseum.org
www.fitzmuseum.cam.ac.uk/er
http://repositories.cdlib.org/nelc/uee
Free Egyptology journals online are listed at www.geocities.com/TimesSquare/Alley/ 4482/EEFDigijournals.html.

Chapter 2

The written sources of the earliest dynasties are discussed in Institut Français d'archéologie orientale du Caire 1972, Volume II: 3–13 (in German). T. Wilkinson 2000 translates the annals on the Palermo Stone. For a brief and accessible survey of the Predynastic and Early Dynastic periods, see Kemp 1995. More detailed studies are Adams 1988, Adams & Cialowicz 1997, Midant-Reynes 2000 and 2003 (more up-to-date, in French), Spencer 1993, Trigger 1983, Wengrow 2006, and T. Wilkinson 1999. Midant-Reynes & Tristant eds. 2008 gives an idea of the ongoing debates.

On the ideological foundations of the newly emerged state, see Kemp 1989 or 2006, part I. For early kingship, see Baines 1995, and for the earliest writing, Baines 2004. For the history of Egyptian scripts, see W. Davies 1987, and consult Collier & Manley 2003 to teach yourself hieroglyphs.

For Nubia in the period, see O'Connor 1993: 10–23; on Babylonian developments in the Uruk period, see Van De Mieroop 2007a: 19–40. For a survey of Egyptian art, see Robins 1997.

Websites

The website http://xoomer.alice.it/francescoraf/ contains abundant information and illustrations on Late Predynastic and Early Dynastic Egypt. For the tombs at Abydos, see www.dainst.org/index_51_en.html# and http://egyptsites.wordpress.com/2009/02/12/abydos-desert-sites.

Chapter 3

For a translation of a wide selection of texts from the Old Kingdom, see Strudwick 2005. Wente 1990 contains a number of letters from the period. A survey of the written sources appears in Institut Français d'archéologie orientale du Caire 1972, Volume II: 15–52 (in English and French).

Redford ed. 2001, Volume 2: 585–601 (by various authors) and Stadelmann 1995 give succinct overviews of the 3rd to 5th dynasties. A very detailed survey is Vercoutter 1992 (in French). Kemp 1983 contains an important discussion of the period. Malek 1986 is an extensively illustrated review of the economy and society. Metropolitan Museum of Art 1999 discusses many aspects of the history and art of the Old Kingdom, with numerous photographs.

On the pyramids, see Lehner 1997. Dodson & Hilton 2004 provides reconstructions of royal family trees. Leprohon 1995 discusses the administration of Egypt.

For later traditions on Imhotep see Wildung 1977. Parkinson 1998 provides translations of many of the tales involving Old Kingdom figures. Other translations can be found in Lichtheim 1978 (including the Great Sphinx stele of Amenhotep II) and Simpson ed. 2003.

Websites on the pyramids

www.gizapyramids.org/code/emuseum.asp, which has links to many other websites, www.mfa.org/giza, and http://www.pbs.org/wgbh/nova/pyramid/.
For the city around Giza pyramids: www.aeraweb.org/lost_city_home.asp.
For Unas pyramid: www.pyramidtextsonline.com/.
Officials' mastabas: www.osirisnet.net/mastabas/e_mastabas.htm.
www.oxfordexpeditiontoegypt.com

Chapter 4

A wide range of inscriptions from the 6th dynasty is translated in Strudwick 2005, and Lichtheim 1988 gives translations of some biographies of the First Intermediate Period. Schenkel 1965 provides a full record of inscriptions from the 7th to 11th dynasties (in German). For a general survey of the written evidence for the First Intermediate Period, see Institut Français d'archéologie orientale du Caire 1972, Volume II: 53–62 (in French).

Seidlmayer 2000 is an up-to-date survey of the period, while Franke 2001a is an accessible brief discussion. Vandersleyen 1995 contains a detailed account of the available information (in French).

On Pepynakht-Heqaib see Habachi 1956, and on Nubian mercenaries see Fischer 1961. On Balat in Dakhla oasis, see Valloggia 1999.

For translations of the literary texts regarding the First Intermediate Period, see Lichtheim 1973, Parkinson 1998, or Simpson ed. 2003. Assmann 2002: 81–114 discusses the atmosphere of doom created by the textual record about the First Intermediate Period. The *Admonitions of Ipuwer* is translated in Lichtheim 1973: 149–63, Parkinson 1998: 166–99, and Simpson ed. 2003: 188–210.

On mortuary texts, see Hornung 1999b. Full English translations of the Pyramid Texts appear in Allen 2005, and of the Coffin Texts in Faulkner 2004. For the concept of democratization of the afterlife, see M. Smith 2009.

Chapter 5

Parkinson 1991 gives a rich survey of writings from the Middle Kingdom. For private inscriptions, see Lichtheim 1988. Wente 1990 includes letters from the period. Amenemhat II's annals are translated into English in Guo 1999. Senusret I's are published in French by Postel & Régen 2005. Allen 2002 is a full publication of the Heqanakht papyri. For a general survey of the papyri of the Middle Kingdom, see Institut Français d'archéologie orientale du Caire, Volume II: 63–72.

Franke 1995 and 2001b provide brief discussions of the period. Callender 2000 is more detailed, while Vandersleyen 1995 (in French) and Grajetzki 2006 give thorough surveys. Bourriau 1988 presents a collection of Middle Kingdom works of art and other objects, and useful essays. Wildung 1984 (published in both German [1984a] and French [1984b]) is a well-illustrated survey. The book edited by Quirke in 1991 contains several important articles, including Bourriau's study of regional traditions, Franke's discussion of the power of local elites, and Quirke's of royal succession in the 13th dynasty.

On urban planning and the layout of Nubian forts, see Kemp 2006: 211–44. Richards 2005 and Seidlmayer 2007 provide a fundamentally different view of the structure of Middle Kingdom Egyptian society. Szpakowska 2008 writes a social history of the town of Lahun on the basis of archaeological and textual material. Murnane 1977 is the basic study on co-regencies throughout Egyptian history. Blyth 2006 provides a history of the Amun temple at Karnak.

On the tombs of Beni Hassan, see Shedid 1994.

Kemp 1993 contains a very useful survey of contact with foreign countries. For the excavations of the Red Sea port at Mersa Gawasis, see Bard & Fattovitch 2007. On the "Nubian kings" see Morkot 2000: 54–5. The best work on Egypt's relations with Asia is still Helck 1971 (in German). Allen 2008 provides the first reconstruction of Khnumhotep III's account of a voyage to Byblos.

On the Osiris cult, see Mojsov 2005 and Otto 1968.

Parkinson 2002 gives a systematic overview of Middle Kingdom literature and an in-depth study of the poetics of Egyptian literature. Parkinson 1998 translates most texts of the period into English. Alternative collections are Lichtheim 1973 and Simpson ed. 2003. For the legal action on the Brooklyn Papyrus, see Quirke 1990: 127–54.

Websites

Lahun: www.kahun.ucl.ac.uk/main.html.

Beni Hassan tombs: http://egyptsites.wordpress.com/2009/02/14/beni-hasan/ and http://
alain.guilleux.free.fr/beni_hassan/necropole_beni hassan.html.

Semna dispatches: www.thebritishmuseum.ac.uk/explore/highlights/highlight_objects/
aes/t/the_semna_dispatches.aspx.

13th-dynasty   lawsuit: www.brooklynmuseum.org/opencollection/objects/3369/
Historical_Papyrus_in_Five_Pieces/image/8190/side.

Chapter 6

Many sources are translated in Redford 1997, while Ryholt 1997 gives a complete catalogue of the inscriptions of the kings from dynasties 13 to 17.

Quirke 2001 is a brief survey of the Second Intermediate Period; see also his study
of the Hyksos from 2007. Bourriau 2000 is longer and sums up recent ideas. Vandersleyen
1995 contains a detailed account of the available information (in French). Ryholt 1997
presents a comprehensive study with controversial conclusions. Oren ed. 1997 includes
several important papers on the Hyksos. The volume edited by Hein in 1994 contains
many images and a good discussion of many topics (in German). Polz 2007 treats the
17th dynasty in detail.

For Avaris see Bietak 1995, 1997, and 2001. On Tell el-Yahudiyya, see Holladay
2001. Polz 2006 shows that the presence of Hyksos inscriptions south of Thebes does
not indicate political control, and Quirke 2007 argues that the Hyksos filled a political
void in the north of Egypt. For the peaceful relations between the Hyksos and Thebes,
see Giveon 1983.

Bonnet 2000 and 2004 (in French) give detailed information on the excavations at
Kerma. His 2006 book with Valbelle provides a brief overview in English. For Kushite
raids in Egypt, see W. Davies 2003a and 2003b (in French).

Loprieno 1998 argues that Nehesy is not a Nubian. For the 17th dynasty, see Polz
2001. On Deir el-Ballas, see Lacovara 1997.

Redford 1997 translates later accounts on the Hyksos. Verbrugghe & Wickersham
1996 provide more extensive passages of Manetho and Josephus (pp. 139–40, 157–8,
160–3). Assmann 1997: 28–33 and Loprieno 2003 discuss aspects of the Hyksos portrayal in Josephus. The tale of Apepi and Seqenenra is translated in Simpson ed. 2003:
69–71.

For Egyptian gods, see R. Wilkinson 2003, and for the Rhind papyrus, see Robins
& Shute 1987.

Websites

For Avaris: www.auaris.at/html/index_en.html, for the 17th-dynasty tombs at Dra abu
el-Naga: www.dainst.org/index.php?id=55&sessionLanguage=en.

Chapter 7

Textual sources for the study of New Kingdom history are described in Institut Français d'archéologie orientale du Caire, Volume II: 73–106 (in English, French, and German). Sethe & Helck eds. 1906–58 is a massive collection of written sources of the 18th dynasty with transcriptions of the hieroglyphic texts and translations into German.

A recent survey of the period covered in this chapter is Bryan 2000. Vandersleyen 1995 contains a detailed account of the available information (in French). Troy 2001 is a brief summary.

For a portrayal of the eastern Mediterranean world at the time of the New Kingdom, see Van De Mieroop 2007b.

A detailed discussion of warfare and its impact on New Kingdom Egypt is Spalinger 2005. Redford 2003 is a study of Thutmose III's Syrian campaigns. Grandet 2008 argues for a much smaller role of militarism in the period.

For Egypt's administration of Nubia, see S. Smith 1995 and Morkot 2001. Morris 2005 gives a detailed survey of relations with all neighboring territories.

For New Kingdom bureaucracy, see Bryan 2006, Hayes 1973, and van den Boorn 1988; for foreign influences, Schneider 2003a.

Many well-illustrated books deal with the artistic and architectural remains of the period. Some examples are: Hornung 1990 for the Valley of the Kings; Hodel-Hoenes 2000 for Theban Tombs; and Lauffray 1979 and Schwaller de Lubicz 1999 for the Amun temple at Karnak.

Several early 18th-dynasty kings have been subjects of book-length studies. For Ahmose, see Barbotin 2008. Very much has been written on Hatshepsut, not all of it of high quality. The exhibition catalogue Roehrig 2005 has an up-to-date text and many illustrations. Maruéjol 2007 has appeared since then. For Thutmose III, see Cline and O'Connor eds. 2006, for Amenhotep II, der Manuelian 1987, and for Thutmose IV, Bryan 1991.

N. Davies 1943 contains the full publication of the tomb of Rekhmira.

Websites

Partial visual reconstructions of the tomb of Rekhmira can be found at: www.cs. dartmouth.edu/farid/egypt/rekhmira.html,   www.pbs.org/wgbh/nova/egypt/explore/ rekhmire.html, www.digitalegypt.ucl.ac.uk/religion/opening.gif.

For a translation of *The Duties of the Vizier*, see www.digitalegypt.ucl.ac.uk/administra-tion/dutiesviziertrans.html.

Other websites with information on tombs in the Valley of the Kings and other areas of western Thebes are:

www.thebanmappingproject.com

www.osirisnet.net/e_centra.htm.

For Deir el-Bahri, http://oi.uchicago.edu/gallery/asp_egypt_bahri/.

www.maat-ka-ra.de/english/personen/senenmut/senenmut_hatschepsut.htm reproduces the graffiti thought to represent Hatshepsut and Senenmut.

http://oi.uchicago.edu/gallery/tve_tpp/index.php has old views of various parts of Thebes.

For Medinet Gurob, see www.digitalegypt.ucl.ac.uk/gurob/index.html.

Chapter 8

Cumming 1982, 1983, and 1984, and B. Davies 1992, 1994, and 1995 provide English translations of the German ones published in Sethe and Helck eds. 1906–58. Murnane 1995 has English translations of numerous late-18th-dynasty texts.

One author has used the term "Amarnamania" to describe the scholarly and semi-scholarly output on the period (Eaton-Krauss 2002). For a two-decade-old survey of the vast bibliography (2,013 titles), see Martin 1991.

For Amenhotep III, see Cline and O'Connor eds. 1998, Cabrol 2000, and the nicely illustrated exhibition catalogue, Kozloff and Bryan 1992. For his deification, see L. Bell 1985, Bickel 2002, and W. Johnson 1990. Murnane 1977: 123–67 and 231–3 gives a systematic survey regarding the question of the co-regency, with a negative answer for its existence. W. Johnson 1990 and 1996 argues the opposite, but Dorman 2007 counters his art-historical arguments.

For Amenhotep, son of Hapu, see Wildung 1977. For the tomb of Ramose, see Hodel-Hoenes 2000.

Moran 1992 contains full English translations of the Amarna letters. Many books and articles deal with them. The work of M. Liverani is especially important, for example, 1990 and 2004. Cohen & Westbrook eds. 2000 is a collection of interesting studies of the material.

Eaton-Krauss 1990 reviews opposing ideas about Akhenaten in scholarly literature, focusing on two widely read monographs on the king: Redford 1984 and Aldred 1988. Her article of 2002 discusses more recent works. Of the numerous works on Akhenaten and his reforms, Hornung 1999c is highly recommended. Kemp 1989: 261–317 and Kemp 2006: 311–12 and 326–30 have very interesting discussions of Akhetaten. On Akhenaten's possible tomb at Thebes, see Grimm and Schoske eds. 2001. For scholarly and non-scholarly analyses of Akhenaten in modern times, see Montserrat 2000. Assmann 1997 is a powerful defense of Akhenaten's importance in the history of monotheism. Leprohon 1985 discusses the return to normalcy.

Many well-illustrated catalogues of exhibitions of Amarna art works exist, for example, Do. Arnold 1996 and Silverman et al. 2006.

Websites

On Malqata: www.waseda.jp/prj-egypt/sites/MP-E.html.
For Akhetaten: www.amarnaproject.com/.
http://amarna.ieiop.csic.es/maineng.html gives photographs of Amarna letters.
For Tutankhamun's and other Theban tombs http://griffith.ashmus.ox.ac.uk/.
For Ramose's tomb: www.osirisnet.net/tombes/nobles/ramose/e_ramose.htm and www.pbs.org/wgbh/nova/egypt/explore/ramosemai.html.
For Horemheb's tomb see www.comune.bologna.it/museoarcheologico/informaz/informa1.htm and for Saqqara tombs in general http://euler.slu.edu/~bart/egyptian-html/tombs/Saqqara-Tombs-NK.html and www.saqqara.nl/.

Chapter 9

Kenneth A. Kitchen has provided a massive collection of the inscriptions of the 19th and 20th dynasties in hieroglyphic text, translation, and commentary. The volumes 1993a, 1993b, 1996a, 1998, and 2000 deal with the period of this chapter. B. Davies 1997 provides a selection of the most important texts of the 19th dynasty. Frood 2007 translates officials' biographies; Kitchen 2000 collects all known non-royal inscriptions of the period.

For a brief description of the 19th dynasty, see Kitchen 2001a. More detailed is Van Dijk 2000, and Vandersleyen 1995 provides a thorough survey (in French).

On Sety I, see Hornung 1991 and Brand 2000. On Rameses II, see Kitchen 1982 (a book-length study) and 2001b (very brief). Habachi 1969 discusses his deification. Murnane 1990 details the relations between Hittites and Egyptians, and Beckman 1999 translates some of the correspondence. For the treaty between Egypt and Hatti, see Edel 1997; easily accessible English translations appear in Beckman 1999: 96–100 (cuneiform version) and Kitchen 1996a: 79–85, or B. Davies 1997: 97–116 (hieroglyphic version).

For Nefertari, see McDonald 1996 and Schmidt & Willeitner 1994 (in German). Setne Khaemwaset's stories in Demotic literature are translated in Lichtheim 1980: 125–51 (see 132–3 for story in the netherworld), and Simpson ed. 2003: 453–91 (see 461–3 for story in the netherworld).

For the discussion of Egypt's administration of Syria, I follow Weinstein 1981. Morris 2005 gives information on the other conquered territories as well. For Asiatic foreigners in Egypt, see Redford 1992: 224–37, and on foreign words in the Egyptian language, see Hoch 1994. For the international style in art, see Feldman 2005. Egypt's cosmopolitan character is discussed in Kemp 2006: 292–6 and Schneider 2003a.

For the administration of the period, see Leprohon 1995 and O'Connor 1983. For Piramesse, see Pusch 1993, Pusch & Herold 1999, and Rehren & Pusch 2005 (on glassmaking).

The tombs in western Thebes are discussed in numerous publications, many of them lavishly illustrated. See, for example, Hawass 2006, Reeves and Wilkinson 1996, and Weeks 2001. For KV 5, see Weeks 2000. On Deir el-Medina, see Andreu 2002 (in French), Bierbrier 1982, McDowell 1999, and Romer 1984. For the erotic papyrus, see O'Connor 2001.

Websites

For Abydos under the 19th dynasty: http://egyptsites.wordpress.com/category/upper-egypt/abydos-upper-egypt/.
Luxor's hypostyle hall: http://history.memphis.edu/hypostyle/index.htm.
For 19th-dynasty tombs:
www.getty.edu/conservation/field_projects/nefertari/
www.osirisnet.net/tombes/pharaons/nefertari/e_nefertari_01.htm
www.osirisnet.net/tombes/artisans/sennedjem1/e_sennedjem1_01.htm

Deir el Medina material is accessible through www.leidenuniv.nl/nino/dmd/dmd.html
and www.waseda.jp/prj-egypt/sites/DeM/DeM-E.html has images of the site.

For examples of ostraca and the Turin erotic papyrus: www.bubastis.be/art/musee/
turin_08.html.

A satirical papyrus is shown on www.britishmuseum.org/explore/highlights/highlight_
image.aspx?image=ps257175.jpg&retpage=15590).

Chapter 10

A rich collection of written material for the period up to the reign of Rameses III is
provided in Kitchen 2003 and 2008. B. Davies 1997 and Peden 1994a give selections
from the most important texts.

For brief descriptions of the late 19th dynasty and the 20th dynasty, see Kitchen
2001a and Grandet 2001. More detailed is Van Dijk 2000, and Vandersleyen 1995
provides a thorough survey (in French). Some monographs on individual reigns are
Grandet 1993 (Rameses III; in French) and Peden 1994b (Rameses IV).

On the crises facing the 20th dynasty, see Vernus 2003. Tomb robberies are discussed there and in Bierbrier 1982 and McDowell 1990. B. Davies 1997 and Peden
1994a translate many of the sources on them. For evidence on temple robberies, see
Goelet 1996. S. Redford 2002 discusses the harem conspiracy; the papyrus document-
ing it is translated in Peden 1994a: 195–210. Vernus 1995 (in French) discusses changes
in the ideology of divine intervention in the human world. The collapse of the international system of the Late Bronze Age is the topic of numerous books and articles (cf.
Van De Mieroop 2007b: 235–54 and add Bachhuber & Roberts eds. 2009).

Many scholarly disagreements exist about the political history of this period. For the
relationship between Saptah and Bay, see Schneider 2003b (in German). The end of
the New Kingdom is especially problematic. The reconstruction presented here follows
Kitchen 2009, Wente 1967, and numerous others. An alternative view, based on the
work of Jansen-Winkeln (for example, 1992, in German) has found many followers, for
example, Taylor 1998 and Van Dijk 2000.

Translations of Wenamun's story are available in Lichtheim 1976: 224–30 and
Simpson ed. 2003: 116–24. An important study is Baines 1999. See also Schipper 2005
(in German).

Websites on Medinet Habu

www.bluffton.edu/~sullivanm/egypt/thebes/medhabu/medhabu.html
www.ancient-egypt.co.uk/medinet%20habu/index.htm

Chapter 11

For source material of the 21st to 24th dynasties, see Institut Français d'archéologie
orientale du Caire, Volume II: 107 22.

General surveys of the period: Kitchen 1996b, first published in 1973, was the earliest in-depth discussion of the period. Detailed surveys are Černý 1975 and I. Edwards 1982. O'Connor 1983 has very important insights. For briefer overviews, see Dodson 2001, Mysliwiec 2000, and Taylor 2000. Broekman et al. eds. 2009 gives an idea of the many debates on the period. K. Wilson 2005 is a detailed analysis of the equation of Sheshonq I with the biblical Shishak.

For Tanis, see Stierlin & Ziegler 1987 and Yoyotte 1987. For Libyan cultural influences in the period, see Leahy 1985 (22nd–24th dynasties) and Jansen-Winkeln 2001 (21st dynasty; in German). For the Libyan identity, see Baines 1996.

On God's Wives of Amun, see Giton & Leclant 1977, Robins 1993, and Ayad 2009.

On Kush, see Brooklyn Museum 1978, D. Edwards 2004, Kendall 1982, Morkot 2000, Redford 2004, Taylor 1991, Török 1997, and Wildung 1997. Diverging recent interpretations of the Katimala inscription are Darnell 2006 and Zibelius-Chen 2007. On the cemetery at Hillat el-Arab, see I. Liverani 2004.

Websites

For the Third Intermediate Period in general: www.cesras.org/Prd/TIP/TIP-start.html.
On Tanis: http://egyptsites.wordpress.com/2009/03/03/san-el-hagar-tanis/.
On el-Hibeh: http://neareastern.berkeley.edu/hibeh/index.htm.
Images of the Bubastite Portal: http://dlib.etc.ucla.edu/projects/Karnak/feature/BubastitePortal.
Re-excavation of TT320 cache: www.tt320.org.
Materials from Kush: www.mfa.org/collections/search_art.asp?coll_package=26155.

Chapter 12

Gyles 1959: 3–12 gives a survey of the published textual material for the period discussed here, up to 50 years ago. For Demotic material, see Institut Français d'archéologie orientale du Caire 1972, Volume III: 83–110 (in Italian and German); much more is published today. Eide et al. 1994 translates Nubian sources. Ray 1988 lists sources for the first Persian period. Lloyd 1975–88 is the most detailed English analysis of Herodotus's writings on Egypt.

For the entire period discussed in this chapter, see Lloyd 1983 and Ray 2001a.

For detailed descriptions of the Nubian 25th dynasty, see James 1991, Kitchen 1996b, Morkot 2000, Redford 2004, and Török 1997. A brief survey is Kitchen 2001c. Hegazy & Weilittner 1990/1 provides a brief discussion of Mentuemhat. Bonnet & Valbelle 2006 discusses the Nubian statues of Kushite kings in detail. Robins 1997, chapter 12, describes the unique features of 25th-dynasty art.

For the Saite 26th dynasty, see James 1991, Lloyd 2000a, and Spalinger 2001.

On the navy, see Lloyd 2000b. For fortresses, see Di. Arnold 1999. Boardman 1999 discusses Greeks in Egypt, and Rowe 1938 provides evidence on generals supervising them. Der Manuelian 1994, Loprieno 2003, and Ritner 2008 study interest in the past in this era. The *Memphite Theology* is translated in Lichtheim 1973: 51–7.

Persians: Briant 2002 is the most comprehensive study of the empire in general. For Egypt specifically, see Bresciani 1985 and 2001, Lloyd 1994, Mysliwiec 2000, and Ray 1988. Primary sources of the entire Persian empire are translated in Brosius 2000 and Kuhrt 2007. On the Red Sea canal, see Redmount 1995. For the development of the oases, see Chauveau 2001 and 2003, and Wuttmann 2001 and 2003. For a translation of the Aramaic documents about the destruction of the Jewish temple at Elephantine, see Kuhrt 2007: 855–9.

On the Apis cult, see Thompson 1988. J. Johnson 1994 discusses Persian attitudes toward Egyptian culture.

For the *Petition of Petiese*, see Griffith 1909, Volume 3: 64–112, M. Smith 2001, and Vittmann 1998 (in German).

Websites

General information on the period is available on the websites www.metmuseum.org/TOAH/HD/lapd/hd_lapd.htm and www.livius.org/egypt.html.

Chapter 13

The literature on Greco-Roman Egypt is very extensive and often written by scholars trained as classicists and Greco-Roman historians. Bagnall 1995 provides a good introduction to papyrological sources. Somtutefnakht's biography is translated in Lichtheim 1980: 41–4 and Kuhrt 2007: 458–9.

For the entire period discussed in this chapter, see Bagnall & Rathbone 2004, and Bowman 1986.

Ptolemaic Egypt: Bowman & Samuel 2009, Errington 2008, and Hölbl 2001 survey political history. Lewis 1986a provides case studies of archival analyses.

Roman Egypt: Ritner 1998 gives a concise survey of political history. Bagnall 1993, Lewis 1986b, and Parsons 2007 discuss aspects of economy, society, and culture; Frankfurter 1998 studies religion.

On Alexandrian architecture, see McKenzie 2007. For Meroe, see Morkot 2000, Török 1997, Welsby 2002, and Wildung & Kroeper 2006.

On Demotic literature, see Quack 2009 (detailed study in German), Tait 1996, 2001a, and 2001b (brief surveys). Hoffmann & Quack 2007 provides German translations of most of the corpus; Lichtheim 1980 and Simpson ed. 2003 give selections. Gozzoli 2006: 274–9 discusses Greek influence on Demotic stories. Griffiths 1970 translates Plutarch's *On Isis and Osiris*.

For the economy, see Manning 2007 and Rathbone 2007.

For the Menches archive, see Lewis 1986a, Ryholt 2005, and Verhoogt 1997. Crawford 1971 studies the entire village of Kerkeosiris. For Manetho, see Gozzoli 2006: 191–226 and Verbrugghe & Wickersham 1996.

For the end of Egyptian writing, see Houston, Baines, & Cooper 2003 and Stadler 2008.

Websites

For the excavations at Alexandria, see www.cealex.org/.

For images of Philae, see www.bluffton.edu/~sullivanm/egypt/philae/philae.html and www.philae.nu/philae/landing.html.

http://nubie-international.fr/#page100000 contains much information on Meroe. www.trismegistos.org/ gives scholarly information on written sources in all languages of the period.

Epilogue

For the memory of Egypt in European tradition, see Curran 2007 and Mojsov 2005; in Islamic tradition, see El Daly 2005 and Haarmann 1996.

Glossary

Anubis a god of the dead, primarily responsible for mummification and guiding the dead on their path to the netherworld.

Aten god of the sun disk whose cult became the sole focus of official attention in the reign of Akhenaten.

***Benben* stone** the sacred stone set up in Ra's temple at Heliopolis that symbolized the first matter the sun god created. Several other monuments, such as the pyramids, evoked the *benben* stone in their form.

Canaan the area of western Asia closest to Egypt, more or less the region of modern Israel and Palestine.

canopic jars the name given to four containers used to hold the organs of dead persons. From the New Kingdom on the jar stoppers were shaped like the heads of Horus's sons.

Caria coastal region in the southwest of Anatolia from which Egypt drew mercenaries in the Late Period.

Cartonnage papier-mâché-like wrapping of dead human and animal bodies made from layers of linen or discarded papyri, stiffened with plaster.

Cartouche modern designation of an ancient Egyptian symbol of royalty, an oval with the king's name inscribed.

Cataract zone of narrow channels and rapids in the Nile Valley where navigation is difficult and dangerous.

Cenotaph Egyptologists use the term to indicate symbolic structures associated with the afterlife. They include chapels unrelated to a tomb containing steles to commemorate a dead person.

Cylinder seal a small cylindrical stone carved with a design that becomes visible only when rolled on clay. The object is typical for Near Eastern art and appeared in Egypt in a few early periods only.

Deben Egyptian measure of weight, approximately 90 grams, used as an exchange unit.

Determinative sign placed at the end of a word in Egyptian writing to clarify its general nature, for example, that it is a verb of motion.

Diodorus 1st-century-BC Greek historian who wrote a massive world history, including one book on Egypt.

Dynasty in Egyptian history this term is used to group together a succession of kings who were often, but not always, from the same family and who governed from the same capital. The dynastic division of Egyptian history in use today was the work of Manetho in the 3rd century BC.

Flavius Josephus historian of the 1st century AD who in his works on the Jews and their culture included information about Egyptian history that he took mostly from Manetho.

Hathor goddess often represented as a cow or as a woman with a cow's head who was the patroness of dancing and music.

Hatti designation of the land of the Hittites (in modern Turkey) in the 2nd millennium BC.

Hippodamian grid-plan city plan developed by the Greek Hippodamus in the 5th century in which the streets are laid out in a regular grid pattern.

Horus the falcon god who was the son of Osiris and Isis and the patron of the Egyptian king.

Hurrian language spoken in northern Syria and parts of Anatolia in the 2nd millennium BC. The poorly known language was written in the cuneiform script and is attested in Egypt in one of the Amarna letters.

Ideogram term to refer to a sign in the Egyptian scripts that renders an entire word rather than a syllable or a single letter. Many scholars prefer the term logogram.

Irtjet area either in Lower Nubia or between the second and third cataracts.

Ka a central element in the Egyptian conception of the human person. Everyone has a *ka*, that is, a vital force that contains his or her essence. In the case of kings the *ka* makes royal divinity real.

Khentyamentiu jackal-headed god of Abydos who became identified with Osiris.

Khnum ram god who was sometimes represented as a potter creating humankind from clay.

Kush the Egyptian term to refer to the region south of the first cataract in general. The name can identify more specifically the area south of the second cataract where the Kingdom of Kush existed from the First Intermediate Period to the early New Kingdom. Kush also was the home of the rulers of the 25th dynasty.

KV abbreviation for Kings' Valley. All tombs have a fixed number attached to the term KV; for example, Tutankhamun's is KV 62.

Levant region of western Asia adjoining the Mediterranean coast from northern Syria to southern Palestine.

Maat a complex Egyptian concept of order and balance in the universe. When there is *maat*, there is truth, justice, correct social behavior, and much more. *Maat* is represented as a feather. A crucial royal duty was the preservation of *maat*.

Mammisi modern scholarly designation of a Late Period and Greco-Roman Period sacred building in which king or god supposedly spent the first weeks after birth under the protection of the gods.

Mandulis Lower Nubian deity whose cult was prominent at Philae in the Roman era.

Manetho Egyptian priest who in the 3rd century BC wrote *Aegyptiaca*, a history of his country in the Greek language. The text is partly preserved from later quotations only, but remains the basis for our dynastic division of Egyptian history.

Mastaba tomb tomb whose superstructure has the squat shape of a bench.

Medjay nomads of the eastern desert, identified with the archaeologically known "Pan-grave" people.

Mesopotamia the region centered on modern Iraq where a series of advanced states and cultures developed at the same time as ancient Egypt. In several periods the states of Mesopotamia and Egypt had direct contacts, both peaceful and military.

Min male fertility god normally represented with an erect phallus.

Mittanni ancient name of the state that dominated the region of northern Syria in the 15th and 14th centuries.

Nomarch official in charge of a nome. In Intermediate periods nomarchs could be virtually independent rulers.

Nome administrative subdivision of Egypt. By the 5th dynasty the 22 nomes of Upper Egypt were fixed. The arrangement of the 20 Lower Egyptian nomes is only certain in the Ptolemaic and Roman periods.

Opet-festival annual festival starting in the New Kingdom in order to renew the king's association with his divine *ka*, and involving a procession from Karnak to Luxor and back.

Oracle a divine pronouncement in reply to a question posed to the statue. The oracles of various Egyptian gods are known from at least the New Kingdom on. In later times in particular the oracle of Amun acquired enormous importance.

Osiris god strongly associated with fertility, who was the ruler of the Netherworld and the father of the god Horus. The relationship between Osiris and Horus was the model of that between dead and living kings. Abydos in Upper Egypt and Busiris in Lower Egypt were his main cult centers.

Ostracon potshard or stone flake used to write or draw on (plural: ostraca).

Ptah patron god of artisans often represented as a bearded man wrapped in a mortuary cloak.

Ptolemaic period the period when descendants of the Macedonian-Greek conquerors of Egypt held kingship over the land, 332–330 BC.

Pylon the massive gateways standing in front of ancient Egyptian temples. For large temples, notably the Amun temple at Karnak, scholars give conventional numbers to the pylons.

Qanat Persian system of underground tunnels for the transport of water in desert environments.

QV abbreviation for Queens' Valley. All tombs have a fixed number attached to the term QV; for example, Nefertari's is QV 66.

Ra sun god. Throughout Egyptian history he ranked among the most prominent deities of the pantheon.

Retenu Egyptian name for the region of Syria-Palestine. Upper Retenu was northern Palestine, and Lower Retenu Syria.

Saff tomb Arabic term for a tomb characterized by a row of pillars in the facade of the cliff in which it was dug. The form was used on the west bank of Thebes from the Late Old Kingdom to the 11th dynasty.

Scarab a type of seal carved in the shape of a scarab beetle whose flat side often contains a brief inscription. This type of object appeared from the First Intermediate Period to the Ptolemaic period. In the Middle Kingdom it was used to make impressions of the owner's name on soft materials such as clay; in later times it was mostly used as an amulet.

Sed-festival festival of renewal of kingship, which originally included a physical test.

Serdab Arabic word for cellar, used to designate the enclosed room in Old Kingdom mortuary complexes where the statues of the dead were placed.

Serekh upright relief rectangle into which the name of a king was written with a vertical pattern in the bottom half.

Seshat goddess of writing and all types of record keeping. Her name may mean "the female scribe."

Seth god of the desert and the foreign world, and the embodiment of confusion. He usurped kingship from the god Horus, and the perpetual battle between Horus and Seth was an important motif in Egyptian mythology.

Sothis also called Sirius or Dog Star. Its rising on the eastern horizon just before sunrise after 70 days of invisibility, around July 19th in the modern calendar, indicated the beginning of the year in the Egyptian calendar.

Talatat Arabic word used to designate the blocks of stone used in Akhenaten's reign for quick building. A *talatat* measures about three spans and only weighs some 50 kilograms.

Thoth god of wisdom and scribe of the gods, represented as an ibis or a baboon, or as a man with such an animal head.

Tjehenu or Tjemhu Egyptian terms to refer to the region of the western desert and its inhabitants, conventionally called Libyans in modern scholarship.

TT abbreviation for Theban Tomb. To refer to the tombs of western Thebes scholars use TT with fixed numbers; for example, Rekhmira's tomb is TT 100.

Tumulus earthen mound piled on top of burials.

Uraeus cobra-shaped symbol on the headdresses of kings, queens, and some gods to indicate their royal status.

Vizier highest official after the king first attested in the 3rd dynasty. His duties could include any aspect of the state administration and justice.

Wawat Egyptian term for Lower Nubia, the region between the first and second cataracts.

Yam area of Nubia reached by Egyptian travelers in the Late Old Kingdom, either located south of the third cataract around Kerma or farther upriver.

King List

The list presented here is selective and omits the names of individual rulers about whom little or nothing is known. It follows the chronology of Shaw (ed.) 2000: 479–83, with minor adjustments. All dates before the Late Period are approximate.

ca. 3400–3000	**Late Predynastic**
ca. 3400–3000	Late Naqada period
ca. 3200–3000	*Dynasty 0*
	King Scorpion
	Narmer, etc.
ca. 3000–2686	**Early Dynastic Period**
ca. 3000–2890	*1st dynasty*
	Aha
	Djer
	Djet
	Qa'a, etc.
ca. 2890–2686	*2nd dynasty*
	Hetepsekhemwy
	Peribsen
	Khashemwy, etc.
ca. 2686–2160	**Old Kingdom**
ca. 2686–2613	*3rd dynasty*
ca. 2686–2648	Djoser

ca. 2648–2640	Sekhemkhet
ca. 2640–2637	Khaba
ca. 2637–2613	Huni
ca. 2613–2494	*4th dynasty*
ca. 2613–2589	Sneferu
ca. 2589–2566	Khufu
ca. 2566–2558	Djedefra
ca. 2558–2532	Khafra
ca. 2532–2503	Menkaura
ca. 2503–2498	Shepseskaf
ca. 2494–2345	*5th dynasty*
ca. 2494–2487	Userkaf
ca. 2487–2475	Sahura
ca. 2475–2455	Neferirkara
ca. 2455–2448	Shepseskara
ca. 2448–2445	Raneferef
ca. 2445–2421	Nyuserra
ca. 2421–2414	Menkauhor
ca. 2414–2375	Djedkara
ca. 2375–2345	Unas
ca. 2345–2181	*6th dynasty*
ca. 2345–2323	Teti
ca. 2323–2321	Userkara
ca. 2321–2287	Pepy I
ca. 2287–2278	Merenra
ca. 2278–2184	Pepy II
ca. 2184–2181	Nitiqret
ca. 2181–2160	*7th and 8th dynasties*
	Numerous kings from Memphis, often called Neferkara

ca. 2160–2055   First Intermediate Period

ca. 2160–2025	*9th and 10th dynasties*
	Khety
	Merykara, etc.
ca. 2125–2055	*Early 11th dynasty*
ca. 2125–2112	Sehertawy Intef I
ca. 2112–2063	Wahankh Intef II
ca. 2063–2055	Nakhnebtepnefer Intef III

ca. 2055–1650   Middle Kingdom

ca. 2055–1985	*Later 11th dynasty*
ca. 2055–2004	Mentuhotep II
ca. 2004–1992	Mentuhotep III
ca. 1992–1985	Mentuhotep IV

ca. 1985–1773	*12th dynasty*
ca. 1985–1956	Amenemhat I
ca. 1956–1911	Senusret I
ca. 1911–1877	Amenemhat II
ca. 1877–1870	Senusret II
ca. 1870–1831	Senusret III
ca. 1831–1786	Amenemhat III
ca. 1786–1777	Amenemhat IV
ca. 1777–1773	Sobekneferu
ca. 1773–after 1650	*13th dynasty*
	More than 60 kings

ca. 1700–1550   Second Intermediate Period

ca. 1700–1650	*14th dynasty*
	Minor rulers in northern Egypt
ca. 1650–1550	*15th dynasty*
	Salitis
	Khyan
	Apepi, etc.
ca. 1650–1580	*16th dynasty*
	Minor rulers
ca. 1650–1550	*17th dynasty*
	Intef
	Seqenenra Taa
	Kamose, etc.

ca. 1550–1069   New Kingdom

ca. 1550–1295	*18th dynasty*
ca. 1550–1525	Ahmose
ca. 1525–1504	Amenhotep I
ca. 1504–1492	Thutmose I
ca. 1492–1479	Thutmose II
ca. 1479–1425	Thutmose III
ca. 1473–1458	Hatshepsut
ca. 1427–1400	Amenhotep II
ca. 1400–1390	Thutmose IV
ca. 1390–1352	Amenhotep III
ca. 1352–1336	Amenhotep IV/Akhenaten
?–?	Neferneferuaten
ca. 1336–1327	Tutankhamun
ca. 1327–1323	Ay
ca. 1323–1295	Horemheb
ca. 1295–1186	*19th dynasty*
ca. 1295–1294	Rameses I

ca. 1294–1279	Sety I
ca. 1279–1213	Rameses II
ca. 1213–1203	Merenptah
ca. 1203–1194	Sety II
ca. 1203–1200	Amenmessu
ca. 1194–1188	Saptah
ca. 1188–1186	Tausret
ca. 1186–1069	*20th dynasty*
ca. 1186–1184	Sethnakht
ca. 1184–1153	Rameses III
ca. 1153–1147	Rameses IV
ca. 1147–1143	Rameses V
ca. 1143–1136	Rameses VI
ca. 1136–1129	Rameses VII
ca. 1129–1126	Rameses VIII
ca. 1126–1108	Rameses IX
ca. 1108–1099	Rameses X
ca. 1099–1069	Rameses XI

ca. 1069–715   Third Intermediate Period

ca. 1069–945	*21st dynasty*
ca. 1069–1043	Smendes
ca. 1043–1039	Amenemnisu
ca. 1039–991	Psusennes I
ca. 993–984	Amenope
ca. 984–978	Osorkon I
ca. 978–959	Siamun
ca. 959–945	Psusennes II
ca. 945–715	*22nd dynasty*
ca. 945–924	Sheshonq I
ca. 924–889	Osorkon II
ca. 890	Sheshonq II
ca. 889–874	Takelot I
ca. 874–850	Osorkon III
ca. 850–825	Takelot II
ca. 825–773	Sheshonq III
ca. 773–767	Pimay
ca. 767–730	Sheshonq V
ca. 730–715	Osorkon IV
ca. 818–715	*23rd dynasty*
	Rulers from multiple centers
ca. 727–715	*24th dynasty*
ca. 727–720	Tefnakht
ca. 720–715	Bakenrenef
ca. 747–715	*Early 25th dynasty*
ca. 747–715	Piy

ca. 715–332	**Late Period**
ca. 715–656	*Later 25th dynasty*
ca. 715–702	Shabaqo
ca. 702–690	Shabitqo
ca. 690–664	Taharqo
ca. 664–656	Tanutamani
664–525	*26th dynasty*
664–610	Psamtek I
610–595	Nekau II
595–589	Psamtek II
589–570	Haaibra
570–526	Ahmose II
526–525	Psamtek III
525–404	*27th dynasty*
525–522	Cambyses
522–486	Darius I
486–465	Xerxes I
465–424	Artaxerxes I
424–405	Darius II
405–359	Artaxerxes II
404–399	*28th dynasty*
404–399	Amyrtaios
399–380	*29th dynasty*
399–393	Nepherites I
393–380	Hakor
380	Nepherites II
380–343	*30th dynasty*
380–362	Nectanebo I
362–360	Teos
360–343	Nectanebo II
343–332	*31th dynasty*
343–338	Artaxerxes III Ochus
338–336	Arses
336–332	Darius III Codoman

332–30 BC	**Ptolemaic Period**
332–305	*Macedonian dynasty*
332–323	Alexander
323–317	Philip Arrhidaeus
317–305	Alexander IV
305–30	*Ptolemaic dynasty*
305–285	Ptolemy I Soter I
285–246	Ptolemy II Philadelphus
246–221	Ptolemy III Euergetes I
221–205	Ptolemy IV Philopater

205–180	Ptolemy V Epiphanes
180–145	Ptolemy VI Philometer
145	Ptolemy VII Neos Philopater
170–116	Ptolemy VIII Euergetes II
116–107	Ptolemy IX Soter II
107–88	Ptolemy X Alexander I
88–80	Ptolemy IX Soter II
80	Ptolemy XI Alexander II
80–51	Ptolemy XII Neos Dionysos
51–30	Cleopatra VII Philopater
51–47	Ptolemy XIII
47–44	Ptolemy XIV
44–30	Ptolemy XV Caesarion

30 BC–AD 395*   **Roman Period**

30 BC–AD 14	Augustus
69–79	Vespasian
98–117	Trajan
117–138	Hadrian
306–337	Constantine I
379–395	Theodosius

*Only the Roman emperors mentioned in the text are included.

Bibliography

Adams, Barbara (1988) *Predynastic Egypt*, Princes Risborough: Shire.

Adams, Barbara, and Krzysztof Cialowicz (1997) *Protodynastic Egypt*, Princes Risborough: Shire.

Albright, William Foxwell (1940) *From the Stone Age to Christianity – Monotheism and the Historical Process*, Baltimore: Johns Hopkins University Press.

Albright, William Foxwell (1960) *The Archaeology of Palestine*, Harmondsworth, Middlesex: Penguin Books.

Aldred, Cyril (1988) *Akhenaten. King of Egypt*, New York and London: Thames & Hudson.

Allen, James P. (2002) *The Heqanakht Papyri*, New York: Metropolitan Museum of Art.

Allen, James P. (2005) *The Ancient Egyptian Pyramid Texts*, Atlanta: Society of Biblical Literature.

Allen, James P. (2008) "The Historical Inscription of Khnumhotep at Dahshur: Preliminary Report," *Bulletin of the American Schools of Oriental Research* 352: 29–39.

Allen, James P. (2009) "The Amarna Succession," in P. J. Brand and L. Cooper, eds., *Causing his Name to Live: Studies in Egyptian History and Epigraphy in Memory of William J. Murnane*, Leiden: Brill: 9–20.

Altenmüller, Hartwig (1980) "Markt," *Lexikon der Ägyptologie* 3: 1191–4.

Altenmüller, Hartwig (2001) "Trade and Markets," in Redford, ed. 2001: Vol. 3: 445–50.

Andreu, Guillemette, ed. (2002) *Les artistes de Pharaon: Deir el-Médineh et la Vallée des Rois*, Turnhout: Brepols.

Arnold, Dieter (1991) *Building in Egypt. Pharaonic Masonry*, New York: Oxford University Press.

Arnold, Dieter (1999) *Temples of the Last Pharaohs*, New York: Oxford University Press.

Arnold, Dorothea (1996) *The Royal Women of Amarna: Images of Beauty from Ancient Egypt*, New York: Metropolitan Museum of Art.

Arnold, Dorothea (2005) "The Destruction of the Statues of Hatshepsut from Deir el-Bahri," in Roehrig, ed. 2005: 270–6.

Asheri, David, Alan Lloyd, and Aldo Corcella (2007) *A Commentary on Herodotus: Books I–IV*, Oxford: Oxford University Press.

Assmann, Jan (1975) *Ägyptische Hymnen und Gebete*, Zurich and Munich: Artemis Verlag.

Assmann, Jan (1997) *Moses the Egyptian. The Memory of Egypt in Western Monotheism*, Cambridge, MA: Harvard University Press.

Assmann, Jan (2002) *The Mind of Egypt. History and Meaning in the Time of the Pharaohs*, New York: Metropolitan Books.

Ayad, Mariam (2009) *God's Wife, God's Servant. The God's Wife of Amun (ca. 740–525 BC)*, London: Routledge.

Bachhuber, Christoph, and R. Gareth Roberts, eds. (2009) *Forces of Transformation. The End of the Bronze Age in the Mediterranean*, Oxford: Oxbow Books.

Bagnall, Roger S. (1993) *Egypt in Late Antiquity*, Princeton: Princeton University Press.

Bagnall, Roger S. (1995) *Reading Papyri, Writing Ancient History*, London: Routledge.

Bagnall, Roger S., and Dominic W. Rathbone (2004) *Egypt from Alexander to the Early Christians: An Archaeological and Historical Guide*, Los Angeles: The J. Paul Getty Museum.

Baines, John (1995) "Origins of Egyptian Kingship," in D. O'Connor and D. P. Silverman, eds., *Ancient Egyptian Kingship*, Leiden: Brill: 95–156.

Baines, John (1996) "Contextualizing Egyptian Representations of Society and Ethnicity," in J. S. Cooper and G. Schwartz, eds., *The Study of the Ancient Near East in the 21st Century: Proceedings of the William Foxwell Albright Memorial Conference*, Winona Lake: Eisenbrauns: 339–84.

Baines, John (1999) "On *Wenamun* as a Literary Text," in J. Assmann and E. Blumenthal, eds., *Literatur und Politik im pharaonischen und ptolemäischen Ägypten*, Cairo: Institut Français d'Archéologie Orientale: 209–33.

Baines, John (2004) "The Earliest Egyptian Writing: Development, Context, Purpose," in S. D. Houston, ed., *The First Writing. Script Invention as History and Process*, Cambridge: Cambridge University Press: 150–89.

Baines, John (2007) *Visual & Written Culture in Ancient Egypt*, Oxford: Oxford University Press.

Baines, John (2008) "On the Evolution, Purpose and Forms of Egyptian Annals," in E. M. Engel et al., eds., *Zeichen aus dem Sand: Streiflichter aus Ägyptens Geschichte zu Ehren von Günter Dreyer*, Wiesbaden: Harrassowitz Verlag: 19–40.

Baines, John, and Jaromír Malek (2000) *Cultural Atlas of Ancient Egypt*, New York: Facts on File.

Baines, John R., Edward F. Wente, and Peter F. Dorman (2009) "Egypt, Ancient," *Encyclopædia Britannica Online*.

Barbotin, Christophe (2008) *Ahmosis et le début de la XVIIIe dynastie*, Paris: Pygmalion.

Bard, Kathryn A. (1994) *From Farmers to Pharaohs: Mortuary Evidence for the Rise of Complex Society in Egypt*, Sheffield: Sheffield Academic Press.

Bard, Kathryn A., ed. (1999) *Encyclopedia of the Archaeology of Ancient Egypt*, London: Routledge.

Bard, Kathryn A. (2008) *An Introduction to the Archaeology of Ancient Egypt*, Oxford: Blackwell Publishing.

Bard, Kathryn A., and Rodolfo Fattovich (2007) *Harbor of the Pharaoh to the Land of Punt*, Naples: Università degli studi di Napoli "L'Orientale".

Barnett, R. D. (1975) "The Sea Peoples," *The Cambridge Ancient History*, Vol. II/2, 3rd edn., Cambridge: Cambridge University Press: 359–78.

Beckman, Gary (1999) *Hittite Diplomatic Texts*, 2nd edn., Atlanta: Scholars Press.

Bell, Barbara (1971) "The Dark Ages in Ancient History. I. The First Dark Age in Egypt," *American Journal of Archaeology* 71: 1–26.

Bell, Lanny (1985) "Luxor Temple and the Cult of the Royal Ka," *Journal of Near Eastern Studies* 44: 251–94.

Bickel, Susanne (2002) "Aspects et fonctions de la déification d'Amenhotep III," *Bulletin de l'Institut Français d'Archéologie Orientale* 102: 63–90.

Bierbrier, Morris L. (1982) *The Tomb-builders of the Pharaohs*, London: British Museum Publications.

Bietak, Manfred (1994) "Historische und archäologische Einführung," in Hein, ed. 1994: 17–57.

Bietak, Manfred (1995) *Avaris: The Capital of the Hyksos. Recent Excavations at Tell el-Dab`a*, London: British Museum Press.

Bietak, Manfred (1997) "The Center of Hyksos Rule: Avaris (Tell el-Dab`a)," in Redford, ed. 1997: 87–139.

Bietak, Manfred (2001) "Dab`a, Tell ed-," in Redford, ed. 2001: Vol. 1: 351–4.

Björkman, Gun (1964) "Egyptology and Historical Method," *Orientalia Suecana* 13: 9–33.

Blackman, A. M. (1941) "The Stela of Shoshenk, Great Chief of the Meshwesh," *Journal of Egyptian Archaeology* 27: 83–95.

Blankenberg-Van Delden, C. (1969) *The Large Commemorative Scarabs of Amenhotep III*, Leiden: Brill.

Bleiberg, Edward (1995) "The Economy of Ancient Egypt," in Sasson, ed. 1995: 1373–85.

Blumenthal, Elke, Ingeborg Müller, and Walter F. Reineke, eds. (1984) *Urkunden der 18. Dynastie: Übersetzung zu den Heften 5–16*, Berlin: Akademie-Verlag.

Blyth, Elizabeth (2006) *Karnak: Evolution of a Temple*, London and New York: Routledge.

Boardman, John (1999) *The Greeks Overseas*, 4th edn., London: Thames & Hudson.

Bonnet, Charles (2000) *Édifices et rites funéraires à Kerma*, Paris: Errance.

Bonnet, Charles (2004) *Le temple principal de la ville de Kerma et son quartier religieux*, Paris: Errance.

Bonnet, Charles, and Dominique Valbelle (2006) *The Nubian Pharaohs. Black Kings on the Nile*, Cairo and New York: American University of Cairo Press.

Bourriau, Janine (1988) *Pharaohs and Mortals: Egyptian Art in the Middle Kingdom*, Cambridge: Cambridge University Press.

Bourriau, Janine (1991) "Patterns of Change in Burial Customs During the Middle Kingdom," in Quirke, ed. 1991: 3–20.

Bourriau, Janine (2000) "The Second Intermediate Period (c. 1650–1550 BC)," in Shaw, ed. 2000: 184–217.

Bowman, Alan K. (1986) *Egypt after the Pharaohs 332 BC–AD 642: From Alexander to the Arab Conquest*, London: British Museum Publications.

Bowman, Alan K., and Alan Edouard Samuel (2009) "Macedonian and Ptolemaic Egypt (332–30)," *Encyclopædia Britannica Online*.

Brand, Peter (2000) *The Monuments of Seti I: Epigraphic, Historical and Art Historical Analysis*, Leiden: Brill.

Breasted, James H. (1906) *Ancient Records of Egypt*, 5 vols., Chicago: University of Chicago Press.

Bresciani, Edda (1985) "The Persian Occupation of Egypt," in I. Gershevitch, ed., *The Cambridge History of Iran*, Cambridge: Cambridge University Press: 502–28.

Bresciani, Edda (2001) "Thirty-first Dynasty," in Redford, ed. 2001: Vol. 2: 276–7.

Briant, Pierre (2002) *A History of the Persian Empire*, Winona Lake: Eisenbrauns.

Broekman, G. P. F., R. J. Demarée, and O. E. Kaper, eds. (2009) *The Libyan Period in Egypt: Historical and Cultural Studies into the 21st–24th Dynasties*, Leiden: Nederlands Instituut voor het Nabije Oosten.

Brooklyn, Museum (1978) *Africa in Antiquity: The Arts of Ancient Nubia and the Sudan*, Brooklyn: Brooklyn Museum.

Brosius, Maria (2000) *The Persian Empire from Cyrus II to Artaxerxes I*, London: London Association of Classical Teachers.

Bryan, Betsy M. (1991) *The Reign of Thutmose IV*, Baltimore: Johns Hopkins University Press.

Bryan, Betsy M. (1996) "In Women Good and Bad Fortune Are on Earth. Status and Role of Women in Egyptian Culture," in A. Capel and G. Markoe, eds., *Mistress of the House. Mistress of Heaven. Women in Ancient Egypt*, New York: Hudson Hill Press: 25–46.

Bryan, Betsy M. (2000) "The 18th Dynasty before the Amarna Period (c. 1550–1352 BC)," in Shaw, ed. 2000: 207–64.

Bryan, Betsy M. (2006) "Administration in the Reign of Thutmose III," in Cline and O'Connor, eds. 2006: 69–122.

Bunnens, Guy (1990) "I Filistei e le invasioni dei Popoli del Mare," in D. Musti, ed., *Le origini dei Greci. Dori e mondo egeo*, Rome: Laterza: 227–56.

Burkard, Günter, and Heinz J. Thissen (2008) *Einführung in die altägyptische Literaturgeschichte. Bd. 2. Neues Reich*, Münster: Lit Verlag.

Burroughs, William James (2007) *Climate Change: A Multidisciplinary Approach*, Cambridge: Cambridge University Press.

Butzer, Karl W. (1984) "Long-Term Nile Flood Variation and Political Discontinuities in Pharaonic Egypt," in J. D. Clark and S. A Brandt, eds., *From Hunters to Farmers: The Causes and Consequences of Food Production in Africa*, Berkeley: University of California Press: 102–12.

Butzer, Karl W. (1997) "Sociopolitical Discontinuity in the Near East c. 2200 BCE: Scenarios from Palestine and Egypt," in H. N. Dalfes et al. eds., *Third Millennium BC Climate Change and Old World Collapse*, Berlin: Springer: 245–96.

Cabrol, Agnès (2000) *Amenhotep III: Le Magnifique*, Monaco: Rocher.

Callender, Gae (2000) "The Middle Kingdom Renaissance (c. 2055–1650 BC)," in Shaw, ed. 2000: 148–83.

Caminos, Ricardo (1954) *Late-Egyptian Miscellanies*, London: Oxford University Press.

Caminos, Ricardo (1958) *The Chronicle of Prince Osorkon*, Rome: Pontificium Institutum Biblicum.

Černý, J. (1953–4) "Prices and Wages in Egypt in the Ramesside Period," *Cahiers d'histoire mondiale* 1: 903–21.

Černý, J. (1975) "Egypt: From the Death of Ramesses III to the End of the Twenty-first Dynasty," *The Cambridge Ancient History*, Vol. II/2, 3rd edn., Cambridge: Cambridge University Press: 606–57.

Chace, Arnold (1927) *The Rhind Mathematical Papyrus, British Museum 10057 and 10058*, Oberlin: Mathematical Association of America.

Champollion, Jean-François (1836) *Grammaire égyptienne*, Paris: Typ. de Firmin Didot frères.

Chauveau, Michel (2000) *Egypt in the Age of Cleopatra*, Ithaca: Cornell University Press.

Chauveau, Michel (2001) "Les qanats dans les ostraca de Manâwir," in P. Briant, ed., *Irrigation et drainage dans l'Antiquité, qanats et canalisations souterraines en Iran, en Égypte et en Grèce*, Paris: Collège de France: 137–42.

Chauveau, Michel (2003) "The Demotic Ostraca of Ayn Manawir," *Egyptian Archaeology* 22: 38–40.

Clarysse, Willy (1992) "Some Greeks in Egypt," in J. H. Johnson, ed., *Life in a Multi-Cultural Society: Egypt from Cambyses to Constantine and Beyond*, Chicago: Oriental Institute of the University of Chicago: 51–7.

Clayton, Peter (1994) *Chronicle of the Pharaohs: The Reign-by-Reign Record of the Rulers and Dynasties of Ancient Egypt*, New York: Thames and Hudson.

Cline, Eric, and David O'Connor, eds. (1998) *Amenhotep III: Perspectives on His Reign*, Ann Arbor: University of Michigan Press.

Cline, Eric, and David O'Connor (2003) "The Mystery of the 'Sea Peoples'," in D. O'Connor and S. Quirke, eds., *Mysterious Lands*, London: UCL Press: 107–38.

Cline, Eric, and David O'Connor, eds. (2006) *Thutmose III: A New Biography*, Ann Arbor: University of Michigan Press.

Cohen, Raymond, and Raymond Westbrook, eds. (2000) *Amarna Diplomacy: The Beginnings of International Relations*, Baltimore: John Hopkins University Press.

Collier, Mark, and Bill Manley (2003) *How to Read Egyptian Hieroglyphs. A Step-by-step Guide to Teach Yourself*, rev. edn., Berkeley: University of California Press.

Crawford, Dorothy J. (1971) *Kerkeosiris; an Egyptian Village in the Ptolemaic Period*, Cambridge: Cambridge University Press.

Cumming, Barbara (1982) *Egyptian Historical Records of the Later Eighteenth Dynasty*, Fascicle 1, Warminster: Aris & Phillips.

Cumming, Barbara (1983) *Egyptian Historical Records of the Later Eighteenth Dynasty*, Fascicle 2, Warminster: Aris & Phillips.

Cumming, Barbara (1984) *Egyptian Historical Records of the Later Eighteenth Dynasty*, Fascicle 3, Warminster: Aris & Phillips.

Curran, Brian A. (2007) *The Egyptian Renaissance: The Afterlife of Ancient Egypt in Early Modern Italy*, Chicago: University of Chicago Press.

Darnell, John Coleman (2006) *The Inscription of Queen Katimala at Semna*, New Haven: Yale Egyptological Seminar.

Davidovits, Joseph, and Margie Morris (1988) *The Pyramids: An Enigma Solved*, New York: Dorset Press.

Davies, Benedict G. (1992) *Egyptian Historical Records of the Later Eighteenth Dynasty*, Fascicle 4, Warminster: Aris & Phillips.

Davies, Benedict G. (1994) *Egyptian Historical Records of the Later Eighteenth Dynasty*, Fascicle 5, Warminster: Aris & Phillips.

Davies, Benedict G. (1995) *Egyptian Historical Records of the Later Eighteenth Dynasty*, Fascicle 6, Warminster: Aris & Phillips.

Davies, Benedict G. (1997) *Egyptian Historical Inscriptions of the Nineteenth Dynasty*, Jonsered: Paul Åströms förlag.

Davies, Norman de Garis (1943) *The Tomb of Rekh-mi-re` at Thebes*, New York: Metropolitan Museum of Art.

Davies, W. V. (1987) *Egyptian Hieroglyphs*, London: British Museum Publications.

Davies, W. Vivian (2003a) "Kush in Egypt: A New Historical Inscription," *Sudan and Nubia* 7: 52–4.

Davies, W. Vivian (2003b) "Kouch en Égypte: Une nouvelle inscription historique à El-Kab," *Bulletin de la Société Française d'Égyptologie* 157: 38–44.

Delia, Robert (1979) "A New Look at Some Old Dates: A Re-Examination of the Twelfth-Dynasty Double Dated Inscriptions," *Bulletin of the Egyptological Seminar* 1: 15–28.

Delia, Robert (1982) "Doubts about Double Dates and Coregencies," *Bulletin of the Egyptological Seminar* 4: 55–69.

Depuydt, Leo (1995) "Murder in Memphis: The Story of Cambyses' Mortal Wounding of the Apis Bull," *Journal of Near Eastern Studies* 54: 119–26.

der Manuelian, Peter (1987) *Studies in the Reign of Amenophis II*, Hildesheim: Gerstenberg.

der Manuelian, Peter (1994) *Living in the Past. Studies in the Archaism of the Egyptian Twenty-sixth Dynasty*, London: Paul Kegan International.

de Sélincourt, Aubrey (1972) *Herodotus. The Histories*, Suffolk: Penguin.

Devauchelle, D. (1995) "Le sentiment anti-perse chez les anciens Égyptiens," *Transeuphratène* 9: 67–80.

Devauchelle, D. (1998) "Un problème de chronologie sous Cambyses," *Transeuphratène* 15: 9–17.

Dodson, Aidan (2001) "Third Intermediate Period," in Redford, ed. 2001: Vol. 3: 388–94.

Dodson, Aidan, and Dyan Hilton (2004) *The Complete Royal Families of Ancient Egypt*, London: Thames & Hudson.

Dorman, Peter F. (1988) *The Monuments of Senenmut*, London and New York: Kegan Paul International.

Dorman, Peter F. (2005) "The Proscription of Hatshepsut," in Roehrig, ed. 2005: 267–9.

Dorman, Peter F. (2007) "The Long Coregency Revisited: Architectural and Iconographic Conundra in the Tomb of Kheruef," in P. J. Brand and J. van Dijk, eds., *Causing his Name to Live: Studies in Egyptian History and Epigraphy in Memory of William J. Murnane*, Leiden: Brill: 65–82.

Dziobek, Eberhard (1992) *Das Grab des Ineni: Theben Nr. 81*, Mainz: Zabern.

Eaton-Krauss, M. (1990) "Akhenaten vs Akhenaten," *Bibliotheca Orientalis* 47: 541–59.

Eaton-Krauss, M. (2002) "Akhenaten Redux," *Chronique d'Égypte* 57: 93–107.

Eaton-Krauss, M., and Rolf Krauss (2001) Review of Gabolde 1998, *Bibliotheca Orientalis* 58: 91–7.

Edel, Elmar (1994) *Die ägyptisch-hethitische Korrespondenz aus Bogazköi in babylonische und hethitische Sprache*, Opladen: Westdeutscher Verlag.

Edel, Elmar (1997) *Der Vertrag zwischen Ramses II. von Ägypten und Ḫattušili III. von Hatti*, Berlin: Gebr. Mann Verlag.

Edgerton, William F. (1951) "The Strikes in Ramses III's Twenty-ninth Year," *Journal of Near Eastern Studies* 10: 137–45.

Edwards, I. E. S. (1971), "The Early Dynastic Period in Egypt," *The Cambridge Ancient History*, Vol. I/2, 2nd edn., Cambridge: Cambridge University Press: 1–70.

Edwards, I. E. S. (1982), "From the Twenty-second to the Twenty-fourth Dynasty," *The Cambridge Ancient History*, Vol. III/1, 2nd edn., Cambridge: Cambridge University Press: 534–81.

Edwards, David N. (2004) *The Nubian Past. An Archaeology of the Sudan*, London and New York: Routledge.

Eide, Tormod, Tomas Hägg, Richard Holton Pierce, and László Török (1994) *Fontes Historiae Nubiorum. Vol. I. From the Eighth to the Mid-fifth Century BC*, Bergen: Department of Classics.

El Daly, Okasha (2005) *Egyptology: The Missing Millennium. Ancient Egypt in Medieval Arabic Writings*, London: UCL Press.

Errington, R. Malcolm (2008) *A History of the Hellenistic World, 323–30 BC*, Oxford: Blackwell Publishing.

Faulkner, R. O. (2004) *The Ancient Egyptian Coffin Texts*, Oxford: Aris & Phillips.

Feldman, Marian H. (2005) *Diplomacy by Design: Luxury Arts and an "International Style" in the Ancient Near East, 1400–1200 BCE*, Chicago: University of Chicago Press.

Fischer, Henry G. (1961) "The Nubian Mercenaries of Gebelein during the First Intermediate Period," *Kush* 9: 44–80.

Foster, Ann L. (2001) "Forts and Garrisons," in Redford, ed. 2001: Vol. 1: 552–9.

Frandsen, Paul J. (1990) "Editing Reality: The Turin Strike Papyrus," in S. Israelit-Groll, ed., *Studies in Egyptology Presented to Miriam Lichtheim* Vol. I, Jerusalem: Magness Press: 166–99.

Franke, Detlef (1986) "Verwandtschaftsbezeichnungen," *Lexikon der Ägyptologie* 6: 1032–6.

Franke, Detlef (1991) "The Career of Khnumhotep III of Beni Hasan and the So-called 'Decline of the Nomarchs," in Quirke, ed. 1991: 51–67.

Franke, Detlef (1995) "The Middle Kingdom in Egypt," in Sasson, ed. 1995: 735–48.

Franke, Detlef (2001a) "First Intermediate Period," in Redford, ed. 2001: Vol. 1: 526–32.

Franke, Detlef (2001b) "Middle Kingdom," in Redford, ed. 2001: Vol. 2: 393–400.

Frankfort, Henri (1948) *Kingship and the Gods, a Study of Ancient Near Eastern Religion as the Integration of Society & Nature*, Chicago: University of Chicago Press.

Frankfurter, David (1998) *Religion in Roman Egypt: Assimilation and Resistance*, Princeton: Princeton University Press.

Frood, Elizabeth (2007) *Biographical Texts from Ramessid Egypt*, Leiden and Boston: Brill.

Gabolde, Marc (1998) *D'Akhenaton à Toutânkhamon*, Lyon: Université Lumière-Lyon 2, Institut d'archéologie et d'histoire de l'antiquité.

Gabolde, Marc (2001) "Das Ende der Amarnazeit," in Grimm & Schoske, eds. 2001: 9–41.

Gillen, Tood J. (2005) "The Historical Inscription on Queen Hatshepsut's *Chapelle Rouge*," *Bulletin of the Australian Centre for Egyptology* 16: 7–28.

Giton, Michel, and Jean Leclant (1977) "Gottesgemahlin," *Lexikon der Ägyptologie* 2: 792–812.

Giveon, Raphael (1983) "The Hyksos in the South," in *Fontes atque Pontes. Eine Festgabe für Helmut Brunner* (Ägypten und Altes Testament 5), Wiesbaden: Harrassowitz: 155–61.

Goelet, Ogden Jr. (1996) "A New 'Robbery' Papyrus: Rochester MAG 51.346.1," *Journal of Egyptian Archaeology* 82: 107–27.

Gozzoli, Roberto B. (2006) *The Writing of History in Ancient Egypt During the First Millennium BC (ca. 1070–180 BC). Trends and Perspectives*, London: Golden House Publications.

Grajetzki, Wolfram (2006) *The Middle Kingdom of Ancient Egypt: History, Archaeology and Society*, London: Duckworth.

Grandet, Pierre (1993) *Ramsès III: Histoire d'un règne*, Paris: Pygmalion.

Grandet, Pierre (2000) "L'exécution du chancelier Bay," *Bulletin de l'Institut Français d'Archéologie Orientale* 100: 339–45.

Grandet, Pierre (2001) "New Kingdom. Twentieth Dynasty," in Redford, ed. 2001: Vol. 2: 538–43.

Grandet, Pierre (2008) *Les Pharaons du Nouvel Empire (1550–1069 av. J.-C.). Une pensée stratégique*, Monaco: Rocher.

Griffith, F. L. (1909) *Catalogue of the Demotic Papyri in the John Rylands Library Manchester*, 3 vols., Manchester and London. Manchester University Press.

Griffiths, J. Gwyn (1970) *Plutarch's de Iside et Osiride; Edited with an Introduction, Translation and Commentary*, Cardiff: University of Wales Press.

Grimal, Nicolas (1981) *La stèle triomphale de Pi('ankh)y au Musée du Caire, JE 48862 et 47086–47089*, Cairo: Institut Français d'Archéologie Orientale.

Grimal, Nicolas (1992) *A History of Ancient Egypt*, Oxford: Blackwell.

Grimal, Nicolas (1995) "Corégence et association au trône: l'Enseignement d'Amenemhat Ier," *Bulletin de l'Institut Français d'Archéologie Orientale* 95: 273–80.

Grimm, Alfred, and Sylvia Schoske, eds. (2001) *Das Geheimnis des goldenen Sarges: Echnaton und das Ende der Amarnazeit*, Munich: Staatliches Museum Ägyptischer Kunst.

Güterbock, Hans Gustav (1956) "The Deeds of Suppiluliuma as Told by his Son, Mursili II," *Journal of Cuneiform Studies* 10: 41–68, 75–98, and 101–30.

Guo, Dantong (1999) "The Inscription of Amenemhet II from Memphis: Transliteration, Translation and Commentary," *Journal of Ancient Civilizations* 14: 45–66.

Gyles, Mary Francis (1959) *Pharaonic Policies and Administration, 663 to 323 BC*, Chapel Hill: University of North Carolina Press.

Haarmann, U. (1996) "Medieval Muslim Perceptions of Pharaonic Egypt," in A. Loprieno, ed., *Ancient Egyptian Literature: History and Forms*, Leiden & New York: E. J. Brill: 605–27.

Habachi, Labib (1956) "Hekaib. The Deified Governor of Elephantine," *Archaeology* 9: 8–15.

Habachi, Labib (1969) *Features of the Deification of Ramesses II*, Glückstadt: J. J. Augustin.

Harris, J. R. (1973) "Nefertiti Rediviva," *Acta Orientalia* 35: 5–13.

Hassan, Fekri A. (1997) "Nile Floods and Political Disorder in Early Egypt," in H. N. Dalfes et al., eds., *Third-Millennium-BC Climate Change and Old World Collapse*, Berlin: Springer: 1–24.

Hassan, Fekri A. (2007) "Draughts, Famine and the Collapse of the Old Kingdom. Re-Reading Ipuwer," in Z. A. Hawass and J. Richards, eds., *The Archaeology and Art of Ancient Egypt: Essays in Honor of David B. O'Connor*, Cairo: Conseil Suprême des Antiquités de l'Égypte, Vol. 1: 357–77.

Hawass, Zahi (2006) *The Royal Tombs of Egypt: The Art of Thebes Revealed*, New York: Thames & Hudson.

Hayes, William C. (1955) *A Papyrus of The Late Middle Kingdom*, New York: The Brooklyn Museum.

Hayes, William C. (1973) "Egypt: Internal Affairs from Tuthmosis I to the Death of Amenophis III," *The Cambridge Ancient History*, Vol. II/1, 3rd edn., Cambridge: Cambridge University Press: 313–416.

Hegazy, Elsayed, and J. Weilittner (1990/1) "Montuemhat. A Man of His Time," *Journal of the Ancient Chronology Forum* 4: 55–7.

Hein, Irmgard, ed. (1994) *Pharaonen und Fremde: Dynastien im Dunkel*, Vienna: Eigenverlag der Museen der Stadt Wien.

Helck, Wolfgang (1968) *Geschichte des alten Ägypten*, Leiden: Brill.

Helck, Wolfgang (1971) *Die Beziehungen Ägyptens zu Vorderasien im 3. und 2. Jahrtausend v. Chr*, 2nd edn., Wiesbaden: Harrassowitz.

Helck, Wolfgang (1993) "Das Hyksos-Problem," *Orientalia* 62: 60–6.

Helck, Wolfgang, Eberhard Otto, and Wolfhart Westendorf, eds. (1975–92) *Lexikon der Ägyptologie*, 7 vols., Wiesbaden: Harrassowitz.

Hoch, James E. (1994) *Semitic Words in Egyptian Texts of the New Kingdom and Third Intermediate Period*, Princeton: Princeton University Press.

Hodel-Hoenes, Sigrid (2000) *Life and Death in Ancient Egypt: Scenes from Private Tombs in New Kingdom Thebes*, Ithaca and London: Cornell University Press.

Hoffmann, Friedhelm, and Joachim Friedrich Quack (2007) *Anthologie der demotischen Literatur*, Berlin: LIT Verlag.

Hölbl, Günther (2001) *A History of the Ptolemaic Empire*, London and New York: Routledge.

Holladay, John S. Jr. (2001) "Yahudiyya, Tell el-," in Redford, ed. 2001: Vol. 3: 527–9.

Hornung, Erik (1990) *The Valley of the Kings: Horizon of Eternity*, New York: Timken.

Hornung, Erik (1991) *The Tomb of Pharaoh Seti I* (photos Harry Burton), Zurich: Artemis Verlag.

Hornung, Erik (1992) *Idea into Image. Essays on Ancient Egyptian Thought*, New York: Timken.

Hornung, Erik (1999a) *History of Ancient Egypt*, Edinburgh: Edinburgh University Press.

Hornung, Erik (1999b) *The Ancient Egyptian Books of the Afterlife*, Ithaca: Cornell University Press.

Hornung, Erik (1999c) *Akhenaten and the Religion of Light*, Ithaca: Cornell University Press.

Hornung, Erik, Rolf Krauss, and David A. Warburton, eds. (2006) *Ancient Egyptian Chronology*, Leiden and Boston: Brill.

Houston, Stephen, John Baines, and Jerrold Cooper (2003) "Last Writing: Script Obsolescence in Egypt, Mesopotamia, and Mesoamerica," *Comparative Studies in Society and History* 45: 430–79.

Institut Français d'archéologie orientale du Caire (1972) *Textes et langages de l'Égypte pharaonique. Cent cinquante années de recherches 1822–1972. Hommage à Jean-François Champollion*, Cairo, 3 vols.

James, T. G. H. (1991) "Egypt: The Twenty-fifth and Twenty-sixth Dynasties," *The Cambridge Ancient History*, Vol. III/2, 2nd edn., Cambridge: Cambridge University Press: 677–747.

Jansen-Winkeln, Karl (1992) "Das Ende des Neuen Reiches," *Zeitschrift für ägyptische Sprache und Altertumskunde* 119: 22–37.

Jansen-Winkeln, Karl (2001) "Der thebanische 'Gottesstaat'," *Orientalia* 70: 153–82.

Janssen, Jac. J. (1975a) *Commodity Prices from the Ramessid Period*, Leiden: Brill.

Janssen, Jac. J. (1975b) "Prolegomena to the Study of Egypt's Economic History During the New Kingdom," *Studien zur altägyptischen Kultur* 3: 127–85.

Johnson, Janet H. (1994) "The Persians and the Continuity of Egyptian Culture," in H. Sancisi-Weerdenburg et al., eds., *Achaemenid History VIII. Continuity and Change*, Leiden: Nederlands Instituut voor het Nabije Oosten: 149–59.

Johnson, W. Raymond (1990) "Images of Amenhotep III in Thebes: Styles and Intentions," in L. Berman, ed., *The Art of Amenhotep III: Art Historical Analysis*, Cleveland: Cleveland Museum of Art: 28–46.

Johnson, W. Raymond (1996) "Amenhotep III and Amarna: Some New Considerations," *Journal of Egyptian Archaeology* 82: 65–82.

Kaiser, Werner (1990) "Zur Entstehung des gesamtägyptischen Staates," *Mitteilungen des Deutschen Archäologischen Instituts. Abteilung Kairo* 46: 287–99.

Kaplony, P. (1977) *Rollsiegel des Alten Reiches*, Vol. 1: Brussels: Fondation Egyptologique.

Kemp, Barry J. (1983) "Old Kingdom, Middle Kingdom and Second Intermediate Period c. 2686–1552 BC," in Trigger, Kemp, O'Connor, and Lloyd 1983: 71–182.

Kemp, Barry J. (1989) *Ancient Egypt. Anatomy of a Civilization*, London and New York: Routledge.

Kemp, Barry J. (1995) "Unification and Urbanization of Ancient Egypt," in Sasson, ed. 1995: 679–90.

Kemp, Barry J. (2006) *Ancient Egypt. Anatomy of a Civilization*, 2nd edn., London and New York: Routledge.

Kendall, Timothy (1982) *Kush: Lost Kingdom of the Nile*, Brockton, MA: Brockton Art Museum/Fuller Memorial.

Kitchen, K. A. (1982) *Pharaoh Triumphant: The Life and Times of Ramesses II, King of Egypt*, Warminster: Aris & Phillips.

Kitchen, K. A. (1993a) *Ramesside Inscriptions Translated and Annotated. Translations I. Ramesses I, Sethos I, and Contemporaries*, Oxford: Blackwell.

Kitchen, K. A. (1993b) *Ramesside Inscriptions Translated and Annotated. Notes and Comments I. Ramesses I, Sethos I, and Contemporaries*, Oxford: Blackwell.

Kitchen, K. A. (1996a) *Ramesside Inscriptions Translated and Annotated. Translations II. Ramesses II, Royal Inscriptions*, Oxford: Blackwell.

Kitchen, K. A. (1996b) *The Third Intermediate Period in Egypt, 1100–650 BC*, 2nd edn. with supplement, Warminster: Aris & Phillips.

Kitchen, K. A. (1998) *Ramesside Inscriptions Translated and Annotated. Notes and Comments II. Ramesses II, Royal Inscriptions*, Oxford: Blackwell.

Kitchen, K. A. (2000) *Ramesside Inscriptions Translated and Annotated. Translations III. Ramesses II, His Contemporaries*, Oxford: Blackwell.

Kitchen, K. A. (2001a) "New Kingdom. Nineteenth Dynasty," in Redford, ed. 2001: Vol. 2: 534–8.

Kitchen, K. A. (2001b) "Ramesses II," in Redford, ed. 2001: Vol. 3: 116–18.

Kitchen, K. A. (2001c) "Twenty-fifth Dynasty," in Redford, ed. 2001: Vol. 3: 457–61.

Kitchen, K. A. (2003) *Ramesside Inscriptions Translated and Annotated. Translations IV. Merenptah and the Late Nineteenth Dynasty*, Oxford: Blackwell.

Kitchen, K. A. (2008) *Ramesside Inscriptions Translated and Annotated. Translations V. Setnakht, Ramesses III, and Contemporaries*, Oxford: Blackwell.

Kitchen, Kenneth A. (2009) "The Third Intermediate Period in Egypt: An Overview of Fact & Fiction," in Broekman et al., eds. 2009: 161–201.

Kozloff, Arielle P., and Betsy M. Bryan (1992) *Egypt's Dazzling Sun: Amenhotep III and His World*, Cleveland: Cleveland Museum of Art.

Krauss, Rolf (1978) *Das Ende der Amarnazeit*, Hildesheim: Gerstenberg.

Krauss, Rolf (1997) "Nefertiti's Ende," *Mitteilungen des Deutschen Archäologischen Instituts. Abteilung Kairo* 53: 209–19.

Kuhrt, Amélie (2007) *The Persian Empire. A Corpus of Sources from the Achaemenid Period*, London and New York: Routledge.

Lacovara, Peter (1997) *The New Kingdom Royal City*, London and New York: Kegan Paul International.

Lauer, Jean-Philippe (1989) "Le problème de la construction de la Grande pyramide," *Revue d'Égyptologie* 40: 91–111.

Lauffray, J. (1979) *Karnak d'Égypte, domaine du divin*, Paris: Éditions du Centre national de la Recherche scientifique.

Lawton, Ian, and Chris Ogilvie-Herald (1999) *Giza. The Truth*, London: Virgin Publishing.

Leahy, A. (1985), "The Libyan Period in Egypt: An Essay in Interpretation," *Libyan Studies* 16: 51–65.

Lehner, Mark (1997) *The Complete Pyramids*, London: Thames & Hudson.

Leprohon, Ronald J. (1985) "The Reign of Akhenaten Seen through the Later Royal Decrees," *Mélanges Gamal Eddin Mokhtar*, Cairo: Institut français d'archéologie orientale: Vol. 2: 93–103.

Leprohon, Ronald J. (1995) "Royal Ideology and State Administration in Pharaonic Egypt," in Sasson, ed. 1995: 273–87.

Lewis, Naphtali (1986a) *Greeks in Ptolemaic Egypt. Case Studies in the Social History of the Hellenistic World*, Oxford: Clarendon.

Lewis, Naphtali (1986b) *Life in Egypt under Roman Rule*, Oxford: Oxford University Press.

Lichtheim, Miriam (1973) *Ancient Egyptian Literature. A Book of Readings*, Vol. I: *The Old and Middle Kingdoms*, Berkeley: University of California Press.

Lichtheim, Miriam (1976) *Ancient Egyptian Literature. A Book of Readings*, Vol. II: *The New Kingdom*, Berkeley: University of California Press.

Lichtheim, Miriam (1980) *Ancient Egyptian Literature. A Book of Readings*, Vol. III: *The Late Period*, Berkeley: University of California Press.

Lichtheim, Miriam (1988) *Ancient Egyptian Autobiographies Chiefly of the Middle Kingdom: A Study and an Anthology*, Freiburg: Universitätsverlag; Göttingen: Vandenhoeck & Ruprecht.

Lipinska, Jadwiga (2001) "Hatshepsut," in Redford, ed. 2001: Vol. 2: 85–7.

Liverani, Irene (2004) "Hillat el-Arab," in Welsby & Anderson, eds. 2004: 138–40.

Liverani, Mario (1990) "A Seasonal Pattern for the Amarna Letters," in T. Abusch et al., eds., *Lingering over Words. Studies in Ancient Near Eastern Literature in Honor of William L. Moran*, Atlanta: Scholars Press: 337–84.

Liverani, Mario (2004) *Myth and Politics in Ancient Near Eastern Historiography*, Ithaca: Cornell University Press.

Lloyd, Alan B. (1975–88) *Herodotus, Book II*, 3 vols., Leiden: E. J. Brill.

Lloyd, Alan B. (1983) "The Late Period, 664–323 BC," in Trigger, Kemp, O'Connor, and Lloyd 1983: 279–364.

Lloyd, Alan B. (1994) "Egypt 404–332 BC," *The Cambridge Ancient History*, Vol. VI, 2nd edn., Cambridge: Cambridge University Press: 337–60.

Lloyd, Alan B. (2000a) "The Late Period (664–332 BC)," in Shaw, ed. 2000: 369–94.

Lloyd, Alan B. (2000b) "Saite Navy," in G. J. Olivier et al., eds., *The Sea in Antiquity*, BAR International Series 899, Oxford: 81–91.

Loprieno, Antonio (1998) "Nhsj, 'der Südländer'?," in H. Guksch and D. Polz, eds., *Stationen: Beiträge zur Kulturgeschichte Ägyptens: Rainer Stadelmann gewidmet*, Mainz: P. von Zabern: 211–17.

Loprieno, Antonio (2003) "Views of the Past in Egypt during the First Millennium BC," in J. Tait, ed., *"Never Had the Like Occurred": Egypt's View of Its Past. Encounters with Ancient Egypt*, London: UCL Press: 139–54.

Malek, Jaromir (1986) *In the Shadow of the Pyramids. Egypt During the Old Kingdom*, London: Orbis.

Manley, Bill (1996) *The Penguin Historical Atlas of Ancient Egypt*, London: Penguin Books.

Manning, Joseph G. (2007) "Hellenistic Egypt," in W. Scheidel, I. Morris and R. Saller, eds., *The Cambridge Economic History of the Greco-Roman World*, Cambridge: Cambridge University Press: 434–59.

Maruéjol, Florence (2007) *Thoutmosis III et la corégence avec Hatchepsout*, Paris: Pygmalion.

Martin, Geoffrey Thorndike (1991) *A Bibliography of the Amarna Period and its Aftermath: The Reigns of Akhenaten, Smenkhkare, Tutankhamun and Ay (c. 1350–1321 BC)*, London: Kegan Paul.

McDonald, John K. (1996) *House of Eternity: The Tomb of Nefertari*, Los Angeles: Getty Conservation Institute and J. Paul Getty Museum.

McDowell, A. G. (1990) *Jurisdiction in the Workmen's Community of Deir el-Medina*, Leiden: Nederlands Instituut voor het Nabije Oosten.

McDowell, A. G. (1999) *Village Life in Ancient Egypt. Laundry Lists and Love Songs*, Oxford: Oxford University Press.

McKenzie, Judith S. (2007) *The Architecture of Alexandria and Egypt, c. 300 BC–AD 700*, New Haven and London: Yale University Press.

Metropolitan Museum of Art (1999) *Egyptian Art in the Age of the Pyramids*, New York: Metropolitan Museum of Art.

Meyer, Christine (1989) "Zur Verfolgung Hatschepsuts durch Thutmosis III.," in A. Altenmüller and R. Germer, eds., *Miscellanea Aegyptologica. Wolfgang Helck zum 75. Geburtstag*, Hamburg: Archäologisches Institut der Universität Hamburg: 119–26.

Midant-Reynes, Béatrix (2000) *The Prehistory of Egypt from the First Egyptians to the First Pharaohs*, Oxford: Blackwell.

Midant-Reynes, Béatrix (2003) *Aux Origines de l'Égypte. Du Néolithique à l'émergence de l'État*, Paris: Fayard.

Midant-Reynes, B., and Y. Tristant, eds. (2008) *Egypt at Its Origins 2*, Leuven: Peeters.

Moeller, Nadine (2006) "The First Intermediate Period: A Time of Famine and Climate Change?'" *Ägypten und Levante* 15: 153–67.

Mojsov, Bojana (2005) *Osiris: Death and Afterlife of a God*, Oxford: Blackwell.

Montserrat, Dominic (2000) *Akhenaten: History, Fantasy, and Ancient Egypt*, New York: Routledge.

Moran, William (1992) *The Amarna Letters*, Baltimore: Johns Hopkins University Press.

Moreno García, Juan Carlos (1997) *Études sur l'administration, le pouvoir et l'idéologie en Égypte, de l'Ancien au Moyen Empire*, Liège: C.I.P.L.

Morenz, Ludwig D. (1996) *Beiträge zur Schriftlichkeitskultur im Mittleren Reich und der 2. Zwischenzeit*, Wiesbaden: Harrassowitz.

Morenz, Siegfried (1969) *Prestige-Wirtschaft im alten Ägypten*, Munich: Verlag der Bayerischen Akademie der Wissenschaften.

Morkot, Robert (2000) *The Black Pharaohs*, London: Rubicon Press.

Morkot, Robert (2001) "The Egyptian Empire in Nubia in the Late Bronze Age (c. 1550–1070 BCE)," in S. Alcock et al., eds., *Empires. Perspectives from Archaeology and History*, Cambridge: Cambridge University Press: 227–51.

Morris, Ellen Fowles (2005) *The Architecture of Imperialism: Military Bases and the Evolution of Foreign Policy in Egypt's New Kingdom*, Leiden and Boston: Brill.

Murnane, William J. (1977) *Ancient Egyptian Coregencies*, Chicago: The Oriental Institute of the University of Chicago.

Murnane, William J. (1981) "In Defense of the Middle Kingdom Double Dates," *Bulletin of the Egyptological Seminar* 3: 73–82.

Murnane, Willliam J. (1990) *The Road to Kadesh*, 2nd edn., Chicago: The Oriental Institute of the University of Chicago.

Murnane, William J. (1995) *Texts from the Amarna Period in Egypt*, Atlanta: Society of Biblical Literature.

Murnane, William J. (2001) "Co-regency," in Redford, ed. 2001: Vol. 1: 307–11.

Mysliwiec, Karol (2000) *The Twilight of Ancient Egypt. First Millennium BCE*, Ithaca and London: Cornell University Press.

Obsomer, Claude (1995) *Sésostris Ier: Étude chronologique du règne*, Brussels: Éditions Safran.

O'Connor, David (1983) "New Kingdom and Third Intermediate Period," in Trigger, Kemp, O'Connor, and Lloyd 1983: 183–278.

O'Connor, David (1993) *Ancient Nubia: Egypt's Rival in Africa*, Philadelphia: The University Museum of Archaeology and Anthropology.

O'Connor, David (2001) "Eros in Egypt," *Archaeology Odyssey*, September–October, 2001, http://fontes.lstc.edu/~rklein/Documents/eros_in_egypt.htm.

O'Connor, David (2009) *Abydos: Egypt's First Pharaohs and the Cult of Osiris*, London: Thames & Hudson.

O'Connor, David, and Andrew Reid, eds. (2003) *Ancient Egypt in Africa*, London: UCL Press.

O'Mara, P. F. (1996) "Was There an Old Kingdom Historiography? Is It Datable?," *Orientalia* 65: 197–208.

Oren, Eliezer D., ed. (1997) *The Hyksos: New Historical and Archaeological Perspectives*, Philadelphia: University Museum, University of Pennsylvania.

Otto, Eberhard (1968) *Egyptian Art and the Cults of Osiris and Amon*, London: Thames & Hudson.

Parkinson, R. B. (1991) *Voices from Ancient Egypt: An Anthology of Middle Kingdom Writings*, London: British Museum Press.

Parkinson, R. B. (1998) *The Tale of Sinuhe and Other Ancient Egyptian Poems 1940–1640 BC* (Oxford World's Classics), Oxford: Oxford University Press.

Parkinson, Richard (1999) *Cracking Codes. The Rosetta Stone and Decipherment*, London: British Museum Press.

Parkinson, R. B. (2002) *Poetry and Culture in Middle Kingdom Egypt: A Dark Side to Perfection*, London: Continuum.

Parkinson, Richard (2005) *The Rosetta Stone*, London: British Museum Press.

Parkinson, Richard, and Stephen Quirke (1995) *Papyrus*, London: British Museum Press.

Parsons, Peter J. (2007) *The City of the Sharp-Nosed Fish: Greek Lives in Roman Egypt*, London: Weidenfeld & Nicolson.

Peden, A. J. (1994a) *Egyptian Historical Inscriptions of the Twentieth Dynasty*, Jonsered: Paul Åströms förlag.

Peden, A. J. (1994b) *The Reign of Ramesses IV*, Warminster: Aris & Phillips.

Polz, Daniel C. (2001) "Seventeenth Dynasty," in Redford, ed. 2001: Vol. 3: 273–4.

Polz, Daniel C. (2006) "Die Hyksos Blöcke aus Gebelên; zur Präsenz der Hyksos in Oberägypten," in E. Czerny et al., eds., *Timelines: Studies in Honour of Manfred Bietak*, Dudley, MA: Peeters: Vol. I: 239–48.

Polz, Daniel C. (2007) *Der Beginn des Neuen Reiches: zur Vorgeschichte einer Zeitenwende*, Berlin: Walter de Gruyter.

Porter, Bertha, Rosalind L. B. Moss, Ethel W. Burney, Jaromír Málek (1929–) *Topographical Bibliography of Ancient Egyptian Hieroglyphic Texts, Reliefs, and Paintings,* Oxford: Griffith Institute.

Posener, Georges (1936) *La première domination perse en Égypte,* Cairo: Institut français d'archéologie orientale.

Postel, Lilian, and Isabelle Régen (2005) "Annales héliopolitaines et fragments de Sésostris Ier réemployés dans la porte de Bâb al-Tawfiq au Caire," *Bulletin de l'Institut français d'archéologie orientale* 105: 229–93.

Préaux, Claire (1977) *Le monde hellénistique,* Vol. II, Paris: Presses universitaires de France.

Pritchard, James B., ed. (1969) *Ancient Near Eastern Texts Relating to the Old Testament,* 3rd edn., Princeton: Princeton University Press.

Pusch, Edgar B. (1993) "'Pi-Ramesse-geliebt-von-Amun, Hauptquartier Deiner Streitwagen'. Ägypter und Hethiter in der Delta-Residenz der Ramessiden," in A. Eggebrecht, ed., *Pelizaeus-Museum Hildesheim. Die Ägyptische Sammlung,* Mainz: Verlag Philip von Zabern: 126–43.

Pusch, Edgar B., and Anja Herold (1999) "Qantir/Pi-Ramesses," in Bard, ed. 1999: 647–9.

Quack, Joachim Friedrich (2009) *Einführung in die altägyptische Literaturgeschichte III: Die demotische und gräko-ägyptische Literatur,* 2nd edn., Berlin: LIT Verlag.

Quirke, Stephen (1990) *The Administration of Egypt in the Late Middle Kingdom: The Hieratic Documents,* New Malden: SIA.

Quirke, Stephen (1991) "Royal Power in the Thirteenth Dynasty," in Quirke, ed. 1991: 123–39.

Quirke, Stephen, ed. (1991) *Middle Kingdom Studies,* New Malden: SIA.

Quirke, Stephen (2001) "Second Intermediate Period," in Redford, ed. 2001: Vol. 3: 261–5.

Quirke, Stephen (2007) "The Hyksos in Egypt 1600 BCE: New Rulers without an Administration," in H. Crawford, ed., *Regime Change in the Ancient Near East and Egypt: from Sargon of Agade to Saddam Hussein,* Oxford: Oxford University Press for The British Academy: 123–39.

Rathbone, Dominic W. (2007) "Roman Egypt," in W. Scheidel, I. Morris and R. Saller, eds., *The Cambridge Economic History of the Greco-Roman World,* Cambridge: Cambridge University Press: 698–719.

Ray, John D. (1988), "Egypt 525–404 BC," *The Cambridge Ancient History,* Vol. IV, 2nd edn., Cambridge: Cambridge University Press: 254–86.

Ray, John D. (2001a), "Late Period. An Overview," in Redford, ed. 2001: Vol. 2: 267–72.

Ray, John D. (2001b), "Thirtieth Dynasty," in Redford, ed. 2001: Vol. 2: 275–6.

Redford, Donald B. (1984) *Akhenaten. The Heretic King,* Princeton: Princeton University Press.

Redford, Donald B. (1986) *Pharaonic King-Lists, Annals, and Day-Books: A Contribution to the Study of the Egyptian Sense of History,* Mississauga: Benben.

Redford, Donald B. (1992) *Egypt, Canaan, and Israel in Ancient Times,* Princeton: Princeton University Press.

Redford, Donald B. (1997) "Textual Sources for the Hyksos Period," in Oren, ed. 1997: 1–44.

Redford, Donald B., ed. (2001) *The Oxford Encyclopedia of Ancient Egypt,* Oxford: Oxford University Press. Available online, http://www.oxford-ancientegypt.com.

Redford, Donald B. (2003) *The Wars in Syria and Palestine of Thutmose III*, Leiden: Brill.

Redford, Donald B. (2004) *From Slave to Pharaoh. The Black Experience of Ancient Egypt*, Baltimore and London: Johns Hopkins University Press.

Redford, Susan (2002) *The Harem Conspiracy: The Murder of Ramesses III*, Dekalb: Northern Illinois University Press.

Redmount, Carol A. (1995) "The Wadi Tumilat and the 'Canal of the Pharaohs',") *Journal of Near Eastern Studies* 54: 127–35.

Reeves, Nicholas, and Richard H. Wilkinson (1996) *The Complete Valley of the Kings: Tombs and Treasures of Egypt's Greatest Pharaohs*, New York: Thames & Hudson.

Rehren, Thilo, and Edgar B. Pusch (2005) "Late Bronze Age Glass Production at Qantir-Piramesses, Egypt," *Science* 17, June 2005, Vol. 308: 1756–8.

Richards, Janet (2005) *Society and Death in Ancient Egypt. Mortuary Landscapes of the Middle Kingdom*, Cambridge: Cambridge University Press.

Riemer, Heiko (2008) "Interactions Between the Desert and the Nile Valley. Introduction," in Midant-Reynes & Tristant, eds. 2008: 565–8.

Ritner, Robert K. (1984) "A Property Transfer from the Erbstreit Archives," in H.-J. Thissen and K.-Th. Zauzich, eds., *Grammata demotika: Festschrift für Erich Lüddeckens zum 15. Juni 1983*, Würzburg: Zauzich: 171–87.

Ritner, Robert K. (1998) "Egypt under Roman Rule: The Legacy of Ancient Egypt," *The Cambridge History of Egypt*, Vol. 1, *Islamic Egypt, 640–1517*, Cambridge: Cambridge University Press: 1–33.

Ritner, Robert K. (2008) "Libyan vs. Nubian as the Ideal Egyptian," in S. E. Thompson and P. der Manuelian, eds., *Egypt and Beyond. Essays Presented to Leonard H. Lesko*, Providence: Department of Egyptology and Ancient Western Asian Studies, Brown University: 305–14.

Robins, Gay (1993) *Women in Ancient Egypt*, London: British Museum Press.

Robins, Gay (1997) *The Art of Ancient Egypt*, Cambridge, MA: Harvard University Press.

Robins, Gay, and Charles Shute (1987) *The Rhind Mathematical Papyrus*, London: British Museum Publications.

Roehrig, Catharine H., ed. (2005) *Hatshepsut: From Queen to Pharaoh*, New York: Metropolitan Museum of Art; New Haven: Yale University Press.

Romer, John (1984) *Ancient Lives: Daily Life in Egypt of the Pharaohs*, New York: Holt, Rinehart, and Winston.

Roth, Ann Macy (2005) "Erasing a Reign," in Roehrig, ed. 2005: 277–81.

Rougé, Emmanuel vicomte de (1867) "Extraits d'un mémoire sur les attaques dirigées contre l'Égypte par les peuples de la mer Méditerranée vers le XIVe siècle avant notre ère," *Revue archéologique* 2e serie 7: 38–81.

Rowe, Alan (1938) "New Light on Objects Belonging to Generals Potasimto and Amasis," *Annales du Service des Antiquités de l'Égypte* 38: 157–95.

Ryholt, K. S. B. (1997) *The Political Situation in Egypt During the Second Intermediate Period, c. 1800–1550 BC*, Copenhagen: Museum Tusculanum Press.

Ryholt, Kim (2005) "On the Contents and Nature of the Tebtunis Temple Library: A status report," in S. Lippert and M. Schentuleit, eds., *Tebtunis und Soknopaiu Nesos: Leben im römerzeitlichen Fajum*, Wiesbaden: Harrassowitz: 141–70.

Sandars, N. K. (1985) *The Sea Peoples*, rev. edn., London: Thames & Hudson.

Sarna, Nahum M. (1986) *Exploring Exodus. The Heritage of Biblical Israel*, New York: Schocken Books.

Sasson, Jack M., ed. (1995) *Civilizations of the Ancient Near East*, 4 vols., New York: Charles Scribner's Sons.

Schaefer, Alisa (1986) "Zur Entstehung des Mitregentschaft als Legitimationsprinzip von Herrschaft," *Zeitschrift für Ägyptische Sprache und Alterumskunde* 113: 44–55.

Schenkel, Wolfgang (1965) *Memphis, Herakleopolis, Theben: die epigraphischen Zeugnisse der 7.–11. Dynastie*, Wiesbaden. Harrassowitz.

Schipper, Bernd Ulrich (2005) *Die Erzählung des Wenamun: ein Literaturwerk im Spannungsfeld von Politik, Geschichte und Religion*, Fribourg and Göttingen: Academic Press; Vandenhoeck & Ruprecht.

Schmidt, Heike C., and Joachim Willeitner (1994) *Nefertari: Gemahlin Ramses' II*, Mainz: P. von Zabern.

Schneider, Thomas (1994) *Lexikon der Pharaonen*, Zurich: Artemis Verlag.

Schneider, Thomas (2003a) "Foreign Egypt: Egyptology and the Concept of Cultural Appropriation," *Ägypten und Levante* 13: 155–61.

Schneider, Thomas (2003b) "Siptah und Beja: Neubeurteilung einer historischen Konstellation," *Zeitschrift für ägyptische Sprache und Altertumskunde* 130: 134–46.

Schneider, Thomas (2006) "The Relative Chronology of the Middle Kingdom and the Hyksos Period," in Hornung et al., eds. 2006: 168–96.

Schwaller de Lubicz, R. A. (1999) *The Temples of Karnak*, Rochester, VT: Inner Traditions.

Schwartz, Jacques (1948) "Les conquérants perses et la littérature Égyptienne," *Bulletin de l'Institut Français d'Archéologie Orientale* 48: 65–80.

Seidlmayer, Stephan (2000) "The First Intermediate Period (c. 2160–2055)," in Shaw, ed. 2000: 118–47.

Seidlmayer, Stephan (2001) *Historische und moderne Nilstände. Pegelablesungen des Nils von der Frühzeit bis in die Gegenwart*, Berlin: Achet Verlag.

Seidlmayer, Stephan (2007) "People at Beni Hassan: Contributions to a Model of Ancient Egyptian Rural Society," in Z. A. Hawass and J. Richards, eds., *The Archaeology and Art of Ancient Egypt: Essays in Honor of David B. O'Connor*, Cairo: Conseil Suprême des Antiquités de l'Égypte, Vol. 2: 351–68.

Sethe, Kurt (1930) *Urgeschichte und älteste religion der Ägypter*, Leipzig: Deutsche morgenländische Gesellschaft.

Sethe, Kurt, and Wolfgang Helck, eds. (1906–58) *Urkunden des ägyptischen Altertums IV: Urkunden der 18. Dynastie*, 22 vols., Leipzig: Hinrichs; Berlin: Akademie Verlag.

Shaw, Ian, ed. (2000) *The Oxford History of Ancient Egypt*, Oxford: Oxford University Press.

Shaw, Ian, and Paul T. Nicholson (1995) *The British Museum Dictionary of Ancient Egypt*, London: British Museum Press.

Shedid, Abdel Ghaffar (1994) *Die Felsgräber von Beni Hassan in Mittelägypten*, Mainz: P. von Zabern.

Silberman, Neil Asher (1998) "The Sea Peoples, the Victorians and Us: Modern Social Ideology and Changing Archaeological Interpretations of the Late Bronze Age Collapse," in S. Gitin et al., eds., *Mediterranean Peoples in Transition. Thirteenth to Early Tenth Centuries BCE*, Jerusalem: Israel Exploration Society: 268–75.

Silver, Morris (2004) "Modern Ancients," in R. Rollinger and C. Ulf, eds., *Commerce and Monetary Systems in the Ancient World: Means of Transmission and Cultural Interaction*, Munich: Franz Steiner Verlag: 65–87.

Silverman, David P., Josef W. Wegner, and Jennifer Houser Wegner (2006) *Akhenaten and Tutankhamun: Revolution and Restoration*, Philadelphia: University of Pennsylvania Museum of Archaeology and Anthropology.

Simpson, William K., ed. (2003) *The Literature of Ancient Egypt*, 3rd edn., New Haven and London: Yale University Press.

Smith, Craig B. (2004) *How the Great Pyramid Was Built*, Washington: Smithsonian Books.

Smith, Mark (2001) "Papyrus Rylands IX" in Redford, ed. 2001: Vol. 3: 24.

Smith, Mark (2009) "Democratization of the Afterlife," in J. Dieleman and W. Wendrich, eds., *UCLA Encyclopedia of Egyptology*, Los Angeles. Available online http://repositories.cdlib.org/nelc/uee/1147.

Smith, S. Tyson (1995) *Askut in Nubia: The Economics and Ideology of Egyptian Imperialism in the Second Millennium BC*, London and New York: Kegan Paul International.

Spalinger, Anthony J. (2001) "Twenty-sixth Dynasty," in Redford, ed. 2001: Vol. 2: 272–4.

Spalinger, Anthony J. (2005) *War in Ancient Egypt*, Oxford: Blackwell.

Spencer, A. J. (1993) *Early Egypt: The Rise of Civilisation in the Nile Valley*, London: British Museum Press.

Stadelmann, Rainer (1995) "Builders of the Pyramids," in Sasson, ed. 1995: 719–34.

Stadler, Martin Andreas (2008) "On the Demise of Egyptian Writing," in J. Baines et al., eds., *The Disappearance of Writing Systems*, London: Equinox: 157–82.

Stierlin, Henri, and Christiane Ziegler (1987) *Tanis: vergessene Schätze der Pharaonen*, Munich: Hirmer.

Strudwick, Nigel C. (2005) *Texts from the Pyramid Age*, Leiden and Boston: Brill.

Szpakowska, Kasia (2007) *Daily Life in Ancient Egypt: Reconstructing Lahun*, Oxford: Blackwell.

Tait, W. John (1996) "Demotic Literature: Forms and Genres," in A Loprieno, ed., *Ancient Egyptian Literature: History and Forms*, Leiden: E. J. Brill: 175–87.

Tait, John (2001a) "Setna Khaemwase Cycle," in Redford, ed. 2001: Vol. 3: 271.

Tait, John (2001b) "Demotic Literature," in Redford, ed. 2001: Vol. 1: 378–81.

Taylor, John (1991) *Egypt and Nubia*, London: British Museum Press.

Taylor, John H. (1998) "Nodjmet, Payankh and Herihor: The End of the New Kingdom Reconsidered," in C. Eyre, ed., *Proceedings of the Seventh International Congress of Egyptologists, Cambridge, 3–9 September 1995*, Leuven: Peeters, 1143–55.

Taylor, John (2000) "The Third Intermediate Period (1069–664 BC)," in Shaw, ed. 2000: 300–68.

Thompson, Dorothy J. (1988) *Memphis Under the Ptolemies*, Princeton: Princeton University Press.

Török, László (1997) *The Kingdom of Kush. Handbook of the Napatan-Meroitic Civilization*, Leiden: Brill.

Trigger, Bruce G. (1983) "The Rise of Egyptian Civilization," in Trigger, Kemp, O'Connor, and Lloyd 1983: 1–70.

Trigger, Bruce G., (2003) *Understanding Early Civilizations: A Comparative Study*, Cambridge: Cambridge University Press.

Trigger, B. G., B. J. Kemp, D. O'Connor, and A. B. Lloyd (1983) *Ancient Egypt. A Social History*, Cambridge: Cambridge University Press.

Troy, Lana (2001) "New Kingdom: Eighteenth Dynasty to the Amarna Period," in Redford, ed. 2001: Vol. 2: 525–31.

Valloggia, Michel (1999) "Dakhla Oasis. Balat," in Bard, ed. 1999: 216–19.

Van De Mieroop, Marc (1997) "On Writing a History of the Ancient Near East," *Bibliotheca Orientalis* 54: 285–305.

Van De Mieroop, Marc (2004) "Economic Theories and the Ancient Near East," in R. Rollinger and C. Ulf, eds., *Commerce and Monetary Systems in the Ancient World:*

Means of Transmission and Cultural Interaction, Munich: Franz Steiner Verlag: 54–64.

Van De Mieroop, Marc (2007a) *A History of the Ancient Near East, ca. 3000–323 BC*, 2nd edn. Oxford: Blackwell.

Van De Mieroop, Marc (2007b) *The Eastern Mediterranean in the Age of Ramesses II*, Oxford: Blackwell.

van den Boorn, G. P. F. (1988) *The Duties of the Vizier. Civil Administration in the Early New Kingdom*, London and New York: Kegan Paul International.

Vandersleyen, Claude (1995) *L'Égypte et la vallée du Nil, Tome 2. De la fin de l'Ancien Empire à la fin du Nouvel Empire*, Paris: Presses universitaires de France.

Vandier, Jacques (1936) *La famine dans l'Égypte ancienne*, Cairo: Imprimerie de l'Institut français d'archéologie orientale.

Van Dijk, Jacobus (2000) "The Amarna Period and the Later New Kingdom (c. 1351–1069)," in Shaw, ed. 2000: 272–313.

Vandorpe, Katelijn (2002a) *The Bilingual Family Archive of Dryton, his Wife Apollonia and their Daughter Senmouthis*, Brussels: Koninklijke Vlaamse Academie van Belgie voor Wetenschappen en Kunsten.

Vandorpe, Katelijn (2002b) "Apollonia, a Businesswoman in a Multicultural Society (Pathyris, 2nd–1st Centuries BC)," in H. Melaerts and L. Mooren, eds., *Le rôle et le statut de la femme en Égypte hellénistique, romaine et byzantine*, Leuven: Peeters: 325–36.

Verbrugghe, Gerald P., and John M. Wickersham (1996) *Berossos and Manetho, Introduced and Translated: Native Traditions in Ancient Mesopotamia and Egypt*, Ann Arbor: University of Michigan Press.

Vercoutter, Jean (1992) *L'Égypte et la vallée du Nil. Tome I. Des origines à la fin de l'Ancien Empire*, Paris: Presses universitaires de France.

Verhoogt, A. M. F. W. (1997) *Menches, Komogrammateus of Kerkeosiris: The Doings and Dealings of a Village Scribe in the Late Ptolemaic Period (120–110 BC)*, New York: Brill.

Verner, Miroslav (2001) *The Pyramids*, New York: Grove Press.

Vernus, Pascal (1995) "La grande mutation idéologique du Nouvel Empire: Une nouvelle théorie du pouvoir politique. Du demiurge face à sa creation," *Bulletin de la Société d'Égyptologie de Genève* 19: 70–95.

Vernus, Pascal (2003) *Affairs and Scandals in Ancient Egypt*, Ithaca: Cornell University Press.

Vittmann, Günter (1998) *Der demotische Papyrus Rylands 9*, Wiesbaden: Harrassowitz.

Von Beckerath, Jürgen (1964) *Untersuchungen zur politischen Geschichte der Zweiten Zwischenzeit in Ägypten*, Glückstadt: J.J. Augustin.

Von Beckerath, Jürgen (1968) "Die 'Stele der Verbannten' im Museum des Louvre," *Revue d'Égyptologie* 20: 7–36.

Von Beckerath, Jürgen (1997) *Chronologie des pharaonischen Ägypten*, Mainz: Von Zabern.

Wainwright, G. A. (1927) "El Hibeh and esh Shurafa and the Connection with Herakleopolis and Cusae," *Annales du Service des Antiquités de l'Égypte* 27: 76–104.

Weeks, Kent R., ed. (2000) *KV 5: A Preliminary Report on the Excavation of the Tomb of the Sons of Rameses II in the Valley of the Kings*, Cairo: American University in Cairo Press.

Weeks, Kent R., ed. (2001) *The Treasures of the Valley of the Kings: Tombs and Temples of the Theban West Bank in Luxor*, Cairo: American University in Cairo Press.

Weinstein, James M. (1981) "The Egyptian Empire in Palestine: A Reassessment," *Bulletin of the American Schools for Oriental Research* 241: 1–28.

Welsby, Derek A. (2002) *The Kingdom of Kush. The Napatan and Meroitic Empire*, London: British Museum Press.

Welsby, Derek A., and Julie R. Anderson, eds. (2004) *Sudan: Ancient Treasures, an Exhibition of Recent Discoveries from the Sudan National Museum*, London: British Museum Press.

Wengrow, David (2006) *The Archaeology of Early Egypt. Social Transformation in North-East Africa 10,000 to 2650 BC*, Cambridge: Cambridge University Press.

Wenke, Robert J. (2009) *The Ancient Egyptian State: The Origins of Egyptian Culture (c. 8000–2000 BC)*, Cambridge: Cambridge University Press.

Wente, Edward F. (1967) "On the Chronology of the Twenty-first Dynasty," *Journal of Near Eastern Studies* 26: 155–76.

Wente, Edward F. (1990) *Letters from Ancient Egypt*, Atlanta: Society of Biblical Literature.

Widmer, Werner (1975) "Zur Darstellung der Seevölker am Grossen Tempel von Medinet Habu," *Zeitschrift für ägyptische Sprache und Altertumskunde* 102: 67–77.

Wildung, Dietrich (1977) *Egyptian Saints. Deification in Pharaonic Egypt*, New York: New York University Press.

Wildung, Dietrich (1984a) *Sesostris und Amenemhet: Ägypten im Mittleren Reich*, Munich: Hirmer.

Wildung, Dietrich (1984b) *L'âge d'or de l'Égypte. Le Moyen Empire*, Fribourg: Office du Livre.

Wildung, Dietrich (1997) *Sudan: Ancient Kingdoms of the Nile*, Paris and New York: Flammarion.

Wildung, Dietrich, and Karla Kroeper (2006) *Naga Royal City of Ancient Sudan*, Berlin: Staatliche Museen zu Berlin.

Wilkinson, Richard H. (2003) *The Complete Gods and Goddesses of Ancient Egypt*, London: Thames & Hudson.

Wilkinson, Toby (1999) *Early Dynastic Egypt*, London and New York: Routledge.

Wilkinson, Toby (2000) *Royal Annals of Ancient Egypt*, London and New York: Kegan Paul International.

Wilkinson, Toby (2003) *Genesis of the Pharaohs*, London: Thames & Hudson.

Wilson, John A. (1956) *The Culture of Ancient Egypt*, Chicago: University of Chicago Press.

Wilson, Kevin (2005) *The Campaign of Pharaoh Shoshenq I into Palestine*, Tübingen: Mohr Siebeck.

Wuttmann, Michel (2001) "Les qanats de 'Ayn Manâwîr (oasis de Kharga, Égypte)," in P. Briant, ed., *Irrigation et drainage dans l'Antiquité, qanats et canalisations souterraines en Iran, en Égypte et en Grèce*, Paris: Collège de France: 109–36.

Wuttmann, Michel (2003) "Ayn Manawir," *Egyptian Archaeology* 22: 36–7.

Yoyotte, Jean (1987) *Tanis: l'or des pharaons*, Paris: Ministère des affaires étrangères.

Zibelius-Chen, Karola (2007) Review of Darnell 2006, *Bibliotheca Orientalis* 64: 377–87.

Index